THE

EFL

DIRECTORY

8th edition

EUROPA ☆ PAGES

SUMMERSDALE

103432726

Summersdale Publishers
46 West Street
Chichester
West Sussex
PO19 1RP
England

Email: summersdale@summersdale.com

Published in association with:
Europa Pages
PO Box 1369
Ascot
Berks.
SL5 7YH
England

Email: efl@europa-pages.co.uk

ISBN 1 84024 282 5

A CIP catalogue record for this book is available from the British Library.

Printed and bound in Great Britain.

Note:
Whilst every effort has been made to ensure the accuracy of all information contained in this directory, neither Europa Pages nor Summersdale Publishers can accept any liability for any loss or damage resulting from omissions or inaccuracies, relating to telephone numbers, addresses, wording, spacing, or positioning of any listing, advertisement or other material, regardless of how caused.

CONTENTS

PART I

LEARNING ENGLISH IN BRITAIN......................................5

Why you should learn English in Britain..........................6
How to use this book..7

Britain and its Language Regions............................16

Region 1:   *West Country*..17
Region 2:   *South of England*....................................29
Region 3:   *London*..48
Region 4:   *South East England*................................82
Region 5:   *Wales*...101
Region 6:   *Heart of England*...................................108
Region 7:   *Middle England*......................................120
Region 8:   *East Anglia*..124
Region 9:   *North West*...134
Region 10:   *Yorkshire & Humberside*......................142
Region 11:   *Northumbria & Cumbria*.......................149
Region 12:   *Scotland*..154

EFL Correspondence Courses..................................162

EFL Examinations..170

PART II

TEACHING ENGLISH AS A FOREIGN LANGUAGE (TEFL).....181

TEFL Qualifications 182
TEFL Course Directory.......................................187
TEFL Distance Learning Courses....................209
Useful TEFL Addresses.....................................216

cont..

PART III

GENERAL INFORMATION..219

    Directory of EFL Publishers in the UK........................220

    Directory of EFL Internet Sites............................228

    Au Pair Work...243

    A-Z of ELT Acronyms...250

    Work Placements...253

    Accommodation.......................................254

    Useful Addresses...255

PART I

LEARNING ENGLISH IN BRITAIN

English as a Foreign Language Courses (EFL)

WHY YOU SHOULD LEARN ENGLISH IN BRITAIN

✓ *Intensive Practice:* Unlike learning English in your own country, you will have the opportunity of using the language outside the classroom - shopping, taking trains, going to the restaurant, all enable you to practise your language skills. What better way could there be for making fast progress?

✓ *Home of English:* Britain is the original home of English, and many of the language's best known writers were British - Shakespeare, Thomas Hardy, Charles Dickens to name but a few. In Britain you will learn "correct" English, enabling you to be understood world-wide.

✓ *Wide Range of Courses:* Britain offers hundreds of courses, and you are sure to find exactly what you need. Whether it is a junior course with activities or an intensive executive programme in a specialist field, Britain has something for you!

✓ *Rich History and Culture:* Britain has a wealth of history and culture, which means that wherever you choose to stay you will find interesting old towns, fine museums and beautiful stately homes. All this coupled with Royal pageantry and tradition, which will help to make your stay entertaining and memorable.

✓ *Safe Destination:* Britain is a safe place to live and study - an ideal location for children and women travelling alone.

✓ *Britain is Easy to Reach:* For Europeans Britain is only a few hours away, and can be reached by plane, boat or even the Channel Tunnel. So why travel for hours with all the extra expense and fatigue, when Britain is on your doorstep?
  For those from outside Europe, travelling to Britain is also easy, thanks to numerous international airports, offering direct flights to nearly all parts of the globe.
   Also, Britain makes the ideal base for exploring the rest of Europe, as the UK has some of the cheapest flights and holiday packages to be found!

So, for fast language progress, in a safe and interesting environment make Britain your first choice!

HOW TO USE THIS BOOK

The schools in this directory are divided into 12 geographic regions (shown on page 16), each with an introduction to the area and its sights.

Each of these regions is then divided into two categories:

1)   Private schools /organisations   2)   State colleges/ universities

NB: There is a separate chapter covering TEFL courses in Britain. In the TEFL chapter, schools are listed by alphabetical order only.

A = *Adult Courses* (usually from ages 17 years +)

J = *Junior Courses.* (often with activities.)

1-1 = *One-to-one tuition* only (tailor-made courses, set at your own pace and for your own requirements. Often held in the teacher's home.)

** = Price includes accommodation

Numbers shown are the months when the courses are offered:
eg: 1-12 means January to December, 7-8 equals July and August only.
So a school with: A: 1-12 J: 7-8 offers Adult courses all year, and junior courses in the summer time only.

Specialist Courses:

B=Business/Commerce	**T**=Travel/Tourism
F=Finance/Banking	**H**=Hotel/Catering
C=Computing/IT	**E**=English for Academic Purposes

Course Recognition / Accreditation:

GBC = British Council
Baselt = British Association of State English Language Teaching
Arels = Association of Recognised English Language Services
Baleap = British Association of Lecturers in English for Academic Purposes

We recommend that you select the region in which you would like to study, based on your personal tastes (i.e. whether you prefer cities, the countryside, or the seaside), and then write-off to 3 or 4 schools for complete details and their latest prices. (A sample letter is shown on the following page to help you.)

You should study this information carefully, making a note of details such as class sizes, hours of study per week, exams offered and facilities available, before making your final decision.

Any prices or information quoted in this book are correct at the time of going to press, but could change before you arrive in Britain. It is therefore essential you check with the schools directly before embarking on your course.

✉ **Sample Letter to Schools:**

Your Name & Address
Date

Dear Sir/ Madam,

I have seen your entry in Europa Pages' EFL Directory, and would be grateful if you could send me further information about your English courses.

My details:

I would like to start my course on:_____*(date)* and stay until _____*(date)*.

I have studied English for _____ years.

Age _____

 Nationality _____

Yours faithfully,

Your Name

☏ **How to telephone from abroad:**

If you are telephoning from abroad, dial your international access code, then 44 followed by the telephone number minus the first zero
e.g. 01234 567890 becomes + 44 1234 567890

POURQUOI ON DEVRAIT APPRENDRE L'ANGLAIS EN GRANDE BRETAGNE

✓ *Pratique intensive:* A la différence d'apprendre l'anglais dans son propre pays, on aura l'occasion d'utiliser l'anglais en dehors de la classe, faisant ainsi de rapides progrès.

✓ *Berceau de la langue anglaise:* La Grande Bretagne est le pays d'origine de l'anglais, donc le seul où l'on apprend un anglais "correcte".

✓ *Enorme variété de cours:* La Grande Bretagne offre des centaines de stages/ cours et l'on peut être sûr d'en trouver un "taillé sur mesure".

✓ *Histoire et culture:* La Grande Bretagne est un pays riche en histoire et culture, ce qui fait que tout point de destination a quelque chose d'interessant à offrir: vieilles cités, d'excellents musées et magnifiques manoirs etc.

✓ *Sécurité:* La Grande Bretagne est un pays à haut coefficient de sécurité pour y vivre et y étudier. Point important pour enfants ou femmes voyageant seules.

✓ *La Grande Bretagne est d'accès facile:* D'Europe elle n'est qu'à quelques heures, et les aéroports internationaux ont des vols directs en provenance du monde entier.

Alors, pour un progrès rapide dans la connaissance de l'anglais, dans un environment sûr et intéressant, choisissez la Grande Bretagne avant tout autre pays anglophone!

UTILISATION DU LIVRE

Les écoles sont divisées en 12 régions géographiques (voir page 16) chacune avec une introduction sur la région et ses points d'intérêt. Ensuite, chaque région est divisée en 2 catégories:

1)   Ecoles privées / Organisations
2)   Enseignement Supérieur / Universités

A: *Adult Courses:* Cours pour adultes (d'habitude 17 ans +)
J: *Junior Courses:* Cours pour enfants . ils offrent généralement des activités pour les jeunes
1-1: Leçons particulières: cours "sur mesure" selon l'aptitude et le niveau individuels.
** = L'hébergement est inclus dans le prix.

Les numéros représentent les mois durant lesquels les cours sont offerts. Exemple: 1-12 veut dire de janvier à décembre, 7-8 juillet et août uniquement.

Donc une école avec: A: 1-12 J: 7-8 offre des cours pour adultes toute l'année et des cours pour enfants en été seulement.

B=Business/Commerce	**T**=Travel/Tourism
F=Finance/Banking	**H**=Hotel/Catering
C=Computing/IT	**E**=English for Academic Purposes

Nous recommandons que vous choisissiez la région où vous aimeriez étudier, puis écrire à 3 ou 4 écoles pour détails complets et prix. (Un exemple de lettre est procuré page 8 pour vous aider.)

Etudiez toute information reçue avec soin, notant la grandeur des groupes, les heures d'enseignements, les examens offerts, facilités etc avant de prendre une décision.

Les prix et les renseignements donnés dans ce livre sont corrects lors de la publication de ce livre, mais pourraient changer avant que vous n'arriviez en Grande Bretagne. Il est donc impératif de vérifier avec les écoles directement avant de commencer votre stage.

ES GIBT GUTE GRÜNDE, ENGLISCH IN ENGLAND ZU LERNEN.

✓ *Intensive Sprachpraxis:* Sie haben die Möglichkeit, Ihre Englischkenntnisse einzusetzen, wenn Sie den Klassenraum verlassen. Dadurch werden schnelle Fortschritte erzielt.

✓ *Hier ist Englisch zuhause:* England ist die ursprüngliche Heimat der englischen Sprache. Nur hier haben Sie die Möglichkeit, "richtiges" Englisch zu lernen.

✓ *Großes Kursangebot:* England bietet hunderte von Kursen an. Sie können sicher sein, den für Sie Richtigen zu finden.

✓ *Große Geschichte und Kultur:* England ist reich an Geschichte und Kultur, was bedeutet, daß Sie überall interessante alte Städte, schöne Museen und prächtige Bauten vorfinden.

✓ *Sicheres Ziel:* England ist ein sicheres Land, zum Wohnen und zum Lernen. Diese Tatsache macht aus England ein ideales Ziel für alleinreisende Frauen und Kinder.

✓ *England ist leicht zu erreichen:* Für Europäer ist England nur ein paar Stunden entfernt. Personen aus außereuropäischen Ländern haben durch die beiden internationalen Flughäfen mit weltweiten Direktverbindungen keine Schwierigkeiten, nach England zu reisen.

Ihre Wahl sollte also auf England fallen, wenn Sie schnelle Fortschritte in einem sicheren und interessanten Umfeld machen wollen!

DIE HANDHABUNG DIESES BUCHES

Die Schulen in diesem Buch sind in 12 geographische Regionen unterteilt (wie auf Seite 16 dargestellt). Jede dieser Regionen wird in einer Zusammenfassung vorgestellt.

Jede dieser Regionen wird wiederum in 2 Untergruppen geteilt:

1) Private Schulen / Private Organisationen 2) Staatliche Schulen / Universitäten

A= *Adult Courses:* Erwachsenenbildung (normalerweise ab 17 Jahren)
J=*Junior Courses:* Jugendausbildung
1-1 = Einzelunterricht. Kurse auf Ihre individuellen Bedürfnisse zugeschnitten.
** = Unterkunft in Schulgeld inbegriffen.

Die Zahlen geben die Monate an, in denen der Kurs angeboten wird. z.B.: 1-12 bedeutet Januar bis Dezember, 7-8 steht für Juli und August. Eine Schüle mit A:1-12 J:7-8 bietet Erwachsenenkurse ganzjährig an, Jugendausbildung nur im Sommer.

B=Business/Commerce	**T**=Travel/Tourism
F=Finance/Banking	**H**=Hotel/Catering
C=Computing/IT	**E**=English for Academic Purposes

Wir empfehlen Ihnen, sich zunächst eine Region herauszusuchen, in der Sie am liebsten lernen möchten, um dann 3-4 Schulen anzuschreiben mit der Bitte, Ihnen detaillierte Informationen und ihre Preislisten zuzusenden (einen Musterbrief zu Ihrer Hilfe finden Sie auf S. 8).

Das Informationsmaterial sollten Sie sorgfältig prüfen. Machen Sie sich Notizen zur Klassengröße, Stundenanzahl, Prüfungen, usw, bevor Sie sich für einen Kurs entscheiden.

Bitte beachten Sie ebenso: Alle in diesem Buch genannten Preise sind mit

Stand des Drucks, können sich aber geändert haben, bevor Sie in England eintreffen. Darum ist es unerläßlich, daß Sie die Preise direkt mit den Schulen absprechen, bevor Sie sich zum Kurs anmelden.

RAZONES PARA APRENDER INGLES EN GRAN BRETAÑA

✓ *Práctica intensiva:* Al contrario de aprender el idioma en su país, hay muchas oportunidades de utilizar el idioma fuera de las clases, haciendo así un progreso muy rápido.

✓ *Tierra del inglés verdadero:* Gran Bretaña es el país donde nació el idioma y donde se aprende un inglés tradicional o puro.

✓ *Gran variedad de cursos:* Gran Bretaña ofrece muchísimos cursos asegurando que se puede encontrar exactamente lo que se necesita.

✓ *Historia y cultura:* Gran Bretaña es un país rico en historia y cultura. En cualquier sitio donde se encuentre el visitante puede admirar sus antiguas ciudades, museos y magníficos castillos.

✓ *Seguridad:* Gran Bretaña es un país donde se puede vivir y estudiar sin peligro personal. Punto importante para jóvenes y mujeres que viajan solos.

✓ *Acceso fácil:* Para los que vienen de Europa, Gran Bretaña está tan sólo a unas horas de viaje. Para visitantes de otros países, los aeropuertos ofrecen vuelos directos desde y hacia casi todas partes del mundo.

¡ Para hacer progresos rápidos, en un ambiente interesante y seguro, Gran Bretaña es el número uno !

COMO UTILIZAR ESTE LIBRO

Las escuelas están divididas en 12 categorías geográficas (ver página 16), cada una con una introducción a la región donde se encuentran y sus puntos de interés.

Cada región está dividida en 2 categorías de escuelas:

1) Escuelas Privadas 2) Universidades

A= *Adult Courses:* Cursos para adultos (generalmente 17 años+)

J=*Junior Courses:* Cursos para jóvenes. Estos cursos ofrecen actividades además de los cursos.

1-1= lecciones particulares: Cursos "hechos a medidas" según el nivel o requerimiento individual.

** = alojamiento incluido en el precio

Los números indican los meses durante los cuales los cursos están en oferta. ej: 1-12 indica enero a diciembre, 7-8 tan sólo julio y agosto.
Asi un colegio con A: 1-12 J: 7-8 ofrece cursos para adultos todo el año y para jóvenes tan sólo en verano.

B=Business/Commerce	**T**=Travel/Tourism
F=Finance/Banking	**H**=Hotel/Catering
C=Computing/IT	**E**=English for Academic Purposes

Recomendamos que Vd elija la región donde le gustaría estudiar y escriba a 3 ó 4 colegios para detalles más concretos, precios y ofertas. (Un ejemplo de esto está en la página 8 para ayudarle).

Es necesario estudiar las informaciones con cuidado, tomando nota del tamaño de las clases, horas de estudio, exámenes en oferta, facilidades etc. antes de tomar una decisión.

Los precios y las informaciones dados en este libro son correctos en el momento de su publicación pero pueden cambiar. Por eso es imperativo verificar con los colegios antes de matricularse en un curso.

PERCHÈ CONVIENE STUDIARE L'INGLESE IN GRAN BRETAGNA.

✓ *Pratica intensiva:* diversamente da quando imparate l'inglese nel vostro paese, qui avrete l'opportunità di usarlo al di fuori della classe, il che vi porterà a fare rapidi progressi.

✓ *La culla della lingua inglese:* l'inglese ebbe origine in Gran Bretagna ed è qui che imparerete a parlarlo correttamente.

✓*Una ampia gamma di corsi:* la Gran Bretagna offre centinaia di corsi tra cui sicuramente troverete quello più adatto alle vostre esigenze.

✓ *Ricca storia e cultura:* la Gran Bretagna è un paese ricco di storia e di cultura, perciò dovunque sceglierete di andare avrete la possibilità di visitare centri storici, importanti musei e stupende residenze nobiliari.

✓ *Una meta sicura:* in Gran Bretagna potrete vivere e studiare sentendovi al sicuro; questo paese è infatti il luogo ideale sia per i ragazzi che per le donne che viaggiano da sole.

✓ *La Gran Bretagna è facile da raggiungere:* per gli europei, la Gran Bretagna si trova solo a poche ore di distanza, ma anche coloro che abitano al di fuori dell' Europa scopriranno che raggiungere la Gran Bretagna è facile grazie agli aeroporti, i quali offrono voli diretti da/ e per ogni parte del mondo.

Per fare rapidi progressi nell' apprendimento della lingua inglese, in un luogo sicuro e ricco di attrazioni, fate dunque della Gran Bretagna la vostra scelta di prim' ordine!

COME USARE QUESTO LIBRO

Troverete le scuole elencate geograficamente sotto 12 regioni diverse (vedi pagina 16) ognuna delle quali contiene un' introduzione alla zona e ai suoi luoghi di interesse.
Sotto ogni regione troverete inoltre 2 categorie:

1) Scuole/ Organizzazioni Private 2) Collegi/ Universita' dello Stato

A= *Adult Courses:* Corsi per adulti (generalmente dai 17 anni in su)
J=*Junior Courses:* Programme di studi per giovani, questi corsi spesso includono attività d'animazione.
1-1= corsi individuali personalizzati atti a soddisfare al meglio le esigenze del singolo individuo.
** = sistemazione compresa nel prezzo

I numeri indicano i messi in cui i corsi sono offerti, per esempio, 1-12 vuol dire da Gennaio a Dicembre, 7-8 vuol dire in Luglio e in Agosto unicamente.

Allora, una scuola che indica A: 1-12, J: 7-8, offre dei corsi per adulti tutto l'anno e programmi di studi per giovani solo nella stagione estiva.

B=Business/Commerce   T=Travel/Tourism
F=Finance/Banking   H=Hotel/Catering
C=Computing/IT   E=English for Academic Purposes

Vi consigliamo di scegliere prima la regione in cui volete studiare e successivamente di scrivere a circa 3 o 4 scuole in modo da ricevere informazioni dettagliate sui corsi e sui prezzi (troverete una lettera come esempio a pagina 8).

Prima di decidere quale corso frequentare, è bene prendere in considerazione i seguenti punti: numero di studenti per classe, ore di studio settimanali, esami che è possibile sostenere, servizi offerti etc.

NB: i prezzi e dati contenuti in questo libro sono corretti al momento della pubblicazione, ma potrebbero subire variazioni successivamente. Vi preghiamo quindi di contattare le scuole direttamente, prima di iscrivervi ad uno dei corsi elencati.

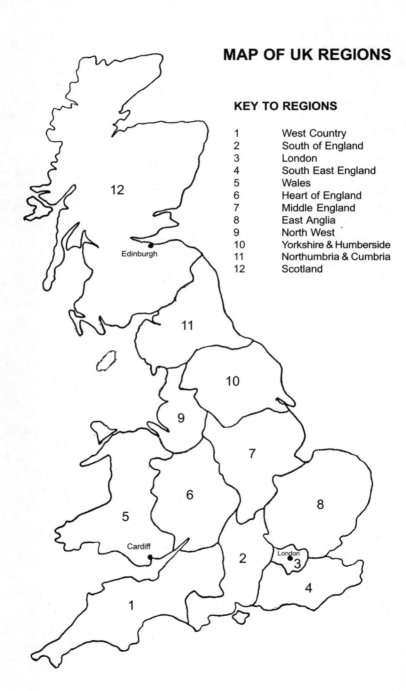

MAP OF UK REGIONS

KEY TO REGIONS

1	West Country
2	South of England
3	London
4	South East England
5	Wales
6	Heart of England
7	Middle England
8	East Anglia
9	North West
10	Yorkshire & Humberside
11	Northumbria & Cumbria
12	Scotland

1 WEST COUNTRY

Bath
Exeter
Plymouth Torquay
Penzance

Includes Cornwall, Devon, Somerset, Western Dorset, Wiltshire, Isles of Scilly.

With 600 miles of coastline, beautiful countryside, two National Parks (Dartmoor and Exmoor), many historic cities and a vast choice of outdoor activities, the West Country is an ideal destination.

The beautiful city of Bath, with its Roman baths and splendid Georgian architecture, is the most popular city in the region. Salisbury, with its magnificent cathedral, has a street of 14th century houses said to be the oldest in Europe.

There is much to see and enjoy in this region, which inspired many great writers over the centuries, from Thomas Hardy to Daphne du Maurier to Agatha Christie.

De splendides côtes, une très belle campagne et beaucoup de villes d'intérêt historique font de cette région une destination idéale tout au cours de l'année grâce au climat plus chaud que dans le reste du Royaumme Uni.

Herrliche Küsten, wunderschöne Landschaft und viele historische Städte machen diese Region das ganze Jahr über zu einem perfekten Ziel für Besucher, nicht zuletzt auch aufgrund des milderen Klimas.

Costas magníficas, campos preciosos y muchas ciudades de interés turístico hacen de esta región un punto de destinación ideal para visitantes durante todo el año, gracias a su clima templado.

Lo splendido litorale, la bella campagna e molte città storiche rendono questa regione la meta ideale per il turista in ogni periodo dell' anno, grazie al clima più mite.

 SIGHTS

Roman Baths Museum
Roman baths with hot spring and Roman monuments.
Pump Room, Abbey Church Yard, Bath.
Tel: 01225 461111

Tate Gallery, St. Ives.
Major new gallery, featuring painting and sculptures from the area.
Porthmeor Beach, St. Ives.
Tel: 01736 796226

Stonehenge
Mysterious ring of monoliths, 9 miles north of Salisbury.

Tintagel Castle
Medieval ruins from the legend of King Arthur. Tintagel. Tel: 01840 770328

For further information on these or other sights, contact the West Country Tourist Board, 60 St. David's Hill, Exeter. EX4 4SY Tel: 01392 76351

DIRECTORY OF EFL BOOKSELLERS IN THIS REGION:

(NB: Many bookshops hold a good selection of EFL material, even if they are not listed below. Moreover, if the particular book you are looking for is not in stock, they can order it for you.)

Blackwell's University Bookshop
University of Exeter
Stocker Road, Exeter EX4 4QA
Tel: 01392 259456 Fax: 01392 411207
Web: http://bookshop.blackwell.co.uk

The Bookshop
2 Barras Street, Liskeard PL14 6AD
Tel: 01579 342112 Fax: 01579 342112

Green Leaf Bookshop
82 Colston Street, Bristol, BS1 5BB
Tel: 0117 9211369 Fax: 0117 9211368

Jervis Books
3 Eugene Road, Paignton TQ3 2PF
Tel: 01803 523388 Fax: 01803 523388

Marjons Bookshop
College of St Mark & St John
Derriford Road, Plymouth PL6 8BH
Tel: 01752 636856 Fax: 01752 636855

Ottakar's Bookstore
95-96 Pydar Street, Truro TR1 2BD
Tel: 01872 225765 Fax: 01872 225766
Web: http://www.ottakars.co.uk

Ottakar's Bookstore
37 Middle Street, Yeovil BA20 1LG
Tel: 01935 479832 Fax: 01935 413506
Web: http://www.ottakars.co.uk

Ottakar's Bookstore
42 High Street, Barnstaple EX31 1BZ
Tel: 01271 374 433 Fax: 01271 374 466
Web: http://www.ottakars.co.uk

Ottakar's Bookstore
20/22 Fore Street, Tiverton EX16 6LH
Tel: 01884 242511 Fax: 01884 253501
Web: http://www.ottakars.co.uk

Ottakar's Bookstore
79 Courtenay St, Newton Abbot TQ12 2QH
Tel: 01626 365050 Fax: 01626 360587
Web: http://www.ottakars.co.uk

Ottakar's Bookstore
9 New Canal, Salisbury SP1 2AA
Tel: 01722 414060 Fax: 01722 413340
Web: http://www.ottakars.co.uk

Ottakar's Bookstore
45 South Street, Dorchester DT1 1DQ
Tel: 01305 257123 Fax: 01305 257182
Web: http://www.ottakars.co.uk

S.B.C. News & Books
1 West Street, Somerton TA11 7PS
Tel: 01458 274880 Fax: 01458 274810

Serendip Fine Books
11 Broad Street, Lyme Regis DT7 3QD
Tel: 01297 442594 Fax: 01297 443036

Truro Bookshop
18 Frances Street, Truro TR1 3DW
Tel: 01872 272185 Fax: 01872 225032
Web: http://www.cornwallbooks.com

Waterstone's
48-49 High Street, Exeter EX4 3DJ
Tel: 01392 218392 Fax: 01392 493797
Web: http://www.waterstones.co.uk

Waterstone's
27-29 College Green, Bristol BS1 5TD
Tel: 0117 925 0511 Fax: 0117 929 8462
Web: http://www.waterstones.co.uk

Waterstone's
Roman Gate, 252 High Street
Exeter EX4 3PZ
Tel: 01392 423044 Fax: 01392 438714
Web: http://www.waterstones.co.uk

Waterstone's
4-5 Milsom Street, Bath BA1 1DA
Tel: 01225 448515 Fax: 01225 429188
Web: http://www.waterstones.co.uk

A➤Z   DIRECTORY OF COURSES IN THIS REGION

PRIVATE SCHOOLS / ORGANISATIONS

Ashburn English Language Centre
Lurgecombe,
Ashburton TQ13 7HT
Tel: 01364 652266   Fax: 01364 652062
Email: jb@english1to1.softnet.co.uk
http://www.soft.net.uk/english1to1

Bailbrook College
39 London Road West,
Bath BA1 7JD
Tel: 01225 855100   Fax: 01225 855270
Email: marketing@bailbrook.com
http://www.bailbrook.com

Barnes Educational Services
12 Lodge Hill,
Westbury-Sub-mendip BA5 1ES
Tel: 01749 870709   Fax: 01749 870743
Email: peter@barnes-educational.co.uk
http://www.barnes-educational.co.uk

Bath Academy
27 Queen Square,
Bath BA1 2HX
Tel: 01225 334577   Fax: 01225 482414
Email: principal@bathacademy.co.uk
http:// www.bathacademy.co.uk

Bath Studio
Tongaat, Beechen Cliff Road
Bath BA2 4QR
Tel: 01225 443320   Fax: 01225 443320
Email: english@bathstudio.com
http://www.bathstudio.com
See display for further details

BELAF Language Study Holidays
Banner Lodge, Cherhill
Calne SN11 8XR
Tel: 01249 812551   Fax: 01249 821533
Email: belaf@aol.com
http://welcome.to/belaf

Bell Language School
Henley Lodge, Weston Road
Bath BA1 2XT
Tel: 01225 426255   Fax: 01225 445716
Email: info@bell-schools.ac.uk
http://www.bellbath.com

BATH STUDIO

Custom-designed courses in Bath.

1-1 and private groups.

General English and Business English.

Recreation to suit your interests.

Comfortable accommodation in your tutor's or host family's home.

Partners welcome.

Tongaat, Beechen Cliff Road
Bath BA2 4QR

Tel/Fax: +44 (0) 1225 443320
Email: english@bathstudio.com
Web: http://www.bathstudio.com

Boscastle Language School
Tremorvah, Fore Street
Boscastle PL35 0AU
Tel: 01840 250636   Fax: 01840 250616
Email: Jdrawingboard@aol.com
http://www.seeksouthwest.co.uk/learnenglish

Bridge International School of English
3 Bennett St.,
Bath BA1 2QQ
Tel: 01225 465453   Fax: 01225 442867
Email: bridge.bath@dial.pipex.com
http://www.bridge-bath.co.uk

Britannia Academy of Languages
Park Hill House, 1 Parkhill Road
Torquay TQ1 2AY
Tel: 01803 201703   Fax: 01803 201726
Email: english@bal.uk.com
http://www.bal.uk.com

Business & Medical English Services
Wellington Back, 21 Canynge Rd
Bristol BS8 3JZ
Tel: 0117 974 2951   Fax: 0117974 2778
Email: e-ínfo@bmes.co.uk
http://www.bmes.co.uk

Canning School, Bath
1 Brock St.,
Bath BA1 2LN
Tel: 01225 335323   Fax: 01225 444572
Email: enquiry@canning.co.uk
http://www.canning.co.uk

Channel School of English
Bicclescombe Park,
Ilfracombe EX34 8JN
Tel: 01271 862834 Fax: 01271 865374
Email: help@country-cousins.com
http://www.country-cousins.com

Churchill House English Home Tuition
Courses - See South East display for details

Cornwall Executive English
Gambia, 4 St Saviours Lane,
Padstow PL28 8BD
Tel: 01841 533791 Fax: 01841 533843
Email: Neil.Vivian@btopenworld.com
http://www.executivecornwall.com

Cornwall Language Services
39 High Cross St.,
St. Austell PL25 4AN
Tel: 01726 74873 Fax: 01726 64551
Email: ianproctor@hotmail.com

Culture-Link UK
2 Keast Ct, Heron Clse
Weymouth DT3 6SX
Tel: 01305 834166
Email: RachelTouray@aol.com

Cynara Training Ltd
2 Peacock, West Overton
Marlborough SN8 4HD
Tel: 0870 746 9338 Fax: 01672 861159
Email: info@cynara.uk.com

Devon Plus English Centre
1 Victoria Road,
Exmouth EX8 1DL
Tel: 01395 227171 Fax: 01395 227172
Email: devonplus@zoom.co.uk
http:// www.devonplus.freeuk.com

Devon School of English
The Old Vicarage, 1 Lower Polsham Road
Paignton TQ3 2AF
Tel: 01803 559718 Fax: 01803 551407
Email: europapages@devonschool.co.uk
http://www.devonschool.co.uk

Dialogue
Coteleigh, Northfield Rd
Minehead TA24 5QH
Tel: 01643 703161 Fax: 01643 708754
Email: dialogue_uk@yahoo.co.uk

Direct Learning
71 High Street,
Saltford BS31 3EW
Tel: 01225 872530 Fax: 01225 872530
Email: ep@directlearning.co.uk
http://www.directlearning.co.uk
See display for further details

English at Wartha Manor
The Lizard,
Helston TR12 7NR
Tel: 01326 290084 Fax: 01326 290084
Email: e@eaton.co.uk

English Centre Salisbury
The Duchess of Albany Building, Ox Row
Salisbury SP1 1EU
Tel: 01722 412711 Fax: 01722 414604
Email: telceng@aol.com
http://www.telc.co.uk

English Experience (The)
4, Nether Cerne,
Dorchester DT2 7AJ
Tel: 01300 341929 Fax: 01300 341929
Email: info@englishex.com
http://www.englishex.com

English in Exeter
42 Longbrook St.,
Exeter EX4 6AE
Tel: 01392 666419 Fax: 01392 433739
Email: exeter@skola.co.uk
http://www.skola.co.uk/englishinexeter

English Language Centre, Bristol
44 Pembroke Road, Clifton
Bristol BS8 3DT
Tel: 0117 973 7216 Fax: 1179239638
Email: elcbristol@compuserve.com
http://www.elcbristol.co.uk

EnglishStudent.com
PO Box 1565,
Wedmore BS28 4YA
Tel: 01934 712470 Fax: 01934 713426
Email: andy@englishstudent.com
http://www.englishstudent.com

Exeter Academy
64 Sylvan Road,
Exeter EX4 6HA
Tel: 01392 430303   Fax: 01392 437309
Email: english@exeteracademy.co.uk
http://www.exteracademy.co.uk

Focus - Cornwall
31, New Road, Newlyn
Penzance TR18 5PZ
Tel: 01736 365553   Fax: 01736 365553
Email: focus-cornwall@cwcom.net
http://www.focus-cornwall.co.uk

Foreign Student Services
19 Haddington Road, Stoke
Plymouth PL2 1RR
Tel: 01752 569462   Fax: 01752 569462
Email: linda.m.green@btinternet.com

Globe English Centre
31 St. David's Hill,
Exeter EX4 4DA
Tel: 01392 271036   Fax: 01392 427559
Email: study@globeenglish.co.uk
http://www.GlobeEnglish.co.uk

Inlingua Torquay
84 Union Street,
Torquay TQ2 5PY
Tel: 01803 380592   Fax: 01803 380592
Email: info@inlinguatorquay.co.uk
http://www.inlinguatorquay.co.uk

International College - Sherborne School
Newell Grange,
Sherborne DT9 4EZ
Tel: 01935 814743   Fax: 01935 816863
Email: reception@sherborne-ic.net
http://www.sherborne-ic.net

International House Bath
Trim St,
Bath BA1 1HB
Tel: 01225 448840   Fax: 01225 448842
Email: info@ih-westengland.co.uk
http://www.westengland.co.uk

International House, Torquay
13 Castle Road,
Torquay TQ1 3BB
Tel: 01803 299691   Fax: 01803 291946
Email: info@ih-westengland.co.uk
http://www.ih-westengland.co.uk

International Language Academy
Castle Circus, Union St.
Torquay TQ1 3DE
Tel: 01803 297166   Fax: 01803 298184
Email: ilatorq@rmplc.co.uk
http://www.language-academies.co.uk

International School (The)
1-3 Mount Radford Crescent,
Exeter EX2 4EW
Tel: 01392 254102   Fax: 01392 434432
Email: study@internationalschool.co.uk
http://www.internationalschool.co.uk

InTuition Languages - *See London display*
for details

Isca School of English
4 Mount Radford Crescent, PO Box 15
Exeter EX2 4EN
Tel: 01392 255342   Fax: 01392 437320
Email: english@iscaschool.com
http://www.iscaschool.com

Language Project (The)
27 Oakfield Road, Clifton
Bristol BS8 2AT
Tel: 0117 909 0911   Fax: 0117 907 7181
Email: info@languageproject.co.uk
http://www.languageproject.co.uk

Learn English Holdays
The Old Rectory, Pyworthy
Holsworthy EX22 6LA
Tel: 01409 253594   Fax: 01409 253594
Email: info@learnenglishholidays.co.uk
http://www.learnenglishholidays.co.uk

Linguarama
Cheney Court, Ditteridge
Corsham SN13 8QF
Tel: 01225 743557   Fax: 01225 743916
Email: jasonwhite@linguarama.com
http://www.linguarama.com

Living Learning English
10 Burghley Road, St.Andrews
Bristol BS6 5BN
Tel: 0117 909 8324   Fax: 0117 909 2483
Email: livingenglish@aol.com
http://www.livingenglish.com
See display for further details

Lowenva EFL Homestay
31, Parc Godrevy, Pentire
Newquay TR7 1TY
Tel: 01637 879944   Fax: 01637 879944
Email: lowenva@aol.com
http://www.geocities.com/lowenva

Mayflower College of English
36 Pier St.,
Plymouth PL1 3BT
Tel: 01752 673784   Fax: 01752 671537
Email: english@maycoll.co.uk
http://www.maycoll.co.uk

LIVING LEARNING ENGLISH
Homestay Courses

Live & Learn General English or
Business English in your Teacher's Home.

Intensive, 1-1 teaching,
individually designed programme of
study and activities, qualified,
experienced teachers.

City or countryside location.

10 Burghley Road
Bristol BS6 5BN UK
Tel: (44) 117 909 8324
Fax: (44) 117 904 2483
e-mail: livingenglish@aol.com
web: http://www.livingenglish.com

Mercator Schools Ltd
31 High Cross St,
St. Austell PL26 8TG
Tel: 01726 69500   Fax: 01726 69135
Email: principal@mercator-schools.ltd.uk
http://www.mercator-school.ltd.uk

Millfield English Language School
Millfield, Street
Somerset BA16 0YD
Tel: 01458 444334   Fax: 01458 444396
Email: efl@millfield.somerset.sch.uk
http://www.millfield.somerset.sch.uk/

Naish Academic English School
Sidcot School,
Winscombe BS25 1PD
Tel: 01934 843102   Fax: 01934 844181
Email: sidcotad@aol.com
http://www.sidcot.org.uk

OISE Bristol Intensive School of English
1 Lower Park Row,
Bristol BS1 5BJ
Tel: 0117 929 7667   Fax: 0117 925 1990
Email: admissions.bristol@oise.net
http://www.oise.net

Park School (The)
The Park,
Yeovil BA20 1DX
Tel: 01935 423514   Fax: 01935 411257
Email: head@parkschool.com
http://www.parkschool.com

Penhallow Language Holidays
Penhallow, 5 Florizel,
Polruan by Fowey PL23 1PQ
Tel: 01726 870322   Fax: 01726 870322
Email: penhallow@cornwall-county.com
http://users.cornwall-county.com/penhallow/

Penzance English Courses
21 Regent Square,
Penzance TR18 4BG
Tel: 01736 367760   Fax: 01736 367760

Real World English
57A Peverell Park Road, Peverell
Plymouth PL3 4LT
Tel: 01752 703064   Fax: 0870 134 5959
Email: paul@realworldeng.co.uk

RIVIERA ENGLISH SCHOOL

Small school by the sea in beautiful
Torquay, with small classes,
and high standards.

Lots of speaking practice.

Have a look at our prices!

The Old Customs House
Torwood Gardens Road
Torquay TQ1 1EG

Tel: +44 (0)1803 212132
Fax: +44 (0)1803 212139
Email: enquiries@Riviera-English-School.com
http://www.Riviera-English-School.com

Riviera English School
The Old Customs House,
Torwood Gardens Road,
Torquay TQ1 1EG
Tel: 01803 212132   Fax: 01803 212139
Email: enquiries@Riviera-English-School.com
http:// www.Riviera-English-School.com
See display for further details

Salisbury School of English
36 Fowlers Road,
Salisbury SP1 2QU
Tel: 01722 331011   Fax: 01722 328324
Email: info@english-school.co.uk
http://www.english-school.co.uk

Sidcot Language School
32 West Street,
Axbridge BS26 2AD
Tel: 01934 733182   Fax: 01934 844117
Email: office@sidcotlanguageschool.co.uk
http://www.sidcotlanguageschool.co.uk

Sidmouth International School
May Cottage,
Sidmouth EX10 8EN
Tel: 01395 516754   Fax: 01395 579270
Email: efl@sidmouth-int.co.uk
http://www.sidmouth-int.co.uk

Somerset School of English
Moorside, Doverhay
Porlock TA24 8LJ
Tel: 01643 862065   Fax: 01643 863222
Email: somersetenglish@msn.com

St. Antony's-Leweston School
Sherborne DT9 6EN
Tel: 01963 210691   Fax: 01963 210786
Email: st.antony@virgin.net

Suzanne Sparrow Plymouth Language School
72-74 North Road East,
Plymouth PL4 6AL
Tel: 01752 222700   Fax: 01752 222040
Email: peter@sparrow.co.uk
http://www.sparrow.co.uk

Taunton International Study Centre
Taunton School,
Taunton TA2 6AD
Tel: 01823 348100   Fax: 01823 349206
Email: tisc@compuserve.com

Torbay International Academy
Castle Chambers, Union St.
Torquay TQ1 4BS
Tel: 01803 294666   Fax: 01803 294555
Email: info@tia-england.com
http://www.tia-england.com

Torbay Language Centre
Conway Road,
Paignton TQ4 5LH
Tel: 01803 666997   Fax: 01803 666998
Email: TLC@lalschool.org
http://www.lalgroup.com

Torquay International School
15 St. Marychurch Road,
Torquay TQ1 3HY
Tel: 01803 295576   Fax: 01803 299062
Email: europa@tisenglish.co.uk
http://www.tisltd.co.uk

Totnes European School
4 Birdwood Court,
Totnes TQ9 5SG
Tel: 01803 868123   Fax: 01803 868223
Email: selsacs@eclipse.co.uk
http://www.selsacs.co.uk/tes

Totnes School of English
Gate House, 2 High Street
Totnes TQ9 5RZ
Tel: 01803 865722   Fax: 01803 865722
Email: enquiry@totenglish.co.uk
http://www.totenglish.co.uk

Trinity English Language Centre
Trinity College, Stoke Hill
Bristol BS9 1JP
Tel: 0117 968 2803   Fax: 0117 968 7470
Email: elc@trinity-bris.ac.uk
http://www.trinity-bis.ac.uk/elc

Westbury School of English
80 Eastfield Road, Westbury on Trym
Bristol BS9 4AG
Tel: 0117 940 6734   Fax: 0117 962 8786
Email: Brittours@aol.com

WISE (Waldorf Intensive School of English)
Bristol Steiner Waldorf School, Park Place
Clifton, Bristol BS8 1JR
Tel: 0117 929 3561   Fax: 0117 929 3561
Email: wise@wise.ndirect.co.uk
http://www.wise.ndirect.co.uk

STATE COLLEGES / UNIVERSITIES

Bath Spa University College
Newton St. Loe, Bath BA2 9BN
Tel: 01225 875845   Fax: 01225 875501
Email: international-office@bathspa.ac.uk
http://www.bathspa.ac.uk

Chippenham College
Cocklebury Road,
Chippenham SN15 3QD
Tel: 01249 444501

City of Bath College
Avon Street,
Bath BA1 1UP
Tel: 01225 312191   Fax: 01225 328864
Email: intstudent@citybathcoll.ac.uk
http://www.citybathcoll.ac.uk

City of Bristol College
Brunel Centre, Ashley Down Road
Bristol BS7 9BU
Tel: 0117 904 5163   Fax: 0117 904 5180
Email: emmanuel.raud@cityofbristol.ac.uk
http://www.cityofbristol.ac.uk

Cornwall College
Pool TR15 3RD
Tel: 01209 616213   Fax: 01209 616214
Email: languages@cornwall.ac.uk
http://www.cornwall.ac..uk

Exeter College of Further Education
The Language Centre, Hele Road
Exeter EX4 4JS
Tel: 01392 273514

Filton College Bristol
International Students Ctre, Filton Avenue
Bristol BS34 7AT
Tel: 0117 909 2279   Fax: 0117 931 2637
Email: international@filton-college.ac.uk
http://www.filton-college.ac.uk

Marjon International
Derriford Road,
Plymouth PL6 8BH
Tel: 01752 636821   Fax: 01752 636802
Email: inted@marjon.ac.uk
http://www.marjon.ac.uk/about/international_ed/

North Devon College
Old Sticklepath Hill,
Barnstaple EX31 2BQ
Tel: 01271 388121   Fax: 01271 45291

Plymouth College of Further Education
Academic & Continuing Studies, Goschen Ctre
Saltash Road, Plymouth PL2 2DP
Tel: 01752 305290   Fax: 01752 305065
Email: ah@pcfe.ac.uk
http://www.pcfe.ac.uk/

Salisbury College
Southampton Road,
Salisbury SP1 2LW
Tel: 01722 344311   Fax: 01722 344345
Email: enquiries@salisbury.ac.uk
http://www.salisbury.ac.uk

Somerset College of Arts & Technology
Wellington Road,
Tauton TA1 5AX
Tel: 01823 366366   Fax: 01823 366418
Email: jem@somerset.ac.uk
http://www.somerset.ac.uk

Soundwell College, Bristol
St. Stephen's Rd, Kingswood
Bristol BS16 4RL
Tel: 0117 967 5101   Fax: 0117 935 2753
Email: courseinformation@soundwell.ac.uk
http://www.soundwell.ac.uk

South Devon College
Language Centre, Newton Road
Torquay TQ2 5BY
Tel: 01803 386338   Fax: 01803 386333
Email: ddavies@s-devon.ac.uk
http://www.s-devon.ac.uk

St. Austell College
Trevarthian Road,
St. Austell TR1 3ST
Tel: 01726 67911   Fax: 01726 68499

Trowbridge College
College Road,
Trowbridge BA14 0ES
Tel: 01225 766241

Truro College
Haven House, Quay St
Truro TR1 2UY
Tel: 01872 261151   Fax: 01872 261145
Email: pamelas@trurocollege.ac.uk
http://www.trurocollege.ac.uk

University of Bath
English Language Centre, Claverton Down
Bath BA2 7AY
Tel: 01225 323024   Fax: 01225 323135
Email: english@bath.ac.uk
http://www.bath.ac.uk/elc

University of Bristol
Graduate School of Education
35 Berkeley Square, Bristol BS8 1JA
Tel: 0117 928 7093   Fax: 0117925 1537
Email: G.M.Clibbon@bristol.ac.uk
http://www.bristol.ac.uk/Depts/LangCent/
efl/efl.htm

University of Exeter
English Language Centre, The Old Library
Prince of Wales Drive, Exeter EX4 4PT
Tel: 01392 264282   Fax: 01392 264277
Email: elc@exeter.ac.uk
http://www.exeter.ac.uk/elc

University of the West of England
Fac. of Languages, Coldharbour Lane
Frenchay, Bristol BS16 1QY
Tel: 0117 334 2392   Fax: 0117 334 2820
Email: george.mann@uwe.ac.uk
http://www.uwe.ac.uk

Weston College
Knightstone Road,
Weston-super-Mare BS23 2AL
Tel: 01934 411411   Fax: 01934 411410
Email: MKTG@weston.ac.uk
http://www.weston.ac.uk

Weymouth College
Cranford Avenue,
Weymouth DT4 7LQ
Tel: 01305 764733   Fax: 01305 208711
Email: roz_osbourne@weymouth.ac.uk
http://www.weymouth.ac.uk

Institution Name	Availability	Junior Ages	Specials	Price /week	Status
Ashburn English Language Centre	A: 1-12 (1-1 only)		B, E	£495-£900**	
Boilbrook College	A: 1-12		B, F (also aviation)	On application	GBC
Barnes Educational Services	A: 1-12 J: 3-4, 6-8	12-18 yrs	(academic year in UK schools)	£250-£500	
Bath Academy	A: 1-12 J: 7-8	12 yrs +	B, T, F, C, E	£100-£400	BAC
Bath Spa University College	A: 1-12		B, E	£109-169	
Bath Studio	A: 1-12 (1-1 & closed grps only)		B, T	£249-£749**	
BELAF Language Study Holidays	A: 1-12 J: 1-12 (1-1 only)	9-18 yrs		£200-£350**	
Bell Language School	A: 1-12		B	£466-556**/2wks	GBC, Eaquals
Boscastle Language School	A: 1-12 J: 1-12	10-18 yrs	B, T, F, H, C, E	£150-£425	
Bridge International School of English	A: 1-12 J: 7	12-17 yrs	B, E	£105-£180	
Britannia Academy of Languages	A: 1-12 J: 1-12	12-15 yrs	B, C	£125-£210	
Business & Medical English Services	A: 1-12		B	On application	
Canning School, Bath	A: 1-12		B, F, E	£690-£2380	
Channel School of English	A: 5-9 J: 3-9	7-16 yrs	B, E	£280-£320**	GBC, Arels
Churchill House English Home Tuition Courses	A: 1-12 J: 1-12 (1-1 only)	7 yrs +	B, T, F, H, C, E	£450-£780**	
City of Bath College	A: 1-12		B, T, E	£100-£150	GBC, Baselt
City of Bristol College	A: 1-12		E	£18(2hrs)-£160(24hrs)	GBC, Baselt
Cornwall College	A: 1-12		B, T, H, C, E	£85-£130**	
Cornwall Executive English	A: 1-12 (1-1 only)		B	£1165-£1333**	
Cornwall Language Services	A: 1-12 J: 1-12 (1-1 only)	15 yrs+	B, T, H, E	£290-£440**	
Culture-Link UK	A: 7-8 (1-1 only)		T, H, E	£200-£500**	
Devon Plus English Centre	A: 1-12 J: 7-8	14-18 yrs		£160-£570	GBC, Arels

Institution Name	Availability	Junior Ages	Specials	Price /week	Status
Devon School of English	A: 1-12 J: 6-8	11-15 yrs	B, T, F, H, E	£122-£1764	GBC, Arels
Dialogue	A: 1-12			£200-£400**	
Direct Learning	A: 1-12		B, E	£655-£705**	ABLS
English at Wortha Manor	A: 1-12 (1-1 only)		B, E	£745-£1075**	
English Centre Salisbury	A: 1-12 J: 6-8		B	£137-£231 (J: £240**)	
English in Exeter	A: 1-12		E	£70-£150	GBC, Arels
English Language Centre, Bristol	A: 1-12		E	£135-£170	GBC, Arels
Exeter Academy	A: 1-12		B, T, F, H, E	£134-£1130	GBC, Arels
Filton College Bristol	A: 9-7		B, E	£120	GBC, Baselt
Focus - Cornwall	A: 3-8			£130	
Globe English Centre	A: 1-12 J: 1-12	7-18 yrs	B, F, C, E	£100-£295	
Inlingua Torquay	A: 1-12		B	£150-£1350	Inlingua International
International College - Sherborne School	J: 9-6, 7-8	10-17 (yr) 8-17 (summer)		£600-£700**	
International House Bath	A: 1-12 J: 7-8	12-16 yrs	B	£130-£180+	GBC, Arels
International House, Torquay	A: 1-12 J: 7-8	12-16 yrs	B	£130-£170	GBC, Arels
International Language Academy	A: 1-12 J: 1-12	8-15 yrs	B, E	£106-£198	
International School (The)	A: 1-12 J: 6-8	13 -17 yrs	B, E	£150-£250	GBC, Arels
InTuition Languages	A: 1-12 J: 1-12 (1-1 only)	14-18 yrs	B, T, F, C, E	£555-£1040**	GBC, Arels
Isca School of English	A: 1-12 J: 6-8	12-14, 14-17 yrs	B, E	£125-£165 (J: 900**/3wks)	GBC, Arels
Language Project (The)	A: 1-12		B, H, E	£45-£175	GBC
Learn English Holidays	J: 7-8	13-18 yrs		£225-£300**	
Linguarama	A: 1-12		B, T, F, H, C	£825-£1925	GBC, Arels

Institution Name	Availability	Junior Ages	Specials	Price /week	Status
Living Learning English	A: 1-12 J: 1-12 (1-1 only)	10-15 yrs	B, E	£550-£850**	
Lowenva EFL Homestay	A: 1-12 J: 1-12	12-16 yrs	B, T, E	£300-£500**	
Marjon International	A: 6-3		E	£175-£200	GBC, Baselt
Marlborough College Summer School	A: 7-8 J: 7-8	3 yrs +		On application	
Mayflower College of English	A: 1-12 J: 6-8	13-17 yrs	E	£185-£350**	GBC, Arels
Mercator Schools Ltd	A: 1-12 J: 7-8	12-18 yrs	B	£200-£275 approx.	GBC
Millfield English Language School	J: 7-8	10-16 yrs	E	On application	GBC
Mountlands Language School	A: 1-12 J: 7-8			On application	
Naish Academic English School	J: 9-6	10-18 yrs	E	£4995/term**	
OISE Bristol Intensive School of English	A: 1-12		T, E	£150-£900	
Park School (The)	A: 7-8			£250-£400**	
Penhallow Language Holidays	A: 5-10 J: 6-8	8-17 yrs	B, C	£80-£187	
Penzance English Courses	A: 1-12		B, T, E	£105-£420	
Plymouth College of Further Education	A: 9-7		B	£10-£100	
Riviera English School	A: 1-12 J: 7-8	8-15 yrs	B, F, H, E	from £99	
Salisbury College	A: 9-6			£50-£125	GBC, Baselt
Salisbury School of English	A: 1-12 J: 6-8	6-17 yrs	B, E	£131-£179 (adults)	GBC, Arels
Sidcot Language School	J: 7-8	9-16 yrs	E	£399-£440**	
Sidmouth International School	A: 1-12 J: 1-12	8-17 yrs	B, E	£150-£400	GBC
Somerset College of Arts & Technology	A: 1-12			£6.17-£66.67	
Soundwell College, Bristol	A: 1-12 J: 1-12	16 yrs +	B	£125	
South Devon College	A: 1-12		B, T, H	£125-£150	GBC, Arels

Institution Name	Availability	Junior Ages	Specials	Price /week	Status
St. Antony's-Leweston School	J: 9-7	5-18 yrs	B, C, E	£310-£340**	
Suzanne Sparrow Plymouth Language School	A: 1-12 J: 1-12	11-18 yrs	B, E	£140-£260	
Taunton International Study Centre	J: 1-12	9-17 yrs		£495**	
Torbay International Academy	A: 1-12 J: 3-4, 6-9	9-18 yrs	B, T	£170-£224**	
Torbay Language Centre	A: 1-12 J: 6-8	10-18 yrs	B, T	£130-£395**	GBC, Arels
Torquay International School	A: 1-12 J: 1,2	12-17 yrs	B, F, E	£230**+	GBC, Arels, IALC
Totnes European School	A: 1-12 J: 7-8	12-17 yrs	B, H, T, C	£100-£215	GBC, Arels
Totnes School of English	A: 1-12 J: 7-8	10-16 yrs	B, E	£135-£750	
Trinity English Language Centre	A: 1-12 J: by special arrangement		E	£84-£98	
Truro College	A: 1-12			On application	
University of Bath	A: 10-6, 7-9		B, E	£222-£238	Buleap
University of Bristol	A: 1-12		B, E	£640+/mth	Buleap
University of Exeter	A: 1-12		B, E	£190-£200	Buleap
University of the West of England	A: 9-6		B, E	£200-£300	Buleap
Westbury School of English	A: 7-8, 9-6		B	£100-£200 (+ reduced rates for Eastern Europe)	
Weston College	A: 9-6		B	Free-£25	
Weymouth College	A: 9-6			£45-£144	
WISE (Waldorf Intensive School of English) I	J: 7-8			£599**/2wks	

2 SOUTH OF ENGLAND

Includes Berkshire, Buckinghamshire, Eastern Dorset, Hampshire, Isle of Wight, Oxfordshire & the Channel Islands.

An area which offers a great deal of activities and cultural attractions. Oxford, one of Britain's most famous university towns, attracts many visitors wishing to learn English and to enjoy the facilities and attractions on offer. Bournemouth, on the coast, is another, if much younger, seat of learning, with lots of colleges and schools to choose from.

For those who enjoy sailing, the stretch of water between the mainland and the Isle of Wight is world famous, and boats can be hired for both beginners and advanced sailors.

Further inland, the town of Windsor boasts a magnificent castle (weekend residence of the Queen), and the prestigious boys' school of Eton, where some of the country's best known figures have been educated.

Région favorisée par les étudiants étrangers, elle possède la célèbre ville d'Oxford et son université, Windsor avec son château, Eton et sa prestigieuse école de garçons. Accès très facile de Londres et des aéroports internationaux.

Diese Region gehört zu der beliebtesten bei ausländischen Studenten. Hier finden sich Oxford mit dem schönen Stadtkern und der berühmten Universität, und Windsor, mit dem Schloß und Eton, der berühmten Schule. Die gesamte Region ist von London aus sehr leicht zu erreichen.

Región preferida por los estudiantes extranjeros donde se encuentran Oxford, con su famosa universidad, Windsor con su castillo y la prestigiosa escuela de Eton. Acceso muy fácil desde Londres y sus aeropuertos internacionales.

In questa regione prediletta dagli gli studenti stranieri si trovano Oxford, col suo affascinante centro città e famose università; e Windsor, sede dell' omonimo castello, nonché di Eton, il prestigioso collegio per ragazzi. L'interra regione è facilmente raggiungibile da Londra e dai suoi aeroporti internazionali.

 SIGHTS

The town of Oxford is filled with wonderful colleges and charming buildings too numerous to mention. Other sights in the region include:

Blenheim Palace
Birthplace of Winston Churchill, with glorious house by Vanbrugh and gardens by Capability Brown.
Woodstock, Oxfordshire.
Tel: 01993 811091

Windsor Castle
Weekend residence of the Queen, with state apartments, St. George's Chapel and Queen Mary's Dolls' House. Windsor. Berks.

Legoland
European cities and famous landmarks, all made out of Lego! Winkfield Road, Windsor.
Tel: 01753 622222

Didcot Railway Centre
Living museum, recreating the golden age of steam travel.
Great Western Railway, Didcot, Oxfordshire. Tel: 01235 817200

Beaulieu Palace House
Stunning palace containing the National Motor Museum.
Beaulieu, Hampshire. Tel: 01590 612345

HMS Victory & The Mary Rose
Nelson's ship from the battle of Trafalgar, and Henry VIII's ship from 1545, raised from the depths of the sea in 1982.
HM Naval Base, Portsmouth.
Tel: 023 9281 2931

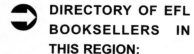

DIRECTORY OF EFL BOOKSELLERS IN THIS REGION:

(NB: Many bookshops hold a good selection of EFL material, even if they are not listed below. Moreover, if the particular book you are looking for is not in stock, they can order it for you.)

Baytree Bookshop Ltd
13 The Precinct, Waterlooville PO7 7DT
Tel: 023 9226 3084 Fax: 023 9225 9069

Beardsall's of Shanklin
53 Regent Street, Shanklin
Isle of Wight PO37 7AE
Tel: 01983 862616 Fax: 01983 867482

Bestsellers
47 Brookley Road, Brockenhurst SO42 7RB
Tel: 01590 622327

Blackwell's
48-51 Broad Street, Oxford OX1 3BQ
Tel: 01865 792792 Fax: 01865 794143
Web: http://bookshop.blackwell.co.uk

Blackwell's
6-12 Kings Road, Reading RG1 3AA
Tel: 0118 959 5555 Fax: 0118 950 9638
Web: http://bookshop.blackwell.co.uk

Bookwise
26Southbourne Grove
Southbourne, Bournemouth BH6 3RA
Tel: 01202 433334 Fax: 01202 417375

Bournemouth English Book Centre
15 Albion Close, Parkstone, Poole BH12 3LL
Tel: 01202 715 555 Fax: 0800 262 266
http://www.bebc.co.uk

Buckinghamshire College Bookshop
Queen Alexandra Road
High Wycombe HP11 2JZ
Tel: 01494 603021 Fax: 01494 524392

College Bookshop
North Road Parkstone, Poole BH14 0LS
Tel: 01202 747600 Fax: 01202 205719

The English Book Centre
26 Grove Street
Summertown, Oxford OX2 7JT
Tel: 01865 514770 Fax: 01865 513924
Web: http://www.ebcoxford.co.uk.

Horizons Bookshop
12-16 Gregories Road
Beaconsfield HP9 1HQ
Tel: 01494 677663 Fax: 01494 676860
Web: http://www.horizonsbooks.com

October Books
4 Onslow Road, Southampton SO14 0JB
Tel: 023 8022 4489 Fax: 023 8022 3916

Ottakar's Bookstore
118 High Street
Newport, Isle of Wight PO30 1TP
Tel: 01983 527927 Fax: 01983 525620
Web: http://www.ottakars.co.uk

Ottakar's Bookstore
102 Curzon Mall, Queensmere Centre
Slough SL1 1DQ
Tel: 01753 694144 Fax: 01753 694288
Web: http://www.ottakars.co.uk

Ottakar's Bookstore
10 Woolgate, Witney OX8 6AP
Tel: 01993 703525 Fax: 01993 772367
Web: http://www.ottakars.co.uk

Ottakar's Bookstore
Units 32-33 Castle Quay
Banbury OX16 5UN
Tel: 01295 270498 Fax: 01295 271660
Web: http://www.ottakars.co.uk

Ottakar's Bookstore
26/28 White Hart Street
High Wycombe HP11 2HL
Tel: 01494 443133 Fax: 01494 443011

Ottakar's Bookstore
72 Midsummer Place
Milton Keynes MK9 3GA
Tel: 01908 395384 Fax: 01908 397847
Web: http://www.ottakars.co.uk

Ottakar's Bookstore
18 Towngate Shopping Centre
Falkland Square, Poole BH15 1ER
Tel: 01202 670000 Fax: 01202 678800
Web: http://www.ottakars.co.uk

Ottakar's Bookstore
115 Commercial Road, Portsmouth PO1 1BU
Tel: 023 9282 1255
Web: http://www.ottakars.co.uk

The Printed Word Book Shop Ltd
7 Wests Centre, St Helier, Jersey JE2 4ST
Tel: 01534 768524 Fax: 01534 768524

Waterstone's
William Baker House Broad Street
Oxford OX1 3AF
Tel: 01865 790212 Fax: 01865 794258
Web: http://www.waterstones.co.uk

Westbourne Bookshop
65 Poole Road, Westbourne
Bournemouth BH4 9BA
Tel: 01202 768626 Fax: 01202 761002

A➡Z DIRECTORY OF COURSES IN THIS REGION

PRIVATE SCHOOLS / ORGANISATIONS

A. Zaccari's English School
67 Wimborne Road,
Bournemouth BH3 7AN
Tel: 01202 311476   Fax: 01202 319080
Email: info@zaccari.co.uk
http://www.zaccari.co.uk

Accent Language School
9-11 Mansell St., St Peter Port
Guernsey GY1 1HG
Tel: 01481 714909   Fax: 01481 715880
Email: accent@guernsey.net
http://www.accent.guernsey.net

Albion International Study Centre
Bocardo House, 24b St Michael's St.
Oxford OX1 2EB
Tel: 01865 244470   Fax: 01865 244112
Email: info@albionschools.co.uk
http://www.albionschools.co.uk

Anderson Executive English
Bona Vista, Chilworth ring Chilworth
Southampton SO16 7HW
Tel: 023 8076 8045
Email: Maryam.Anderson@btinternet.com
http://andersonee.hypermart.net/

Anglo European School of English
77 Lansdowne Road,
Bournemouth BH1 1RW
Tel: 01202 558658   Fax: 01202 552849
Email: admin@angloeuro.org
http://www.angloeuropean.org

Anglo-Continental
29-35 Wimborne Road,
Bournemouth BH2 6NA
Tel: 01202 557414   Fax: 01202 556156
Email: english@anglo-continental.com
http://www.anglo-continental.com

Ardmore Language Group
Hall Place,
Maidenhead SL6 6QR
Tel: 01628 826699   Fax: 01628 829977
Email: mailbox@ardmore.org.uk
http://www.ardmore.org.uk

Aspect Bournemouth
Heliting House, Richmond Hill
Bournemouth BH2 6HT
Tel: 01202 638100   Fax: 01202 438900
Email: enquiries@aspectworld.com
http://www.aspectworld.com

Aspect ILA Bourmouth
Hinton Chambers, Hinton Road
Bournemouth BH1 2EN
Tel: 01202 557522   Fax: 01202 297046
Email: equiries@aspectworld.com
http://www.aspectworld.com

Aspect ILA - Westbourne College
130-136 Poole Road,
Bournemouth BH4 9EF
Tel: 01202 638100   Fax: 01202 438900
Email: enquiries@aspectworld.com
http://www.aspectworld.com

Aspect ILA Oxford - Austen House
108 Banbury Road,
Oxford OX2 6JU
Tel: 01202 638100   Fax: 01202 438900
Email: enquiries@aspectworld.com
http://www.aspectworld.com

Aspect ILA Oxford - Henley House
7 Norham Gardens,
Oxford OX2 6PS
Tel: 01202 638100   Fax: 01202 438900
Email: enquiries@aspectworld.com
http://www.aspectworld.com

BEET Language Centre
Nortoft Road, Charminster
Bournemouth BH8 8PY
Tel: 01202 397721   Fax: 01202 309662
Email: admin@beet.co.uk
http://www.beet.co.uk
See display for further details

Bidbury Greywalls
Greywalls House, Hillbrow
Liss GU33 7QR
Tel: 01730 894246   Fax: 01730 894865
Email: bidbury-greywalls@lineone.net
http://www.bidbury.com.uk

Bidbury Lake
Bidbury Lane, Havant
Hants PO9 3JG
Tel: 023 9248 3217   Fax: 023 92454233
Email: enquiries@bidbury.co.uk
http://www.bidbury.com.uk

Bob Lewis ELT
Fairway, North Hinksey Lane
Oxford OX2 0LY
Tel: 01865 792436   Fax: 01865 243260
Email: bob@oxfree.com
http://www.bob.oxfree.com

BEET LANGUAGE CENTRE

Cambridge University examinations,
General English, Business English,
English for Tourism, Hotel &
Hospitality, Media Studies, university
preparation including IELTS/EAP.

Close links to Bournemouth University,
especially Tourism & Business Faculties.
Teacher Training.

Nortoft Road, Charminster
Bournemouth BH8 8PY

Tel: +44 1202 397721
Fax: +44 1202 309662
E-Mail: admin@beet.co.uk
Website: http://www.beet.co.uk

**Bournemouth Business School
International**
Avon House, 26 St. Peter's Road
Bournemouth BH1 2LW
Tel: 01202 780777   Fax: 01202 780888
Email: info@bbsi.co.uk
http://www.bbsi.co.uk

**Bournemouth International Language
College**
4 Trinity, 161 Old Christchurch Road
Bournemouth BH1 1JU
Tel: 01202 318269   Fax: 01202 318269
Email: efl@bilc.co.uk
http://www.bilk.co.uk

Bournemouth International School
2 Owls Rd,
Bournemouth BH5 1AA
Tel: 01202 393112   Fax: 01202 309638
Email: info@bischool.com
http://www.bischool.com

**Bournemouth One to One English
Language School**
19 Lowther Road,
Bournemouth BH8 8NG
Tel: 01202 257775   Fax: 01202 257775
Email: admin@bournemouth121.com
http://www. bournemouth121.com

Bournemouth School of English
12 St. Stephen's Road,
Bournemouth BH2 6JJ
Tel: 01202 294938   Fax: 01202 294938

BTS
139 Charminster Road,
Bournemouth BH8 8UH
Tel: 01202 521355   Fax: 01202 521355
Email: steve.bts@freenet.co.uk
http://www.englishinbournemouth.co.uk

Burton's English Summer School
Suite 2, 4 Crick Road
Oxford OX2 6QJ
Tel: 01865 512149   Fax: 01865 512149

Bury Lawn School
Soskin Drive, Stantonbury Fields
Milton Keynes MK14 6DP
Tel: 01404 8817028   Fax: 01404 881882
Email: oxenways@aol.com

Business and Legal Homestay
24 Church Lane,
Middle Barton OX7 7BX
Tel: 01869 347130   Fax: 01869 347130
Email: Rnj@btinternet.com
http://www.btinternet.com/~rnj

Centre for International Education
5 Worcester St.,
Oxford OX1 2BX
Tel: 01865 202238   Fax: 01865 202241
Email: info@ceninted.demon.co.uk
http://www.utsinternational.com/cie

**Churchill House English Home Tuition
Courses** - See South East display for details

Collingham Oxford
31 St. Giles,
Oxford OX1 3LF
Tel: 01865 728280   Fax: 01865 240126
Email: principal@collingham.co.uk
http://www.collingham.co.uk

Croeso School Of English
46 Shillito Road,
Parkstone BH12 2BW
Tel: 01202 248160   Fax:
Email: croeso@supanet.com
http://www.croeso.supanet.com

Cultural Fluency
17 Stour Road,
Christchurch BH23 2JT
Tel: 01202 478288   Fax: 01202 483933
Email: enquire@cultural-fluency.com
http://www.cultural-fluency.com

Direct Effect Training & Development Ltd
PO Box 356,
Maidenhead SL6 4YT
Tel: 01628 620727   Fax: 01628 671272
Email: directeffect@free4all.co.uk

Dorset International College
Cambridge House, 7 Knyveton Road
Bournemouth BH1 3QF
Tel: 01202 316611   Fax: 01202 318811
Email: info@dorsetinternationalcollege.co.uk
http://www.dorsetinternationalcollege.co.uk

Eagle International School
'Tiami', 55 Elms Ave, Lilliput
Poole BH14 8EE
Tel: 01202 745175   Fax: 01202 745175
Email: EagleSch@aol.com
http://members.aol.com/eaglesch/

Eckersley School of English
14 Friars Entry,
Oxford OX1 2BZ
Tel: 01865 721268   Fax: 01865 791869
Email: english@eckersley.co.uk
http://www.eckersley.co.uk

ELC London Street
78 London St.,
Reading RG1 4SJ
Tel: 0118 958 2247   Fax: 0118 958 2247
Email: elc@elclondonstreet.co.uk
http://www.elclondonstreet.co.uk
See display for further details

ELT Banbury
49 Oxford Road,
Banbury OX16 9AH
Tel: 01295 263480   Fax: 01295 271658
Email: info@elt-banbury.com
http://www.elt-banbury.com

English Host Holidays
21 Manor Way,
Hayling Island PO11 9JH
Tel: 023 9246 2191   Fax: 023 9246 8227
Email: sizer.ehh@talk21.com
http://www.english-host-holidays.co.uk

English Language Centre
6B Church St.,
Reading RG1 2SB
Tel: 0118 939 1833   Fax: 0118 939 1833
Email: katepepper@ntlworld.com

English Learning Holidays
15 Heatherlea Road, Southbourne
Bournemouth BH6 3HN
Tel: 01202 425846   Fax: 01202 425846
Email: carole@englishlearningholidays.co.uk
http://www.englishlearningholidays.co.uk

English Naturally
22 Fordington Avenue,
Winchester SO22 5AW
Tel: 01962 859700   Fax: 01962 86702
Email: info@english-naturally.com
http://www.english-naturally.com

English Tuition Services
Halgavor House, Broad Layings
Woolton Hill, Newbury RG20 9TT
Tel: 01635 253942   Fax:
Email: Chris_Trinder@compuserve.com
http://ourworld.compuserve.com/homepages/
Chris_Trinder/

English Tutorial Centre (The)
39 Kennett Road, Headington
Oxford OX3 7BH
Tel: 01865 763065   Fax: 01865 454295
Email: clivejenkins@bigfoot.com
http://come.to/tutorials

English Tutorial Centre Oxford (The)
3 All Saints Close, Marcham, Abingdon
Oxford OX13 6PE
Tel: 01865 391193   Fax: 01865 391186
Email: enquiries@tetco.co.uk
http://www. tetco.co.uk

English2Advance
Maple House, 18 Dartmouth Road
Olney MK46 4BH
Tel: 01234 711044   Fax: 01234 714980
Email: info@english2advance.com
http://www.english2advance.com

ETC
24 West Hill Road,
Bournemouth BH2 5PG
Tel: 01202 559044   Fax: 01202 780162
Email: english@etc-inter.net
http://www.etc-inter.net

Eurocentre, Bournemouth
26 Dean Park Road,
Bournemouth BH1 1HZ
Tel: 01202 554426   Fax: 01202 293249
Email: 101317.1242@compuserve.com
http://www.eurocentres.com

Europartner Language Holidays and Group Travel Ltd
Twynham House, 15 Stour Road
Christchurch BH23 1PL
Tel: 01202 480266   Fax: 01202 480266
Email: europartner-xch@bigfoot.com

European Summer School of Arts & Languages at Oxford
69-71 Oxford St.,
Woodstock OX20 1TJ
Tel: 01993 812547   Fax: 01993 812547
Email: theatre.oxford@virgin.net

Eurospeak
Greyfiars Centre, 64 Friar St.
Reading RG1 1EH
Tel: 0118 979 2221   Fax: 0118 979 2221
Email: info@eurospeak.org.uk
http://www.eurospeak.org.uk

Face to Face
Damson Cottage, Lower End
Leafield OX8 5QQ
Tel: 01993 878276   Fax: 01993 878589
Email: fleur@iggulden7.freeserve.co.uk

Gornall School of English
Llandaff Court, 41g Corn St.,
Witney OX8 7DQ
Tel: 01993 706541   Fax: 01993 706541
Email: gornallschool@1gornall.freeserve.co.uk

Greylands School of English.
315-317 Portswood Road,
Southampton SO17 2LD
Tel: 023 8031 5180   Fax: 023 8058 6684
Email: info@greylands.co.uk
http://www.greylands.co.uk

Habyn Hill House
Rogate,
Petersfield GU31 5HN
Tel: 01730 821820   Fax: 01730 821820
Email: pam.wilkinson@habyn.freeserve.co.uk

Harrow House International Colleges
Harrow Drive,
Swanage BH19 1PE
Tel: 01929 424421   Fax: 01929 427175
Email: karin.abarrow@lds.co.uk
http://www.harrowhouse.com
See display for further details

HARROW HOUSE INTERNATIONAL COLLEGES

Harrow House International Colleges in Swanage and London, the top language school organisation in England, offer year round educational and vacational courses for adult and junior students with college and homestay accommodation.

Harrow Drive, Swanage,
Dorset BH19 1PE

Tel: +44 1929 424421
Fax: +44 1929 427175
Email: karin.abarrow@lds.co.uk
Web: http://www.harrowhouse.com

Heathfield School for Girls
London Road,
Ascot SL5 8BQ
Tel: 01344 885197   Fax: 01344 882235
Email: heathfield.summer@which.net

Homelingua
Gordon House, 276 Banbury Rd,
Oxford OX2 7ED
Tel: 01865 557555   Fax: 01865 557545
Email: info@homelingua.com
http://www.homelingua.com

Homestay English Learning
270 Castle Lane West,
Bournemouth BH8 9TU
Tel: 01202 523652   Fax: 01202 248195
Email: woolrych@aol.com

Inter-Continental Communications
91 Emmbrook Road,
Wokingham RG41 1JN
Tel: 0118 979 3893   Fax: 0118 979 3893
Email: info@iccommunications.com
http://iccommunications.com

Interlingua - Jersey
Sunnyfield, Rue de la Lourderie La Rocque
JERSEY JE3 9SG
Tel: 01534 852590   Fax: 01534 856727
Email: interjer@itl.net
http://itl.net/go/to/linguaj

Interlink School of English
126 Richmond Park Road,
Bournemouth BH8 8TH
Tel: 01202 290983   Fax: 01202 291141
Email: english@ilse.co.uk
http://www.ilse.co.uk

International College of English
27, Chalton Lane, Clanfield
Portsmouth PO8 0PP
Tel: 023 9259 6989   Fax: 023 9259 6989
Email: mel596989@aol.com

International Quest
50 Oxford St.,
Southampton SO50 8QJ
Tel: 02380 338858   Fax: 01280 338848
Email: english@internationalquest.co.uk
http://www.internationalquest.co.uk

InTuition Languages- *See London display for details*

Jersey School of English
17-19 Don St., St. Helier
Jersey JE2 3YS
Tel: 01534 758895   Fax: 01534 758869
Email: wordcraf@itl.net
http://user.itl.net/~wordcraf/jsebro.html

King's Junior School
282 Iford Lane, Tuckton
Bournemouth BH6 5NQ
Tel: 01202 293535   Fax: 01202 293922
Email: kings@lds.co.uk
http://www.kings-group.co.uk

King's School of English
58 Braidley Road,
Bournemouth BH2 6LD
Tel: 01202 293535   Fax: 01202 293922
Email: marketing@kingsschool.uk.com
http://www.kings-group.co.uk

King's School Oxford
St Joseph's Hall, Temple Road
Temple Cowley, Oxford OX4 2UJ
Tel: 01865 711829   Fax: 01865 747791
Email: info@kingsoxford.co.uk
http://www.kingsoxford.co.uk

Lake School of English Oxford
14 Park End St.,
Oxford OX1 1JQ
Tel: 01865 724312   Fax: 01865 251360
Email: europa@englishinoxford.com
http://www.englishinoxford.com
See display for further details

THE LAKE SCHOOL OF ENGLISH OXFORD

Great Teaching: dynamic classes
Great Atmosphere: personal attention
Great Location: central Oxford
Great Service: accommodation and
university placement service
Great Reputation: academic excellence
Great Value: lots included,
no hidden extras

14 Park End Street, Oxford OX1 1JQ

Tel: +44 1865 724312
Fax: +44 1865 251360
Email: europa@englishinoxford.com
Web: www.englishinoxford.com

Language Management
21 Byron Avenue,
Winchester SO22 5AT
Tel: 01962 853943   Fax: 01962 853943
Email: info@langman.co.uk
http://www.langman.co.uk

Language Specialists International
1-13 Lord Montgomery Way,
Portsmouth PO1 2AH
Tel: 02392 291811   Fax: 02392 750435
Email: contact@lsi-international.co.uk
http://www.lsi-international.co.uk

Leander Grey & Associates Ltd.
5 Robins Way,
Christchurch BH23 4AW
Tel: 01425 276591
Email: leandergrey@btconnect.com
http://www.leandergrey.co.uk

Learn English
46 Shillito Road, Parkstone
Bournemouth BH12 2BW
Tel: 0797 986 1870   Fax: 01202 248160
Email: info@taranet.co.uk
http://www.learn-english.uk.com

Lewis School of English
33 Palmerston Road,
Southampton SO14 1LL
Tel: 023 8022 8203   Fax: 023 80231395
Email: alistair@lewis-school.co.uk
http://www.lewis-school.co.uk

Lines Languages
Heid des Chenes 75, 4620 Fleron
BELGIUM (HQ address)
Tel: 0032 477 13 41 48   Fax: 0032 87 34 17 34
Email: lines.info@swing.be
http://www.lines.ac
Courses held at schools in Berkshire & Surrey

Lingua Travel English & Educational
33 Crawford Close, Earley
Reading RG6 7PE
Tel: 0118 966 1291   Fax: 0118 935 1101
Email: colinhennell@aol.com

Link Education & Guardian Service
14, Busby Close, Clanfield
Bampton OX18 2RD
Tel: 01367 810478   Fax: 01367 810478

Live in Languages Ltd
11 Derwent Drive,
Burnham SL1 6HT
Tel: 01628 661315   Fax: 01628 661315
Email: james@liveinlanguages.co.uk
http://www. liveinlanguages.co.uk

Lymington Language
Compass House, 50 Gosport Street
Lymington SO41 9BB
Tel: 01590 672881   Fax: 01590 676001
Email: admin@lymlang.com
http://www.lymlang.com

Meridian School of English
9 Yarborough Road, Southsea
Portsmouth PO5 3DZ
Tel: 023 9281 6023   Fax: 023 9283 3438
Email: meridian@meridsch.demon.co.uk
http://www.meridsch.demon.co.uk

MLS International College
MLS House, 8 Verulam Place,
Bournemouth BH1 1DW
Tel: 01202 291556   Fax: 01202 293846
Email: admin@mls-college.co.uk
http://www.mls-college.co.uk

MLS International College
8 / 9 Verulam Place,
Bournemouth BH1 1DW
Tel: 01202 291556   Fax: 01202 293846
Email: mls@mls.softnet.co.uk

MM Oxford Study Services Ltd.
44 Blenheim Drive,
Oxford OX2 8BQ
Tel: 01865 513788   Fax: 01865 311988
Email: english@mmoxford.co.uk
http://www.mmoxford.co.uk
Courses held at Hertford College & St.Hugh's

New Horizons
40 Dalmeny Road, Southbourne
Bournemouth BH6 4BW
Tel: 01202 425298   Fax: 01202 425298

Newbold College
St. Mark's Road, Binfield
Bracknell RG42 4AN
Tel: 01344 407421   Fax: 01344 407405
Email: admissions@newbold.ac.uk
http://www.newbold.ac.uk

Newbury Hall
Enborne Road,
Newbury RG14 6AD
Tel: 01635 36879   Fax: 01635 48400
Email: info@oise.co.uk
http://www.oise.net

OISE Central Reservations
OISE House, Binsey Lane
Oxford OX2 0EY
Tel: 01865 258300   Fax: 01865 726726
Email: info@oise.co.uk
http://www.oise.net

OISE Oxford Intensive School of English
13-15 High Street,
Oxford OX1 4EA
Tel: 01865 247272   Fax: 01865 723648
Email: admissons.oxford@oise.net

**Olcote Guardianships & Language
Services**
Olcote, 6 Oakley Lane,
Oakley, Nr Basingstoke RG23 7HP
Tel: 01256 780774   Fax: 01256 780774
Email: info@olcote.co.uk
http://www.olcote.co.uk

Oxford Academy
18 Bardwell Road,
Oxford OX2 6SP
Tel: 01865 512174   Fax: 01865 553751
Email: info@oxac.co.uk
http://www.oxac.co.uk

Oxford County Courses at Millbrook House
Millbrook House, Milton,
Abingdon OX14 4EL
Tel: 01235 831237   Fax: 01235 821556
Email: millbrook@millbrookhouse.org.uk
http://www.millbrookhouse.org.uk

Oxford English Centre
66 Banbury Road,
Oxford OX2 6PR
Tel: 01865 516162   Fax: 01865 310910
Email: info@oxfordenglish.co.uk
http://www.oxfordenglish.co.uk

Oxford House School of English
67 High St., Wheatley
Oxford OX33 1XT
Tel: 01865 874786   Fax: 01865 873351
Email: oxford.house@dial.pipex.com
http://www.oxford.house.co.uk

Oxford Language Centre
Threeways House, George St.
Oxford OX1 2BJ
Tel: 01865 240111   Fax: 01865 247259
Email: olc@abacuscollege.net
http://www.abacuscollege.net

Oxford Language Institute
6 Bickerton Road,
Headington OX3 7LS
Tel: 01865 741069   Fax: 01865 741069

Oxford Language Training
9 Blue Boar St.,
Oxford OX1 4EZ
Tel: 01865 205077   Fax: 01865 793088
Email: olt@dial.pipex.com
http://www.olt.co.uk

Oxford Study Centre
40 Cumnor Hill,
Oxford OX2 9HB
Tel: 01865 865354   Fax: 01865 862783
Email: g.philip@easynet.co.uk
http://easynet.co.uk/oxstudy/

Oxford Tutorials
25 Lakeside,
Oxford OX2 8JF
Tel: 01865 514433   Fax: 01865 514433
Email: oxford.tutorials@ukgateway.net
http://www.oxford-tutorials-edu.co.uk

OxfordLife
55 Meadow Close, Farmoor
Oxford OX2 9PA
Tel: 01865 863748   Fax: 01865 864679
Email: oxfordlife@aol.com
http://www.oxfordlife.uk.com

Padworth College
Padworth,
Reading RG7 4NR
Tel: 0118 983 2644   Fax: 0118 983 4515
Email: info@padworth.com
http://www.padworth.com

Parkland International
Leighton Park School, Shinfield Road
Reading RG2 7DH
Tel: 0118 931 3214   Fax: 0118 931 3224
Email: jna@parklang.demon.co.uk
http://www.parklang.co.uk

Personal English Tutors
19 Sandford Park,
Charlbury OX7 3TH
Tel: 01608 811342   Fax: 07980 678854
Email: info@p-e-t.co.uk
http://www.p-e-t.co.uk
See display for further details

PERSONAL ENGLISH TUTORS

Study English in Oxford.
One-to-One tuition in the Host-
Tutor's home. Total immersion in
the English language. Courses
tailored to your individual needs.
Fully qualified and experienced
teachers in beautiful homes.

19, Sandford Park,
Charlbury, Oxfordshire. OX7 3TH

Tel: +44 1608 811342
Fax: +44 7980 678854
Email: info@p-e-t.co.uk
Website: http://www.p-e-t.co.uk

Scanbrit School of English
22 Church Road,
Bournemouth BH6 4AT
Tel: 01202 428252   Fax: 01202 428926
Email: info@scanbrit.co.uk
http://www.scanbrit.co.uk
See display for further details

SCANBRIT SCHOOL OF ENGLISH

Situated adjacent to sandy beach in
major resort of Bournemouth.
Tuition all-year - all levels.
Caring homestays near School.
Excellent value
(£170/wk inclusive of tuition,
single room & meals).
Varied interesting social programme.

22 Church Road, Southbourne,
Bournemouth BH6 4AT

Tel: +44 1202 428252
Fax: +44 1202 428926
Email: info@scanbrit.co.uk
Web: http://www.scanbrit.co.uk

Pippins Home-Stays
1 Brode Close,
Abingdon OX14 2QJ
Tel: 01235 525520   Fax: 01235 525520
Email: terry@pippins-stays.freeserve.co.uk
http://www.pippins-stays.freeserve.co.uk

Red Dragon Languages Consultancy
109 Victoria Road,
Bournemouth BH1 4RS
Tel: 01202 398879   Fax: 01202 566764
Email: redragonlanguages@hotmail.com
http://www.rdlc.co.uk

Regent Oxford
90 Banbury Road,
Oxford OX2 6JT
Tel: 01865 515566   Fax: 01865 512538
Email: oxford@regent.org.uk
http://www.regent.org.uk

Richard Language College
43-45 Wimborne Road,
Bournemouth BH3 7AB
Tel: 01202 555932   Fax: 01202 555874
Email: enquiry@rlc.co.uk
http://www.rlc.co.uk

Shane English School, Oxford
5 Cambridge Terrace,
Oxford OX1 1UP
Tel: 01865 246620   Fax: 01865 246857
Email: info@saxoncourt.com
http://www.shane-english.co.uk

SILC UK
26 Queen Street,
Maidenhead SL6 1HZ
Tel: 01628 781444   Fax: 01628 781 196
Email: silcuk@silc.fr

Southbourne School of English
30 Beaufort Road, Southbourne
Bournemouth BH6 5AL
Tel: 01202 422022   Fax: 01202 4171108
Email: details@southbourneschool.co.uk
http://www.southbourneschool.co.uk

Southern College
81 Lansdowne Road,
Bournemouth BH1 1RP
Tel: 01202 780010   Fax: 01202 780009

Speak & Learn Languages
154a Castle Hill,
Reading RG1 7RP
Tel: 0118 958 1103   Fax: 1189393227
Email: speak_learn@netmatters.co.uk
http://www.speakandlearnlanguages.com

Spires International
Linch Hill Leisure Park, Stanton Harcourt
Oxford OX8 1BB
Tel: 01865 882443   Fax: 01865 882870
Email: info@spiresinternational.co.uk
http://www.spiresinternational.co.uk

St. Brelade's College
Mont Les Vaux, St. Aubin
JERSEY JE2 8AF
Tel: 01534 741305   Fax: 01534 741159
Email: sbc@itl.net
http://www.st-brelades-college.co.uk

St. Clare's, Oxford
139 Banbury Road,
Oxford OX2 7AL
Tel: 01865 552031   Fax: 01865 553751
Email: marketing@stclares.ac.uk
http://www.stclares.ac.uk

St. George's International Summer School
Windsor Boy's School, 1 Maidenhead Road
Windsor SL4 5EH
Tel: 01753 863882   Fax: 01753 833186

Swan School of English
111 Banbury Road,
Oxford OX2 6JX
Tel: 01865 553201   Fax: 01865 552923
Email: english@swanschool.com
http://www.swanschool.com
See display for further details

THE SWAN SCHOOL OF ENGLISH
OXFORD

Quality courses for students
and teachers. British Council and
EAQUALS accreditation guarantees
highest standards.

General English, 25+ Courses
Business English
Overseas Teachers' Courses
One-to-One Tuition, Special Courses
Exam Preparation.

111 Banbury Road, Oxford OX2 6JX
Tel: 01865 553201   Fax: 01865 552923

E-mail: english@swanschool.com
Website: http://www.swanschool.com

TEC Poole Language School
Newfoundland House, The Quay
Poole BH15 1HJ
Tel: 01202 686675   Fax: 01202 686675
Email: info@tecpoole.co.uk
http://www.tecpoole.co.uk

Thames Valley Cultural Centres
15 Park St.,
Windsor SL4 1LU
Tel: 01753 852001   Fax: 01753 831165
Email: english@tvcc.demon.co.uk

Thornton College
Convent of Jesus & Mary,
Milton Keynes MK17 0HJ
Tel: 01280 812610   Fax: 01280 824042

Trinity School
Buckeridge Road,
Teignmouth TQ14 8LY
Tel: 01626 774138   Fax: 01626 771541
Email: trinsc123@aol.com
http://www.trinityschool.co.uk

Triple Alliance English Language Services
67 Radley Road, Abingdon
Oxford OX14 3PN
Tel: 01235 528575   Fax: 01235 520373
Email: kate@triplealliance.co.uk
http://www.triplealliance.dabsol.co.uk

Typically English
143 Hollow Way,
Oxford OX4 2NE
Tel: 01865 775854   Fax: 01865 775854
Email: typenglish@aol.com

Vacational Studies
Pepys' Oak, Tydehams
Newbury RG14 6JT
Tel: 01635 523333   Fax: 01635 523999
Email: vacstuds@vacstuds.com
http://www.vacstuds.com

Wessex Academy School of English
84/86 Bournemouth Road, Parkstone
Poole BH14 0HA
Tel: 01202 744700   Fax: 01202 716266
Email: office@wessexacademy.co.uk
http://www.wessexacademy.co.uk

Westbourne English Language School
24 Westover Road,
Bournemouth BH1 2BZ
Tel: 01202 294054   Fax: 01202 294054
Email: welschool@bournemouth-net.co.uk
http://www.artisan-inter.net/wels/

Westway Language Centre
176 Friar Street,
Reading RG1 1HE
Tel: 0118 956 0610   Fax: 0118 951 0910
Email: impact@future-impact.co.uk
http://www.impactraining.co.uk/

White House Guardianships
34 Talbot Road,
Bournemouth BH9 2JF
Tel: 01202 521100   Fax: 01202 776509
Email: guardianship@white-house-education.co.uk
http://www.white-house.education.co.uk

Winchester School of English
Beaufort House, 49 Hyde St.
Winchester SO23 7DX
Tel: 01962 851844   Fax: 01962 851844
Email: english@winchestersoe.co.uk
http://www.winchestersoe.co.uk

Windsor English Language Centre
51 Albany Road,
Windsor SL4 1HL
Tel: 01753 866966   Fax: 01753 866966
Email: info@WindsorEnglishLanguageCentre.co.uk
http://www.WindsorEnglishLanguageCentre.co.uk

Windsor Schools
21 Osborne Road,
Windsor SL4 3EG
Tel: 01753 858995   Fax: 01753 831726
Email: info@windsorschools.co.uk
http://www.windsorenglish.com

STATE COLLEGES / UNIVERSITIES

Abingdon & Witney College
Wootton Road,
Abingdon OX14 1GG
Tel: 01235 555585   Fax: 01235 553168
Email: inquiry@abingdon-witney.ac.uk
http://www.abingdon-witney.ac.uk

Amersham & Wycombe College
High Wycombe Campus, Spring Lane
Flackwell Heath, High Wycombe HP7 9HN
Tel: 01494 735555   Fax: 01494 735577
Email: Amcintyre@amersham.ac.uk
http://www.amersham.ac.uk

Aylesbury College
Oxford Road,
Aylesbury HP21 8PD
Tel: 01296 434111

Basingstoke College of Technology
Worthing Road,
Basingstoke RG21 8TN
Tel: 01256 306350   Fax: 01256 306444
Email: Annabel.Stowe@bcot.ac.uk
http://www.bcot.ac.uk

Bournemouth & Poole College of Further Education
International Operations, Lansdown Centre
Bournemouth BH1 3JJ
Tel: 01202 205656   Fax: 01202 205991
Email: intops.bpcfe@dial.pipex.com
http://www.thecollege.co.uk

Bracknell & Wokingham College
Montague House, Broad St.
Wokingham RG40 1AU
Tel: 0118 902 9150   Fax: 0118 902 9160
Email: international@bracknell.ac.uk
http://www.bracknell.ac.uk

Brockenhurst College
Lyndhurst Road, Brockenhurst
Hampshire SO42 7ZE
Tel: 01590 23565

East Berkshire College
Claremont Road,
Windsor SL4 3AZ
Tel: 01753 793000   Fax: 01753 793119
Email: audreyrenton@eastberks.ac.uk
http://www.eastberks.ac.uk

East Berkshire College
Boyn Hill Avenue,
Maidenhead SL6 4FZ
Tel: 01753 793000   Fax: 01753 793432

East Berkshire College
Station Road,
Langley SL3 8BY
Tel: 01753 793000

Eastleigh College
Chestnut Avenue,
Eastleigh SO50 5HT
Tel: 023 8032 6326   Fax: 023 80399912
Email: sdowner@eastleigh.ac.uk
http://www.eastleigh.ac.uk

English Language Support Centre
Millbrook Centre, Mill End Road
High Wycombe HP12 4BA
Tel: 01494 522021   Fax: 01494 522021

Farnborough College
Boundary Road,
Farnborough GU14 6SB
Tel: 01252 407307   Fax: 01252 407041
Email: info@farn-ct.ac.uk
http://www.farn-ct.ac.uk

Highbury College of Technology
Dovercourt Road, Cosham
Portsmouth PO6 2SA
Tel: 023 9238 3131

Isle of Wight College
Medina Way, Newport
Isle of Wight PO30 5TA
Tel: 01983 526631   Fax: 01983 522803
Email: Jeanetteh@iwightc.ac.uk
http://iwightc.ac.uk

Milton Keynes College
Chaffron Way Centre, Woughton Campus
West Leadenhall, Milton Keynes MK6 5LP
Tel: 01908 684444

Newbury College
Oxford Road,
Newbury RG13 1PQ
Tel: 01635 42824

North Oxfordshire College & School of Art
Broughton Road,
Banbury OX16 9QA
Tel: 01295 252221

Oxford Brookes University
International Centre for English Language
Studies, Gipsy Lane Campus, Headington
Oxford OX3 0BP
Tel: 01865 483874   Fax: 01865 484377
Email: icels@sol.brookes.ac.uk
http://www.brookes.ac.uk/sol/home/icels.html

Oxford College of Further Education
City Centre Campus, Oxpens Road
Oxford OX1 1SA
Tel: 01865 269268   Fax: 01865 269412
Email: enquiries_oxford@oxfe.ac.uk
http://www.oxfe.ac.uk

Reading College & School of Arts & Design
Crescent Road,
Reading RG1 5RQ
Tel: 0118 967 5442   Fax: 0118 967 5441
Email: spargoc@reading-college.ac.uk
http://www.reading-college.ac.uk

South Downs College
College Road, Purbrook Way
Havant PO7 8AA
Tel: 023 9279 7979   Fax: 023 92356124
Email: college@southdowns.ac.uk
http://www.southdowns.ac.uk

Southampton City College
St. Mary Street,
Southampton SO14 1AR
Tel: 023 8048 4848   Fax: 023 8057 7473
Email: information@southampton-city.ac.uk
http://www.southampton-city.ac.uk

University of Buckingham
Hunter St.,
Buckingham MK18 1EG
Tel: 01280 820377   Fax: 01280 820391
Email: gerry.loftus@buck.ac.uk

University of Portsmouth
Language Centre, Park Building
King Henry I Street, Portsmouth PO1 2DZ
Tel: 023 9284 6112   Fax: 023 9284 6156
Email: language.centre@port.ac.uk
http://www.port.ac.uk/english@portsmouth
See display for further details

UNIVERSITY OF PORTSMOUTH
LANGUAGE CENTRE

Historical port and seaside - London 80
minutes - direct ferries to Continent.
Mix with British students.
Free Internet / Email.
Prize-winning business English publications.
Start any month.
Excellent exam results.
Courses for teachers of English.

Park Building, King Henry I Street,
Portsmouth PO1 2DZ

Tel: +44 23 9284 6112
Fax: +44 23 9284 6156
Email: language.centre@port.ac.uk
http://www.port.ac.ukenglish@portsmouth

University of Reading
School of Linguistics & Applied Lang. Studies
Whiteknights, PO Box 241
Reading RG6 6WB
Tel: 0118 931 8511   Fax: 1189756506
Email: SLALS@reading.ac.uk
http://www.rdg.ac.uk/AcaDepts/cl/SLALS/
index.htm

University of Southampton
Language Centre, Highfield
Southampton SO17 1BJ
Tel: 023 8059 2222   Fax: 023 80593849

Institution Name	Availability	Junior Ages	Specials	Price /week	Status
A. Zaccari's English School	A: 1-10 J: 1-10	14-15 yrs	B, T, H	£77-£375	
Abingdon & Witney College	A: 9-7		B, E	£130 max.	
Accent Language School	A: 1-12 J: 7-9	12-18 yrs	B, F, H, E	£180-£325**	ABLS
Albion International Study Centre	A: 1-12 J: 1-12	8-16 yrs	B, T, F, E	£130-£300	EuroInternatsBeratung member
Amersham & Wycombe College	A: 9-6		B	£9.20 (4/hrs wk)	
Anderson Executive English	A: 1-12		B, T, F, H	£1466**	
Anglo European School of English	A: 1-12 J: 4, 6-8	15 yrs +	B, T, F, H, C, E	£70-£170 approx.	GBC, Arels
Anglo-Continental	A: 1-12 J: 1-2, 6-8	10-15 yrs	B, T, F, H, E	£95-£1040	GBC, Arels
Ardmore Language Group	J: 4, 6-8	9-17 yrs		£250-£400**	
Aspect Bournemouth	A: 1-12		B, H, T, F, E	£199-£277**	
Aspect ILA Bournemouth	A: 1-12			On application	
Aspect ILA Bournemouth - Westbourne College	A: 1-12		B, E	£200-£260+**	GBC, Arels
Aspect ILA Oxford - Austen House	A: 1-12			On application	GBC, Arels
Aspect ILA Oxford - Henley House	A: 1-12		B, E	On application	GBC, Arels
Basingstoke College of Technology	A: 1-12		B	£5050 (EU) £11 (non-EU)	
BEET Language Centre	A: 1-12		B, T, F, H, E	£112-£160	GBC, Arels
Bidbury Greywalls	A: 3-12 J: 7-8 (mostly 1-1)	14-18 yrs	B, T, F, E	£450-£810	GBC
Bidbury Lake	A: 1-12		B, F	£450-£810	
Bob Lewis ELT	A: 1-12 (1-1 only)		B, F	£500-£825	
Bournemouth & Poole College of Further Education	A: 1-12		E	£100-£150	GBC, Baselt
Bournemouth Business School International	A: 1-12		B, T, F, H, C, E	£130-£210	GBC, Arels
Bournemouth International Language College	A: 1-12		B, T, F, H, C, E	£125-£900	

Institution Name	Availability	Junior Ages	Specials	Price /week	Status
Bournemouth International School	A: 1-12 J: 3-4, 7-8	14-15 yrs		£112-£125	GBC, Arels, Relsa
Bournemouth One to One English Language School	A: 1-12		B, T, F, H, C, E	£890-£1490**	
Bracknell & Wokingham College	A: 9-7		B, T, E	£90-£100	Baselt
BTS	A: 1-12			£59-£85	
Business and Legal Homestay	A: 1-12		B, F, E	£600-£750**	
Centre for International Education	A: 1-12 J: 1-12	8-15 yrs	B, E	£150-£200	GBC, Arels
Churchill House English Home Tuition Courses	A: 1-12 J: 1-12 (1-1 only)	7 yrs +	B, T, F, H, C, E	£450-£780**	
Collingham Oxford	A: 1-12 J: 1-12	13 yrs +	B	£295-£485**	
Direct Effect Training & Development Ltd	A: 1-12		B, T, F, H	Price on application	
Dorset International College	A: 1-12 J: 1-12	12-16 yrs	B, E	£20-£185	GBC, AQA
Eagle International School	J: 7-8	11-17 yrs		On application	GBC, Arels
East Berkshire College	A: 1-12		B, H, T, C, E	£100-£250	
Eckersley School of English	A: 1-12		B, E	£170-£210	GBC, Arels
ELC London Street	A: 1-12 J: 6-8	10 yrs +	B, T, F, H	On application	
ELT Banbury	A: 1-12 J: 7-8	10-20 yrs	B, F (also aviation)	£150-/1wk, £4600/36wks	GBC, Arels
English Host Holidays	A: 1-12 J: 1-12 (1-1 only)	11-16 yrs		£150-£500	
English Language Centre	A: 1-12		B	£10-£60	
English Language Support Centre	A: 9-6			£4.25 (2hrs) £25.50 (6hrs)	
English Learning Holidays	A: 1-12 J: 1-12 (1-1 only)	15 yrs +		from £400**	
English Tuition Services	A: 1-12 J: 1-12 (mostly 1-1)	12-15 yrs	C	£300-£400**	
English Tutorial Centre (The)	A: 1-12 J: 1-12	5-15 yrs	B, T, F, H, C, E	£265	
ETC	A: 1-12 J: 3-4, 7-8	10-17 yrs	B, T, F, H, C, E	£70-£800	

Institution Name	Availability	Junior Ages	Specials	Price /week	Status
Eurocentre, Bournemouth	A: 1-12 J: 1, 6-8	12-16 yrs	B, E	£125-£300+ (J: includes **)	
Europartner Language Holidays and Group Travel Ltd	A: 1-5, 9-12 J: 6-8	11-17 yrs		£340-£560**	
European Summer School of Arts & Languages	A: 7-8			£370**	
Eurospeak	A: 1-12			£32-£36	
Face to Face	A: 1-12 J: 7-9	15-18 yrs	B, T, H, C, E	£850-£1200**	
Farnborough College	A: 9-6			£17-£70	
Gornall School of English	A: 1-12		B, E	£80-£130	
Greylands School of English.	A: 1-12 J: 7-8	14-17 yrs		£103-£170	GBC, Arels
Habyn Hill House	A: 1-12 J: 5-9		B, F, E	£500-£700**	
Harrow House International Colleges	A: 1-12 J: 1-11	8-17 yrs	B, T, H, C, E	£225-£313**	GBC, Arels, DFEE
Heathfield School for Girls	J: 7-8	8-18 yrs		£500** (approx.)	GBC, Baselt
Homelingua	A: 1-12 (1-1 only)		B	On application	
Homestay English Learning	A: 1-12 (1-1 only)			On application	
Inter-Continental Communications	A: 1-12			£200-£1450**	
Interlingua - Jersey	A: 1-12 J: 1-12	9-21 yrs	B, T, F, E	£175-£750	
Interlink School of English	A: 1-12 J: 7-8	14-16 yrs		£90-£140	GBC, Arels
International College of English	A: 1-12 J: 1-12	6-18 yrs	B	£100-£130	
International Quest	A: 1-12 J: 1-12	7 yrs +		On application	
Intuition Languages	A: 1-12 J: 1-12 (1-1 only)	14-18 yrs	B, T, F, C, E	£555-£1040**	GBC, Arels
Isle of Wight College	A: 1-12 J: 6-8	12-16 yrs	B, T, H, C, E	£55-£178	
Jersey School of English	A: 1-12		B	£195-£950	
King's Junior School	J: 1-12	9-15 yrs		£235-£280**	

Institution Name	Availability	Junior Ages	Specials	Price /week	Status
King's School of English	A: 1-12 J: 6-8	9-17 yrs	B, C, E	£116-£333	GBC, Arels
King's School Oxford	A: 1-12		B, C, E	£189-£367**	GBC, Arels
Lake School of English Oxford	A: 1-12 J: 7-8	11-16 yrs	B, C, E	£260-£260	GBC, Arels
Language Management	A: 1-12		B, T, F, H, C, E	£850 (20hrs 1-1) £1850 (30hrs grp.of 4)	
Language Specialists International	A: 1-12		B, T, F, C, E	£110-£1200	GBC, Arels
Leander Grey & Associates Ltd.	A: 1-12 J: 1-12 (1-1 only)	8 yrs +	B, F, C, E	£500-£600**	
Learn English	A: 1-12 J: 4-6 (1-1 only)	12-16 yrs	B	£320-£395**	
Lewis School of English	A: 1-12 J: 7-8	12-17 yrs	B, T, E	£83-£156	GBC, Arels
Lines Languages	J: 7-8	8-18 yrs		£680-£700**	GBC, Arels
Lingua Travel English & Educational	A: 1-12 (1-1 only)		B, T, F, H, E	£19/hr	HPN
Link Education & Guardian Service	A: 1-12 J: 1-12			On application	ABLS
Live in Languages Ltd	A: 1-12 (1-1 only)		B, T, F, H, C, E	£568-£1185**	GBC, Arels
Lymington Language	A: 1-12		B, E	£260-£750	
Meridian School of English	A: 1-12 J: 7-8	12-17 yrs	B	£46-£112	GBC, Arels
MLS International College	A: 1-12		B, T, C, F, E	£120-£185	
MLS International College	A: 1-12 J: 7-8	14-17 yrs	B, T, F, H, C, E	£135-£1560	GBC, Arels
MM Oxford Study Services Ltd.	A: 7-8 J: 7-8	13-16 yrs		£400** (approx.)	GBC, Arels
New Horizons	A: 1-12		B, T, H, E	£225-£296 (15hrs)**	
Newbold College	A: 1-12		E	£270**	GBC
Newbury Hall	J: 1-12	11-16 yrs		£315-£650**	
OISE Central Reservations	A: 1-12 J: 1-12	7-18 yrs	B, F, E	£150-£1150	
OISE Oxford Intensive School of English	A: 1-12		B	£405-£1270**	GBC

Institution Name	Availability	Junior Ages	Specials	Price /week	Status
Olcote Guardianships & Language Services	A: 1-12 J: 1-12	8 yrs +	B, H	£450-£655**	
Oxford Academy	A: 1-12		B, F, E	£230-£500	
Oxford Brookes University	A: 1-12 J: 7-8	Closed grps only	B, T, C, E	£8.50-£217	GBC, Baself
Oxford College of Further Education	A: 1-12 J: 7-8	14+ yrs	B, T, F, H, C, E	£87-£120	
Oxford County Courses at Millbrook House	J: 1-11	7-15 yrs	E	£350-£480**	
Oxford English Centre	A: 1-12 J: 1-2, 6-9	14-17 yrs	B, T, F, C, E	£140-£870	
Oxford House School of English	A: 1-12		B, T, F, H, E	£170-£1140	GBC, Arels
Oxford Language Centre	A: 1-12 J: 4, 7, 8		B, C, E	On application	
Oxford Language Training	A: 1-12		B, C, E	£130-£190	GBC, Arels
Oxford Study Centre	A: 7-9 J: 6,7,9	12-16 yrs		£270-£590**	GBC, Arels
Oxford Tutorials	A: 1-12 J: 7-9	14-16 yrs	B, E	£235-£260**	GBC, Arels
Oxfordlife	A: 1-12 J: 6-9	12-16 yrs		£295-£550**	ABLS
Podworth College (Girls only - except summer)	A/J: 1-12	14-25yrs (9-16 summer)	B, E	£400**	GBC, Arels
Parkland International	J: 7-8	11-17 yrs		£460**	GBC, Arels
Personal English Tutors	A: 1-12 J: 1-12 (1-1 only)	14-15 yrs	B, T, F, E	£255-£915**	ABLS
Pippins Home-Stays	J: 1-12	11-17 yrs		£125-£250**	
Reading College & School of Arts & Design	A: 1-12		E	£105	
Red Dragon Languages Consultancy	A: 1-12		B, T, H, E	£70-£400	BLS
Regent Oxford	A: 1-12		B, F, C, E	£117-£1240	GBC, Arels
Richard Language College	A: 1-12 J: 6-8	11-17 yrs	B	£119-£150	GBC, Eaquals
Scanbrit School of English	A: 1-12			£99-£132	GBC, Arels
Shane English School, Oxford	A: 1-12		B, E	£100-£185	

Institution Name	Availability	Junior Ages	Specials	Price/week	Status
SILC UK	A: 1-12 J: 1-12	9-18 yrs		£150-£500**	
South Downs College	A: 9-6			£1.70 (2hrs/wk)	
Southampton City College	A: 9-6		B, C	£3 (home)-£100 (overseas)	
Southbourne School of English	A: 1-12 J: 6-8	10 yrs +	B, H	£121-£330	GBC, Arels
Speak & Learn Languages	A: 1-12 J: 1-12 (1-1 only)	11-15 yrs	B, E	£50-£1500	
St. Brelade's College	A: 1-12 J: 2-10	9-18 yrs	B	£230-£730	
St. Clare's, Oxford	A: 1-12 J: 7-8	10-16 yrs	B, F, C, E	£300-£1000	GBC, Arels
Swan School of English	A: 1-12		B	£220-£960	GBC, Arels, Eaquals
TEC Poole Language School	A: 1-12		B, T, F, H	£110-£180	
Thames Valley Cultural Centres	A: 7-8 J: 6-8	10-17 yrs		£275-£450**	GBC, Arels
Thornton College	J: 6-8			£330-£500**	
Trinity School	A: 1-12 J: 1-12	12-18 yrs	B, T, H, C	£400-£1280**	GBC
Triple Alliance English Language Services	A: 1-12 J: 1-12	12 yrs +	B	£120 (1-1 £540**)	
University of Portsmouth	A: 1-12		B, C, E	£121.20-£200	GBC, Baselt
University of Reading	A: 1-12		E	£210	Boleap
Vocational Studies	J: 7-8	11-17 yrs		£465**	GBC, Arels
Wessex Academy School of English	A: 1-12		B, T	£62-£155	GBC, Arels
Westbourne English Language School	A: 1-12 J: 1-12	5-16 yrs	B, T, F, E	£90-£240 (more for business)	
Westway Language Centre	A: 1-12		T, C	£30-£45	
White House Guardianships	placements in UK schools and colleges	8 yrs +		On application	
Winchester School of English	A: 1-12		B	£133-£144	GBC, Arels
Windsor English Language Centre	A: 1-12			£69-£139	GBC
Windsor Schools	A: 1-12		B, T, F, H, C, E	£17-£50	

3 LONDON

Includes the Greater London area.

A vibrant city which has it all: monuments, museums, art galleries, cathedrals, palaces, theatres, shops, restaurants, night-clubs. The list is endless, for this large capital city caters for all tastes.

The theatres in the West End offer a wide variety of entertainment, from the world's longest running play, The Mousetrap, to world-class opera and Andrew Lloyd-Webber hits such as Sunset Boulevard and Cats.

Vibrant street fashions, black taxis, red double-decker buses: they are all to be found in London.

For those wishing to learn English in London, there are many schools to choose from, and of course the city is well served by its two international airports, Heathrow and Gatwick.

Londres: Une cité vibrante qui pourvoit à tous les goûts: musées, théâtres, magasins et boîtes de nuit; la liste est infinie. On peut assiter à un spectacle d'Andrew Lloyd-Webber, prendre un taxi noir bien Londonien, acheter des articles mode "dernier cri" pour lesquels Londres est célèbre. Une énorme gamme de cours est constamment offerte et la capitale est desservie par les aéroports d'Heathrow et de Gatwick.

Diese lebhafte Stadt bietet für alle etwas: Museen, Theater, Geschäfte und Bars, die Liste ist endlos. Man kann ein Andrew Lloyd-Webber Musical besuchen, im berühmten schwarzen Taxi fahren oder sich nach dem letzten Schrei einkleiden, wofür London bekannt ist. Es wird eine große Anzahl von Sprachkursen angeboten. Natürlich ist London von den Fluhäfen Heathrow und Gatwick leicht zu erreichen.

Londres: Una ciudad llena de vida que ofrece algo de interés para cada visitante: museos, teatros, almacenes y salas de fiestas; la lista es interminable. Se puede, ver desde un espectáculo musical de Andrew Lloyd Webber, hasta viajar en un taxi típico Londinense o comprar articulos de moda por los que Londres es muy famoso. Hay muchísimos cursos en oferta y la capital tiene los aeropuertos internacionales de Heathrow y Gatwick.

Città brulicante, Londra ha da molto da offrire ad ogni genere di visitatore: musei, teatri, negozi e night club; l'elenco è infinito. Si puo godere di un musical di Andrew Lloyd-Webber, viaggiare in uno dei suoi tipici taxi neri, i cabs, o acquistare un capo all' ultima moda per cui Londra è famosa.

C'è una ampia gamma di corsi di lingua tra cui scegliere e, ovviamente, la città è servita dagli aeroporti di Heathrow e Gatwick.

SIGHTS

Really far too numerous to list! They include:

Madame Tussaud's
Famous wax-works museum, including the chamber of horrors! Underground Station: Baker Street.

The British Museum
One of the world's greatest museums, housing over 4 million artefacts. Underground Station: Russell Square/ Holborn.

The National Gallery
Fine collection of Western paintings from 13th - 19th century. Includes works by Van Gogh, da Vinci and Renoir. Underground Station: Leicester Square/ Charing Cross.

Buckingham Palace
Permanent residence of the Queen, with regular changing of the guard at 11.30am. Entry into the palace is allowed for 2 months in the summer. Underground Station: St. James's Park/ Green Park

Houses of Parliament & Big Ben
The ornate clock tower and seat of government. Underground Station: Westminster.

For further information contact the London Tourist Board and Convention Bureau, 26 Grosvenor Gardens, London. SW1W 0DU.

 DIRECTORY OF EFL BOOKSELLERS IN THIS REGION:

(NB: Many bookshops hold a good selection of EFL material, even if they are not listed below. Moreover, if the particular book you are looking for is not in stock, they can order it for you.)

Blackwell's
100 Charing Cross Rd, London WC2H 0JG
Tel: 020 7292 5100 Fax: 020 7240 9665
Web: http://bookshop.blackwell.co.uk

Bookshop Limited
177 Malden Road, Cheam SM3 8QY
Tel: 020 8641 0481 Fax: 020 8641 0481
Web: http://www.bookshopltd.com

Centerprise Bookshop
136 Kingsland High Street, Dalston
London E8 2NS
Tel: 020 7254 9632 Fax: 020 7923 1951

The Children's Bookshop
1 Red Lion Parade, Bridge Street
Pinner HA5 3JD
Tel: 020 8866 9116 Fax: 020 8866 9116
Web: http://www.thechildrensbookshop.com

Dar Al-Taqwa Ltd
7A Melcombe Street, London NW1 6AE
Tel: 020 7935 6385 Fax: 020 7224 3894
Web:http://www.daraltaqwa.com

Eastside Books Ltd
178 Whitechapel Road, London E1 1BJ
Tel: 020 7247 0216 Fax: 020 7377 6120

The European Bookshop
5 Warwick Street, London W1R 5RA
Tel: 020 7734 5259 Fax: 020 7287 1720
Web: http://www.eurobooks.co.uk

Fielders
54 Wimbledon Hill Road, Wimbledon
London SW19 7PA
Tel: 020 8946 5044 Fax: 020 8944 1320
Web:http://www.fielders.co.uk

The Greek Bookshop
29 Doveridge Gardens, London N13 5BJ
Tel: 020 8882 1910 Fax: 020 8882 1910
Web: http://www.thegreekbookshop.com

Harrow School Book Shop
7 High Street, Harrow-on-the-Hill HA1 3HU
Tel: 020 8872 8212 Fax: 020 8872 8014

Heath Educational Book Supplies
Willow Hse, Willow Walk, Sutton SM3 9QQ
Tel: 020 8644 7788 Fax: 020 8641 3377

Index Bookcentre
16 Electric Avenue, London SW9 8JX
Tel: 020 7274 8342 Fax: 020 7274 8351
Web: http://www.indexbooks.co.uk

Keltic
154 Southampton Row, Bloomsbury
London, WC1B 5AX
Tel: 020 7278 6110 Fax: 020 7278 6110
http://www.keltic.co.uk

The Kilburn Bookshop
8 Kilburn Bridge, Kilburn High Road
London NW6 6HT
Tel: 020 7328 7071 Fax: 020 7372 6474

The Learning Centre Bookshop
Hammersmith & West London College
Gliddon Road, London W14 9BL
Tel: 020 7565 1244 Fax: 020 8741 2491

LCL International Ltd
104-106 Judd Street, London WC1H 9NT
Tel. 020 7837 0486 Fax: 020 7833 9452
Web: http://www.lclib.com

Ottakar's Bookstore
Units 5/6, High Road, Wood Green
Shopping Centre, London N22 6YD
Tel: 020 8889 3777 Fax: 020 8889 9895
Web: http://www.ottakars.co.uk

Ottakar's Bookstore
The Glades Shopping Centre
Bromley BR1 1DJ
Tel: 020 8460 6037 Fax: 020 8460 6036
Web: http://www.ottakars.co.uk

Ottakar's Bookstore
26 Church Street, Enfield EN2 6BE
Tel: 020 8363 6060 Fax: 020 8363 6464
Web: http://www.ottakars.co.uk

Ottakar's Bookstore
70 St Johns Road, London SW11 1PT
Tel: 020 7978 5844 Fax: 020 7978 5855

Ottakar's Bookstore
77 High Street, Staines TW18 4PQ
Tel: 01784 490404 Fax: 01784 490229
Web: http://www.ottakars.co.uk

Ottakar's Bookstore
6-6A Exchange Centre Putney
London SW15 1TW
Tel: 020 8780 2401 Fax: 020 8780 0861
Web: http://www.ottakars.co.uk

Parents Centre Activities
745/747 Barking Road, London E13 9ER
Tel: 020 8552 9993 Fax: 020 8471 2589

Prospero Book Cafe
19 Church Lane, Leytonstone Town Centre
London E11 1HG
Tel: 020 8539 9040 Fax: 020 8539 9042
Web: http://www.prosperobookcafe.com

The Riverside Bookshop
18/19 Hay's Galleria, London Bridge City,
Tooley Street, London SE1 2HD
Tel: 020 7378 1824 Fax: 020 7407 5315
Web: http://www.riversidebookshop.com

W & G Foyle Ltd
113-119 Charing Cross Road
London WC2H 0EB
Tel: 020 7437 5660 Fax: 020 7434 1580

Waterstone's
Goldsmiths' College, New Cross
London SE14 6NW
Tel: 020 8469 0262 Fax: 020 8694 2279
Web: http://www.waterstones.co.uk

Waterstone's
The Grand Building, Trafalgar Square
London WC2N 5EJ
Tel: 020 7839 4411 Fax: 020 7839 1797
Web: http://www.waterstones.co.uk

Waterstone's
203-206 Piccadilly, London W1V 9LE
Tel: 020 7851 2400 Fax: 020 7851 2401
Web: http://www.waterstones.co.uk

Waterstone's
128 Camden High St., London NW1 0NB
Tel: 020 7284 4948 Fax: 020 7482 3457
Web: http://www.waterstones.co.uk

Waterstone's
266 Earls Court Road, London SW5 9AS
Tel: 020 7370 1616 Fax: 020 7244 6641
Web: http://www.waterstones.co.uk

Waterstone's
150 Kings Road, London SW3 3NR
Tel: 020 7351 2023 Fax: 020 7351 7709
Web: http://www.waterstones.co.uk

Waterstone's
82 Gower Street, London WC1E 6EQ
Tel: 020 7636 1577 Fax: 020 7580 7680
Web: http://www.waterstones.co.uk

Waterstone's
11 Islington Green, London N1 2XH
Tel: 020 7704 2280 Fax: 020 7704 2152
Web: http://www.waterstones.co.uk

Waterstone's
121 Charing Cross Rd, London WC2H 0EA
Tel: 020 7434 4291 Fax: 020 7437 3319

Waterstone's
193 Kensington High St., London W8 6SH
Tel: 020 7937 8432 Fax: 020 7938 4970
Web: http://www.waterstones.co.uk

Waterstone's
St Mary's Road, London W5 5RF
Tel: 020 8840 6205 Fax: 020 8840 6729
Web: http://www.waterstones.co.uk

Waterstone's
2-6 Hill Street, Richmond TW10 6UA
Tel: 020 8332 1600 Fax: 020 8940 2595
Web: http://www.waterstones.co.uk

West End Lane Books
277 West End Lane, London NW6 1QS
Tel: 020 7431 3770 Fax: 020 7431 7655

A➡Z DIRECTORY OF COURSES IN THIS REGION

PRIVATE SCHOOLS / ORGANISATIONS

Abceda.com
22 Glyn Mansions,
London W14 8XH (correspondence only)
Tel: 020 7603 9243   Fax: 020 7602 3006
Email: mike@abceda.com
http://www.abceda.com

About English London Limited
5 Usborne Mews,
London SW8 1LR
Tel: 020 7587 0272   Fax: 020 7587 0272
Email: about@englishlondon.co.uk
http://www.englishlondon.co.uk
See display for further details

ABOUT ENGLISH LONDON Ltd

Learn English in London, birthplace of the modern English language.

Stay in your tutor's home.

Learn and absorb everyday conversation and tour a city rich in English tradition and culture.

5 Usborne Mews
London SW8 1LR

Tel: +44 (0)20 7587 0272
Fax: +44 (0)20 7587 0272
Email: about@englishlondon.co.uk
Web: http://www.englishlondon.co.uk

Academy International School of English
3 Queen's Gardens, Bayswater
London W2 3BA
Tel: 020 7262 7481   Fax: 020 7262 0854
Email: info@central-london-english.co.uk
http://www.central-london-english.co.uk

Academy of Professional Studies (APS)
114-115 Tottenham Court Road,
London W1T 5AH
Tel: 020 7388 8126   Fax: 020 7388 8127
Email: enquiries@apslondon.co.uk
http://www.apslondon.co.uk

Active Learning
4a King St,
London W6 0QA
Tel: 020 8748 6665   Fax: 020 8748 6773
Email: info@activ.org

Advanced English at Queenslea
18 Geneva Road,
Kingston-upon-Thames KT1 2TW
Tel: 020 8546 6381   Fax:
Email: subs@queenslea.co.uk
http://www.queenslea.co.uk

AEP Academy English Programmes
33 St. Mary's Rd, Ealing
London W5 5RG
Tel: 020 8840 4712   Fax: 020 8840 4677
Email: aeplondon@aol.com
http://www.aep-london.co.uk

Alpha International School of English
Meridian House, Greenwich High Road
Greenwich, London SE10 8TL
Tel: 020 8853 5697   Fax: 020 8858 5553
Email: english@alpha-int.co.uk
http://www.alpha-int.co.uk
See display for further details

AMI Progressive Language Services
444a Edgware Road,
London W2 1EG
Tel: 020 7724 4407   Fax: 020 7724 6809
Email: ami@anja.demon.co.uk
http://www.anja.demon.co.uk

Anglo European Study Tours (AEST)
8 Celbridge Mews,
London W2 6EU
Tel: 020 7229 4435   Fax: 020 7792 8717
Email: anglo@aest.co.uk
http://www.aest.co.uk

Angloschool
146 Church Road,
London SE19 2NT
Tel: 020 8653 7285   Fax: 020 8653 9667
Email: english@angloschool.co.uk
http://www.angloschool.co.uk
See display for further details

Aspect ILA London
3-4 Southampton Place,
London WC1A 2DA
Tel: 01202 638100   Fax: 01202 438900
Email: enquiries@aspectworld.com
http://www.aspectworld.com

Avalon School of English
Avalon House, 8 Denmark Street,
London WC2H 8LS
Tel: 020 7379 1998   Fax: 0207 916 5261
Email: paul.weeks@avalonschool.co.uk
http://www.avalonschool.co.uk
See display for further details

Bales Language School
742 Harrow Road, Kensal Green
London W10 4AA
Tel: 020 8960 5899   Fax: 020 8960 8296
Email: principal@balescollege.co.uk
http://www.balescollege.co.uk

Bell Language School
34 Fitzroy Square,
London W1P 6BP
Tel: 020 7637 8338   Fax: 020 7637 4811
Email: info@bell-schools.ac.uk
http://www.belllondon.com

Beltring Language Courses
Capel House, 83 Kew Green
Richmond TW9 3AH
Tel: 020 8940 5240   Fax: 020 8940 5340
Email: beltlang@aol.com

School of English

English Speaking Courses, Central London

- 85% Speaking & Listening

- 15% Reading & Writing

- Class size: average 8, max. 12

Other Services:

▸ **Exam preparation:**
   Cambridge PET to Proficiency
   (Average Pass Rate 85%: Proficiency Pass Rate 100%)
   English for Business; Travel and Tourism; IELTS

▸ **Cafe & study centre, roof garden, free internet access**

▸ **English homestay accommodation and airport pickup**

▸ **Social programme & UK excursions**

CAMBRIDGE EXAM PASS PROMISE
FREE LESSONS IF YOU FAIL
(Terms and conditions apply)

Avalon School of English Limited

www.avalonschool.co.uk

Tel: ++44 (0) 20 7379 1998

8 Denmark Street, London WC2H 8LS

Email: paul.weeks@avalonschool.co.uk

Fax: ++ 44 (0) 20 7916 5261

Berlitz
321 Oxford St.,
London W1A 3BZ
Tel: 020 7408 2474   Fax: 020 7493 4429

Better English!
31 St. James's Ave,
London N20 0JS
Tel: 020 8368 7660   Fax: 020 8368 7660
Email: info@betterenglish.net
http://www.betterenglish.net

Britannia Academy of English
1517a London Road,
Norbury SW16 4AE
Tel: 020 8239 1515   Fax: 020 8239 1551
Email: study@britanniaacademy.co.uk
http://www.britanniaacademy.co.uk

Bromley Language Centre
240 High St.,
Bromley BR1 1PQ
Tel: 020 8464 5149   Fax: 020 8325 2276
Email: bromlang@yahoo.co.uk
http://www.bromleylanguage.freeserve.co.uk
See display for further details

BROMLEY LANGUAGE CENTRE

Friendly, professional school,
family atmosphere.
Small classes & personal attention.
Green residential area
(15 mins from Central London).
Visa assistance.
Accommodation service.
Cambridge Examinations.
Start any Monday
Member UK Institute of Linguists.

240 High Street, Bromley, Kent BR1 1PQ

Tel: +44 (0)20 8464 1883 or 5149
Fax: + 44 (0)20 8325 2276
Email: bromlang@yahoo.co.uk
http://www.bromleylanguage.freeserve.co.uk

Bromley School of English
2 Park Road,
Bromley BR1 3HP
Tel: 020 8313 0308   Fax: 020 8313 3957
Email: info@bromleyschool.com
http://www.bromleyschool.com

Brudenell School of English
15a The Mall, Ealing
London W5 2PJ
Tel: 020 8566 5710   Fax: 020 8566 5720
Email: joan@brudenell.uk.com
http://www.brudenell.uk.com
See display for further details

Burlington School of English
1-3 Chesilton Road,
London SW6 5AA
Tel: 020 7736 9621   Fax: 020 7371 8131
Email: marketing@burlingtonschool.co.uk
http://www.burlington-school.co.uk

Callan School of English
139 - 143 Oxford St.,
London W1R 1TD
Tel: 020 7437 4573   Fax: 020 7494 3204
Email: csl@callan.co.uk
http://www.callan.co.uk

Cambridge School of English
7-11 Stukeley St., Covent Garden
London WC2B 5LB
Tel: 020 7242 3787   Fax: 020 7242 3626
Email: info@cambridgeschool.co.uk
http://www.cambridgeschool.co.uk

Camden College of English
61 Chalk Farm Road,
London NW1 8AN
Tel: 020 7482 5380   Fax: 020 7284 4347
Email: stu@camdencollege.demon.co.uk
http://www.camdencollege.com

Canning
4 Abingdon Road,
London W8 6AF
Tel: 020 7937 3233   Fax: 020 7937 1458
Email: enquiry@canning.co.uk
http://www.canning.co.uk

Cavendish College
35-37 Alfred Place,
London WC1E 7DP
Tel: 020 7580 6043   Fax: 020 7255 1591
Email: learn@cavendish.ac.uk
http://www.cavendish.ac.uk

Central School of English
1 Tottenham Court Road,
London W1T 1BB
Tel: 020 7580 2863   Fax: 020 7255 1806
Email: enquiry@centralschool.co.uk
http://www.centralschool.co.uk

Chelsea SW6 School of English Ltd
2 Michael Road
London SW6 2AD
Tel: 020 7610 6116   Fax: 020 7384 0253
Email: chelseaschool@aol.com

**Churchill House English Home Tuition
Courses -** *See South East display for details*

Cites
5 Stile Parade, Chiswick High Road
London W4 3AG
Tel: 020 8747 9696   Fax: 020 8747 1188
Email: info@cites.co.uk
http://www.cites.co.uk

City of London College
Neil House, 7 Whitechapel Road
London E1 1DU
Tel: 020 7247 2166   Fax: 020 7247 1226
Email: Registrar@clc-london.ac.uk
http://www.clc-london.ac.uk

CL English Language School
170 Westminster Bridge Road,
London SE1 7RW
Tel: 020 7633 9460   Fax: 020 7633 9460
Email: info@clenglish.co.uk
http://www.clenglish.co.uk

Clark's International Summer School
13 Friern Park,
London N12 9DE
Tel: 020 8445 7049   Fax: 020 8445 6681
Email: clarksissc@aol.com
http://members.aol.com/clarksissc/

College of Central London
73 Great Eastern Street,
London EC2A 3HR
Tel: 020 7833 0987   Fax: 020 7837 2959
Email: ccl@btinternet.com
http://www.central-college.co.uk

Communicaid Group (The)
21-25 Earl Street,
London EC2A 2AL
Tel: 020 7426 8400   Fax: 020 7426 8408
Email: info@communicaid.com
http://www.communicaid.com

Computing and Business College
Metropolitan Business Centre, Suite B010
Enfield Road, London N1 5AZ
Tel: 020 7923 7466   Fax: 020 7249 0500
Email: cbcedu@aol.com

Conversation Piece
120 Windermere Road,
London W5 4TH
Tel: 020 8579 4567   Fax: 020 8579 3352
Email: lc@conversation-piece.co.uk
http://www.conversation-piece.co.uk

Covent Garden Language Centre
Africa House, 64-78 Kingsway
London WC2B 6AH
Tel: 020 7831 9820   Fax: 020 7831 9830
Email: cglc@LALschool.org

Crest Schools of English
192b Station Road,
Edgware HA8 7AR
Tel: 020 8952 8040   Fax: 020 8952 4980
Email: info@crestschools.com
http://www.crestschools.com

Dean College of London
97-101 Seven Sisters Road, Holloway
London N7 7QP
Tel: 020 7281 4461   Fax: 020 7281 7849
Email: deancollegeUK@aol.com

East Finchley School of English
197 High Road,
London N2 8AJ
Tel: 020 7794 9410   Fax: 020 7431 7703
Email: clockie@efse.com
http://www.efse.com

Ebury Executive English
132 Ebury St.,
London SW1W 9QQ
Tel: 020 7730 3991   Fax: 020 7730 1794
Email: EburyEE@aol.com

Eden House College
46 Oxford Street,
London W1D 1BE
Tel: 020 7637 5959   Fax: 020 7637 2442
Email: enquiries@edenhouse.co.uk
http://www.edenhouse.co.uk

Edgware Academy of Languages
205 Edgware Road,
London W2 1ES
Tel: 020 7262 0944   Fax: 020 7262 0948
Email: info@english-courses.co.uk
http://www.english-courses.co.uk

Edwards Language School
38 The Mall, Ealing
London W5 3TJ
Tel: 020 8566 3684   Fax: 020 8566 4911
Email: edwardslang@btinternet.com
http://www.edwards-language-school.com

EF International School of English
74 Roupell St.,
London SE1 8SS
Tel: 020 7401 8399   Fax: 020 7401 3717
Email: languages.gb@ef.com
http://www.ef.com

ELS Language Centres
3 Charing Cross Rd,
London WC2H 0HA
Tel: 020 7976 1066   Fax: 020 7976 1055
Email: elsuk@compuserve.com
http://www.els-london.com

ELT
18 Old Town,
London SW4 0LB
Tel: 020 7622 7254   Fax: 020 7627 2016
Email: eltlondon@aol.com
http://www.englangtrain.co.uk

ELT English Language Tuition
1 Childs Lane, Crystal Palace
London SE19 3RZ
Tel: 020 8771 4611   Fax: 020 8771 1918
Email: info@eltlondon.com
http://www.eltlondon.com

Embassy CES London
Froebel College, Roehampton Institute
Roehampton Lane, London SE15 5PJ
Tel: 020 8392 3692   Fax: 020 8392 3731
Email: london@embassyces.com
http://www.embassyces.com

English [OutThere!]
10 Coptic Street, Bloomsbury
London WC1A 1NH
Tel: 020 7813 1633   Fax: 020 7813 1634
Email: info@EnglishOutThere.co.uk
http://www.EnglishOutThere.co.uk

English and Cultural Studies Centres
40 Village Road,
Enfield EN1 2EN
Tel: 020 8360 4118   Fax: 020 8364 1854
Email: JPicci8918@aol.com
http://members.aol.com/JPicci8918

English for Serious Purposes
16 Highcliffe, 32 Albemarle Road
Beckenham BR3 5HJ
Tel: 020 8650 6942
Email: simon-read@esp-beckenham.demon.co.uk

English Language Institute
Royal Waterloo House, 51-55 Waterloo Rd
London SE1 8TX
Tel: 020 7928 0029   Fax: 020 7401 2231
Email: lcceli@aol.com
http://www.londoncitycollege.com

English School at the Chelsea Centre
World's End Place, King's Road
London SW10 0HE
Tel: 020 7376 5901   Fax: 020 7376 5901
Email: english.lessons@btinternet.com
http://www.theenglishchool.co.uk

English Studio (The)
54 Uxbridge Road, Shepherd's Bush
London W12 8LP
Tel: 020 8735 0565   Fax: 020 8740 0699
Email: info@the-englishstudio.com
http://www.the-englishstudio.com

Eurocentres London Central
56 Eccleston Square,
London SW1V 1PH
Tel: 020 7834 4155   Fax: 020 7834 1866
Email: vic-info@eurocentres.com
http://www.eurocentres.com

Eurocentres, Lee Green
21 Meadowcourt Road,
London SE3 9EU
Tel: 020 8318 5633   Fax: 020 8318 9057
Email: sgibbons@eurocentres.com
http://www.eurocentres.com

European Business School
Summer Courses, Regent's College
Inner Circle, Regent's Park, London NW1 4NS
Tel: 020 7487 7495   Fax: 020 7487 7602
Email: markhamt@regents.ac.uk
http://www.regents.ac.uk

European Language Skills
Roman House, 9/10 College Road
London E3 5AN
Tel: 020 8983 3363   Fax: 020 8980 2627

**European Language Studies
International Ltd**
Commonwealth Hall, Cartwright Gardens
London WC1H 9EB
Tel: 020 7388 9095   Fax: 020 7388 9095
Email: elsi@dial.pipex.com

Evendine College
22 Grosvenor Gardens,
London SW1W 0DH
Tel: 020 7730 4070   Fax: 020 7881 0852
Email: evendine@evendine.com
http://www.evendine.com

Excel Communications Ltd
51 Tweedy Road,
Bromley BR1 3NH
Tel: 020 8466 7070   Fax: 020 8466 5111
Email: walton@excel.bdx.co.uk

Excel English
The Hall, 8 Muswell Hill
London N10 3TD
Tel: 020 8365 2485   Fax: 020 8442 1143
Email: info@excelenglish.co.uk
http://www.excelenglish. co.uk

ExploreUKLand (EUKL)
Acorn House, 74-94 Cherry Orchard Rd,
Croydon CR9 6DA
Tel: 020 8664 8831   Fax: 020 8665 5855
Email: admin@exploreukland.co.uk
http://www.exploreukland.co.uk
See display for further details

ExploreUKLand (EUKL)

Professional, imaginative teaching designed with you in mind.

Language courses for corporate clients and individuals/groups with qualified teachers in comfortable surroundings tailor-made to suit your needs.

Acorn House,
74-94 Cherry Orchard Road
Croydon, Surrey CR9 6DA

Tel: +44 (0)20 8664 8831
Fax: +44 (0)20 8665 5855
E-mail: Admin@exploreukland.co.uk
Website: http://www.exploreukland.co.uk

Frances King School of English
77 Gloucester Road,
London SW7 4SS
Tel: 020 7870 6533   Fax: 020 7341 9771
Email: info@francesking.co.uk
http://www.francesking.co.uk

Friendly Tutors Online Tuition
2, Firethorn Close,
Edgware HA8 9GF
Tel: 020 8201 0128   Fax:
Email: contact@friendlytutors.co.uk
http://www.friendlytutors.co.uk

GEOS English Academy London
16-20 New Broadway, Ealing
London W5 2XA
Tel: 020 8566 2188   Fax: 020 8566 2011
Email: languages@euroaccents.co.uk
http://www.euroaccents.co.uk

Golders Green College
11 Golders Green Road,
London NW11 8DY
Tel: 020 8731 0963   Fax: 020 8455 6528
Email: teachertraining@ggcol.fsnet.co.uk
http://www.clct.co.uk/ttc

Hampstead School of English
553 Finchley Road,
London NW3 7BJ
Tel: 020 7794 3533   Fax: 020 7431 2987
Email: info@hampstead-english.ac.uk
http://www.hampstead-english.ac.uk

Harrow House International College London
103 Palace Road, Hampton Court
London KT8 9DU
Tel: 01929 424421   Fax: 01929 427175
Email: karin.abarrow@lds.co.uk
http://www.harrowhouse.com
See display in South England for details

Holborn English Language Services
14 Soho Street,
London W1D 3DN
Tel: 020 7734 9989   Fax: 020 7437 1302
Email: english@holborn.co.uk
http://www.holborn-english.co.uk

Homestay Providers' Association (HPA)
PO Box 2431,
Romford RM6 6BZ
Tel: 020 8262 2617   Fax: 020 8262 2617
Email: enquiry@hpa.org.uk
http://www.hpa.org.uk

International Community School - I.C.S.
4 York Terrace East, Regent's Park
London NW1 4PT
Tel: 020 7935 1206   Fax: 020 7935 7915
Email: skola@easynet.co.uk
http://www.skola.co.uk

International House
106 Piccadilly,
London W1V 9FL
Tel: 020 7491 2598   Fax: 020 7409 0959
Email: info@ihondon.co.uk
http://www.ihlondon.com

International Language Academy
457-463 Caledonian Road,
London N7 9BA
Tel: 020 7700 6438   Fax: 020 7697 5753
Email: ilalond@rmplc.co.uk
http://www.language-academies.com

InterNexus London
Regent's College, Inner Circle
Regent's Park, London NW1 4NS
Tel: 020 7487 7489   Fax: 020 7487 7409
Email: london@internexus.to
http://www.internexus.to

InTuition Languages
4 Ravey Street,
London EC2A 4QP
Tel: 020 7739 4411   Fax: 020 7729 0933
Email: learn@intuitionlang.com
http://www.intuitionlang.com
See display for further details

ISIS Greenwich School of English
259 Greenwich High Road,
Greenwich SE10 8NB
Tel: 020 8293 1444   Fax: 020 8293 1199
Email: info@isisgroup.co.uk
http://www.isisgroup.co.uk

Kensington Academy of English
86 Old Brompton Road,
London SW7 3LQ
Tel: 020 7584 7580   Fax: 020 7584 2637
Email: info@kensingtonacademy.com
http://www.kensingtonacademy.com

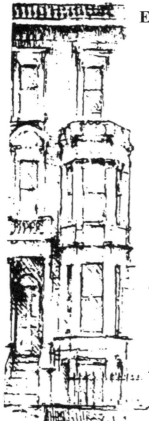

Kensington Academy of English
69 Notting Hill Gate,
London W11 3JS
Tel: 020 7221 6665   Fax: 020 7243 1730
Email: info@kensingtonacademy.com
http://www.kensingtonacademy.com

Key Languages
Douglas House, 16-18 Douglas Street
Westminster, London SW1P 4PB
Tel: 020 7630 6113   Fax: 020 7630 6114
Email: keylanguages@keylanguages.demon.co.uk

King Street College
47, Shepherd's Bush Green,
London W12 8PS
Tel: 020 8749 6780   Fax: 020 8742 9649
Email: info@kingstreet.co.uk
http://www.kingstreet.co.uk
See display for further details

King Street College
4 Hammersmith Broadway,
London W6 7AL
Tel: 020 8748 0971   Fax: 020 8741 1098
Email: info@kingstreet.co.uk
http://www.kingstreet.co.uk
See display for further details

King's School of English, (London)
25 Beckenham Road,
Beckenham BR3 4PR
Tel: 020 8650 5891   Fax: 020 8663 3224
Email: info@kingslon.co.uk
http://www.kingslon.co.uk

Kingsley School of English
4 Wellgarth Road,
London NW11 7HR
Tel: 020 8458 6058   Fax: 020 8458 6058
Email: info@kingsleyschoolofenglish.co.uk
http://www.kingsleyschoolofenglish.co.uk

Kingston Hill School of English
6 Sussex Road,
New Malden KT3 3PY
Tel: 020 8401 2899   Fax: 020 8401 2899
Email: registrar@kingstonhill.com
http://www.kingstonhill.com

Kingswood Learning & Leisure Group
Linton House, 164-180 Union St.
London SE1 0LH
Tel: 020 7922 1234   Fax: 020 7928 7733
Email: sales@campbeaumont.com
http://www.campbeaumont.com

Language Link
21 Harrington Road,
London SW7 3EU
Tel: 020 7225 1065   Fax: 020 7584 3518
Email: languagelink@compuserve.com
http://www.languagelink.co.uk

Language Link
181 Earls Court Rd,
London SW5 9RB
Tel: 020 7225 1065   Fax: 020 7584 3518
Email: languagelink@compuserve.com
http://www.languagelink.co.uk

Language Network
PO Box 55, Tinkers Hill
Furneux Pelham SG9 0TP
Tel: +49 30 45027649   Fax: +49 30 45027649
Email: info@LanguagesForLife.com
http://www.languagesForLife.com

Language Quest
Suite 405, Bondway Commercial Centre
71 Bondway, London SW8 1SQ
Tel: 020 7820 7503   Fax: 020 7733 8290
Email: evelyn_ono@hotmail.com

Language Studies International
19-21 Ridgmount St,
London SW7 3EU
Tel: 020 7467 6500   Fax: 020 7323 1736
Email: lon@lsi.edu
http://www.lsi.edu

Language Studies International
13 Lyndhurst Terrace,
London NW3 5QA
Tel: 020 7794 8111   Fax: 020 7431 5681
Email: ham@lsi.edu
http://www.lsi.edu

Learn English the Easy Way
3 Selborne Rd,
Croydon CR0 5JQ
Tel: 020 8688 4427   Fax:
Email: learneasy02@hotmail.com
http://www.learnenglishtheeasyway.com

Leicester Square School of English
22 Leicester Square,
London WC2H 7LE
Tel: 020 7839 7772   Fax: 020 7839 2377
Email: neelisha@lsse.ac.uk
http://www.lsse.ac.uk

Lesson One School of English
22-30 Keeley Road,
Croydon CR0 1TE
Tel: 020 8760 1907   Fax: 020 8760 5071
Email: learn@lesson-one.co.uk
http://www.lesson-one.co.uk

LETS (London English Teaching Services) Ltd
15, Westbourne Terrace,
London W2 3UN
Tel: 020 7402 5933   Fax: 020 7229 2904
Email: information@lets-english.co.uk
http://www.lets-english.co.uk
See display for further details

LETS (LONDON ENGLISH TEACHING SERVICES) Ltd

1-1 intensive courses, fortnightly.
Executives & other professionals
Comfortable central London hotel
Individual language needs our speciality
Enjoyable hard work
Friendly experienced teachers
Socialize with English people
Fee includes accommodation & lunch

15 Westbourne Terrace, London W2 3UN

Tel: +44 (0) 20 7402 5933
Fax: +44 (0) 20 7229 2904
Email: information@lets-english.co.uk
Web: http://www.lets-english.co.uk

Lilian Bishop School of English
1 Harrington Road,
London SW7 3ES
Tel: 020 7591 0345   Fax: 020 7591 3922
Email: sales@lilianbishop.com
http://www.lilianbishop.com

Linguarama Ltd.
8 Queen St.,
London EC4N 1SP
Tel: 020 7236 7206   Fax: 020 7236 1992
Email: londoncity@linguarama.com
http://www.linguarama.com/english/index.html

LITE, Piccadilly
1 Sherwood Street, Piccadilly Circus
London W1V 7RA
Tel: 020 7439 2240   Fax: 020 7439 2260
Email: info@litepiccadilly.com
http://www.litepiccadilly.com

London Academy
George House, 75b George St.,
Croydon CR0 1LD
Tel: 020 8686 8111   Fax: 020 8686 0373
Email: jon.reeves@lineone.net

London English Language Academy
77-83 The Broadway, West Ealing
London W13 9BP
Tel: 020 8579 9661   Fax: 020 8579 3919
Email: info@london-english-language-academy.co.uk
http://www.london-english-language.academy.co.uk

London Film Academy
The Old Church, 52a Walham Grove
London SW6 1QR
Tel: 020 7386 7711   Fax: 020 7381 6116
Email: info@londonfilmacademy.com
http://www.londonfilmacademy.com

London Institute of Technology and English
11A Pratt Street, Camden Town
London NW1 0AE
Tel: 020 7284 2559   Fax: 020 7267 4187
Email: Study@Lite11.freeserve.co.uk

London Language & Drama School, StarTek Associates
30 Brondesbury Park,
London NW6 7DN
Tel: 020 8830 0074   Fax: 020 8830 4992
Email: enquiries@startek-uk.com
http://www.startek-uk.com

London Life English
30, Fryent Way, Kingsbury
London NW9 9SB
Email: enq@london-life-english.co.uk
http://www.london-life-english.co.uk

London Meridian College
67-83 Seven Sisters Road,
London N7 6BU
Tel: 020 7561 7077   Fax: 020 7561 7078
Email: registrar@meridiancollege.co.uk
http://www.meridiancollege.co.uk

London School of English
15 Holland Park Gardens,
London W14 8DZ
Tel: 020 7603 1656   Fax: 020 7603 5021
Email: quality@londonschool.com
http://www.londonschool.com

London School of Management
43-47 New Broadway, Ealing
London W5 5AH
Tel: 020 8567 4355   Fax: 020 8810 0215
Email: lsm@cableinet.co.uk
http://www.lsm.ac..uk

London Skills Institute (The)
1st Floor, College House,
67-83 Seven Sisters Road
London N7 6BU
Tel: 020 7317 9020   Fax: 020 7317 9021
Email: registrar@tlsi.co.uk
http://www.tlsi.co.uk

London Study Centre
Munster House, 676 Fulham Road
London SW6 5SA
Tel: 020 7731 3549   Fax: 020 7731 6060
Email: lsc.uk@compuserve.com
http://www.londonstudycentre.com

Management International
63-69 Eltham Road,
London SE12 8UF
Tel: 020 8852 1261   Fax: 020 8297 0514
Email: info@managementinternational.co.uk
http://managementinternational.co.uk

Marble Arch Intensive English - M.A.I.E.
21 Star St.,
London W2 1QB
Tel: 020 7402 9273   Fax: 020 7724 2219
Email: skola@easynet.co.uk
http://www.skola.co.uk

Mayfair School of English
45 Oxford St.,
London W1R 2DZ
Tel: 020 7437 9941   Fax: 020 7494 3611
Email: enquiries@mayfairschool.co.uk
http://www.mayfairschool.co.uk

Mayfair School of English
27a James St., Covent Garden
London WC2 8PA
Tel: 020 7240 8889   Fax: 020 7379 6917
Email: enquiries@mayfairschool.co.uk
http://www.mayfairschool.co.uk

Metropole College
7 Praed Street, Paddington
London W2 1NJ
Tel: 020 7706 2685   Fax: 020 7706 2723
Email: metropole_college_edu@msn.com
http://www.metropolecollege.com

Milner School of English
32 Worple Road Mews,
London SW19 4DB
Tel: 020 8944 8800   Fax: 020 8944 8266
Email: milner.school@virgin.net
http://www.milnerschool.co.uk

Netherhall International College
18b Netherhall Gardens,,
London NW3 5TH
Tel: 020 7794 1122   Fax: 020 7794 8455
Email: secretary@nic.netherhall.org.uk
http://www.nic-netherhall.co.uk

NetLearn Languages
28 Appledore Avenue,
Ruislip HA4 0UU
Tel: 020 8845 5555   Fax: 07092 106305
Email: enquiries@netlearnlanguages.com
http://www.netlearnlanguages.com

Norwood English
20 Hadley Gardens, Norwood Green
Southall UB2 5SQ
Tel: 020 8893 6253   Fax: 020 8893 6253
Email: norwoodeng@aol.com
http://members.aol.com/norwoodeng/

OISE London Intensive School of English
19-23 Oxford St.,
London W1R 1RF
Tel: 020 7494 3456   Fax: 020 7494 3366
Email: admissions.london@oise.net

Our World English Schools
3 High View Court, 65 Horniman Drive
London SE23 3BZ
Tel: 020 8291 5978   Fax: 020 8291 5978
Email: bookings@ourworld-english.demon.co.uk
http://www.ourworld-english.demon.co.uk
Courses held at Dulwich College

Oxford English Homestays
Head Office: No.11, 7 Elm Park Gardens,
London SW10 9QG
Tel: 07905 285566   Fax:
Email: info@english-homestays.co.uk
http://www.english-homestays.co.uk

Oxford House College
28 Market Place, Oxford Circus
London W1W 8AW
Tel: 020 7580 9785   Fax: 020 7323 4582
Email: english@oxfordhouse.co.uk
http://wwww.oxfordhousecollege.co.uk

Passport Language Schools
37 Park Road,
Bromley BR1 3HJ
Tel: 020 8464 6925   Fax: 020 8466 5928
Email: courses@passport.uk.com
http://www.passport.uk.com

Polyglot Language Centre
214 Trinity Road,
London SW17 7HP
Tel: 020 8767 9113   Fax: 020 8767 9104
Email: english@polyglot.co.uk
http://www.polyglot.co.uk
See display for further details

POLYGLOT LANGUAGE CENTRE

Maximum 10 students per class.

General English, Business English, 1-1, Cambridge Examinations and IELTS.

Small, friendly school in green, residential area with easy access to Central London (10mins to Victoria).

214 Trinity Road, London SW17 7HP

Tel: +44 (0) 20 8767 9113
Fax: +44 (0) 20 8767 9104
E-Mail: english@polyglot.co.uk
Website: http://www.polyglot.co.uk

Princes College
36 New Oxford Street,
London WC1A 1EP
Tel: 020 7636 4052   Fax: 020 7637 7291
Email: enquiries@princescollege.com
http://www.princescollege.com
See display for further details

PRINCES COLLEGE

Well-known school in the heart of London.

Recognised by the Association of British Language Schools (ABLS).

English courses prepare for Cambridge PET/FCE/CAE/CPE Examinations.

Open all year: £180/4wks.
£740/1 academic yr.

36 New Oxford Street
London WC1A 1EP

Tel: +44 (0) 20 7636 4052
Fax: +44 (0) 20 7637 7291
Email: enquiries@princescollege.com
Website: www.princescollege.com

Purley Language College Ltd
14 Brighton Road, Purley CR8 3AB
Tel: 020 8660 5060   Fax: 020 8668 4022
Email: enquiries@purleycollege.com
http://www.purleycollege.com

Queens English
166 West Barnes Lane,
Motspur Park KT3 6LR
Tel: 020 8949 0594   Fax: 020 8949 0594
Email: vittoria@queens-english.co.uk
http://www.queens-english.co.uk
See display for further details

Radcliffe College
185 Oxford St.,
London W1R 1TA
Tel: 020 7734 4214   Fax: 020 7734 4218
Email: cambridge@radcliffe-college.com
http://www.radcliffecollege.co.uk
See display for further details

Radcliffe College
53 Oxford St.,
London W1R 1RD
Tel: 020 7494 1083   Fax: 020 7494 1084
Email: cambridge@radcliffe-college.com
http://www.radcliffecollege.co.uk
See display for further details

Regent London
12 Buckingham St, London WC2N 6DF
Tel: 020 7872 6620   Fax: 020 7872 6630
Email: london@regent.org.uk
http://www.regent.org.uk

Richmond English Language Institute
American International University in London
Queens Road, Richmond TW10 6JP
Tel: 020 8332 9000   Fax: 020 8332 1596
Email: enroll@richmond.ac.uk
http://www.richmond.ac.uk

Richmond Language Training Centre
32 Hill Street,
Richmond-upon-Thames TW9 1TW
Tel: 020 8332 7732   Fax: 020 8332 7732
Email: info@rlt.co.uk
http://www.rlt.co.uk
See display for further details

RLI Language Services
122 Coldershaw Road,
London W13 9DT
Tel: 020 8567 3988   Fax: 020 8840 9287
Email: info@language-tuition.co.uk
http://www.language-tuition.co.uk
See display for further details

RLI LANGUAGE SERVICES

RLI is a tuition and short course centre for adults based in London.

We offer one to one language tuition at all levels, specialist language tuition and home tuition courses.

122 Coldershaw Road
London W13 9DT

Tel: +44 (0) 20 8567 3988
Fax: +44 (0) 20 8840 9287

Email: info@language-tuition.co.uk
Web: http://www.language-tuition.co.uk

QUEENS ENGLISH

166 West Barnes Lane, Motspur Park, Surrey KT3 6LR
Tel: 0044 (0)20 8949 0594   Fax: 0044 (0)20 8949 0594
Email: info@queens-english.co.uk   http://www.queens-english.co.uk

- ☑ Our courses achieve results fast and effectively.
- ☑ We want you to improve your level of English quickly and with results that last in time.
- ☑ We prepare for all the Cambridge exams.
- ☑ You can expect qualified, experienced, mother tongue teachers.
- ☑ We can help you with your accommodation and Visa applications.
- ☑ We promise small classes and a friendly environment.
- ☑ All levels welcome.
- ☑ Business and One-to-One courses available.
- ☑ Homestay Courses.
- ☑ Contact us for free advice.

Cambridge

Examinations

RICHMOND LANGUAGE TRAINING CENTRE

- GENERAL ENGLISH
- ACADEMIC ENGLISH
- BUSINESS ENGLISH

All levels of ability
Small Group & Individual tuition
Social Programme - sport, activity and excursion programme
4-week modules throughout the year

RLT is located in elegant surroundings close to the River Thames and within 20 minutes of central London

RLT Admissions
32 Hill Street, Richmond-Upon-Thames
Surrey TW9 1TW

Tel: +44 (0)20 8948 3333
Fax: +44 (0)20 8332 7732
Email: info@rlt.co.uk   www.rlt.co.uk

Sels College
64-65 Long Acre, Covent Garden
London WC2E 9SX
Tel: 020 7240 2581   Fax: 020 7379 5793
Email: english@sels.co.uk
http://www.sels.co.uk
See display for further details

Shane English School London
59 South Molton St.,
London W1K 5SN
Tel: 020 7499 8533   Fax: 020 7499 9374
Email: marketing@shane-english.co.uk
http://www.shane-english.co.uk

St Giles International London Central
154 Southampton Row,
London WC1B 5AX
Tel: 020 7837 0404   Fax: 020 7837 4099
Email: londoncentral@stgiles.co.uk
http://www.stgiles-international.com

St Giles International London Highgate
51 Shepherds Hill,
London N6 5QP
Tel: 020 8340 0828   Fax: 020 8348 9389
Email: londonhighgate@stgiles.co.uk
http://www.stgiles-international.com

St. George International
76 Mortimer St.,
London W1N 7DE
Tel: 020 7299 1700   Fax: 020 7299 1711
Email: info@stgeorges.co.uk
http://www.stgeorges.co.uk

St. George's College
182 Seven Sisters Road,
London N7 7PX
Tel: 020 7263 7842   Fax: 020 7281 9789

St. John's Wood School of English
126 Boundary Road,
London NW8 0RH
Tel: 020 7624 1925   Fax: 020 7328 6877
Email: sjw-school@dial.pipex.com
http://www.sjw-school.co.uk
See display for further details

St John's Wood School Of English

SJW School London offers Intensive General
English Courses and Cambridge University
examination courses for adults only -
the minimum age is 18.
There are 10 classrooms.

The maximum number of students in each
class on Maincourse and on Cambridge
University Examination Courses is 8.

Small classes are essential for rapid progress,
and maximum student/teacher contact.

All courses are 25 hours per week,
and cost £180 per week.

SJW IS ACCREDITED BY THE **BRITISH COUNCIL**

Local homestay or hotel accommodation
can easily be arranged.

126, Boundary Road, London NW8 0RH
Tel: 44 207 624 1925 Fax: 44 207 328 6877
Email: sjw-school@dial.pipex.com
Web: http://www.sjw-school.co.uk

St. Patrick's International College
24 Great Chapel St.,
London W1F 8FS
Tel: 020 7734 2156   Fax: 020 7287 6282
Email: info@st-patricks.ac.uk
http://www.st-patricks.ac.uk

Stanfords School of English
1517A London Road, Norbury
London SW16 4AE
Tel: 020 8679 1116   Fax: 020 8764 4141
Email: enquiries@stanfordsschoolofenglish.co.uk
http://www.stanfordsschoolofenglish.co.uk

Stanton School of English
167 Queensway,
London W2 4SB
Tel: 020 7221 7259   Fax: 020 7792 9047
Email: study@stanton-school.co.uk
http://www.stanton-school.co.uk

Summer School of English
12 Courthope Road,
Wimbledon SW19 7RD
Tel: 020 8947 0328   Fax: 020 8296 8655
Email: SSofE@aol.com
http://www.summerschoolofenglish.co.uk

SuperStudy UK
1-3 Manor Parade, Sheepcote Road
Harrow HA1 2JN
Tel: 020 8861 5322   Fax: 020 8861 5169
Email: superstudy@btinternet.com
http://www.superstudy.com

Swandean School of English
2nd Floor, Broadway House,
112-134 The Broadway
Wimbledon, London SW19 1RL
Tel: 020 8543 5150   Fax: 020 8540 1416
Email: study@swandean.co.uk
http://www.swandean.co.uk/wimbledon

TTI School of English
148-150 Camden High Street,
London NW1 0NE
Tel: 020 7419 2300   Fax: 020 7419 2299
Email: Info@ttischool.com
http://www.ttischool.com

Twickenham Language Studies
4 York St.,
Twickenham TW1 3LD
Tel: 020 8744 0959   Fax: 020 8744 0959
Email: info@twickenhamlanguagestudies.co.uk
http://www.twickenhamlanguagestudies.co.uk

Twin Towers School of English
Abacus House, 53-55 Ballards Lane
London N3 1XP
Tel: 020 8343 3567   Fax: 020 8343 1196
Email: info@twintowers.co.uk
http://www.twintowers.co.uk

United International College
10-12 James St.,
London W1M 5HN
Tel: 020 7495 6667   Fax: 020 7495 6668
Email: registrar@uiclondon.com
http://www.uiclondon.com

Unity College
81-89 Fortress Road, Kentish Town
London NW5 1AG
Tel: 020 7482 3349   Fax: 020 7267 7067

University College Kensington
53 Uxbridge Street,
London W8 7TQ
Tel: 0207 243 4000   Fax: 0207 243 1484
Email: admissions@lcuck.ac.uk
http://www.lcuck.ac.uk

Victoria School of English
28 Graham Terrace, Sloane Square
London SW1W 8JH
Tel: 020 7730 1333   Fax: 020 7823 4175
Email: english@victoria-school.demon.co.uk
http://www.victoriaschool.co.uk

Waterloo School of English
124 Cornwall Road,
London SE1 8TQ
Tel: 020 7401 9889   Fax: 020 7401 9559
Email: study@waterlooschoolELT.co.uk
http://www.waterlooschoolELT.co.uk

Wellington Study Centre
1 Wellington Terrace, Turnpike Lane
London N8 0PX
Tel: 020 8889 1208   Fax: 020 8889 1208
Email: welstudy@clara.net
http://home.clara.net/welstudy

Wimbledon Language School
126 Wimbledon Park Road,
London SW18 5UE
Tel: 020 8874 7401   Fax: 020 8874 7401
Email: info@wimbledonls.co.uk
http://www.wimbledonls.co.uk

Wimbledon School of English
41 Worple Road,
London SW19 4JZ
Tel: 020 8947 1921   Fax: 020 8944 0275
Email: principal@wimbledon-school.ac.uk
http://www.wimbledon-school.ac.uk

World Intuition
PO Box 2189,
Woodford Green IG9 5WS
Tel: 020 8504 7549
Email: info@worldintuition.com
http://www.worldintuition.com

Young English Studies
21 Star Street,
London W2 1QB
Tel: 020 7402 9273   Fax: 020 7724 2219
Email: skola@easynet.co.uk
http://www.skola.co.uk

STATE COLLEGES / UNIVERSITIES

Acton & West London College
Mill Hill Road, Acton
London W3 8UX
Tel: 020 8231 6220   Fax: 020 8993 2725
Email: susie.kusnierz@wlc.ac.uk
http://www.westlondoncollege.ac.uk

Barnet College
Montagu Road,
London N2 0JY
Tel: 020 8266 4365   Fax: 020 8202 6727
Email: int_enq@barnet.ac.uk
http://www.barnet.ac.uk

Barnet College
Wood St.,
Barnet EN5 4AZ
Tel: 020 8440 6321   Fax: 020 8441 5236
Email: stsald@barnet.ac.uk
http://www.barnet.ac.uk

Birkbeck- University of London
Fac. of Continuing Education, 26 Russell Square
London WC1B 5DQ
Tel: 020 7631 6674   Fax: 020 7631 6688
Email: english@fce.bbk.ac.uk
http://www.bbk.ac.uk/fce

Bromley College
Rookery Lane,
Bromley BR2 8HE
Tel: 020 8295 7031   Fax: 020 8295 7051
Email: international@bromley.ac.uk
http://www.bromley.ac.uk/
See display for further details

Carshalton College
Nightingale Road,
Carshalton SM5 2EJ
Tel: 020 8770 6800   Fax: 020 8770 6887

City and Islington College
383 Holloway Road,
London NR7 0RN
Tel: 020 7700 9333   Fax: 020 7700 9222
Email: jwalsh@candi.ac.uk
http://www.candi.ac.uk

English as a Foreign Language

Full or Part-time courses

Cambridge PET, First, Advanced, Proficiency taught by fully trained teachers.

• New vocational courses available from September
• Modern multi-media suite
• Competitive rates
• Green field site close to Central London

Contact: Peter Reeves or Chantal Milnes
Tel: 020 8295 7031
Fax: 020 8295 7051

E-mail: international@bromley.ac.uk

BROMLEY COLLEGE
of Further & Higher Education

Bromley College
Rookery Lane, Bromley,
Kent BR2 8HE

www.bromley.ac.uk

City of Islington College
Finsbury Park Ctre, Prah Rd
London N4 2RA
Tel: 020 7288 4922   Fax: 020 7359 8769
Email: celta@candi.ac.uk
http://www.candi.ac.uk

City of Westminster College
25 Paddington Green,
London W2 1NB
Tel: 020 7723 8826   Fax: 020 7258 2700
Email: customer.services@cwc.ac.uk
http://www.cwc.ac.uk

City University
Room A251, Northampton Square,
London EC1V 0HB
Tel: 020 7040 5060   Fax: 020 7040 8575
Email: c.kretschmer@city.ac.uk
http://www.city.ac.uk/languages

College of North West London
Kilburn Centre, Priory Park Road
London NW6 7UJ
Tel: 020 8208 5131   Fax: 020 8208 5151
Email: international.admin@cnwl.ac.uk
http://www.cnwl.ac.uk

Croydon Continuing Education & Training Service
South Norwood Centre, Sandown Rd
London SE25 4XE
Tel: 020 8656 6620   Fax: 020 8662 1828

Croydon School of English
8 Whyteleafe Road,
Caterham CR3 5EE
Tel: 020 8686 9191   Fax: 020 8667 0078
Email: cets@clara.co.uk

Enfield College
Hertford Road,
Enfield EN3 5HA
Tel: 020 8443 3434   Fax: 020 8805 5898

English Centre for Internatiaonal Students
Hampstead Garden Suburb, Central Square
London NW11 7BN
Tel: 020 8455 8176   Fax: 020 8455 4448
Email: ec.hgsi@virgin.net
http://www.hgsi.ac.uk

Epping Forest College
Borders Lane,
Loughton IG10 3SA
Tel: 020 8504 8311   Fax: 020 8502 0186
Email: shutchin@epping-forest.ac.uk
http://epping-forest.ac.uk

Goldsmith's College (University of London)
ELU, Lewisham Way New Cross
London SE14 6NW
Tel: 020 7919 7402   Fax: 020 7919 7403
Email: m.miller@gold.ac.uk
http://www.goldsmiths.ac.uk/elu

Greenwich Community College
Kidbrooke School, Corelli Road
London SE3 8EP
Tel: 020 8331 1900   Fax: 020 8319 8040
Email: info@woolwich.ac.uk
http://www.woolwich.ac.uk

Hackney Community College
Shoreditch Campus, Falkirk Street
London N1 6HQ
Tel: 020 8613 9123   Fax: 020 7613 9003

Hammersmith & West London College
Gliddon Road, Barons Court
London W14 9BL
Tel: 020 8563 0063   Fax: 020 8563 8247
Email: cic@hwlc.ac.uk
http://www.hwlc.ac.uk

Harrow College
Temple House, 221-225 Station Road
Harrow HA1 2XL
Tel: 020 8909 6594   Fax: 020 8909 6061
Email: lkoten@harrow.ac.uk
http://www.harrow.ac.uk

Hounslow Community Education
The Civic Centre, Lampton Road
Hounslow TW3 4DN
Tel: 020 8862 5388   Fax: 020 8862 5064
Email: info@education.hounslow.gov.uk
http://www.hounslowlea.org.uk

Institute of Education
University of London, CCS, 20 Bedford Way
London WC1H 0AL
Tel: 020 7612 6504   Fax: 020 7612 6177
Email: m.scott@ioe.ac.uk
http://www.ioe.ac.uk

Kensington & Chelsea College
Marlborough Ctre, Sloane Ave
London SW3 3AP
Tel: 020 7589 2044   Fax: 020 7589 1772
Email: n.cooke@kcc.ac.uk
http://www.kcc.ac.uk

King's College London
English Language Ctre, Strand
London WC2R 2LS
Tel: 020 7848 1600   Fax: 020 7848 1601
Email: elc@kcl.ac.uk
http://www.kcl.ac.uk/elc

Kingston Community Adult Education & Training
King Charles Centre, King Charles Road
Surbiton KT5 9AL
Tel: 020 8547 6875   Fax: 020 8547 6874
Email: gill.ellis@rbk.kingston.gov.uk
http://www.kingston.gov.uk/adulteducation

Kingston University
English Language Support Programme
School of Languages, Penrhyn Road
Kingston-upon-Thames KT1 2EE
Tel: 020 8547 7863   Fax: 020 8547 7388
Email: B.Atherton@kingston.ac.uk
http://www.kingston.ac.uk

Lambeth College
Brixton Centre, 56 Brixton Hill
London SW2 1QS
Tel: 020 7501 5000   Fax: 020 7501 5325
Email: admissions@lambethcollege.ac.uk

Language Centre at the London Institute
65 Davies St,
London W1K 5DA
Tel: 020 7514 7261   Fax: 020 7514 7265
Email: language-centre@linst.ac.uk
http://www.linst.ac.uk/language
See display for further details

THE LANGUAGE CENTRE AT THE LONDON INSTITUTE

- Academic English for university preparation
- General English throughout the year
- Specialist English, Executive and one-to-one tuition
- English Plus Art and Design - short and long courses
- Accommodation in host families or student residences
- Central London location

The Language Centre at The London Institute
65 Davies Street
London
W1K 5DA

tel: +44 (0) 20 7514 7261
fax: +44 (0) 20 7514 7265
Email: language-centre@linst.ac.uk
website: http://www.linst.ac.uk/language

Lewisham College
EFL Dept., Lewisham Way
London SE4 1UT
Tel: 020 8694 3295   Fax: 020 8694 3349
http://www.lewisham.ac.uk

London Guildhall University
English Language Centre, Old Castle St.
London E1 7NT
Tel: 020 7320 1251   Fax: 020 7320 1253
Email: elc@lgu.ac.uk
http://www.lgu.ac.uk/elc

Middlesex University
White Hart Lane, Tottenham
London N17 8HR
Tel: 020 8411 6722   Fax: 020 84116655
Email: p.fanning@mdx.ac.uk
http://www.ilrs.mdx.ac.uk/lang/eng_non

Morley College
61 Westminster Bridge Road,
London SE1 7HT
Tel: 020 7928 8501   Fax: 020 7928 4074
Email: enquiries@morleycollege.ac.uk
http://morleycollege.ac.uk

NESCOT
Reigate Road, Ewell
Epsom KT17 3DS
Tel: 020 8394 3267   Fax: 020 8394 3030
Email: eflnescot@nescot.ac.uk
http://www.nescot.ac.uk/inter.html

Newham College of Further Education
High Street South, East Ham
London E6 3AB
Tel: 020 8257 4293   Fax: 020 8257 4306
Email: pam.fleisch@newham.ac.uk

Queen Mary & Westfield College
Learning Development & Continuing Ed. Unit
Mile End Road, London E1 4NS
Tel: 020 7882 5526   Fax: 020 8983 5857
Email: a.l.d.evison@qmw.ac.uk
http://www.learndev.qmw.ac.uk/elss/

Redbridge College
Little Heath,
Romford RM6 4XT
Tel: 020 8548 7436   Fax: 020 8599 8224
Email: info@redbridge.essex.sch.uk

Richmond Adult Community College
Clifden Road,
Twickenham TW1 4LT
Tel: 020 8891 5907   Fax: 020 8892 6354
Email: efl@racc.ac.uk
http://www.racc.ac.uk

Richmond Upon Thames College
Egerton Road,
Twickenham TW2 7SJ
Tel: 020 8607 8000   Fax: 020 8744 9738
Email: courses@richmond-utcoll.ac.uk
http://www.richmond-utcoll.ac.uk

Roehampton Institute London
International Unit, Roehampton Lane
London SW15 5PH
Tel: 020 8392 3151   Fax: 020 8392 3717
Email: L.Thomas@roehampton.ac.uk
http://www.roehampton.ac.uk

SCOLA Community College
St Nicholas Way,
Sutton SM1 1EA
Tel: 020 8770 6901   Fax: 020 8770 6933
Email: scola@suttonlea.org

SOAS
University of London, 4 Gower St.
London WC1E 6HA
Tel: 020 7580 8272   Fax: 020 7631 3043
Email: english@soas.ac.uk
http://www.soas.ac.uk/elu

South Bank University
English Language Services, Caxton House
103 Borough Road, London SE1 0AA
Tel: 020 7815 6409   Fax: 020 7815 6464
Email: langleg@sbu.ac.uk
http://www.sbu.ac.uk/caxton

South Thames College
50-52 Putney Hill,
London SW15 6QX
Tel: 020 8918 7380   Fax: 020 8918 7347
Email: eis@south-thames.ac.uk
http://www.south-thames.ac.uk

Southgate College
High Street, Southgate
London N14 6BS
Tel: 020 8982 5050   Fax: 020 8982 5051
Email: admiss@southgate.ac.uk
http://www.southgate.ac.uk

Southwark College
The Cut,
London SE1 8LE
Tel: 020 7815 1600   Fax: 020 7261 1301
Email: info@southwark.ac.uk
http://www.southwark.ac.uk

Stanmore College
Elm Park,
Stanmore HA7 4BQ
Tel: 020 8420 7759   Fax: 020 8420 6502
Email: jtissier@stanmore.ac.uk

Thames Valley University
St Mary's Road, Ealing
London W5 5RF
Tel: 020 8579 5000   Fax: 020 8566 1353
Email: learning.advice@tvu.ac.uk
http://www.tvu.ac.uk

**Thomas Calton Community Education
Centre**
Alpha St.,
London SE15 4NX
Tel: 020 7639 6818

Tower Hamlets College
Poplar Centre, Poplar High Street
London E14 0AF
Tel: 020 7538 5888   Fax: 020 7538 9153

University College London
UCL Language Centre, 136 Gower St.
London WC1E 6BT
Tel: 020 7679 7722   Fax: 020 7383 3577
Email: m.farina@ucl.ac.uk
http://www.ulc.ac.uk/language-centre/

University of North London
European and Language Services
236-250 Holloway Road
London N7 6PP
Tel: 020 7753 5106   Fax: 020 7753 5112
Email: els@unl.ac.uk
http://www.unl.ac.uk/els

University of Westminster
309 Regent Street,
London W1B 2UW
Tel: 020 7915 5401   Fax: 020 7911 5001
Email: efl@wmin.ac.uk
http://www.wmin.ac.uk/efl

Uxbridge College
Park Road,
Uxbridge UB8 1NQ
Tel: 01895 853300   Fax: 01895 853377
Email: pmcann@uxbridge.ac.uk
http://www.uxbridge.ac.uk

Waltham Forest College
Forest Road,
London E17 4JB
Tel: 020 8501 8091   Fax: 020 8501 8001
Email: international@waltham.ac.uk
http://www.waltham.ac.uk

West Thames College
London Road,
Isleworth TW7 4HS
Tel: 020 8326 2000   Fax: 020 8569 7787
Email: info@west-thames.ac.uk
http://www.west-thames.ac.uk

Westminster Adult Education Service
Amberley Road Centre, Amberley Road
London W9 2JJ
Tel: 020 7289 2183   Fax: 020 7641 8140
Email: info@waes.ac.uk
http://www.waes.ac.uk

Westminster Kingsway College
School of Languages, Peter St.
London W1V 4HS
Tel: 020 7437 8536   Fax: 020 7287 0711
Email: linda.roberts@westking.ac.uk
http://www.westking.ac.uk

Institution Name	Availability	Junior Ages	Specials	Price /week	Status
Abceda.com	A: 1-12			£38-£45	
About English London Limited	A:1-12 (1-1 only)		B, F	£583-£958**	
Academy International School of English	A: 1-12		B, T, H	£50-£150	
Academy of Professional Studies (APS)	A: 1-12		B	On application	
Active Learning	A: 1-12			On application	GBC
Acton & West London College	A: 9-7		E	Free-£88	
AEP Academy English Programmes	A: 1-12 (1-1 only)		B, T, F, E	£550-£780**	
Alpha International School of English	A: 1-12 J: 6-8	12 yrs +		£24-£88	
AMI Progressive Language Services	A: 1-12 (mostly 1-1 for execs)		B	On application	
Anglo European Study Tours (AEST)	A: 1-11 J: 6-8	10-18 yrs		£250-£500**	GBC, Arels
Angloschool	A: 1-12		B	£125-£190	GBC, Arels, Eaquals
Aspect ILA London	A: 1-12		B, C, E	£125-£205 (summer)	GBC, Arels
Avalon School of English	A: 1-12 J: 6-9	12-16 yrs	B, T, C, E	£37.50 - £60	
Boles Language School	A: 1-12 J: 1-12	11 yrs +	B, F, C, E	£50-£195**	
Barnet College	A: 1-12		B, T	£3+	GBC, Baselt
Barnet College	A: 1-12		B, T, C, E	On application	GBC, Baselt
Bell Language School	A: 1-12		B	£1012/2wks, £2916/12wks	GBC, Eaquals
Belhring Language Courses	A: 1-12 (1-1 only)		B, F, E	£1200-1500**	ABLS
Better English!	A: 1-12 J: 1-12 (1-1 only)	14 yrs +	B, T, E	£420**	
Birkbeck- University of London	A: 9-6		B, E	£5-£50	
Britannia Academy of English	A: 1-12 J: 7-8	15 yrs +	B	£29-£60	GBC
Bromley College	A: 1-12		B	£90-£120	

Institution Name	Availability	Junior Ages	Specials	Price /week	Status
Bromley Language Centre	A: 1-12 J: 3-4, 7-8	11-15 yrs	B, E	£54 (longer courses) - £78	
Bromley School of English	A: 1-12 J: 7-8	8-15 yrs	B	£100-£160	
Brudenell School of English	A: 1-12		B, E	£50 (£100 summer)	
Burlington School of English	A: 1-12 J: 6-7	14-18 yrs	B, T, F, E	£49-£129	GBC
Callan School of English	A: 1-12			£26-£92	
Cambridge School of English	A: 1-12		B	£45-£490	GBC, Arels
Camden College of English	A: 1-12			£65-£145	GBC, Arels
Canning	A: 1-12		B, F	£1100-£2500	GBC
Carshalton College	A: 1-12			On application	
Cavendish College	A: 1-12		B, H, T, F, C, E	£55-£65	
Central School of English	A: 1-12		B	£90-£250	
Churchill House English Home Tuition Courses	A: 1-12 J: 1-12 (1-1 only)	7 yrs +	B, T, F, H, C, E	£450-£780**	
City of Islington College	A: 9-6		B, T, C	£12-£18	
City of London College	A: 1-12		B, T, C, E	£50	
City of Westminster College	A: 1-12		B, F, E	On application	
City University	A: 8, 9			£200-£450	
CL English Language School	A: 1-12			£33-£95	ABLS
Clark's International Summer School	J: 7-8	13-18 yrs		£265**	
College of Central London	A: 1-12 J: 7-8	14-15 yrs	B, T, F, H, C	£28-£60	
College of North West London	A: 9-6		B, C, E	£20-£75	GBC, Baselt
Communicaid Group (The)	A: 1-12		B, T, F, H, C, E	£1370-£1870	
Computing and Business College	A: 1-12 J: 9-6	12-16 yrs	B, T, H, C	£20-£25	

Institution Name	Availability	Junior Ages	Specials	Price /week	Status
Conversation Piece	A: 1-12 J: 1-12 (1-1 only)	4-15 yrs	B, T, F, H, C	£20-£750	
Crest Schools of English	A: 1-12		B, T, F, H, C, E	£30-£125	GBC, Arels
Croydon Continuing Education & Training Service	A: 9-7			£10-£37.50	
Croydon School of English	A: 1-12			£32.50-£40	
Dean College of London	A: 1-12		B	£50-£70	
East Finchley School of English	A: 9-8 J: 7	10-16 yrs	B, T, H, E'	£17-£45	
Ebury Executive English	A: 1-12		B, T, F, H, C, E	£450-£1650	
Eden House College	A: 1-12 J: 1-12	15-18 yrs	B, C, E	£18-£40	
Edgware Academy of Languages	A: 1-12			£15-£30	
Edwards Language School	A: 1-12		B	£185	GBC, Arels
EF International School of English	A: 1-12		B (as 1-1)	£265** (summer)	GBC, Arels
ELS Language Centres	A: 1-12		B	£240-£310** (summer)	GBC, Arels
ELT	A: 1-12		B, T, E	£20-£90	GBC, Arels, ABLS
ELT English Language Tuition	A: 1-12 J: 6-7	11-15 yrs	B, F	£16-£48	
Embassy CES London	A: 1-12			£105-£235	GBC, Arels
Enfield College	A: 1-12			£4 (EU) £8 (non-EU)	
English [OutThere!]	A: 1-12			£23-£50	
English and Cultural Studies Centres	A: 4, 6-8 J: 4, 6-8	10-16 yrs		£248-£389**	
English Centre for International Students	A: 1-12		B, T, E	£15-£75	Baselt
English for Serious Purposes	A: 1-12		E	Negotiable	
English Language Institute	A: 1-12		B, T, H, E	£120-£185	GBC, Arels
English School at the Chelsea Centre	A: 1-12 J: 6-8	10-16 yrs	B	£22-£50	

Institution Name	Availability	Junior Ages	Specials	Price /week	Status
English Studio (The)	A: 1-12		B	£15-£45	
Epping Forest College	A: 9-6			£2.40-£44	
Eurocentres London Central	A: 1-12 J: 7-8	14-16 yrs	B	£180-£207	
Eurocentres, Lee Green	A: 1-12 J: 1, 7-8	14-16 yrs	B	£191	
European Business School	A: 6-8		B, F, E	£230	
Evendine College	A: 1-12 J: 1-12	10-15 yrs	B, T, C, E	£30-£100	
Excel Communications Ltd	A: 1-12		B, F, C, E	£100-£200+	GBC
Excel English	A: 1-12		B, E	£93-£150+	GBC, Arels
ExploreUK.and (EUKL)	A: 1-12 J: 1-12	9-15 yrs	B, T, F, H, C, E	£49-£70	
Frances King School of English	A: 1-12		B, F, E	£50-£1470	GBC, Arels
GEOS English Academy London	A: 1-11 J: 6-8	13-18 yrs	E	£135-£175	GBC, Arels
Golders Green College	A: 1-12		B, C	£35-£100	
Goldsmith's College (University of London)	A: 1-12		E	£194-£233	Baleap
Hammersmith & West London College	A: 1-12		B, T	£50-£75	GBC, Baselt
Hampstead School of English	A: 1-12 J: 6-8	10-15 yrs	B, T, E	£72-£180	
Harrow College	A: 1-12		B, T	£50 max.	GBC, Baselt
Harrow House International College London	A: 1-12		B, C, E	£265-£305**	GBC, Arels
Holborn English Language Services	A: 1-12		B	£25-£69	
Homestay Providers' Association (HPA)	A: 1-12 J: 1-12	9-16 yrs	B, T, F, H, C, E	£90-£2000**	
Hounslow Community Education	A: 1-12		B	free-£3	
International Community School - I.C.S.	J: 1-12	3-17 yrs		£235-£265	GBC, Arels
International House	A: 1-12		B, H, T, F, E	£152.50-£515	

Institution Name	Availability	Junior Ages	Specials	Price /week	Status
International Language Academy	A: 1-12 J: 7-8	8-15 yrs	B, E	£129-£160	
InterNexus London	A: 1-12		B, E	£164-£228	GBC, Arels
InTuition Languages	A: 1-12 (1-1 only)		B, T, F, H, C, E	£555-£1040**	GBC, Arels
ISIS Greenwich School of English	J: 7-8	9-18 yrs		On application	GBC, ALTO, FIYO
Kensington & Chelsea College	A: 1-12		B, E	£50-£75	GBC, Baselt
Kensington Academy of English	A: 1-12 J: 6-9	10-15 yrs	B, E	£67-£170	BAC
Kensington Academy of English	A: 1-12 J: 6-9	10-15 yrs	B, E	£67-£170	BAC
King Street College	A: 1-12		B	£20-£90	
King Street College	A: 1-12		B	£20-£90	
King's College London	A: 1-12		E	£133-£294	Baleap
King's School of English, (London)	A: 1-12			£120-£192	GBC, Arels
Kingsley School of English	A: 9-6		B	£17.50-£37.50	
Kingston Community Adult Education & Training	A: 1-12			£10.63	
Kingswood Learning & Leisure Group	J: 1-12	9-16 yrs		£388-£463**	
Lambeth College	A: 1-12			On application	
Language Centre at the London Institute (The)	A: 1-12		B, F, E	£148-£1200	GBC, Baselt
Language Link	A: 1-12		B, T, F, C, E	£190/2wks, £690/12wks	GBC, Arels
Language Link	A: 1-12		B, T, F, C, E	£190/2wks, £690/12wks	GBC, Arels
Language Network	A: 1-12 J: 7-8	11-18 yrs	B	£75-£355	
Language Quest	A: 1-12 J: 1-12	7-14 yrs	B, T, F, H, C, E	£12-£62	
Language Studies International	A: 1-12		B	£125-£160	GBC, Arels
Language Studies International	A: 1-12		B	£125-£160	GBC, Arels

Institution Name	Availability	Junior Ages	Specials	Price /week	Status
Learn English the Easy Way	A: 1-12 (1-1 only)			£225-£375 (£400-£550**)	
Leicester Square School of English	A: 1-12		E	£42-£100	GBC, Arels
LETS (London English Teaching Services) Ltd	A: 1-12		B, F, E	On application.	
Lewisham College	A: 1-7, 9-12		B	Free-£44	GBC, Baselt
Lilian Bishop School of English	A: 1-12		B	£25-£69	
Linguarama Ltd.	A: 1-12		B, F	£800+	
London Academy	A: 1-12 J: 6-8	Varies		£34-£40	
London English Language Academy	A: 1-12		B	£15-£35	
London Film Academy	A: 1-12			£225	
London Guildhall University	A: 1-12		B, C, E	£118-£122	
London Language & Drama School, StarTek Associates	A: 1-12		B, E	£101-£247.50	
London Life English	A: 1-12 J: 1-12 (mostly 1-1 only)	11 yrs +	C, E	£380-£715**	
London Meridian College	A: 1-12		B	£350-£699/4wks	
London School of English	A: 1-12		B, F, E	£220	GBC, Arels
London School of Management	A: 1-12		B, T, H, C, E	£16-£36	
London Skills Institute (The)	A: 1-12		B, C	£838/12mths	
London Study Centre	A: 1-12		B	£105/2wks, £1289/48wks	GBC, Arels
Management International	A: 1-12 J: 1-12	13-17 yrs	B, T, F, C, E	£135-£1495	
Marble Arch Intensive English - M.A.I.E.	A: 1-12		B, E	£80-£180	GBC, Arels
Mayfair School of English	A: 1-12		B	£33.15-£150	GBC
Mayfair School of English	A: 1-12		B	£33.15-£150	GBC
Metropole College	A: 1-12 J: 1-12	15 yrs +	C	£60-£100	GBC

Institution Name	Availability	Junior Ages	Specials	Price /week	Status
Middlesex University	A: 1-12		B, E	£54-£240	Baleap
Milner School of English	A: 1-12			£80-£130	GBC, Arels
Morley College	A: 1-12		B, C, E	£15	
NESCOT	A: 1-12			£65 (summer - min.stay 4wks)	GBC, Baselt
Netherhall International College	A: 1-12		B, T, E	£98-£128	GBC
NetLearn Languages	A: 1-12		B, E	299-1675 €	
Newham College of Further Education	A: 9-6			On application	
Norwood English	A: 1-12 J: 1-12	9-15 yrs	B, T, C, E	£350-£950**	
OISE London Intensive School of English	A: 1-12		B, C, E	£67-Various rates	
Our World English Schools	J: 7-8	9-13 & 14-18 yrs		£1250**/2wks, £2890**/6wks	GBC, Arels
Oxford English Homestays	A: 1-12 J: 1-12	16 yrs +	B, T, F, H, C, E	£350-£550**	
Oxford House College	A: 1-12		B, T, C, E	£46-£171	GBC, Arels
Passport Language Schools	J: 6-8	11-17 yrs		£250-£375**	GBC, Arels
Polyglot Language Centre	A: 1-12		B, E	£97-£162	GBC
Princes College	A: 1-12		B	£75	ABLS
Purley Language College Ltd	A: 1-12 J: 1-12	9-15 yrs	B, E	£60+ (£260**)	
Queen Mary & Westfield College	A: 8-9 (EAP ONLY!)		E	£180 approx.	GBC, Baselt
Queens English	A: 1-12 J: 1-12	9-15 yrs	B, F, E	£50-£200	
Radcliffe College	A: 1-12 J: 1-12	9-15 yrs	B, C, E	£40-£65	
Radcliffe College	A: 1-12 J: 1-12	9-15 yrs	B, C, E	£40-£65	
Redbridge College	A: 9-6			£3.70/hr+ range of other fees	
Regent London	A: 1-12		B, T, F, H	£110-£1800	GBC, Arels
Richmond Adult Community College	A: 9-12, 1-6, 7-8		B, T	£17-£49 (£85 summer with activities/excursions)	GBC, Baselt

Institution Name	Availability	Junior Ages	Specials	Price /week	Status
Richmond English Language Institute	A: 1-12		B, C, E	On application	GBC
Richmond Language Training Centre	A: 1-12 J: 6-9	10-15 yrs	B, F	£155-£1260	
Richmond Upon Thames College	A: 9-6		B	£50-£75	GBC, Baselt
RLI Language Services	A: 1-12 (mostly 1-1 only)		B, F, E	£900**	
Roehampton Institute London	A: 1-12			£151-£600	
SCOLA Community College	A: 9-6, 7+8 J: 7	10-14 yrs		£8-£16 approx.	
Sels College	A: 1-12		B, E	£129-£258	GBC, Arels
Shane English School London	A: 1-12 J: 7-8	7-17 yrs	B, T, E	£87-£1700	GBC, Arels
SOAS	A: 9-6		E	£5100 / 30wks	Baleap
South Bank University	A: 4-9		E	On application	Baleap
South Thames College	A: 1-7, 9-12		B, E	£50 +	GBC, Baselt
Southgate College	A: 9-6		B, J, C, E	£3.50-£7 (P/T) £70 (f/T)	
Southwork College	A: 1-3, 4-7, 9-12		B, T, H, E	On application	
St Giles International London Central	A: 1-12		B, E	£109.50-£677	GBC, Arels
St Giles International London Highgate	A: 1-12		B, T, E	£84-£223	GBC, Arels
St. George International	A: 1-12 J: 7-8	10-15 yrs	B, F, E	£126-£1675	
St. George's College	A: 9-6 J: 7-8	12-16 yrs	C	£150	
St. John's Wood School of English	A: 1-12			£180	GBC, Arels
St. Patrick's International College	A: 1-12			£100-£190	GBC, Arels
Stanfords School of English	A: 1-12		C	£29+	
Stanmore College	A: 1-6, 7, 9-12			£20	
Stanton School of English	A: 1-12			£13.44-£71.50	GBC, Arels
Summer School of English	J: 7-8	7-16 yrs		£150 (or £330**)	

Institution Name	Availability	Junior Ages	Specials	Price /week	Status
SuperStudy UK	A: 1-12			£199-£249**	GBC
Swandean School of English	A: 1-12		E	£105-£170	GBC, Arels
Thames Valley University	A: 1-12		E	£150	GBC
Tower Hamlets College	A: 1-12			Variable	
TTI School of English	A: 1-12		B	£25-£45	
Twickenham Language Studies	A: 1-12 J: 1-12	14 yrs +	B, E	£38-£65 (15hrs/wk)	
Twin Towers School of English	A: 1-12		B, E	£750/12wks, £2000/36wks	
United International College	A: 1-12		T, C, E	£42-£165	GBC, Arels
Unity College	A: 1-12			On application	
University College Kensington	A: 1-12			£660+ per course	
University College London	A: 1-12		B, E	£150-£200	GBC, Baselt
University of North London	A: 5-9, 1		E	£125	
University of Westminster	A: 1-4, 7-9		B, T, E	£100	GBC, Baselt
Uxbridge College	A: 1-12		E	£50-£125	GBC, Baselt
Victoria School of English	A: 1-12			£85-£135	GBC, Arels
Waltham Forest College	A: 1, 4, 6, 7, 8, 9		T, H, C	On application	GBC, Baselt
Wellington Study Centre	A: 1-12 J: 7-9	14 yrs +		£25-£42	
West Thames College	A: 9-6			£9-£45	
Westminster Adult Education Service	A: 1-12		B, E	Variable	
Westminster Kingsway College	A: 1-12		B, T, F, H, C, E	£75-£125	GBC, Baselt
Wimbledon School of English	A: 1-12		B, E	£152-£210	GBC, Arels
World Intuition	A: 1-12		B, T, F	£266-£650	
Young English Studies	J: 1-12	11-17 yrs		£240	GBC, Arels

4 SOUTH EAST ENGLAND

Guildford
Dover
Hastings
Brighton   Eastbourne

Includes East & West Sussex, Kent, Surrey.

Its beaches, once a smugglers' meeting place, are dotted with friendly seaside resorts. Brighton, the most famous of this region's resorts, offers entertainment and all year round learning programmes, as do the towns of Eastbourne and Hastings.

With more stately homes and castles than perhaps any region in England, the South East has something for everyone. Canterbury, with its ancient cathedral, the rolling splendour of the Downs, the amusement park at Thorpe are but a few of the varied attractions to be enjoyed.

London is within easy access, making an ideal weekend trip for those wishing to visit the capital. Driving to the area from mainland Europe is now extremely easy thanks to the new Channel Tunnel, and of course traditional ferry transport is also available.

Région aussi favorisée par les étudiants étrangers à cause du grand nombre de cours offerts. Dotée de manoirs historiques et de châteaux, elle est d'accès facile de Londres. Les traversées en provenance du reste de L'Europe sont facilitées par le Tunnel sous la Manche et par bâteaux.

Auch diese Gegend ist bei ausländischen Stundenten sehr beliebt aufgrund des reichhaltigen Kursangebots. Hier finden sich zahlreiche Schlösser und historische Bauten, die alle von London aus sehr leicht zu erreichen sind. Der Kanaltunnel und der Fährbetrieb gewährleisten eine bequeme Anreise vom europäischen Festland.

Otra región preferida por los estudiantes extranjeros por los numerosos cursos de inglés que ofrece. También es una región con mansiones históricas y castillos, además no está lejos de Londres. El Túnel de la Mancha y los varios puertos ofrecen accesos fáciles desde el resto de Europa.

Un' altra regione favorita dagli studenti stranieri, grazie al grande numero di corsi offerti. Questa regione è ricchissima di castelli e palazzi d'interesse storico ed è facilmente raggiungibile da Londra. Il tunnel della Manica e i traghetti offrono comodi collegamenti col resto dell' Europa.

SIGHTS

Leeds Castle
Spectacular setting in lake and
parkland. Leeds, Nr. Maidstone, Kent.
Tel: 01622 765400

Thorpe Park
Water orientated theme park.
Staines Road, Chertsey, Surrey.   Tel:
01932 562633

Chessington World of Adventure
Experience transylvania and the
wild west in this popular amusement
park. Leatherhead Road, Chessington.
Tel: 01372 727227

Brighton Sea Life Centre
Over 35 displays of marine life,
including a whale and dolphin
exhibition, and underwater tunnel.
Brighton. Tel: 01273 604234

For further information contact the
South East England Tourist Board,
The Old Brew House, Warwick Park,
Tunbridge Wells, Kent. TN2 5TU
Tel: 01892 540766

 **DIRECTORY OF EFL
BOOKSELLERS   IN
THIS REGION:**

*(NB: Many bookshops hold a good
selection of EFL material, even if they
are not listed below. Moreover, if the
particular book you are looking for is not
in stock, they can order it for you.)*

Albion Bookshop
13 Mercery Lane, Canterbury CT1 2JJ
Tel: 01227 768631
Web: http://www.cantweb.co.uk/books/albion/

Alphabetstreet Books
9 Overline House, Station Way
Crawley RH10 1JA
Tel: 01293 402040 Fax: 01293 402050
Web: http://www.alphabetstreet.infront.co.uk

Barnett's of Wadhurst
Gordon House, High Street
Wadhurst TN5 6AA
Tel: 01892 783566 Fax: 01892 783566

Bookstack
Unit 67, Arndale Centre
Eastbourne BN21 3NW
Tel: 01323 430554 Fax: 01323 430554

Bookworm
2A Market Place, Faversham ME13 7AG
Tel: 01795 536262

Bookworm Bookshop
22 North Street, Leatherhead KT22 7AT
Tel: 01372 377443 Fax: 01372 812674

Charterhouse Enterprises Ltd
Charterhouse, Godalming GU7 2DH
Tel: 01483 291634 Fax: 01483 291637

Crane Books
High Street, Cranbrook TN17 2AD
Tel: 01580 713567

English Language Bookshop
31 George Street, Brighton BN2 1RH
Tel: 01273 604 864 Fax: 01273 687 280

Harper's Bookshop
64 Grove Road, Eastbourne BN21 4UH
Tel: 01323 731589 Fax: 01323 412838

Mozbooks
Mid Kent College, Horsted Centre
Maidstone Road, Chatham ME5 9UQ
Tel: 01634 400581 Fax: 01634 672142

Ottakar's Bookstore
71 Royal Victoria Place
Tunbridge Wells TN1 2SS
Tel: 01892 520325 Fax: 01892 527481
Web: http://www.ottakars.co.uk

Ottakar's Bookstore
16 Sandgate Road, Folkestone CT20 1DP
Tel: 01303 258888 Fax: 01303 258111
Web: http://www.ottakars.co.uk

Ottakar's Bookstore
Priory Meadow Shopping Centre
Hastings TN34 1PH
Tel: 01424 722253 Fax: 01424 722326
Web: http://www.ottakars.co.uk

Ottakar's Bookstore
Units 4, The Martleys
Crawley RH10 1ES
Tel: 01293 525352
Web: http://www.ottakars.co.uk

Ottakar's Bookstore
182 High Street, Chatham ME4 4AS
Tel: 01634 828929 Fax: 01634 830140
Web: http://www.ottakars.co.uk

Ottakar's Bookstore
37 London Road, East Grinstead RH19 1AW
Tel: 01342 322978 Fax: 01342 315611
Web: http://www.ottakars.co.uk

Ottakar's Bookstore
74/76 South Road, Haywards Heath RH16 4LA
Tel: 01444 453411 Fax: 01444 451932
Web: http://www.ottakars.co.uk

Ottakar's Bookstore
6 Grace Reynolds Walk, Main Sq.
Shopping Centre, Camberley GU15 3SN
Tel: 01276 65227 Fax: 01276 65228
Web: http://www.ottakars.co.uk

Practical Books
14 Western Road, Hove BN3 1AE
Tel: 01273 734602 Fax: 01273 720241
http://www.practicalbooks.fsnet.co.uk

Ronald Edwards Stationers
103 The Street, Rustington BN16 3DP
Tel: 01903 782786 Fax: 01903 783470

Sussex University Bookshop
University of Sussex Falmer
Brighton BN1 9QU
Tel: 01273 678333 Fax: 01273 678286

University College
North Holmes Road, Canterbury CT1 1QU
Tel: 01227 782256 Fax: 01227 786937
Web: http://www.cant.ac.uk/bookshop

University of Surrey Bookshop
Surrey University Press Ltd
Guildford GU2 5XH
Tel: 01483 879169 Fax: 01483 879529
Web: http://www.surrey.ac.uk/bookshop

Waterstone's
Old Town Hall 1-2 Guildhall Street
Folkestone CT20 1DY
Tel: 01303 221979 Fax: 01303 221981
Web: http://www.waterstones.co.uk

Waterstone's
North Terminal Airside
Gatwick RH6 0NP
Tel: 01293 507112 Fax: 01293 507124
Web: http://www.waterstones.co.uk

Waterstone's
71 North Street
Brighton BN1 1ZA
Tel: 01273 206017 Fax: 01273 205616
Web: http://www.waterstones.co.uk

Waterstone's
120 Terminus Road
Eastbourne BN21 3AJ
Tel: 01323 735676 Fax: 01323 738903
Web: http://www.waterstones.co.uk

Wheeler's Bookshop
Red Lion Street
Midhurst GU29 9PB
Tel: 01730 817666 Fax: 01730 817666

Wilmington Bookshop Ltd
55-59A High Street
East Grinstead RH19 3DD
Tel: 01342 323007 Fax: 01342 317097

DIRECTORY OF COURSES IN THIS REGION

PRIVATE SCHOOLS / ORGANISATIONS

ABC English
Woodgate, Blackgate Lane
Henfield BN5 9HA
Tel: 01273 494138   Fax:
Email: moira@bonn25.freeserve.co.uk
http://www.bonn25.freeserve.co.uk/abcenglish

Academy of English Studies, Folkestone
106a Sandgate Road,
Folkestone CT20 2BW
Tel: 01303 210808   Fax: 01303 210809
Email: acaes@btconnect.com
http://www.acaes.co.uk

Anderida English Junior School
Brook Green,
Cuckfield RH17 5JJ
Tel: 01444 454333   Fax: 01444 454333
Email: email@englishjuniorschool.co.uk
http://www.englishschool.co.uk

Anglian School of English
77-83 Norfolk Road,
Margate CT9 2HX
Tel: 01843 293700   Fax: 01843 226014
Email: anglian.school@btinternet.com
http://www.anglianschool.co.uk

B.A.S.E Summer School
139 Beacon Road,
Broadstairs
Tel: 01843 603832
Email: baseone@supanet.com

BEL Centre
26 Nutley Avenue, Saltdean
Brighton BN2 8EB
Tel: 01273 306070   Fax: 01273 300180

Bellerbys College (MW International Summer School)
Lorna House, 103 Lorna Road
Hove BN3 3EL
Tel: 01273 723911   Fax: 01273 328445
Email: info@bellerbys.com
http://www.bellerbys.com/courses/summer.htm
Courses held in Wadhurst

Bethany Summer Language School
Curtisden Green, Goudhurst
Cranbrook TN17 1LE
Tel: 01580 211273   Fax: 01580 212622
Email: admin@bethany.demon.co.uk

Bonnie Cottage
Sacketts Hill,
Broadstairs CT10 2QS
Tel: 01843 866115   Fax: 01843 603163
Email: fraser-reid@supanet.com

Brighton International Summer School
PO Box 2831,
Brighton BN1 6ES
Tel: 01273 555752   Fax: 01273 555752
Email: enquiries@biss-school.com
http://www.biss-school.com

Buckswood ARC Summer Programmes
Westminster House, Bolton Close
Uckfield TN22 1PH
Tel: 01825 760900   Fax: 01825 760911
Email: info@buckswood.com
http://www.buckswood.com

Campana International College
Moor Park House, Moor Park Lane
Farnham GU10 1QP
Tel: 01252 727111   Fax: 01252 712011

Canterbury Language Training
73 Castle St.,
Canterbury CT1 2QD
Tel: 01227 760000   Fax: 01227 764400
Email: office@clt.com
http://www.clt.com

Carl Duisberg Language Centre - Canterbury
26 Oaten Hill,
Canterubry CT1 3HZ
Tel: 01227 764123   Fax: 01227 762575
Email: info@cdccanterbury.co.uk

Channel English Studies
66 Eddington Lane,
Herne Bay CT6 5TR
Tel: 01227 375394   Fax: 01227 367586
Email: info@channel-english.co.uk
http://www.channel-english.co.uk

Charles Eaton College
Southview, 30 Piltdown Way
Eastbourne BN23 8LB
Tel: 01323 760780   Fax: 01323 461112
Email: charleseaton@lineone.net
http://website.lineone.net/~charleseaton
See display for further details

CHARLES EATON COLLEGE OF ENGLISH LANGUAGE

General English courses:
Elementary, Intermediate, Advanced
Small International Classes -
students from all over the world
Seaside Location in Hastings
Friendly Host families close to school
Excellent Activity Programme
Low Prices

Head Office: Southview, 30 Piltdown Way,
Eastbourne BN23 8LB

Tel: 00 44 (0) 1323 760780
Fax: 00 44 (0) 1323 461112
Email: charleseaton@lineone.net
http://website.lineone.net/~charleseaton

Churchill House English Home Tuition Courses
Spencer Square (137),
Ramsgate CT11 9EQ
Tel: 01843 586833   Fax: 01843 584827
Email: ehtc@churchillhouse.co.uk
http://www.churchillhouse.co.uk

Churchill House School of English Language
Spencer Square (137),
Ramsgate CT11 9EQ
Tel: 01843 586833   Fax: 01843 584827
Email: welcome@churchillhouse.co.uk
http://www.churchillhouse.co.uk
See display for further details

Cicero Languages International
42 Upper Grosvenor Road,
Tunbridge Wells TN1 2ET
Tel: 01892 547077   Fax: 01892 522749
Email: enrolments@cicero.co.uk
http://www.cicero.co.uk
See display for further details

Concorde International
Arnett House, Hawks Lane
Canterbury CT1 2NU
Tel: 01227 451035   Fax: 01227 762760
Email: info@concorde.ltd.uk
http://www.concorde.ltd.uk

CHURCHILL HOUSE SCHOOL OF ENGLISH

We offer:
High Cambridge FCE pass rate.
Welcoming host-families.
Excellent social programme.
Picturesque seaside location.
British Council, ARELS, EAQUALS
& ISO 9002 accreditation.
Low prices - from £160 per week
all inclusive.

Spencer Square (137)
Ramsgate, Kent CT11 9EQ

Tel: (0044) 1843 586833
Fax: (0044) 1843 584827
E-mail: welcome@churchillhouse.co.uk
Website: www.churchillhouse.co.uk

CICERO LANGUAGES INTERNATIONAL

Small friendly school, in pleasant 17th
century spa town, near London.

Weekly enrolment, wide variety
of courses for all ages.

Excellent host families, close to school.

Students from all over the world.

42 Upper Grosvenor Road
Tunbridge Wells, Kent TN1 2ET

Tel: +44 (0) 1892 547077
Fax: +44 (0) 1892 522749
Email: enrolments@cicero.co.uk
Website: http://www.cicero.co.uk

Concorde International Home Language Tuition
Arnett House, Hawks Lane
Canterbury CT1 2NU
Tel: 01227 479279   Fax: 01227 479379
Email: info@home-tuition.com
http://www.home-tuition.com

Cultural Linguistic Stays (CLS)
Terracotta, Tanyard Lane
Steyning BN44 3RJ
Tel: 01903 813300   Fax: 01903 813300
Email: cls@fastnet.co.uk
http://www.www.clsenglish.co.uk

East Sussex School of English
92, Portland Road,
Hove BN3 5DN
Tel: 01273 736404   Fax: 01273 770672
Email: esse@mistral.co.uk
http://www.esse-uk.com

Eastbourne International Summer School
Duke's Drive,
Eastbourne BN20 7XL
Tel: 01323 430531   Fax: 01323 430531
Email: h.ho@btinternet.com
http://www.stbedes.co.uk

Eastbourne School of English
8 Trinity Trees,
Eastbourne BN21 3LD
Tel: 01323 721759   Fax: 01323 639271
Email: english@esoe.co.uk
http://www.esoe.co.uk

Echo Language School
23 Rutland Gardens, Hove
Brighton BN3 5PD
Tel: 01273 202802   Fax: 01273 746464
Email: echo@mistral.co.uk

Education Matters
Baytrees, 10a Laton Road,
Hastings TN34 2ET
Tel: 01424 722203   Fax: 01424 722203
Email: jeremy.lucas@tesco.net

EF English First
1-3 Farman Street,
Hove BN3 1AL
Tel: 01273 201412   Fax: 01273 748566
Email: languages.gb@ef.com
http://www. ef.com

EF International School of English
1-2 Sussex Square,
Brighton BN2 1FJ
Tel: 01273 571780   Fax: 01273 691232
Email: languages.gb@ef.com
http://www.ef.com

EF International School of English
74-78 Warrior Square,
Hastings TN37 6BP
Tel: 01424 423998   Fax: 01424 718369
Email: languages.gb@ef.com
http://www.ef.com

Elizabeth Johnson Organisation
Passfield Enterprise Ctre,
Liphook GU30 7SB
Tel: 01428 751933   Fax: 01428 751944
Email: sales@ejo.co.uk
http://www.ejo.co.uk

Embassy CES Hastings
White Rock,
Hastings TN34 1JY
Tel: 01424 720100   Fax: 01424 720323
Email: hastings@embassyces.com
http://www.embassyces.com

Embassy Educational Services (UK) Ltd
7 Wilbury Villas,
Hove BN3 6GB
Tel: 01273 721135   Fax: 01273 326534
Email: embassy@eltchove.bsg.ac.uk

Embassy Language and Training Centre
7 Warrior Square,
St. Leonards-on-Sea TN37 6BA
Tel: 01424 720282   Fax: 01424 431542
Email: embassy@eltchastings.bsg.ac.uk

English for You
25 Wellington Square,
Hastings TN34 1PN
Tel: 01424 717320   Fax: 01424 717320
Email: EnglishForYou@mcmail.com
http://www.EnglishForYou.mcmail.com

English Homestay
Field House, Wayborough Hill
Minster CT12 4HR
Tel: 01843 822088   Fax: 01843 825162
Email: janet@englishhomestay.co.uk
http://www.englishhomestay.co.uk
See display for further details

English Language Anon
Riverside, Iden Lock
Rye TN31 7QE
Tel: 01797 280151   Fax:
Email: sue.marriott@btopenworld.com
http://www.sue.marriott.btinternet.co.uk

English Language Centre
33 Palmeira Mansions,
Brighton & Hove BN3 2GB
Tel: 01273 721771   Fax: 01273 720898
Email: info@elc-brighton.co.uk
http://www.elc-brighton.co.uk

English Plus @ Canterbury
35 Henry Court, Gordon Road,
Canterbury CT1 3PL
Tel: 01227 831041   Fax: 01227 831041
Email: english-plus@hotmail.com
http:// www.englishplus.freeuk.com

English Teacher Direct
10 Montpelier Crescent,
Brighton BN1 3JF
Tel: 01273 324270   Fax: 01273 324270
Email: clive@english-teacher-direct.co.uk
http://www.english-teacher-direct.co.uk

Essential English Homestay
27 Chapel Park Road,
St. Leonards on Sea TN376HR
Tel: 01424 430807   Fax:
Email: MMAILLE100@aol.com

Eurocentres Brighton
Huntingdon House, 20 North St.
Brighton BN1 1EB
Tel: 01273 324545   Fax: 01273 746013
Email: bri-info@eurocentres.com
http://www.eurocentres.com

Express Language Homestay
10 Station Road, Preston Park
Brighton BN1 6SF
Tel: 01273 233239   Fax: 01273 233239
Email: expresslang@mcmail.com
http://www.exlanguage.mcmail.com

FGC School of English
76, Chaffers Mead,
Ashtead KT21 1NH
Tel: 01372 272429   Fax: 01372 277800
Email: FGCUK@btinternet.com
http://www.btinternet.com/~fgcuk

GEOS English Academy
55-61 Portland Road,
Brighton & Hove BN3 5DQ
Tel: 01273 735975   Fax: 01273 732884
Email: info@geos-brighton.com
http://www.geos-brighton.com
See display for further details

GEOS ENGLISH ACADEMY

Our school is friendly, medium-sized
and caring, with host families almost
all within walking distance, a full social
programme, free internet access,
language laboratory, garden,
lounge and kitchen.

55-61 Portland Road,
Brighton & Hove BN3 5DQ

Tel: +44 (0) 1273 735975
Fax: +44 (0) 1273 732884
Email: info@geos-brighton.com
Web: http://www.geos-brighton.com

Grove House Language Centre
Carlton Avenue,
Greenhithe DA9 9DR
Tel: 01322 386826   Fax: 01322 386347
Email: EFL@grovehouse.com
http://www.grovehouse.com

Guildford College
Stoke Park,
Guildford GU1 1EZ
Tel: 01483 448688   Fax: 01483 448689
Email: bmorrison@guildford.ac.uk
http://www.guildford.ac.uk/int/welcom.htm

H.E.L.P.
43 Magdalen Road,
St.Leonards-on-Sea TN37 6EU
Tel: 01424 444407   Fax: 01424 444407
Email: jbhelp@clara.net

Harven School of English
The Mascot, Coley Avenue
Woking GU22 7BT
Tel: 01483 770969   Fax: 01483 740267
Email: harven.school@btinternet.com
http://www.harven.co.uk

HELC - Hastings English Language Centre
St. Helen's Park Road,
Hastings TN34 2JW
Tel: 01424 437048   Fax: 01424 716442
Email: english@helc.co.uk
http://www.helc.co.uk

Home Language International
Reservations Office, 17 Royal Crescent
Ramsgate CT11 9PE
Tel: 01843 851116   Fax: 01843 590300
Email: hli@hli.co.uk
http://www.hli.co.uk

Homestay English Language Programme
86 Childsbridge Lane, Seal
Sevenoaks TN15 0BW
Tel: 01732 763755   Fax:
Email: jamesgodber@freeuk.com
http://www.homestay-english.co.uk

House of English
24 Portland Place,
Brighton BN2 1DG
Tel: 01273 694618   Fax: 01273 674775
Email: info@house-of-english.co.uk
http://www.house-of-english.co.uk

Hove School of English
9 The Drive, Hove
Brighton BN3 3JE
Tel: 01273 723781   Fax: 01273 771222
Email: hse@ukstudies.co.uk
http://www.ukstudies.co.uk

Hurtwood House
Holmbury St. Mary,
Dorking RH5 6NU
Tel: 01483 277416   Fax: 01483 267586
Email: hurtwood2@aol.com
http://www.thesummerschool.com

Individual English
19 St.Peter's Lane,
Canterbury CT1 2BP
Tel: 01227 463871   Fax: 01227 463871
Email: StPetersLane@aol.com

Intensive English Training
3 Haywards,
Crawley RH10 3TR
Tel: 01293 457100   Fax: 01293 40581
Email: iet@langtraining.co.uk
http://www.langtraining.co.uk

**Intensive School of English & Business
Communication**
34 Duke St,
Brighton BN1 1BS
Tel: 01273 384800   Fax: 01273 236872
Email: info@ise.uk.com
http://www.ise.uk.com

Inter-Monde Language Services Ltd
1 Hillary Road,
Farnham GU9 8QY
Tel: 01252 717745   Fax: 01252 717745
Email: language@intermonde.co.uk
http://www.intermonde.co.uk

International House, Folkestone
Highcliffe House, Clifton Gardens
Folkestone CT20 2EF
Tel: 01303 258536   Fax: 01303 851455
Email: ilc@compuserve.com
http://www.ilcgroup.com

International Language Homestays
38 Hawley Square,
Margate CT9 1PH
Tel: 01843 227700   Fax: 01843 223377
Email: info@ilh.com
http://www.ilh.com

InTuition Languages - *See London display
for details*

ISS English Language Academy
58 Chapel Road,
Worthing BN11 1BG
Tel: 01903 211060   Fax: 01903 230129

ITS English School
43-45 Cambridge Gardens,
Hastings TN34 1EN
Tel: 01424 438025   Fax: 01424 438050
Email: itsbest@its-hastings.co.uk
http://www.its-hastings.co.uk

Kent Language & Activity Courses
Pilgrims House, Orchard Street
Canterbury CT2 8BF
Tel: 01227 818228   Fax: 01227 784293
Email: amanda@klac.co.uk
http://www.klac.co.uk

Kent School of English
3/5, 10/12 Granville Avenue,
Broadstairs CT10 1QD
Tel: 01843 874870   Fax: 01843 860418
Email: enquiries@kentschool.co.uk
http://www. kentschool.co.uk

King's School, Rochester
Satis House, Boley Hill
Rochester ME1 1TE
Tel: 01634 843913   Fax: 01634 832493

L.R.G.D. Study Centre
74 Sackville Road,
Hove BN3 3HB
Tel: 01273 771119   Fax: 01273 771119
Email: admin@lrgd.co.uk
http://www.lrgd.co.uk

Language Services Worldwide School
47 Warrior Square,
Hastings TN37 6BG
Tel: 01424 201153   Fax: 01424 201150
Email: mail@language-world.net
http://www.language-world.net

Language Studies International
13 Ventnor Villas,
Hove BN3 3DD
Tel: 01273 722060   Fax: 01273 746341
Email: bri@lsi.edu
http://www.lsi.edu

Languages Plus
135 Kings Road,
Brighton BN1 2HX
Tel: 01273 737657   Fax: 01273 774382
Email: enquiries@languages-plus.co.uk
http://www.languages-plus.co.uk

Learn English in the Garden of England
'Fieldings', The Street
Bearsted ME14 4EX
Tel: 01622 737506   Fax: 01580 737506
Email: Penelope.J.Mitchell@tesco.net
http://www.english-1to1.co.uk

Linguatech, East Kent Itec Ltd
Athanaton House, Victoria Road
Margate CT9 1RD
Tel: 01843 299266   Fax: 01843 226307
Email: 101376.2120@compuserve.com

Living Language Centre
Highcliffe House, Clifton Gardens
Folkestone CT20 2EF
Tel: 01303 258536   Fax: 01303 851455

Logos Linguistics
2 Beaconsfield Road,
Canterbury CT2 7HF
Tel: 01227 766663   Fax: 01227 766663

London House School of English
51 Sea Road,
Westgate-on-Sea CT8 8QL
Tel: 01843 831216   Fax: 01843 832419
Email: lonhou@adept.co.uk
http://www.london-house.co.uk

LTC International College
Compton Park, Compton Place Road
Eastbourne BN21 1EH
Tel: 01323 727755   Fax: 01323 728279
Email: learnenglish@ltccollege.demon.co.uk
http://geos-ltc.com

Margate Language Centre
38 Hawley Square,
Margate CT9 1PH
Tel: 01843 227700   Fax: 01843 227700
Email: mlc@student-reservations.co.uk
http://www.student-reservations.co.uk

Mayfield Academy of English
24 Holland Road,
Hove BN3 1JJ
Tel: 01273 779231   Fax: 02173 207388
Email: info@mayfieldacademy.co.uk
http://www.mayfieldacademy.co.uk

Meads School of English
2 Old Orchard Road,
Eastbourne BN21 4HG
Tel: 01323 734335   Fax: 01323 649512
Email: english@meads.co.uk
http://www.meadsenglish.co.uk

Multi Lingua
Abbot Hse, Sydenham Rd
Guilford GU1 3RL
Tel: 01483 535118   Fax: 01483 534777
Email: mail@multi-lingua.co.uk
http://www.multi-lingua.co.uk

Olivet English Language School
52 Norfolk Square,
Brighton BN1 2PA
Tel: 01273 325839   Fax: 01273 325839
Email: Olivetschl@aol.com
http://www.olivet.co.uk

Pilgrims Ltd
Pilgrims House, Orchard St.
Canterbury CT2 8BF
Tel: 01227 762111   Fax: 01227 459027
Email: sales@pilgrims.co.uk
http://www.pilgrims.co.uk

Pinelands Language Centre
114 St. Helens Down,
Hastings TN34 2AR
Tel: 01424 421506   Fax: 1424 426787
Email: pinelands@compuserve.com

Prestige English Services
10 Park Avenue,
Brixham TQ5 ODT
Tel: 01803 858139
Email: paul@pepes.force9.co.uk
http://www.pepes.force9.co.uk

Reftec Programs Ltd
57 Biggins Wood Road, Cheriton
Folkestone CT19 4NH
Tel: 01303 278698   Fax: 0870 130 32125
Email: info@jobref.com

Regency College
61 Western Road,
Hove BN3 1JD
Tel: 01273 718009   Fax: 01273 718109
Email: info@regencycollege.co.uk
http://www.regencycollege.co.uk
See display for further details

REGENCY COLLEGE

A new, young, friendly and professional school in England's most popular seaside city.

Full range of courses and levels.

Specialists in Cambridge and IELTS exams and university/college entry help.

61 Western Road
Brighton & Hove BN3 1JD

Tel: 01273 718009
Fax: 01273 718109
Email: info@regencycollege.co.uk
Web: http://www.regencycollege.co.uk

ROCHESTER INDEPENDENT COLLEGE - SCHOOL OF ENGLISH -

Specialist school offering Basic to Advanced level classes.
Experienced staff, excellent facilities.
Small group tuition.
Friendly, supportive environment.
Proven record of examination success.
Accommodation available.
45 minutes from Central London.

Star Hill, Rochester, Kent ME1 1XF

Tel: +44 (0) 1634 828115
Fax: +44 (0) 1634 405667
Email: rochester@mcmail.com
Web: http://www.rochester-college.org

Regency School of English
Royal Crescent,
Ramsgate CT11 9PE
Tel: 01843 591212   Fax: 01843 850035
Email: reception@regencyschool.co.uk
http://www.regencyschool.co.uk

Regent Brighton
18 Cromwell Road,
Hove BN3 3EW
Tel: 01273 731684   Fax: 01273 324542
Email: brighton@regent.org.uk
http://www.regent.org.uk

Regent Fitzroy
Northdown House,
Margate CT9 3TP
Tel: 01843 865547   Fax: 01843 869055
Email: fitzroy@regent.org.uk
http://www.regent.org.uk

Regent Language Holidays
40-42 Queen's Road,
Brighton BN1 3XB
Tel: 01273 718620   Fax: 01273 718621
Email: holidays@regent.org.uk
http://www.regent.org.uk
Coures held at St.Swithun's School, St.Mary's College, Penpont Manor, Box Hill School or Teacher's Home

Renaissance Training
12 Poona Road,
Tunbridge Wells TN1 1U
Tel: 01892 538932   Fax: 01892 538932
Email: info@renaissance-training.co.uk
http://www.renaissance-training.co.uk

Rochester Independent College
Star Hill,
Rochester ME1 1XF
Tel: 01634 828115   Fax: 01634 405667
Email: rochester@mcmail.com
http://www.rochester-college.org
See display for further details

Rutland School of English
78 Canterbury Road, Westbrook
Margate CT9 5DF
Tel: 01843 223031   Fax: 01843 231386
Email: rutland.school@btinternet.com

Savoir Faire
Pine Marten, Rannoch Road,
Crowborough TN6 1RB
Tel: 01892 655953   Fax: 01892 654323
Email: enquiries@english4you.org.uk
http://www.english4you.org.uk
See display for further details

School of English Studies, Folkestone
26 Grimston Gardens,
Folkestone CT20 2PX
Tel: 01303 850007   Fax: 01303 256544
Email: info@ses-folkestone.co.uk
http://www.ses-folkestone.co.uk

SEE Europe
16/17 Springfield Lane,
Weybridge KT13 8AW
Tel: 01932 820216   Fax: 01932 820315
Email: see.europe@easynet.co.uk
http://www.see-europe.co.uk

SAVOIR FAIRE

Intensive English Courses in our
Country House in Sussex.

Especially for Executives/Professionals
Small groups (max. 3)
1 hour South of London
Highly qualified, experienced teacher
Made to measure

Pine Marten, Rannoch Road,
Crowborough, East Sussex TN6 1RB

Tel: +44 (0) 1892 655953
Fax: +44 (0) 1892 654323
Email: enquiries@english4you.org.uk
Web: http://www.english4you.org.uk

Skippers Hill Manor Preparatory School
Five Ashes,
Mayfield TN20 6HR
Tel: 01825 830234   Fax: 01825 830234

St George's, England
The Belfrey,
Uckfield TN22 5DB
Tel: 01825 760122   Fax: 01825 760122
Email: learnenglish@stgeorgesengland.com
http://www.stgeorgesengland.com

St Giles International Brighton
3 Marlborough Place,
Brighton BN1 1UB
Tel: 01273 682747   Fax: 01273 689808
Email: stgiles@pavilion.co.uk
http://www.stgiles-international.com

St. Giles Eastbourne
13 Silverdale Road,
Eastbourne BN20 7AJ
Tel: 01323 729167   Fax: 01323 721332
Email: english@stgiles-eastbourne.co.uk
http://www.stgiles-international.com

St. Peter's School of English
St. Alphege Lane,
Canterbury CT1 2EB
Tel: 01227 462016   Fax: 01227 458628
Email: stpeters@dial.pipex.com
http://www.stpeters.co.uk

Stafford House School of English
8/9 Oaten Hill,
Canterbury CT1 3HY
Tel: 01227 452250   Fax: 01227 453579
Email: enquiries@staffordhouse.com
http://www.staffordhouse.com

Surrey Language Training
Sandford House, 39 West Street
Farnham GU9 7DR
Tel: 01252 723494   Fax: 01252 733519
Email: slc@surreylanguage.co.uk
http://www.surreylanguage.co.uk/slc/slc.html

Sussex English Language School
Seadown House, Farncombe Road
Worthing BN11 2BE
Tel: 01903 209244   Fax: 01903 231402
Email: info@selschool.co.uk
http://www. selschool.co.uk

Swandean School of English
12 Stoke Abbott Road,
Worthing BN11 1HE
Tel: 01903 231330   Fax: 01903 200953
Email: study@swandean.co.uk
http://www.swandean.co.uk/worthing

TASIS England
Coldharbour Lane,
ThorpeVillage TW20 8TE
Tel: 01932 565252   Fax: 01932 564644
Email: uksummer@tasis.com
http://www.tasis.com

Twin English Centre, Eastbourne
Gordon Lodge, 25 St. Anne's Road
Eastbourne BN21 2DJ
Tel: 01323 725887   Fax: 01323 730727
Email: ece@twinschool.co.uk
http://www.twinschool.co.uk

Warnborough College
Warnborough House, 8 Vernon Place
Canterbury CT1 3WH
Tel: 01227 762107   Fax: 01227 762108
Email: wc@warnborough.ac.uk
http://www.warnborough.ac.uk

West Sussex School of English
7 High St.,
Steyning BN44 3GG
Tel: 01903 814512   Fax: 01903 812451
Email: info@wsse.uk.com
http://www.wsse.uk.com

YES Education Centre
12 Eversfield Road,
Eastbourne BN21 2AS
Tel: 01323 644038   Fax: 01323 726260
Email: english@yeseducation.co.uk
http://www.yeseducation.co.uk

STATE COLLEGES / UNIVERSITIES

Bexley College
Tower Road,
Belvedere DA17 6JA
Tel: 01322 442331

Brighton College of Technology
Pelham Street,
Brighton BN1 4FA
Tel: 01273 667788   Fax: 01273 667703
Email: info@bricoltech.ac.uk
http://www.bricoltech.ac.uk

Brooklands College
Heath Rd,
Weybridge KT13 8TT
Tel: 01932 797739   Fax: 01932 797800
Email: uover@brooklands.ac.uk
http://www.brooklands.ac.uk

Canterbury Christ Church University College
International Office, North Holmes Road
Canterbury CT1 1QU
Tel: 01227 458459   Fax: 01227 781558
Email: ipol@cant.ac.uk
http://www.cant.ac.uk/io

Canterbury College
The Language Centre, New Dover Road
Canterbury CT1 3AJ
Tel: 01227 766081   Fax: 01227 811101
Email: http://www.cant-col.ac.uk

Chichester College of Arts, Science & Technology
Westgate Fields,
Chichester PO19 1SB
Tel: 01243 536294   Fax: 01243 775783
Email: intunit@chichester.ac.uk
http://www.chichester.ac.uk

Crawley College
College Road,
Crawley RH10 1HR
Tel: 01293 442295   Fax: 01293 442399
Email: crawcol@rmplc.co.uk

East Surrey College
Claremont Road, Gatton Point
Redhill RH1 2JX
Tel: 01737 772611   Fax: 01737 768641
Email: jtaylor@staff.esc.org.uk

Eastbourne College of Arts and Technology
Cross Levels Way,
Eastbourne BN21 2UF
Tel: 01323 637637   Fax: 01323 637472
Email: info@ecat.ac.uk
http://www.ecat.ac.uk/overseas

European Link
Kent Adult Education, Avebury Avenue
Tonbridge TN9 1TG
Tel: 01732 361181   Fax: 01732 361185
Email: kaeselink@aol.com

Hastings College of Arts & Technology
Archery Road,
St. Leonards-on-Sea TN38 0HX
Tel: 01424 445400   Fax: 01424 424804
Email: recept1@hcatintl.co.uk
http://www.hastings.ac.uk

Hilderstone College
St Peter's Road,
Broadstairs CT10 2JW
Tel: 01843 869171   Fax: 01843 603877
Email: info@hilderstone.ac.uk
http://www.hilderstone.ac.uk

Mid Kent College
Oakwood Park Centre, Language Services,
Tonbridge Road
Maidstone ME16 8AQ
Tel: 01622 691555   Fax: 01622 695049
Email: clare.harrison@midkent.ac.uk
http://www.midkent.ac.uk

Northbrook College
International Office,, Union Place
Worthing BN11 1LG
Tel: 01903 606107   Fax: 01903 606113
Email: international@nbcol.ac.uk
http://www.northbrook.ac.uk

Royal Holloway College Language Centre
Royal Holloway College
University of London, Egham TW20 0EX
Tel: 01784 443829   Fax: 01784 477640
Email: language-centre@rhbnc.ac.uk
http://rhbnc.ac.uk/language-centre

South Kent College
European Business & Language Centre,
Maison Dieu Road
Dover CT16 1DH
Tel: 01304 204573   Fax: 01304 204573

Surrey Adult Education Centre
19 Esher Green,
Esher KT10 8AA
Tel: 01372 465374   Fax: 01372 463696

Sussex Downs College
Mountfield Road,
Lewes BN7 2XH
Tel: 01273 483188   Fax: 01273 488974
Email: international@sussexdowns.ac.uk
http://www.sussexdowns.ac.uk

Sussex Language Institute
University of Sussex, Arts A, Falmer
Brighton BN1 9QN
Tel: 01273 678006   Fax: 01273 678476
Email: L.Gunn@sussex.ac.uk
http://www.sussex.ac.uk/langc/efl.html

SYAES Waverley Area
25 West St.,
Farnham GU9 8DH
Tel: 01252 723888   Fax: 01252 712927

Thanet College
International Office, Ramsgate Road
Broadstairs CT10 1PN
Tel: 01843 605014   Fax: 01843 863403
Email: international@thanet.ac.uk
http://www.thanet.ac.uk

Tunbridge Wells Adult Education Centre
Monson Road,
Tunbridge Wells TN1 1LS
Tel: 01892 527317   Fax: 01892 529743

University College Chichester
The Dome, Upper Bognor Road
Bognor Regis PO21 1HR
Tel: 01243 816271   Fax: 01243 816272
Email: g.lloyd@ucc.ac.uk
http://www.ucc.ac.uk

University of Brighton
School of Languages, Falmer
Brighton BN1 9PH
Tel: 01273 643339   Fax: 01273 690710
Email: slweb@bton.ac.uk
http://www.bton.ac.uk/

University of Kent
English Language Unit, Cornwallis West
Building
Canterbury CT2 7NY
Tel: 01227 764000   Fax: 01227 823641
Email: M.J.Hughes@ukc.ac.uk

University of Surrey
English Language Institute,
Guildford GU2 5XH
Tel: 01483 259911   Fax: 01483 259507
Email: eli@surrey.ac.uk

West Kent College
Brook St.,
Tonbridge TN9 2PW
Tel: 01732 358101   Fax: 01732 771415
Email: judyhebert@wkc.ac.uk

Institution Name	Availability	Junior Ages	Specials	Price /week	Status
ABC English	A: 1-12		B, E	On application	
Academy of English Studies, Folkestone	A: 1-12 J: 7-8	13-17 yrs	B, T, F, H, E	£95-£700	
Anderida English Junior School	J: 1-12	7-13 yrs	E	£385-£485**	
Anglian School of English	A: 1-12		B, F	£170-£264**	
B.A.S.E Summer School	J: 7-8	13-17 yrs		£250-£350**	
BEL Centre	J: 7-8			On application	
Bellerbys College (MW International Summer School)	J: 7-8	11-17 yrs		£550-£650**	
Bethany Summer Language School	J: 7			On application	
Brighton College of Technology	A: 1-12		B, T, F, H, C	£3.37-£5.08 (£99-£125 summer)	GBC, Basalt
Brighton International Summer School	J: 6-8	5-12 & 13-18 yrs		£120-£235	Ofsted (for juniors 5-12)
Brooklands College	A: 9-6			£3.90-£13	
Buckswood ARC Summer Programmes	J: 7, 8	7-16 yrs		£495-£535**	FIYTO
Campana International College	A: 1-12 J: 7-8			On application	
Canterbury Christ Church University College	A: 1-12		B, T, E	£174-£235	GBC, Basalt
Canterbury Language Training	A: 1-12		B	£700-£1600	GBC, Arels
Carl Duisberg Language Centre - Canterbury	A: 1-12 J: 4-8	12-16 yrs	B, T, F, H, E	£135-£1429	
Channel English Studies	A: 1-12 J: 1-12 (1-1 only)			On application	
Charles Eaton College	A: 1-8 J: 1-8	10-15 yrs		£150-£240**	
Chichester College of Arts, Science & Technology	A: 1-12 J: 7-8	11-15 yrs	B, T, F, H, C, E	£2.40-£160	GBC, Basalt
Churchill House English Home Tuition Courses	A: 1-12 J: 1-12 (1-1 only)	7 yrs +	B, T, F, H, C, E	£450-£780**	
Churchill House School of English Language	A: 1-12 J: 7-8	8-15 yrs	B, E	£160-£297**	GBC, Arels

Institution Name	Availability	Junior Ages	Specials	Price /week	Status
Cicero Languages International	A: 1-12 J: 7	11-15 yrs	B, E	£72-£1866	GBC, Arels
Concorde International	A: 1-12 J:1, 4, 6-8	8-17 yrs		£98-£194	GBC, Arels
Concorde International Home Language Tuition	A: 1-12 J: 1-12 (1-1 only)	12 yrs +	B, F, C	£495-£895**	
Crawley College	A: 1-12, J: 7-8	12-18 yrs	B, T, H, C, E	£2.50-£50	
Cultural Linguistic Stays (CLS)	A: 1-11 J: 1-11	14-16 yrs		£310-£475**	
East Surrey College	A: 9-6		B	£14-£65	
East Sussex School of English	A: 7-8 J: 7-8	12-15 yrs		£265-£285**	GBC, Arels
Eastbourne College of Arts and Technology	A: 1-12		B, T, H, C, E	£75-£200	GBC, Baselt
Eastbourne International Summer School	J: 3-4, 7-8	7-16 yrs		£435**	
Eastbourne School of English	A: 1-12		B, E	£160-£207	GBC, Arels
Education Matters	A: 1-12 (1-1 only)		B, T, C, E	£575-£875**	
EF International School of English	A: 1-12		B	£230-£285**	GBC, Arels
EF International School of English	A: 1-12			£245-£300**	GBC, Arels
Elizabeth Johnson Organisation	A: 1-12 J: 1-12	8-16 yrs	B	from £150**	GBC, Arels, FIYTO
Embassy CES Hastings	A: 1-12		B	£100-£220	GBC, Arels
Embassy Educational Services (UK) Ltd	A: 1-12 J: 6-8	8-16 yrs	B, T, F, C, E	£200-£400**	
Embassy Language and Training Centre	A: 1-12 J: 1,4, 6-9	10 yrs +		£100-£188+	
English for You	A: 1-12 J: 6-8	12-16 yrs	b	£90	GBC
English Homestay	A: 1-12 (mostly 1-1 but also 2-1 & 3-1)		B, T, E	£350-£575**	
English Language Anon	A: 1-12 (1-1 only)			£44-£315	
English Language Centre	A: 1-12		B, E	On application	

Institution Name	Availability	Junior Ages	Specials	Price /week	Status
English Plus @ Canterbury	A: 1-12		B, T, F, H, C, E	£225-£690	
English Teacher Direct	A: 1-12 J: 1-12 (1-1 only)	9-15 yrs	B, T, F, H, E	£20 min.	
Eurocentres Brighton	A: 1-12		B, E	£132-£206	
Express Language Homestay	A: 1-12 J: 1-12	14 yrs +	B, T	£345+**	
FGC School of English	A: 1-12 J: 1-12	14-17 yrs	B	£299-£350**	
GEOS English Academy	A: 1-12		C	£125-£435	GBC, Arels
Grove House Language Centre	A: 1-12 J: 1-12	12-16 yrs	B, F, E	£150-£675	
Guildford College	A: 9-7		B, C, E	£40 (EU)-£60 (non EU).	
H.E.L.P.	A: 1-12 J: 1-12 (1-1 only)	13 yrs +	B, T, H, C	£265-£355**	
Harven School of English	A: 1-12 J: 6-8	8-17 yrs	E	£65-£549	GBC, Arels, ASSET
Hastings College of Arts & Technology	A: 1-11		B, E	On application	GBC, Baselt
HELC - Hastings English Language Centre	A: 1-12		B, E	£125-£400	GBC, Arels
Hilderstone College	A: 1-12		E	£185-£222	GBC, Baselt, Eaquals
Home Language International	A: 1-12 J: 1-12 (1-1 homestay)	8 yrs +		£470-720**	
Homestay English Language Programme	A: 1-12 (1-1 only)		B, H, T, C	£500-£890**	
House of English	A: 1-12 J: 1-12	12-18 yrs	B	£150	GBC, Arels
Hove School of English	A: 1-12 J: 6-9	8-15 yrs	B, T, F, H, C, E	£50-£500	
Hurtwood House	J: 7-8	11-17 yrs		£780**	GBC, Arels
Individual English	A: 1-12		B, E	£210-£350	
Intensive English Training	A: 1-12		B, T, F, H	£750-£1500	
Intensive School of English & Business Communication	A: 1-12 J: 1, 6-8, 12	8-17 yrs	B, T, C, E	£60-£120	GBC

Institution Name	Availability	Junior Ages	Specials	Price /week	Status
International House, Folkestone	A: 1-12 I: 1-9	12-16 yrs	B, E	£110-220 (J: £245**)	
International Language Homestays	A: 1-12 J: 1-12 (1-1 only)	12-16 yrs	B	£500-£1060**	ABLS
InTuition Languages	A: 1-12 J: 1-12 (1-1 only)	14-18 yrs	B, T, F, C, E	£555-£1040**	GBC, Arels
ISS English Language Academy	A: 3-4, 7-8 J: 7-8			On application	
ITS English School	A: 1-12	8-17	B, F	£135-£150 (more for B course)	GBC, Arels
Kent Language & Activity Courses	J: 5, 7, 8			£525-£616**	
Kent School of English	A: 1-12 J: 1-12	12 yrs +		£170-£1080**	GBC
L.R.G.D. Study Centre	A: 1-12 J: 1-12 (1-1 only)	8 + yrs	E	£384-£694**	GBC, Arels
Language Studies International	A: 1-12			£290+/wks	GBC
Languages Plus	A: 1-12 J: 3/4, 7-8	14-18 yrs	B	£85-£420	
Learn English in the Garden of England	A: 1-12 (1-1 or 1-2)		B	£500-£650**	
Logos Linguistics	A: 1-12 J: 7-8	13-17 yrs	B, E	£245-£625**	
London House School of English	A: 1-12		B	On application	GBC, Arels
LTC International College	A: 1-12 J: 7-8	10-16 yrs		£120-£335 (** for juniors)	GBC, Arels
Margate Language Centre	A: 1-12		B, T, F, H, C, E	£75+	
Mayfield Academy of English	A: 1-12		B	£40-£180	GBC, Arels
Meads School of English	A: 1-12 J: 7-8	10-15 yrs	B, C, E	£45-£180	GBC, Arels
Mid Kent College	A: 9-7		B	£7-£21.25	
Multi Lingua	A: 1-12 6-8	9-16 yrs	B, T, F, C, E	£200 (J: £300**)	GBC, Arels
Northbrook College	A: 1-12		E	£1220/13wks (£160/2wks summer)	

Institution Name	Availability	Junior Ages	Specials	Price /week	Status
Olivet English Language School	A: 1-12 J:1-12	12-16 yrs		£79-£145	GBC
Pilgrims Ltd	A: 7-8 J: 7-8	8-17 yrs	B	£290-£2090	GBC, Arels
Regency College	A: 1-12		B, T, F, H, E	£60-£120	
Regency School of English	A: 1-12 J: 1-12	9-15 yrs	B, T, C, E	£199-£350**	GBC, Arels
Regent Brighton	A: 1-12		B, T, C, E	£81-£285	GBC, Arels
Regent Fitzroy	A: 1-12		B, T, F, H	£180/2wks (15hrs/wk)	GBC, Arels
Regent Language Holidays	J: 3/4, 7-8	10-17 yrs		£895**/2wks	GBC, Arels
Rochester Independent College	A: 1-12		B, E	£105-£320	BAC
Royal Holloway College Language Centre	A: 1-12		B, E	£185-£220	
Rutland School of English	A: 1-12 J: 1-12	9-15 yrs	B	£180-£190**	
Savoir Faire	A: 3-9		B, T, F, H	£495**	HPA
School of English Studies, Folkestone	A: 1-12 J: 3	9-17 yrs	B, H, T, F, C, E	£110-£1325	
SEE Europe	A: 1-12 J: 1-12	8-18 yrs	B	£250-£600**	
St George's, England	A: 1-12		B, E	£250-£350**	
St Giles International Brighton	A: 1-12		B, E	£109.50-£677	GBC, Arels
St. Giles Eastbourne	A: 1-12		B, T, E	£82-£208	GBC, Arels
St. Peter's School of English	A: 1-12			£187-£302**	GBC, Arels
Stafford House School of English	A: 1-12 J: 6-8	14-17 yrs	B	£330-£360**	GBC, Arels
Surrey Language Training	A: 1-12 J: 7-8	11-18 yrs		£95-£215 (J: £566**/2wks)	
Sussex Downs College	A: 1-12		B, T, E	£94-£134	GBC, Bcrselt
Sussex English Language School	A: 1-12		B, E	£100-£130	GBC

Institution Name	Availability	Junior Ages	Specials	Price /week	Status
Sussex Language Institute, University of Sussex	A: 1-12		B, E	£18-£218.25 (£180-£203.25 summer)	Baleap
Swandean School of English	A: 1-12 J: 6-8	12-16 yrs	E	£130-£215	GBC, Arels
TASIS England	J: 7-8			On application	
Tunbridge Wells Adult Education Centre	A: 9-7			£11.60-£13 (4hrs/wk)	
Twin English Centre, Eastbourne	A: 1-12		B	£33	GBC, Arels
University College Chichester	A: 1-12		E	On application	GBC, Baselt
University of Brighton	A: 1-12		B, C, E	£125-£175	GBC, Baselt
Wamborough College	A: 1-12		B, T, F, C, E	£180-£300	
West Kent College	A: 9-6		B	£15 (6hrs)	
West Sussex School of English	A: 2-12		B, E	£160-£995**	GBC, Arels
YES Education Centre	A: 1-12 J: 3-4, 6-9	12-17 yrs		£104-£188	GBC, Arels

5 WALES

Includes Clwyd, Dyfed, Gwent, Gwynedd, Mid, South & West Glamorgan, Powys.

Wales is a country of great contrasts, with a truly beautiful landscape, and offers much for the nature lover. It is also an ideal place for golf enthusiasts, boasting many fine courses.

The country is divided into three regions:
North Wales, with the Snowdonia National Park contains breathtaking scenery: waterfalls, steep passes, lakes and the highest mountains in England and Wales. The coast offers a pleasant alternative.
Mid Wales, with valleys, streams and miles of unspoilt countryside and beautiful sandy beaches on the coastline.
West Wales, with a particularly mild climate, is home of the Pembrokeshire Coastal National Park, with stunning cliffs, sandy beaches, coves and harbours.

Wales is surprisingly easy to get to: it is just 1¾ hours from London to Cardiff, Wales' capital city, and speedy rail and road-links connect Wales to the international airports of Heathrow and Gatwick.

Le Pays de Galles- Un pays charmant qui a de nombreux attraits: des monuments anciens, de beaux paysages et une côte splendide. Cardiff, la capitale, n'est qu'à 1¾ heures de Londres.

Diese reizende Landschaft offeriert eine Vielzahl verschiedener Attraktionen: Denkmäler, schöne Natur und prächtige Küsten. Cardiff, die Hauptstadt, ist nur 1¾ Stunden von London entfernt.

El País de Gales- Un país muy bonito con muchos tipos de diversiones: antiguos monumentos, preciosos paisajes campestres y una costa estupenda. Cardiff, su capital, está a tan sólo 1¾ hora de Londres.

Questo incantevole paese offre diverse attrazioni: monumenti antichi, una campagna lussureggiante e uno splendido litorale. Cardiff, la sua capitale, dista solamente un' ora e tre quarti da Londra.

 SIGHTS

Powys Castle
Beautiful castle, containing treasures from India in the Clive Museum, and outstanding gardens. Nr. Welshpool. Tel: 01938 554336

Snowdonia National Park
840 square miles of outstanding natural beauty. Mid and North Wales.

Maritime Quarter
Marina with shops, restaurants and leisure centre. Swansea.

Portmeirion
Extremely unusual village, famous for being the setting of the 1960's cult television series, "The Prisoner." Gwynedd. Tel: 01766 720228

For further information on these or other sights, contact the Welsh Tourist Board, Brunel House, 2 Fitzalan Road, Cardiff. CF2 1UY Tel: 029 2049 9909

 DIRECTORY OF EFL BOOKSELLERS IN THIS REGION:

(NB: Many bookshops hold a good selection of EFL material, even if they are not listed below. Moreover, if the particular book you are looking for is not in stock, they can order it for you.)

The Anglo American Book Co Ltd
Crown Buildings, Bancyfelin SA33 5ND
Tel: 01267 211880 Fax: 01267 211882
Web: http://www.anglo-american.co.uk

Blackwell's University Bookshop
Cardiff University Union,
Senghennydd Road, Cardiff CF24 4A
Tel: 029 2034 0673 Fax: 029 2038 2533
Web: http://bookshop.blackwell.co.uk

Cambrian Books - Aberystwyth
13 Terrace Road, Aberystwyth SY23 1NY
Tel: 01970 639250 Fax: 01970 639250
Web: http://www.cambrianbooks.com

The Muse
43 Holyhead Road, Bangor LL57 2EU
Tel: 01248 362072 Fax: 01248 362072

Ottakar's Bookstore
14 Guildhall Square, Carmarthen SA31 1PR
Tel: 01267 233330 Fax: 01267 233339
Web: http://www.ottakars.co.uk

Ottakar's Bookstore
26 Great Darkgate Street
Aberystwyth SY23 1DG
Tel: 01970 611222 Fax: 01970 624949
Web: http://www.ottakars.co.uk

Ottakar's Bookstore
159 Commercial Street, Newport NP20 1JQ
Tel: 01633 223977 Fax: 01633 223845
Web: http://www.ottakars.co.uk

Ottakar's Bookstore
38/39 Victoria Centre, Mostyn Street
Llandudno LL30 2NG
Tel: 01492 872287 Fax: 01492 872297
Web: http://www.ottakars.co.uk

Waterstone's
2-8 King Street, Lancaster LA1 1JN
Tel: 01524 61477 Fax: 01524 383748
Web: http://www.waterstones.co.uk

Waterstone's
University of Wales
Taliesin Art Centre, Swansea SA2 8PN
Tel: 01792 281460 Fax: 01792 281463
Web: http://www.waterstones.co.uk

DIRECTORY OF COURSES IN THIS REGION

PRIVATE SCHOOLS / ORGANISATIONS

Business Language Services
Westgate House, 2 Union Road East
Abergavenny NP7 5UW
Tel: 01873 856762   Fax: 01873 855006
Email: blsltd@compuserve.com
http://www.businesslanguageservices.co.uk

Cain Valley School of English
Bridge Street, Llanfyllin
Powys SY22 5AX
Tel: 01691 648008
Email: englishclasses@hotmail.com

Castilla H.C.C.
1st Floor, 5 Princes Drive, Colwyn Bay
Conwy LL29 8LA
Tel: 01492 534616   Fax: 01492 534616
Email: CastillaNW@msn.com
http://www.hcc-castilla.com

CELT- Centre for English Language Teaching Ltd.
6 Salisbury Road,
Cardiff CF24 4AD
Tel: 029 2033 9290   Fax: 029 2033 9515
Email: english@celt.co.uk
http://www.celt.co.uk

Churchill House English Home Tuition Courses - See South East display for details

Country House School of English
Broniwan, Rhydlewis
Llandysul SA44 5PF
Tel: 01239 851261   Fax: 01239 851261
Email: chse@ouvip.com

English at Oak Hollow
Westfield Road,
Saundersfoot SA69 9JL
Tel: 01834 814582   Fax: 01834 814582
Email: enquiries@oakhollow.co.uk
http://www.oakhollow.co.uk

English Study Centre
19-21 Uplands Crescent, Uplands
Swansea SA2 0NX
Tel: 01792 464103   Fax: 01792 472303
Email: info@escwales.co.uk
http://www.englishstudycentre.com

InTuition Languages
See London display for details

Island School of English
Ynys Faelog, Menai Bridge
Gwynedd LL59 5EU
Tel: 01248 716088   Fax: 01248 716088

Languages Direct
61 Charles Street,
Cardiff CF10 2GD
Tel: 029 2041 5800   Fax: 029 2039 7989
Email: languagesdirect@btinternet.com
http://www.languagesdirect.co.uk

Lingualink Language Services
7 Conwy Street,
Rhyl LL18 3ET
Tel: 01745 351168   Fax: 01745 351509
Email: lingualink@iname.com
http:// www.lingualink-uk.com

Meirionnydd Languages
Bodyfuddau,
Trawsfynydd LL41 4UW
Tel: 01766 540553   Fax: 0870 7060207
Email: daf@meirionnydd.force9.co.uk
http://www.meirionnydd.force9.co.uk

New College, Cardiff
Bute Terrace,
Cardiff CF1 2TE
Tel: 029 2046 3355   Fax: 029 20489616

Oaklands Educational Travel Services Ltd
30 Oakland Road, Mumbles
Swansea SA3 4AH
Tel: 01792 539184   Fax: 01792 539185
Email: Abacusaupairs@aol.com

Park House Training Ltd
Hyssington,
Montgomery SY15 6DZ
Tel: 01588 620611   Fax: 01588 620673
Email: enquiries@parkhousetraining.com
http://www.parkhousetraining.com

Regent Trebinshun
Trebinshun House, Nr. Brecon
Powys LD3 7PX
Tel: 01874 730653   Fax: 01874 730843
Email: trebinshun@regent.org.uk
http://www.regent.org.uk

Séjours Linguistiques au Pays de Galles
Myrtle Villa, Waunfawr
Aberystwyth SY23 3QD
Tel: 01970 612 256   Fax: 01970 626 974
Email: aberlangue@aol.com

The Pembrokeshire Retreat - English Language Learning Holidays
Rhos-Y-Gilwen Mansion, Rhoshill
Cilgerran SA43 2TW
Tel: 01239 841387   Fax: 01239 841387
Email: enquiries@retreat.co.uk
http://www.enquiries@retreat.co.uk

STATE COLLEGES / UNIVERSITIES

Aberystwyth, The University of Wales
Language & Learning Ctre, Llandinam
Building Penglais Campus
Aberystwyth SY23 3DB
Tel: 01970 622545   Fax: 01970 622546
Email: language+learning@aber.ac.uk
http://www.aber.ac.uk/language+learning
See display for further details

Barry College
Colcot Road, Barry
Nr. Cardiff CF62 8YJ
Tel: 01446 735162   Fax: 01446 732667

Cardiff University
English Language Centre, 53 Park Place
Cardiff CF10 3AT
Tel: 029 2087 6587   Fax: 029 2023 1968
Email: elt@cardiff.ac.uk
http://www.cardiff.ac.uk/elsis

Ceredigion College of Further & Higher Education
Llanbadarn Campus,
Llanbadarn Fawr SY23 2BP
Tel: 01970 4511

Coleg Glan Hafren
International Office, 27 The Parade
Cardiff CF24 3AB
Tel: 029 2048 9343   Fax: 029 2048 9343
Email: international@glan.hafren.ac.uk
http://www.glan-hafren.ac.uk/eis

Coleg Llysfasi
Rhuthun
Sir Ddinbych LL15 2LB
Tel: 01978 790263   Fax: 01978 790468
Email: admin@llysfasi.ac.uk
http://www.llysfasi.ac.uk

Coleg Menai
Friddoedd Road,
Bangor LL56 4UQ
Tel: 01248 383324   Fax: 01248 370052
Email: carl.mather@menai.ac.uk
http://www.menai.ac.uk

Gwent Tertiary College
Crosskeys Campus, Risca Road
Crosskeys, Gwent NP1 7ZA
Tel: 01495 270295

Llandrillo College International
Rhos-on-Sea,
Colwyn Bay LL28 4HZ
Tel: 01492 542315   Fax: 01492 543052
Email: international@llandrillo.ac.uk
http://www.llandrillo-international.com
See display for further details

North East Wales Institute of Higher Education
Plas Coch, Mold Road
Wrexham LL11 2AW
Tel: 01978 290666

Swansea College
Tycoch Rd,
Swansea SA2 9EB
Tel: 01792 284000   Fax: 01792 284074
Email: p.p.@swancoll.ac.uk
http://www.swancoll.ac.uk

University of Glamorgan
Centre for Language Studies,
Pontypridd CF37 1DL
Tel: 01443 480480   Fax: 01443 480558
Email: jrwalter@glam.ac.uk

Prifysgol Cymru
Aberstwyth
The University of Wales

Promoting Excellence in Teaching and Research

SUMMER IN WALES 2003

ENGLISH LANGUAGE COURSES
ENGLISH FOR UNIVERSITY (PRE-SESSIONAL)
EFL TEACHER DEVELOPMENT COURSES
TRINITY CERT. TESOL

beautiful and secure seaside location
university campus accommodation
big social programme

YEAR-ROUND COURSES

INTERNATIONAL FOUNDATION PROGRAMME
ENGLISH LANGUAGE COURSES
PRE-MASTERS COURSE

Language and Learning Centre
The University of Wales Aberystwyth
Llandinam Building, Penglais Campus
Aberystwyth, Ceredigion SY23 3DB, UK

Tel: +44 (0)1970 622545   Fax: +44 (0) 1970 622546

http://www.aber.ac.uk/language+learning
email: language+learning@aber.ac.uk

The British Association of Lecturers in English for Academic Purposes

THE BRITISH ASSOCIATION OF STATE
ENGLISH LANGUAGE TEACHING

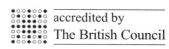

accredited by
The British Council

University of Wales Institute Cardiff
International Foundation Course
Llandaff Campus
Western Ave, Cardiff CF5 2SG
Tel: 029 2041 6161
Email: casowden@uwic.ac.uk

University of Wales, Bangor
ELCOS,
Bangor LL57 2DG
Tel: 01248 382153   Fax: 01248 383784
Email: elcos@bangor.ac.uk
http://www.bangor.ac.uk/english/elcos/
elcos.htm
See display for further details

University of Wales, Lampeter
Lampeter SA48 7ED
Tel: 01570 424746   Fax: 01570 423423

University of Wales, Swansea
Centre for Applied Language Studies,
North Arts
Swansea SA2 8PP
Tel: 01792 295391   Fax: 01792 295641
Email: K.A.Frith@swansea.ac.uk
http://www.swansea.ac.uk/cals/clasx.html

Institution Name	Availability	Junior Ages	Specials	Price /week	Status
Aberystwyth, The University of Wales	A: 1-12		B, E	£148-£200	GBC, Baselt, Baleap
Barry College	A: 9-6			On application	
Business Language Services	A: 1-12 (1-1 only)		B	£85-£1050	
Cain Valley School of English	A: 5-8 J: 7-8 (1-1 only)	12-16 yrs	B, T, E	£300-£400**	Baselt, Baleap
Cardiff University	A: 1-12		E	£135-£185	
Costilla H.C.C.	A: 1-12 J: 1-12	9-16 yrs	B, T, F, H, C, E	£0-£200	
CELT- Centre for English Language Teaching Ltd.	A: 1-12 J: 6-8	13 yrs +	B, T	£85-£150+	GBC
Churchill House English Home Tuition Courses	A: 1-12 J: 1-12 (1-1 only)	7 yrs +	B, T, F, H, C, E	£450-£780**	
Coleg Glan Hafren	A: 9-6		B, C, E	£16-£40	GBC, Baselt
Coleg Llysfasi	A: 9-12, 1-7		B, C	On application	
Coleg Menai	A: 9, 1		B, F, C, E	£100-£180	
Country House School of English	A: 1-12 (1-1 only)		B, T, E	£460-£640**	
English at Oak Hollow	A: 1-12 (1-1 only)		B, T, F, H, C, E	£460-£1015**	
English Study Centre	A: 1-12 J: 6-8	12-17 yrs	B, T, F, H, E	£115-£555	ABLS
Infurion Languages	A: 1-12 J: 1-12 (1-1 only)	14-18 yrs	B, T, F, C, E	£555-£1040-*	GBC, Arels
Island School of English	A: 7-8			On application	
Languages Direct	A: 1-12 J: 6-9	9-15 yrs	B, E	£90-£126+	
Lingualink Language Services	A: 1-12 J: 1-12	5-15 yrs	B, E	£160-£300**	
Llandrillo College International	A: 1-12		B, T, H, C, E	£109-£120	
Merionnydd Languages	A: 1-12 (1-1 only)		E	£200-£300**	
Oaklands Educational Travel Services Ltd	A: 1-12 J: 1-12	7-18 yrs		£175-£205**	
Park House Training Ltd	A: 1-12 (1-1/ executives only)		B, F	from £1000**	GBC
Swansea College	A: 1-12			On application	
University of Glamorgan	A: 7/8			On application	
University of Wales, Bangor	A: 7-9		E	£125-£175 (approx.)	Baleap
University of Wales, Swansea	A: 1-12		B, T, F,H, C, E	£140-£200	GBC, Baselt

6 HEART OF ENGLAND

Stoke on Trent

Birmingham •

Stratford upon Avon

Cheltenham

Includes Gloucestershire, Herefordshire, Shropshire, Staffordshire, Warwickshire, West Midlands & Worcestershire.

This region, which includes Shakespeare's country and the Cotswolds, forms a large part of central England.

Stratford-upon-Avon is the home of Shakespeare and is an excellent point from which to visit other historic towns in the area.

The Cotswolds, to the south, are famous for their beautiful honey-coloured villages and their stately homes and gardens.

In the north, Staffordshire is famous for its potteries and for the open hills of the Peak District.

The "Marches" provide a total contrast: a land of black and white villages, this area offers a wide range of sporting activities.

The city of Birmingham, in the centre of the region, boasts good theatres and shopping facilities. Its international airport has direct flights to over 40 European cities, with onward connections world-wide.

Le berceau de Shakespeare (Stratford-upon-Avon), cette région contient aussi le Staffordshire, bien connu pour ses potteries. Les Cotswolds et Marches offrent de beaux paysages de grand contraste. Accès très facile grâce à l'aéroport international de Birmingham.

Hier findet sich der Geburtsort Shakespeare (Stratford-upon-Avon), ebenso Staffordshire, das für seine Töpfereien bekannt ist. Die Cotswolds und die Marches offerieren wunderschöne, kontrastierende Seiten. Die Region ist dank dem internationalen Flughafen von Birmingham zudem sehr gut zu erreichen.

En esta región donde nació Shakespeare (Stratford-upon-Avon) está también Staffordshire muy conocida por sus alfarerías. Los Cotswolds y Marches ofrecen magnificos paisajes de gran contraste. Toda la región es de acceso muy fácil gracias al aeropuerto internacional de Birmingham.

Oltre a Stratford-upon-Avon, luogo natale di Shakespeare, in questa regione si trova anche lo Staffordshire, noto per i suoi laboratori di ceramiche. I Cotswolds e le Marches offrono stupendi paesaggi ricchi di contrasti e la regione è facilmente accessibile grazie all' aeroporto internazionale di Birmingham.

SIGHTS

Warwick Castle
Magnificent castle set in 60 acres of grounds, with dungeon, state rooms & Madame Tussaud's display.   Warwick. Tel: 01926 495421

Shakespeare's Birthplace
Books, costumes and manuscripts of the Bard.
Stratford-upon-Avon. Tel: 01789 204016

Alton Towers
Large theme park with 125 rides, including Congo River Rapids and Thunderlooper!
Alton. Tel: 01538 702200

Cadbury World
The story of chocolate, with demonstrations (and samples!)
Linden Road, Bourneville, Birmingham.
Tel: 0121 433 4334

For further information on these or other sights, contact the Heart of England Tourist Board, Lark Hill Road, Worcester. WR5 2EF Tel: 01905 763436

 **DIRECTORY OF EFL BOOKSELLERS IN THIS REGION:**

(NB: Many bookshops hold a good selection of EFL material, even if they are not listed below. Moreover, if the particular book you are looking for is not in stock, they can order it for you.)

Burway Books
10 Beaumont Rd, Church Stretton SY6 6BN
Tel: 01694 723388 Fax: 01694 724368
Web: http://www.burwaybooks.co.uk

The Forest Bookshop
8 St John Street, Coleford GL16 8AR
Tel: 01594 833334 Fax: 01594 833446
Web: http://www.forestbk.demon.co.uk

H & H Spalding
60 Main Street
Barton under Needwood DE13 8AA
Tel: 01283 712220 Fax: 01283 716545

Students' Union Bookshop
P O Box 220, The Park
Cheltenham GL50 2QF
Tel: 01242 532808 Fax: 01242 261381

Ottakar's Bookstore
13 Cricklade Street
Cirencester GL7 1JH
Tel: 01285 658998 Fax: 01285 651562
Web: http://www.ottakars.co.uk

Ottakar's Bookstore
6 Cooper Square, Cooper Centre
Burton-on-Trent DE14 1DF
Tel: 01283 566055 Fax: 01283 511383
Web: http://www.ottakars.co.uk

Ottakar's Bookstore
57 Greengate Street, Stafford ST16 2JE
Tel: 01785 222212 Fax: 01785 222213
Web: http://www.ottakars.co.uk

Ottakar's Bookstore
Unit SU11, The Parade
Sutton Coldfield B72 1PD
Tel: 0121 321 2333 Fax: 0121 321 2332
Web: http://www.ottakars.co.uk

Ottakar's Bookstore
12 South Street
Bishop's Stortford CM23 3AT
Tel: 01279 508900 Fax: 01279 506979
Web: http://www.ottakars.co.uk

Ottakar's Bookstore
3 Park Street, Walsall WS1 1LY
Tel: 01922 610922 Fax: 01922 725391
Web: http://www.ottakars.co.uk

Ottakar's Bookstore
66/68 High Street, Bromsgrove B61 8EX
Tel: 01527 833339 Fax: 01527 833773
Web: http://www.ottakars.co.uk

THE
Unit One, Rosevale Business Park
Newcastle-under-Lyme ST5 7QT
Tel: 01782 566566 Fax: 01782 580402
Web: http://www.the.co.uk

Warwick University Bookshop
Arts Centre, University of Warwick
Coventry CV4 7AL
Tel: 024 7652 3388 Fax: 024 7652 3792
Web: http://www.booksack.co.uk

Waterstone's
University of Staffordshire
Station Road, Stoke-on-Trent ST4 2UQ
Tel: 01782 746318 Fax: 01782 844946
Web: http://www.waterstones.co.uk

Waterstone's
Coventry University Earl Street
Coventry CV1 5RG
Tel: 024 7623 0880 Fax: 024 7623 0881
Web: http://www.waterstones.co.uk

Waterstone's
Unit 95, Merryhill Shopping Centre
Brierley Hill DY5 1SJ
Tel: 01384 751551 Fax: 01384 77121
Web: http://www.waterstones.co.uk

Waterstone's
13-15 Victoria Street
Wolverhampton WV1 3TA
Tel: 01902 427219 Fax: 01902 712001
Web: http://www.waterstones.co.uk

Waterstone's
24-26 High Street, Birmingham B4 7SL
Tel: 0121 633 4353 Fax: 0121 633 4300
Web: http://www.waterstones.co.uk

Waterstone's
Birmingham University
Ring Road North, Edgbaston
Birmingham B15 2TP
Tel: 0121 472 3034 Fax: 0121 415 4649
Web: http://www.waterstones.co.uk

 DIRECTORY OF COURSES IN THIS REGION

PRIVATE SCHOOLS / ORGANISATIONS

4Languages
24 Avon Street,
Stratford-upon-Avon CV37 7EU
Tel: 01789 297166
Email: anniegi@aol.com
http://4languages.biz

Abbey College
253 Wells Road,
Malvern Wells WR14 4JF
Tel: 01684 892300   Fax: 01684 892757
Email: abbey@cix.co.uk
http://www.abbey-college.co.uk

Anne Christian Dyson School of English
Saxons Meadow,
Hartlebury DY10 4JE
Tel: 01299 250576   Fax: 01299 250576
Email: Dysnjd@aol.com

Berlitz Language Centre
Paradise Forum,
Birmingham B3 3HJ
Tel: 0121 233 0974   Fax: 0121 233 1236
Email: michael@languagecentres.com
http://www.languagecentres.com

BSNS English
23 Victoria Avenue,
Droitwich Spa WR9 7DF
Tel: 01905 773557   Fax:
Email: chris@bsnsenglish.com
http://www.bsnsenglish.com
See display for further details

BSNS ENGLISH

Qualified and experienced
English teacher offers:

One-to-one English courses.
General/Business English.
Homestay (live with the family)
or hotel accommodation.
Pretty spa town in central England.

Christine Robbins BA (Hons) Dip. M. C.T.E.F.L.A

23 Victoria Avenue, Droitwich Spa
Worcester WR9 7DF

Tel: +44 (0) 1905 773557
E-mail: chris@bsnsenglish.com
Web: http://www.bsnsenglish.com

Ceran Lingua UK - Sherbourne Priors
Watery Lane,
Warwick CV35 8AL
Tel: 01926 624016   Fax: 01926 624390
Email: customer@ceran.com
http://www.ceran.com
Junior courses held in Taunton.

Cheltenham School of English
87 St. George's Rd,
Cheltenham GL50 3DU
Tel: 01242 570000   Fax: 01242 227350
Email: chelteng@eurobell.co.uk
http://www.cheltenglish.co.uk

**Churchill House English Home Tuition
Courses** - *See South East display for details*

Class Languages
Cotswold House, 28 Cambray Place,
Cheltenham GL50 1JN
Tel: 01242 520046 Fax: 01242 256707
Email: enquiries@classlanguages.com
http://www.classlanguages.com

Communicaid English
Canterbury House, 85 Newhall Street
Birmingham B3 1LH
Tel: 0800 1691310 Fax:
Email: info@communicaid.com
http://www.communicaid.com

Concord College
Acton Burnell Hall, Acton Burnell
Shrewsbury SY5 7PF
Tel: 01694 731633 Fax: 01694 731219
Email: summercourse@concordcollegeuk.com
http://www.concordcollegeuk.com/summer/
english.htm

Corinium Language Associates
1-2 Priory Court, Poulton
Nr. Cirencester GL7 5JB
Tel: 01285 851122 Fax: 01285 850544
Email: kathy.wilson@coriniumlanguage.co.uk
http://www.coriniumlanguage.co.uk

Discovery School of English
Alderwood House, Thirlmere Close
Wolverhampton WV6 9DG
Tel: 01902 688261 Fax: 01902 827339
Email: emma@discovery.fsnet.co.uk

English Country School
18 Riverside,
Winchcombe GL54 5JP
Tel: 01242 604067 Fax: 01242 604067
Email: etchells@countryschool.com
http://www.countryschool.com

Entente UK
Austin Court, Bridleyplace, Cambridge Street
Birmingham B1 2NP
Tel: 0121 600 7535 Fax: 0121 600 7544
Email: EntenteUK@aol.com
http://www.ententeuk.com
See display for further details

Euro-Lang Communications
12 The Fairways,
Leamington Spa CV32 6PR
Tel: 01926 426090 Fax: 01926 426090
Email: eurolang@mail.com

Harper School of English
88 Styvechale Ave,
Coventry CV5 6DX
Tel: 024 76 676136 Fax: 024 76 715588
Email: AJandCHarper@compuserve.com

ENGLISH FOR BUSINESS AND INTERNATIONAL TRADE

1 - 16 week programmes designed for intermediate speakers of English who are working in any international trading environment. They are ideal preparation for the Cambridge Business English Certificate.

We offer all support arrangements including homestay or hotel accommodation and cultural programmes. Work experience placements with UK organisations can be arranged if required.

Our centre is in the heart of Birmingham's business and entertainment area. For information about Birmingham, visit the city's website: www.birmingham.gov.uk

ENTENTE UK, Austin Court, Brindleyplace,
Cambridge Street, Birmingham B1 2NP
Tel: +44 121 600 7535   Fax: +44 121 600 7544
E-mail: EntenteUK@aol.com   www.ententeuk.com

Heart of England Language School
50 Russell Terrace,
Leamington Spa CV31 1HE
Tel: 01926 311375 Fax: 01926 338509
Email: enquiries@heartengland.co.uk
http://www.heartengland.co.uk

Home End Farm
Stiffords Bridge, Cradley
Malvern WR13 5NW
Tel: 01886 880240 Fax: 01886 880240
Email: info@english-for-children.co.uk
http://www.english-for-children.co.uk

Inlingua Cheltenham
Rodney Lodge, Rodney Road
Cheltenham GL50 1HX
Tel: 01242 250493 Fax: 01242 250495
Email: info@inlingua-cheltenham.co.uk
http://www.inlingua-cheltenham.co.uk

International Study Programmes
The Manor, Hazleton
Cheltenham GL54 4EB
Tel: 01451 860379 Fax: 01451 860482
Email: Discover@International-Study-Programmes.org.uk
http://International-Study-Programmes.org.uk

InTuition Languages - *See London display for details*

Kingsway English Centre
Northwall House, 11 The Butts
Worcester WR1 3PA
Tel: 01905 27511 Fax: 01905 29712
Email: rick@kingsway-english.com
http://www.kingsway-english.com

Linguarama
1 Elm Court, Arden St.
Stratford-upon-Avon CV37 6PA
Tel: 01789 296535   Fax: 01789 266462
Email: stratford@linguarama.com
http://www.linguarama.com/english/index.html

Lydbury English Centre
Lydbury North SY7 8AU
Tel: 01588 681000 Fax: 01588 681018
Email: enquiry@lydbury.co.uk
http://www.lydbury.co.uk

PGL Adventure
Alton Court, Penyard Lane
Ross-on-Wye HR9 5NR
Tel: 01989 764211 Fax: 01989 765451

Redwood Farmhouse Language Centre
Redwood Farmhouse, St Michaels
Tenbury Wells WR15 8TL
Tel: 1568750314 Fax: 1568750382
Email: redwoodcentre@cs.com
http://www.redwoodcentre.co.uk

Severnvale Academy
25 Claremont Hill,
Shrewsbury SY1 1RD
Tel: 01743 232505 Fax: 01743 272637
Email: enquiry@severnvale.co.uk
http://www.severnvale.co.uk
See display for further details

St. Michael's College
Tenbury Wells WR15 8PH
Tel: 01584 811300   Fax: 01584 811221
Email: st.michaels@ukonline.co.uk
http://www.kingsgroup.com/sme.htm

Stratford-upon-Avon School of English Studies
8 Tiddington Road,
Stratford-upon-Avon CV37 7AE
Tel: 01789 269497 Fax: 01789 262837
Email: stratford.school@btinternet.com
http://www.stratfordschool.com

Swindon Hall Private Language School
Swindon Village,
Cheltenham GL51 9QR
Tel: 01242 523561 Fax: 01242 237001
Email: swindonhalledu@enterprise.net
http://www.cotswold.star.co.uk/swindonhalledu/

Severnvale Academy

■ Severnvale is a small English language school devoted entirely to the teaching of business, examination (especially IELTS, Cambridge and TOEFL) and general English.

■ It is British Council Accredited, and maintains a high level of professionalism, together with the kind of personal attention and friendliness only possible in a school where all staff and students can get to know each other.

■ The maximum number of students is 50 in the all-year adult centre (minimum age 18), and 90 juniors in our completely separate youth centre in July and August.

■ A separate purpose-adapted Business Centre, with self-access office facilities to help clients maintain contact with their businesses at home, is due to open in the next few months.

■ Severnvale is in a beautiful, modernised 18th century building 3 minutes' walk from the centre of Shrewsbury - a lively, modern town (population about 100 000) rich in history, with good entertainment, leisure and sporting facilities and many picturesque old buildings.

■ As the only Accredited school in Shrewsbury, Severnvale has the pick of the best homestay families, but equally excellent hotel accommodation can also be arranged.

25 Claremont Hill, Shrewsbury, Shropshire. SY1 1RD
Tel: +44 1743 232505   Fax: +44 1743 272637
Email: enquiry@severnvale.co.uk   Web: http://www.severnvale.co.uk

Windsor English Centre
Wrekin College,
Wellington TF1 3AR
Tel: 01743 415063   Fax: 01743 415064
Email: theprincipal@windsorenglish.co.uk
http://www.windsorenglish.co.uk

Witchdrum Consulting and Training
26 Exhall Green, Exhall
Coventry CV7 9GL
Tel: 0870 137 0973   Fax: 0870 137 0973
Email: inquiry@witchdrum.com
http://www.witchdrum.com

Wyre English Services
Aldbury House, George Lane, Wyre Piddle
Pershore WR10 2HX
Tel: 01386 553754   Fax: 01386 553754
Email: aldbury@onetel.net.uk

STATE COLLEGES / UNIVERSITIES

Aston University
Language Studies Unit, Aston Triangle
Birmingham B4 7ET
Tel: 0121 359 3611   Fax: 0121 359 2725
Email: lsu@aston.ac.uk

Bilston Community College
Westfield Road, Bilston
Wolverhampton WV14 6ER
Tel: 01902 353877

Birmingham Central College
Wynner house, Bromsgrove Street
Birmingham B5 6RG
Tel: 0121 622 5139   Fax: 0121 622 5872
Email: bccuk@btconnect.com

Bournville College of Further & Higher Education
Bristol Road South,
Birmingham B31 2AJ
Tel: 0121 411 1414

Brasshouse Centre
50 Sheepcote St.,
Birmingham B16 8AJ
Tel: 0121 303 0114   Fax: 0121 464 5375
Email: brasshouse@birmingham.gov.uk
http://www.birmingham.gov.uk/brasshouse
See display for further details

Burton College
Lichfield Street,
Burton -on - Trent DE14 3RL
Tel: 01283 545401   Fax: 01283 515095
Email: cmaca1bu@mail.burton-college.ac.uk

Cheltenham International Language Centre
Dunholme Villa, The Park
Cheltenham GL50 2QF
Tel: 01242 532925   Fax: 01242 532926
Email: cilc@glos.ac.uk
http://www.glos.ac.uk/cilc

Coventry Technical College English Centre
Butts,
Coventry CV1 3GD
Tel: 024 7652 6742   Fax: 024 7652 6743
Email: language@covcollege.ac.uk
http://www.covcollege.ac.uk

Coventry University
International Office, Priory St.
Coventry CV1 5FB
Tel: 024 7688 8674   Fax: 024 7663 2710
Email: int002@coventry.ac.uk
http://www.coventry.ac.uk

Dudley College of Technology
Lexis Language Centre, The Broadway,
Dudley DY1 4AS
Tel: 01384 363422   Fax: 01384 363316
Email: international@dudleycol.ac.uk
http://www.dudleycol.ac.uk

East Birmingham College
Garretts Green Lane,
Birmingham B33 0TS
Tel: 0121 743 4471

East Warwickshire College
Lower Hillmorton Road,
Rugby CV21 3QS
Tel: 01788 541666

Gloscat
Princess Elizabeth Way,
Cheltenham GL51 7SJ
Tel: 01242 532144   Fax: 01242 532196
Email: woodmj@gloscat.ac.uk
http://www.gloscat.ac.uk

Handsworth College
Soho Road, Handsworth
Birmingham B21 9DP
Tel: 0121 551 6031   Fax: 0121 523 4447
Email: l.webster@handsworth.ac.uk
http://www.handsworth.ac.uk

Henley College Coventry
Henley Road, Bell Green
Coventry CV2 1ED
Tel: 024 7662 6300   Fax: 024 76611837
Email: overseas@henley-cov.ac.uk
http://www.henley-cov.ac.uk

Herefordshire College of Technology
Folly Lane,
Hereford HR1 1LS
Tel: 01432 352235

Joseph Chamberlain Sixth Form College
Balsall Heath Road, Highgate
Birmingham CR2 8JJ
Tel: 0121 440 4288

Keele University
English Language Unit,
c/o Dept. of Academic Affairs,
Keele ST5 5BG
Tel: 01782 584293
Email: eltu@keele.ac.uk
http://www.keele.ac.uk/depts/aa/elu

Kidderminster College
Hoo Road,
Kidderminster DY10 1LX
Tel: 01562 820811

North Birmingham College
Aldridge Road, Great Barr
Birmingham B44 8NE
Tel: 0121 360 3543   Fax: 0121 325 0828

North East Worcestershire College
Bromsgrove Campus, Blackwood Road
Bromsgrove B60 1PQ
Tel: 01527 570020

North Warwickshire & Hinckley College
Park House, Riversley Rd
Nuneaton CV11 5QS
Tel: 024 76 382265   Fax: 024 76 382265

Sandwell College
Crocketts Lane,
Smethwick B66 3BU
Tel: 0121 253 6306   Fax: 0121253 6322
Email: ulla.stede@sandwell.ac.uk
http://www.sandwell.ac.uk

Selly Oak Colleges
English Dept., Bristol Road
Birmingham B29 6LQ
Tel: 0121 472 4231   Fax: 0121 472 8852
Email: english@sellyoak.ac.uk
http://www.sellyoak.ac.uk

Shrewsbury College of Arts & Technology
London Road, Main Campus
Schrewsbury SY2 6PR
Tel: 01743 342333   Fax: 01743 342333
Email: infoff@s-cat.ac.uk
http://www.s-cat.ac.uk

Solihull College
Centre for International Development,
Blossomfield Road
Solihull B91 1SB
Tel: 0121 678 7172   Fax: 0121 711 2316
Email: intenqu@solihull.ac.uk

South Birmingham College
Cole Bank Road,
Birmingham B28 8ES
Tel: 0121 778 2311

Staffordshire University
Language Services Unit, College Road
Stoke-on-Trent ST4 2XW
Tel: 01782 294415   Fax: 01782 294760
Email: p.walker@staffs.ac.uk
http://www.staffs.ac.uk/schools/
humanities_and_soc_sciences/languages/
LSU.html

Stoke-on-Trent College
Stoke Rd, Shelton
Stoke-on-Trent ST4 2DG
Tel: 01782 208208   Fax: 01782 603504
Email: dston@stokecoll.ac.uk
http://www.stokecoll.ac.uk

Stourbridge College
Hagley Road,
Stourbridge DY8 1LY
Tel: 01384 78531

Stratford upon Avon College
The Willows North, Alcester Road
Stratford CV37 9QR
Tel: 01789 266245   Fax: 01789 267524
Email: waggott_j@strat-avon.ac.uk

Stroud College
Stratford Road,
Stroud GL5 4AH
Tel: 01453 763424   Fax: 01453 753543
Email: enquire@strouda.demon.co.uk

Sutton Coldfield College of Further Education
Lichfield Road,
Sutton Coldfield B74 2NW
Tel: 0121 355 5671

Tamworth College
Croft St., Upper Gungate
Tamworth B79 8AE
Tel: 01827 310202   Fax: 01827 759437
Email: enquiries@tamworth.ac.uk

University College Worcester
Henwick Grove,
Worcester WR2 6AJ
Tel: 01905 855077   Fax: 01905 855132
Email: s.phillipson@worc.ac.uk
http://www.worc.ac.uk
See display for further details

UNIVERSITY COLLEGE WORCESTER

Quality EFL programmes at attractive
university college in the
heart of England.

General courses in EFL, specialist
programmes in Academic English and
Summer Schools for pre-university
students and adults.

Henwick Grove, Worcester WR2 6AJ

Tel: +44 (0) 1905 855077
Fax: +44 (0) 1905 855132
Email: s.phillipson@worc.ac.uk
Website: http://www.worc.ac.uk

University of Birmingham
EISU, Elmfield House, Bristol Road
Birmingham B29 6LQ
Tel: 0121 415 2285   Fax: 0121415 2270
Email: a.steward@bham.ac.uk
http://www.bham.ac.uk/EISU

University of Central England
Staff and Student Development Department
Baker Building, Perry Barr
Birmingham B42 2SU
Tel: 0121 331 5380   Fax: 0121 331 6389
Email: vicky.schofield@uce.ac.uk
http://lmu.uce.ac.uk/lmu/esu/

University of Warwick
Centre for English Language Teacher
Education
Coventry CV4 7AL
Tel: 024 76 523200   Fax: 024 76 524318
Email: celte@warwick.ac.uk

University of Wolverhampton
School of Humanities, Languages &
Social Sciences
Wulfruna Street, Wolverhampton WV1 1SB
Tel: 01902 322770   Fax: 01902 322 739
Email: efl@wlv.ac.uk
http://www.wlv.ac.uk/efl

Walsall College of Arts and Technology
St Paul's Street,
Walsall WS1 1XN
Tel: 01922 657000   Fax: 01922 657083
Email: sstokes@walcat.ac.uk
http://www.walcat.ac.uk

**Warwickshire College - Shakespeare
School of English Language**
International Office, Warwick New Road,
Leamington Spa CV32 5JE
Tel: 01926 318165   Fax: 01926 427317
Email: wci@warkscol.ac.uk
http://194.66.249.134/uniform2/
international/uinternation.shtml

Wulfrun College
Paget Road,
Wolverhampton WV6 0DU
Tel: 01902 317700

Institution Name	Availability	Junior Ages	Specials	Price /week	Status
4Languages	A: 1-12 (mostly 1-1)		B, T, H, E	£175-£450	
Abbey College	A: 1-11 J: 1-11	8-11, 12-17 yrs	B, T, F, H, C, E	£320-£410**	GBC, Arels
Anne Christian Dyson School of English	A: 3-11		B	£565-£735**	
Berlitz Language Centre	A: 1-12 J: 7-8	8-15 yrs	B, F	£212.50-£1850	
Birmingham Central College	A: 1-12			On application	
Brasshouse Centre	A: 9-8			On application	GBC, Baselt
BSNS English	A: 1-12 (1-1 or 1-2 only)		B, T, H	£445-£575**	
Burton College	A: 9-6			On application	
Ceran Lingua UK - Sherbourne Priors	A: 1-12 J: 3-4, 7-8	10-18 yrs	B	from 880 € **	
Cheltenham International Language Centre	A: 1-12		B, E	£96-£146	GBC, Baselt
Cheltenham School of English	A: 1-12		B, E	On application	GBC, Arels
Churchill House English Home Tuition Courses	A: 1-12 J: 1-12 (1-1 only)	7 yrs +	B, T, F, H, C, E	£450-£780**	
Class Languages	A: 1-12		B, F, E	£100-£1295	
Communicaid English	A: 1-12		B, T, F, H, C, E	£845-£1845	
Concord College	J: 7-8	8-18 yrs		£485**	GBC, Arels
Corinium Language Associates	A: 1-12			£950-£1150	
Coventry Technical College English Centre	A: 1-12		B, E	£75-£100	GBC, Baselt
Coventry University	A: 7-9		E	£230**	
Discovery School of English	A: 6-9 J: 6-9	6-9 yrs	B	£125-£185	
Dudley College of Technology	A: 1-12		B, E	£100-£150 (more for B)	GBC, Baselt

Institution Name	Availability	Junior Ages	Specials	Price /week	Status
English Country School	J: 7-8	7-17 yrs		£550**	GBC, Arels
Entente UK	A: 1-12		B	£450-£1000	
Euro-Lang Communications	A: 1-12 (1-1 only)		B, F	On application	
Gloscat	A: 1-12 J: 7	11-17 yrs	B, T,	£70-£100	GBC, Baselt
Handsworth College	A: 9-6			On application	
Harper School of English	A: 1-6, 10-12		B, T, F, H, E	£278-£954**	
Heart of England Language School	A: 1-12 J: 1-12	13-16 yrs	B, T, F, H, C, E	£220-£1000	
Henley College Coventry	A: 1-12		B	£100-£150	GBC, Baselt
Home End Farm	J: 29	8-15yrs	E	£400**	ABLS
Inlingua Cheltenham	A: 1-12 J: 7	11-16 years	B	£155-£1575	GBC, Arels
International Study Programmes	A: 1-12 J: 1-12 (grps) 7-8 (individuals)	12-18 yrs	B, T, F, H, C, E	£170-£340 **	
InTuition Languages	A: 1-12 J: 1-12 (1-1 only)	14-18 yrs	B, T, F, C, E	£555-£1040**	GBC, Arels
Keele University	A: 4-9		E	£157	GBC, Baselt
Kingsway English Centre	A: 1-12		B	£285-£1035	GBC, Arels
Linguarama	A: 1-12		B, F	£785-£1925	GBC
Lydbury English Centre	A: 1-12		B, F	£675-£1590	GBC, Arels
Prince Phillimore School	A: 1-12 J: 1-9	7-15 yrs		£350-£700**	
Redwood Farmhouse Language Centre	A: 1-12		B, F, E	£285-£1000**	
Sandwell College	A: 9-6		B, C	On application	
Selly Oak Colleges	A: 1-12		E	£263-£100+	

Institution Name	Availability	Junior Ages	Specials	Price /week	Status
Severnvale Academy	A: 1-12 J: 7-8	12-18 yrs	E	£145-£425	GBC, Arels
Shrewsbury College of Arts & Technology	A: 9-6			£112	
St. Michael's College	J: 6-8	10-16 yrs	E	£275-£295**	
Staffordshire University	A: 1-12		E	£95	
Stoke-on-Trent College	A: 1-12		B, C, E	On application	
Stratford upon Avon College	A: 1-12		E	£75-£195	
Stratford-upon-Avon School of English Studies	A: 1-12 J: 1-12	14-17 yrs	B, F	£175-£400+	GBC, Arels
Stroud College	A: 1-6 & 9-12			On application	
University College Worcester	A: 1-12		B, E	£165	
University of Birmingham	A: 1-12		B, E	£150-£175	GBC, Baselt
University of Central England	A: 10-5 (Erasmus/Students of UCE)			On application	
University of Warwick	A: 9-6		E only	On application	Boleap
University of Wolverhampton	A: 1-12		B, T, C, E	£175-£200	GBC, Baselt
Walsall College of Arts and Technology	A: 10-5		B, T, H, C	£101	Provisional Baselt Member
Warwickshire College - Shakespeare School	A: 1-12		B, C	£100-£150	GBC, Baselt
Windsor English Centre	A: 1-12 J: 4, 6-8	12-17 yrs	B, T, H, C, E	£160-£205	
Wyre English Services	A: 1-12 (1-1 only)		B, C, E	£450**	

7 MIDDLE ENGLAND

Includes Derbyshire, Leicestershire, Lincolnshire,
Northamptonshire, Nottinghamshire.

The land of Robin Hood and Sherwood forest, this region has been at the heart of many historic events. Hence the great variety of heritage centres, museums and castles scattered throughout this beautiful part of the country.

The Peak District offers superb outdoor activities as well as craft centres, pretty villages and lovely towns such as the old spa of Buxton with its thermal springs. Together with its seaside resorts, rivers and canals, Middle England is well worth a visit.

La terre de Robin des Bois, cette région a un passé historique très marqué. Le Peak District offre de nombreuses activités en plein air et partout, il y a beaucoup à visiter et à faire.

Dies ist die Heimat Robin Hoods. Die Region hat eine große geschichtliche Vergangenheit. Der Peak District offeriert eine große Auswahl an Freizeitakivitäten, und es gibt viel zu sehen und zu tun in diesem schönen Teil des Landes.

La Tierra de Robin Hood, esta región tiene un pasado histórico muy importante. El Peak District ofrece actividades deportivas y hay mucho que ver y hacer en esta bonita parte de Inglaterra.

Patria di Robin Hood, questa regione possiede un passato particolarmente ricco di storia. Il Peak District offre una ampia gamma di attività all' aria aperta e c'è molto da vedere e da fare in questa parte dell' Inghilterra.

 SIGHTS

Chatsworth House
Built in 1687-1707 and housing a fine collection of pictures, furniture and books. Also contains a farmyard garden & adventure playground. Bakewell, Derbyshire. Tel: 01246 582204

American Adventure
Theme park with more than 100 rides and daily shows.
Pit Lane, Ilkeston. Tel: 01773 531521

Sherwood Forest Country Park & Visitor Centre
Mythical forest of Robin Hood and his merry men!
Edwinstowe, Mansfield.

For further information on these or other sights, contact the East Midlands Tourist Board, Exchequergate, Lincoln. LN2 1PZ. Tel: 01522 531521

 ## DIRECTORY OF EFL BOOKSELLERS IN THIS REGION:

(NB: Many bookshops hold a good selection of EFL material, even if they are not listed below. Moreover, if the particular book you are looking for is not in stock, they can order it for you.)

Blackwell's Academic Bookshop
Loughborough University
Ashby Road, Loughborough LE11 3TT
Tel: 01509 219788 Fax: 01509 219754
Web: http://bookshop.blackwell.co.uk

Blackwell's University Bookshop
Portland Building, University Park
Nottingham NG7 2RD
Tel: 0115 958 0272 Fax: 0115 950 5935
Web: http://bookshop.blackwell.co.uk

Blackwell's University Bookshop
Chaucer Building Goldsmith Street
Nottingham NG1 5LT
Tel: 0115 941 7307 Fax: 0115 941 7311
Web: http://bookshop.blackwell.co.uk

The Book Shop
54 King Street, Southwell NG25 0EN
Tel: 01636 816324 Fax: 01636 816399

Bookworld
8 Central Ave, West Bridgford NG2 5GR
Tel: 0115 945 5655
Web: http://www.book-world.co.uk

Ottakar's Bookstore
297A High Street, Lincoln LN2 1AF
Tel: 01522 540011 Fax: 01522 535035
Web: http://www.ottakars.co.uk

Ottakar's Bookstore
Unit G, Baxtergate Fresuney Place
Grimsby DN31 1QL
Tel: 01472 353212 Fax: 01472 353305
Web: http://www.ottakars.co.uk

Waterstone's
19 Abington Street, Northampton NN1 2AN
Tel: 01604 634854 Fax: 01604 234781
Web: http://www.waterstones.co.uk

Waterstone's
26 Market Street, Leicester LE1 6DP
Tel: 0116 2545858 Fax: 0116 2541049
Web: http://www.waterstones.co.uk

Waterstone's
The Shires, Churchgate, Leicester LE1 4AJ
Tel: 0116 251 6838 Fax: 0116 242 5910
Web: http://www.waterstones.co.uk

Wilkins' Bookshop
12 Market Street, Loughborough LE11 3EP
Tel: 01509 235486 Fax: 01509 266343

A▶Z DIRECTORY OF COURSES IN THIS REGION

PRIVATE SCHOOLS / ORGANISATIONS

Ashbourne Pneu School
St. Monica's House, Windmill Lane
Ashbourne DE6 1EY
Tel: 01335 343294 Fax: 01355 343294

Churchill House English Home Tuition Courses - *See South East display for details*

Clock Tower English Language Centre
218 Leicester Road,
Wigston LE18 1DS
Tel: 0116 281 0786 Fax: 0116 281 0786
Email: mocc@clocktower-elc.freeserve.co.uk
http://www.clocktower-elc.freeserve.co.uk/

Communicaid English
MWB Business Exchange, 15 Wheeler Gate
Nottingham NG1 2NA   Tel: 0800 1691310
Email: info@communicaid.com
http://www.communicaid.com

Derwent Executive Language Centre
Crag Moor, Froggatt Edge, Calver
Hope Valley S32 3ZJ
Tel: 01433 639393 Fax: 01433 639827
Email: info@derwentexeclang.co.uk
http://www.derwentexeclang.co.uk

International Students & Youth Exchanges
PO Box 6, Lane End House, London Road
Leicester LE2 1ZE
Tel: 0116 270 3351 Fax: 0116 2703313

InTuition Languages - *See London display for details*

Oxford College of English Ltd.
14 Shakespeare Road,
Northampton NN1 3QP
Tel: 01604 32647   Fax: 01604 32703

St. Elphin's School
Darley Dale, Matlock DE4 2HA
Tel: 01629 732314   Fax: 01629 733956
Email: admin@st-elphins.co.uk

Students International Ltd
158 Dalby Rd, Melton Mowbray LE13 0BJ
Tel: 01664 481997   Fax: 01664 563332
Email: studentsint@aol.com
http://www.studentsint.com

Wold School of English
Ivy House, Main St, Osgodby
Market Rasen LN8 3PA
Tel: 01673 828539   Fax: 01673 828539
Email: hrosser@fsbdial.co.uk
http://www.woldschool.com

STATE COLLEGES / UNIVERSITIES

Broxtowe College
High Road, Chilwell Beeston
Nottingham NG9 4AH
Tel: 0115 917 5252   Fax: 0115 917 5200
Email: hardimp@broxtowe.ac.uk
http://www.broxtowe.ac.uk

Charles Keene College
Painter St., Leicester LE10 3WA
Tel: 0116 251 6037   Fax: 0116 262 0592
Email: advice@ckeene.ac.uk
http://www.ckeen.ac.uk

Derby Tertiary College
London Road, Wilmorton
Derby DE24 8UG   Tel: 01332 757570

Irwin College
164 London Road, Leicester LE2 1ND
Tel: 0116 255 2648   Fax: 0116 285 4935
Email: irwincoll@aol.com
http://www.cife.org.uk/irwin/index.htm

Leicester Adult Education College
Wellington Street, Leicester LE1 6HL
Tel: 0116 233 4343   Fax: 0116 233 4344
Email: enquiries@leicester-adult-ed.ac.uk
http://www.leicester-adult-ed.ac.uk

New College Nottingham
Clarendon City College, The Adams
Building, Stoney St., Nottingham NG1 2LJ
Tel: 0115 910 4610   Fax: 0115 9104611
Email: internat@ncn.ac.uk
http://www.ncn.ac.uk

North Lincolnshire College
Monks Road, Lincoln LN2 5HQ
Tel: 01522 876286   Fax: 01522 876281
Email: c_platt@nlincs-coll.ac.uk
http://www.nlincs-coll.ac.uk

Northampton College
Language Centre, Booth Lane
Northampton NN3 3RF
Tel: 01604 734567   Fax: 01604 734207
Email: carold@northamptoncollege.ac.uk

Nottingham Trent University
Nottingham Language Centre, Burton St.
Nottingham NG1 4BU
Tel: 0115 848 6156   Fax: 0115 848 6513
Email: nlc@ntu.ac.uk
http://nlc.ntu.ac.uk

Tresham Institute
St. Mary's Road, Kettering NN15 7BS
Tel: 01536 413015   Fax: 01536 413137
Email: international@tresham.ac.uk
http://www.tresham.ac.uk

University College Northampton
Park Campus, Boughton Green Road
Northampton NN2 7AL
Tel: 01604 735500   Fax: 01604 721214
Email: dave.burnapp@northampton.ac.uk
http://www.northampton.ac.uk/home.html

University of Leicester
ELTU, Ken Edwards Building, University Rd
Leicester LE1 7RH
Tel: 0116 252 2845   Fax: 0116 252 5376
Email: language.services@le.ac.uk
http://www.le.ac.uk/international/eltu

University of Loughborough
English Language Study Unit, Ashby Rd
Loughborough LE11 3TU
Tel: 01509 222058   Fax: 01509 223919

University of Nottingham
Centre for English Language Education,
University Park, Nottingham NG7 2RD
Tel: 0115 951 4404   Fax: 0115 951 4992
Email: norma.hazzledine@nottingham.ac.uk
http://www.ccc.nottingham.ac.uk/cele

West Nottinghamshire College
Derby Road, Mansfield NG18 5BH
Tel: 01623 27191
Email: nickfenn@westnotts.ac.uk
http://www.westnotts.ac.uk

Wigston College of Further Education
Station Road, Wigston, Leicester LE18 2DW
Tel: 0116 288 5051   Fax: 0116288 0823
Email: davidh@wigston-college.ac.uk
http://www.wigston-college.ac.uk

Institution Name	Availability	Junior Ages	Specials	Price /week	Status
Ashbourne Pneu School	J: 6-9	4-12 yrs		£85-£100	
Broxtowe College	A: 1-12		B	£75-£100	GBC, Baselt
Charles Keene College	A: 1-12			On application	
Churchill House English Home Tuition Courses	A: 1-12 J: 1-12 (1-1 only)	7 yrs +	B, T, F, H, C, E	£450-£780**	
Clock Tower English Language Centre	A: 7-8 J: 7-8	14 yrs +		On application	GBC
Communicaid English	A: 1-12		B, T, F, H, C, E	£845-£1845	
Derwent Executive Language Centre	A: 1-12 J: 4-10		B, T, F, H, C	£235-£1775	
International Students & Youth Exchanges	A: 6-8 J: 6-8	11-18 yrs		On application	
InTuition Languages	A: 1-12 J: 1-12 (1-1 only)	14-18 yrs	B, T, F, C, E	£555-£1040**	GBC, Arels
Irwin College	A: 1-12 J: 1-12	14 yrs +	B, E	On application	
New College Nottingham	A: 1-12		B, T, C, E	£100-£125	GBC, Baselt
North Lincolnshire College	A: 4, 7-8		B, T	£180**	
Northampton College	A: 9-6			from £11.50	
Nottingham Trent University	A: 1-12		E	£150-£200	GBC, Baselt, Baleap
Oxford College of English Ltd.	A: 1-12 J: 4-8, 10			On application	
Students International Ltd	A: 1-12 J: 6-9	8-16 yrs	H, E	£350-£515**	GBC
Tresham Institute	A: 9-6			£120	GBC, Baselt
University College Northampton	A: 10-6		E	£120	Being validated by GBC/Baselt
University of Leicester	A: 1-12		B, E	£165-£200	
University of Nottingham	A: 1-12		F, E	£165	Baleap
Wigston College of Further Education	A: 1-12		B	£50-£100	GBC, Baselt
Wold School of English	A: 1-12 (mostly 1-1)		B, E	£120-£420	

8 EAST ANGLIA

Includes Bedfordshire, Cambridgeshire, Essex, Hertfordshire, Norfolk, Suffolk.

The spiritual heartland of England's famous painters, Constable and Gainsborough, this is not surprisingly a region of beautiful and romantic landscapes.

Its heritage is reflected in the rich diversity of its cities and monuments: the Roman remains in St. Albans and Colchester and the historic cities of Peterborough and Cambridge, home to one of England's most famous universities.

The whole region is dotted with magnificent cathedrals, churches and stately homes. The flat coastline offers charming villages and plenty of watersport activities. Cross county walks, amusement Parks, all add up to make East Anglia an interesting place for people of all ages.

Une région riche en héritage historique qui contient un grand nombre de monuments, cathédrales et de villes telle que Cambridge, célèbre pour son université. La côte offre beaucoup d'activités sportives et de jolis villages.

Eine Region mit einem reichhaltigen Angebot. Historische Denkmäler, Kathedralen und Städte, wie z.B. Cambridge mit der bekannten Universität finden sich hier. Die Küste läßt viele Wassersportmöglichkeiten zu und ist von malerischen Dörfern gesäumt.

Una región rica en patrimonio histórico con monumentos, castillos y ciudades tal como Cambridge con su famosa universidad. La costa ofrece deportes náuticos y pueblos muy bonitos.

Regione dal ricco passato storico, essa offre molti monumenti, cattedrali e città come Cambridge, famosa per la sua università. La zona costiera offre una grande varietà di sport acquatici e incantevoli paesini.

 SIGHTS

Knebworth House
Set in 250 Acres of parkland, this fine mansion house includes a banqueting hall and attractive formal gardens.   Knebworth, Hertfordshire.   Tel: 01438 812661

Rollerworld/ Quasar
Europe's finest roller-skating centre and Quasar, the laser game. Eastgates, Colchester.
Tel: 01206 868868

Sandringham
The country retreat of the Queen, with house, grounds and museum. King's Lynn, Norfolk. Tel: 01553 772675

Pleasurewood Hills - American Theme Park.
Aladdin's cave, 180-degree cinema and haunted house form just some of the attractions at this large amusement park. Lowestoft, Suffolk. Tel: 01493 441611

For further information on these or other sights, contact the East Anglia Tourist Board, Toppesfield Hall, Suffolk. IP7 5DN
Tel: 01473 822922

 DIRECTORY OF EFL BOOKSELLERS IN THIS REGION:

(NB: Many bookshops hold a good selection of EFL material, even if they are not listed below. Moreover, if the particular book you are looking for is not in stock, they can order it for you.)

Amberstone Bookshop
49 Upper Orwell Street, Ipswich IP4 1HP
Tel: 01473 250675 Fax: 01473 226980

Bertram Books Ltd
The Nest Rosary Road, Norwich NR1 1TF
Tel: 01603 216666 Fax: 01603 611201
Web: http://www.bertrams.com

Boardmans
14-16 North Street
Bishop's Stortford CM23 2LL
Tel: 01279 654033 Fax: 01279 504384

Cambridge International Book Centre
42 Hills Road, Cambridge CB2 1LA
Tel: 01223 365400 Fax: 01223 312607

Cambridge University Press Bookshop
1 Trinity Street, Cambridge CB2 1SZ
Tel: 01223 333325 Fax: 01223 332954
Web: http://www.cup.cam.ac.uk/

Caxton Books
37 Connaught Avenue
Frinton-on-Sea CO13 9PN
Tel: 01255 851505 Fax: 01255 670299

Chambers of Dereham
Under the Town Sign, Dereham NR19 2AP
Tel: 01362 692006 Fax: 01362 691481

County Town Books Ltd
7 High Street, Bedford MK40 1RN
Tel: 01234 341789 Fax: 01234 352252

Felsted Bookshop
Felsted School, Great Dunmow CM6 3JG
Tel: 01371 820257 Fax: 01371 821179

Hammicks Bookshops Online
8 St Peter's Street, St Albans AL1 3LF
Tel: 01727 863781 Fax: 01727 856938
Web: http://www.hammicks-bookshops.co.uk

Heffers
31 St Andrew's Street
Cambridge CB2 3AX
Tel: 01223 568596 Fax: 01223 568593
Web: http://www.heffers.co.uk

Hammicks Bookshops
8 St Peters Street, St Albans AL1 3LF
Tel: 01727 834966 Fax: 01727 864969
Web: http://www.hammicks-bookshops.co.uk

Ottakar's Bookstore
Unit A 36 Buttermarket
Bury St Edmunds IP33 1DW
Tel: O1284 750877 Fax: 01284 750835
Web: http://www.ottakars.co.uk

Ottakar's Bookstore
100 London Road North
Lowestoft NR32 1ET
Tel: 01502 588909 Fax: 01502 585595
Web: http://www.ottakars.co.uk

Ottakar's Bookstore
Unit 45, Eastgate Centre
Basildon SS141AE
Tel: 01268 532255 Fax: 01268 532266
Web: http://www.ottakars.co.uk

Ottakar's Bookstore
76 High Street, Chelmsford CM1 1EY
Tel: 01245 268737 Fax: 01245 268832
Web: http://www.ottakars.co.uk

Ottakar's Bookstore
69 High Street, Brentwood CM14 4RW
Tel: 01277 263202 Fax: 01277 263212
Web: http://www.ottakars.co.uk

Ottakar's Bookstore
11-17 Castle Street, Norwich NR2 1PB
Tel: 01603 767292 Fax: 01603 765761
Web: http://www.ottakars.co.uk

PMA Books
PMA House, Free Church Passage
St Ives PE27 5AY
Tel: 01480 300653 Fax: 01480 496022
Web: http://www.pma-group.co.uk

Study Needs Ltd
Basildon College, Nethermayne
Basildon SS16 5NN
Tel: 01268 532015 Fax: 01268 287660

Waterstone's
University of Luton
Park Square, Luton LU1 3JT
Tel: 01582 402704 Fax: 01582 450906
Web: http://www.waterstones.co.uk

Waterstone's
20-22 Sidney Street, Cambridge CB2 3HG
Tel: 01223 351688 Fax: 01223 355612
Web: http://www.waterstones.co.uk

Waterstone's
University of East Anglia
University Plain, Norwich NR4 7TR
Tel: 01603 453625 Fax: 01603 507950
Web: http://www.waterstones.co.uk

A ➡ Z   DIRECTORY OF COURSES IN THIS REGION

PRIVATE SCHOOLS / ORGANISATIONS

ABC Language Training - Cambridge
18 George IV Street,
Cambridge CB2 1HH
Tel: 01223 302121   Fax: 01223 300889
Email: main@abclanguages.force9.co.uk

Alexanders International School
Bawdsey Manor, Bawdsey
Woodbridge IP12 3AZ
Tel: 01394 411633   Fax: 01394 411357
Email: english@alexandersint.demon.co.uk

Aspect ILA Cambridge
75 Barton Road,
Cambridge CB3 9LJ
Tel: 01202 638100   Fax: 01202 438900
Email: enquiries@aspectworld.com
http://www.aspectworld.com/

Barnardiston Hall Preparatory School
Barnardiston Hall,
nr. Haverhill CB9 7TG
Tel: 01440 786316   Fax: 01440 786355
Email: barnardistonhall@yahoo.co.uk

Bedford Modern School
Manton Lane,
Bedford MK41 7NT
Tel: 01234 364331   Fax: 01234 270951
Email: geoffl@bedmod.co.uk
http://www.bedmod.co.uk

Bedford School Study Centre
67 De Parys Avenue,
Bedford MK40 2TR
Tel: 01234 350861   Fax: 01234 325790
Email: bssc@bedfordschool.beds.sch.uk

Bell Language School
Red Cross Lane,
Cambridge CB2 2QX
Tel: 01223 247242   Fax: 01223 412410
Email: info@bell-schools.ac.uk
http://www.bell-schools.ac.uk

Bell Language School
South Road,
Saffron Walden CB11 3DP
Tel: 01799 522918   Fax: 01799 526949
Email: info@bell-centres.com
http://www.bell-centres.com

Bell Language Schools, Young Learners
Lancaster House, South Road
Saffron Walden CB11 3DP
Tel: 01799 516680   Fax: 01799 516690
Email: info@bell-schools.ac.uk
http://www.bell-schools.ac.uk

Bell Norwich
Bowthorpe Hall, Bowthorpe
Norwich NR5 9AA
Tel: 01603 745615   Fax: 01603 747669
Email: info@bell-schools.ac.uk
http://www.bell-schools.ac.uk

Bury Language School
5 Angel Hill,
Bury St Edmunds IP33 1UZ
Tel: 01284 765511   Fax: 01284 765511
Email: burylangschool@easynet.co.uk
http://www.burylanguageschool.co.uk

Byron School, Cambridge
79 Hills Road,
Cambridge CB2 1PG
Tel: 01223 360740   Fax: 01638 604156
Email: info@byronschool.com
http://www.byronschool.com
See display for further details

*Byron School
Cambridge*

❏ Byron School Cambridge offers intensive courses in classes of no more than six students.

❏ We are a family business situated in the heart of Cambridge, who specialise in courses for students who are serious about learning English.

❏ We also offer on-line video lessons through our website at www.byronschool.com.

79 Hills Road, Cambridge CB8 0ES
Tel: 00 44 1223 360740
Fax: 00 44 1638 604156
Email: info@byronschool.com
Website: www.byronschool.com

Cambridge Academy of English
65 High St., Girton
Cambridge CB3 0QD
Tel: 01223 277230   Fax: 01223 277606
Email: cae@caeco.demon.co.uk
http://www.cambridgeacademy.co.uk

Cambridge Centre for English Studies
Guildhall Chambers, Guildhall Place
Cambridge CB2 3QQ
Tel: 01223 357190   Fax: 01223 301691
Email: cces@ccces.com
http://www.cces.com

Cambridge Centre for Languages
Sawston Hall,
Cambridge CB2 4JR
Tel: 01223 835099   Fax: 01223 837424
Email: ar70@dial.pipex.com
http://www.camlang.co.uk

Cambridge International Study Centre
St Mary's College, 2 Brookside
Cambridge CB2 1JE
Tel: 01223 305698   Fax: 01223 307352
Email: director@stmaryscambridge.com
http://www.stmaryscambridge.com

Cambridge Language & Activity Courses
10 Shelford Park Avenue, Great Shelford
Cambridge CB2 5LU
Tel: 01223 846348   Fax: 01223 844436
Email: will@clc.org.uk
http://www.clac.org.uk

Cambridge Language Services
119b Mill Road,
Cambridge CB1 2AZ
Tel: 01223 312944   Fax: 01223 312944

Cambridge School of Languages
119 Mill Road,
Cambridge CB1 2AZ
Tel: 01223 312333   Fax: 01223 323257
Email: cambridge_school_of_languages_edu@msn.com
http://www.csl.uk.com

Camtours Ltd - English and Russian languages
18 Hurrell Road,
Cambridge CB4 3RH
Tel: 01223 527799   Fax: 01223 527798
Email: main@camtours.demon.co.uk

Central Language School, Cambridge
The Stone Yard Centre, 41B St Andrews St
Cambridge CB2 3AR
Tel: 01223 502004   Fax: 01223 502004
Email: info@central-ls.co.uk
http://www.central-ls.co.uk

Churchill House English Home Tuition
Courses - *See South East display for details*

Colchester English Study Centre
19 Lexden Road,
Colchester CO3 3PW
Tel: 01206 544422   Fax: 01206 761849
Email: info@cesc.co.uk
http://www.cesc.co.uk

EF International School of English
221 Hills Road,
Cambridge CB2 2RW
Tel: 01223 240020   Fax: 01223 412474
Email: languages.gb@ef.com
http://www.ef.com

Embassy CES Newnham
8 Grange Road,
Cambridge CB3 9DU
Tel: 01223 311344   Fax: 01223 461411
Email: cambridge@embassyces.com
http://www.embassyces.com

English Business (The)
23 Queenswood Crescent,
Watford WD25 7DG
Tel: 01923 463384   Fax: 01923 445046
Email: info@theenglishbusiness.co.uk
http://www.theenglishbusiness.co.uk

English Language Holidays
7 Rectory Lane, Wyton
Huntingdon PE28 2AQ
Tel: 01480 463870
Email: christine.d@btinternet.com
http://www.efl.uk.com

Eurocentre, Cambridge
62 Bateman St.,
Cambridge CB2 1LX
Tel: 01223 353607   Fax: 01223 368531
Email: cam-info@eurocentres.com
http://www.eurocentres.com

Euroyouth
301 Westborough Road, Westcliff
Southend-on-Sea SS0 9PT
Tel: 01702 341434   Fax: 01702 330104

Flying Classrooms
14 Bank Street,
Norwich NR2 4SE
Tel: 01603 619091   Fax: 01603 619110
Email: portanglia@flyingclassrooms.com
http://www.flyingclassrooms.com

Friday Bridge School of English
173 March Road, Friday Bridge
Wisbech PE14 0LR
Tel: 01945 860255   Fax: 01945 861088
Email: fbse@freenetname.co.uk
http://www.fbse.org.uk

Homestay Hertfordshire
74 Church Green, St. Peter's St.
St. Albans AL1 3HG
Tel: 01727 868434   Fax:
Email: homestay@stalbans.co.uk
http://www.stalbans.gov.uk/homestay

I H Rickmansworth - ELCO
Lowlands, Chorleywood Road
Rickmansworth WD3 4ES
Tel: 01923 776731   Fax: 01923 774678
Email: efl@elco.co.uk
http://www.elco.co.uk

ICS
26 Pottergate,
Norwich NR2 1DX
Tel: 01603 624021   Fax: 01603 766552
Email: mail@icsenglish.com
http://www.icsenglish.com

International Language Academy
12-13 Regent Terrace,
Cambridge CB2 1AA
Tel: 01223 350519   Fax: 01223 464730
Email: ilacamb@rmplc.co.uk
http://www.language-academies.co.uk

InTuition Languages - *See London display*
for details

Kids Klub
The Lodge, Finborough Hall
Stowmarket IP14 3EF
Tel: 01449 742700   Fax: 01449 742701
Email: maggie@kidsklub.co.uk
http://www.kidsklub.co.uk

Language Studies International
41 Tenison Road,
Cambridge CB1 2DG
Tel: 01223 361783   Fax: 01223 467725
Email: cam@lsi.edu
http://www.lsi.edu

The Language Tree (UK) Ltd
59 Cromer Road,
Holt NR25 6EX
Tel: 01263 711171   Fax: 01263 712199
Email: thelanguagetree@btinternet.com
http://www.members.tripod.com/thelanguagetree

Live & Learn English
149, Parkway,
Welwyn Garden City AL8 6JB
Tel: 01707 320011
Email: live&learn@link-up.u-net.com
http://www.link-up.u-net.com/ lle/lle.htm

Living English
New Oak House, Stevenage Road
Little Wymondley SG4 7JA
Tel: 01438 746467   Fax: 01438 745145
Email: chris@livingenglish.co.uk

New Century Study Ltd
P.O. Box 4275, Danbury
Chelmsford CM3 4UG
Tel: 01245 227215   Fax: 01245 227215

New School of English
52 Bateman St.,
Cambridge CB2 1LR
Tel: 01223 358089   Fax: 01223 315276
Email: newschool@dial.pipex.com
http://www.newschool.co.uk

Norwich Institute for Language Education
PO Box 2000,
Norwich NR2 1LE
Tel: 01603 664473   Fax: 01603 664493
Email: marketing@nile-elt.com
http://www.nile-elt.com

Rectory School of Business English
67 Church Drive, Orton Waterville
Peterborough PE2 5HE
Tel: 01733 239885   Fax: 01733 239885
Email: rectschool@aol.com
http://www.rsbe.co.uk

Select English
15 Station Road,
Cambridge CB1 2JB
Tel: 01223 300529   Fax: 01223 467150
Email: info@selectenglish.co.uk
http://www.selectenglish.co.uk

St Mary's School
Bateman Street,
Cambridge CB2 1LY
Tel: 01223 353253   Fax: 01223 357451
Email: enquiries@stmarys.cambs.sch.uk
http://www.stmarys.cambs.sch.uk/

St. Andrew's
2a Free School Lane,
Cambridge CB3 2QA
Tel: 01223 360040   Fax: 01223 467150
Email: mjm@standrew.demon.co.uk

St. Edmund's College
Old Hall Green, Near Ware
Herts. SG11 1DS
Tel: 01920 821111   Fax: 01920 821111
Email: summer@st-edmundscollege.co.uk
http://www.st-edmundscollege.co.uk

Studio Cambridge
6 Salisbury Villas, Station Road
Cambridge CB1 2JF
Tel: 01223 369701   Fax: 01223 314944
Email: information@studiocambridge.co.uk
http://www.studiocambridge.co.uk

Suffolk Country Courses
The Old Rectory, Hargrave
Bury St.Edmunds IP29 5HH
Tel: 01284 850282   Fax: 01284 850727
Email: paul.johson@itnet.co.uk

T.L.S. - The Language School
Admirals Green, 19 Hudson Way
Norwich NR5 9NJ
Email: tomleseelleur@yahoo.com

Whitehill Estate School of English
Flamstead,
St. Albans AL3 8EY
Tel: 01582 792208   Fax: 01582 715599
Email: alanhardy@whitehillschool.fsnet.co.uk
http://www.whitehillschool.co.uk

STATE COLLEGES / UNIVERSITIES

Anglia Polytechnic University
Centre for English Language Studies,
East Road, Cambridge CB1 1PT
Tel: 01223 417716   Fax: 01223 417717
Email: efl@apu.ac.uk
http://www.apu.ac.uk/efl

Barking College
Dagenham Road, Romford RM7 0XU
Tel: 01708 788014 (ext.2327)

Basildon College
Nethermayne, Basildon SS16 5NN
Tel: 01268 532015

Bedford College
Cauldwell Street, Bedford MK42 9AH
Tel: 01234 291000   Fax: 01234 342674
Email: hweaver@bedford.ac.uk
http://www.bedford.ac.uk

Cambridge Regional College
Newmarket Road, Cambridge CB5 8EG
Tel: 01223 357545

Centre for English Language & British Studies
University of East Anglia, Norwich NR4 7TJ
Tel: 01603 592977   Fax: 01603 250200
Email: ceb@uea.ac.uk
http://www.uea.ac.uk/llt/ceb
See display for further details

Chelmsford College
Moulsham Street, Chelmsford CM2 0JQ
Tel: 01245 265611

Colchester Institute
Sheepen Road,
Colchester CO3 3LL
Tel: 01206 518637   Fax: 01206 518186
Email: efl@colch-inst.ac.uk
http://www.colch-inst.ac.uk

Cranfield University
Language Centre, Silsoe
Bedford MK45 4DT
Tel: 01525 863077   Fax: 01525 863001
Email: s.medaney@cranfield.ac.uk

Great Yarmouth College
Southdown, Great Yarmouth NR31 0ED
Tel: 01493 655261

Harlow College
Velizy Avenue, Harlow CM20 1LH
Tel: 01279 868229

STUDY ENGLISH
at the
Centre for English Language
and British Studies
University of East Anglia

✳ English Language Summer School

✳ Year-round English and Culture Course

✳ Translation and English Courses

We also offer teacher training courses throughout
the year for closed groups

Norwich

...is less than 2 hours from London
...has its own international airport
...offers a range of social and cultural activities
...is a dynamic and safe city

For information please contact:
The Centre for English Language and British Studies (CEB),
University of East Anglia, Norwich NR4 7TJ, UK

Tel: 00-44-1603-592977 Fax: 00-44-1603-250200
Email: ceb@uea.ac.uk Web: http://www.uea.ac.uk/llt/ceb/

Hertford Regional College
Broxbourne Centre, Turnford
Broxbourne EN10 6AE
Tel: 01992 466451

Isle College
Ramnoth Road, Wisbech PE13 0HY
Tel: 01945 582561

Lowestoft College
St. Peter's Street, Lowestoft NR32 2NB
Tel: 01502 583521

Norfolk College of Arts & Technology
Tennyson Avenue, King's Lynn PE30 2QW
Tel: 01553 761144

North Hertfordshire College
Cambridge Road, Hitchin SG4 0JD
Tel: 01462 424323 Fax: 01462 424380
Email: lmachin@nhc.ac.uk

Norwich City College
Ipswich Road, Norwich NR2 2LJ
Tel: 01603 660011

Oaklands College
International Office, St. Peter's Road,
St. Albans AL1 3RX
Tel: 01727 737175 Fax: 01727 737273
Email: international@oaklans.ac.uk
http://www.oaklands.ac.uk

Peterborough College of Adult Education
Brook Street,
Peterborough PE1 1TU
Tel: 01733 761361 Fax: 01733 703545
Email: cwooding@pcae.org.uk

Peterborough Regional College
Park Crescent,
Peterborough PE1 4DZ
Tel: 01733 762249 Fax: 01733 767986
Email: paul.watkins@peterborough.ac.uk
http://www.peterborough.ac.uk

South East Essex College
Carnarvon Road,
Southend on Sea SS2 6LS
Tel: 01702 220448 Fax: 01702 432320
Email: marketing@se-essex-college.ac.uk
http://www.se-essex-college.ac.uk

Suffolk College
Rope Walk, Ipswich IP4 1LT
Tel: 01473 255885

Thurrock College
Woodview, Grays RM16 2YR
Tel: 01375 390099 Fax: 01375 362679
Email: efl@thurrock.ac.uk

University of Essex
ELT Centre, Wivenhoe Park
Colchester CO4 3SQ
Tel: 01206 872217 Fax: 01206 873107
Email: dilly@essex.ac.uk
http://www.essex.ac.uk/eltc

University of Hertfordshire
Hatfield Campus, College Lane
Hatfield AL10 9AB
Tel: 01707 285965 Fax: 01707 285241
Email: English@herts.ac.uk
http://www.herts.ac.uk

University of Luton
EFL Suite, 3rd floor, Vicarage Street
Campus, Vicarage Street, Luton LU1 3AJ
Tel: 01582 743205 Fax: 01582 743221
Email: efl@luton.ac.uk
http://www.luton.ac.uk

West Herts College
Cassio Campus, Langley Road
Watford WD1 3RH
Tel: 01923 812261 Fax: 01923 812284
Email: admissions@westherts.ac.uk
http://westherts.ac.uk

West Suffolk College
Out Risbygate, Bury St Edmunds IP33 3RL
Tel: 01284 701301

Institution Name	Availability	Junior Ages	Specials	Price /week	Status
Alexanders International School	J: 1-12	11-18 yrs	C, E	£385-£440**	
Anglia Polytechnic University	A: 1-8, 10-12		B, T, C, E	£26-£133	GBC, Baselt
Aspect ILA Cambridge	A: 1-12			£128-201	GBC, Arels
Barnardiston Hall Preparatory School	J: 7-8	6-13 yrs		£340**	
Bedford College	A: 9-6			£8-£60	GBC, Baselt
Bedford School Study Centre	J: 1-12			On application	
Bell Language School	A: 1-12		B	£385-£425**	GBC, Eaquals
Bell Language School	A: 1-12 J: 1, 4, 6	11-16 yrs	B, C	£380-£450** (£499** J)	GBC, Eaquals
Bell Language Schools, Young Learners	J: 1, 3, 4, 6-8	8-17 yrs		£380-£590**	GBC, Eaquals
Bell Norwich	A: 1-12		B, E	£198-£273	GBC, Eaquals
Bury Language School	A: 1-12 J: 7-8	16 yrs +	B, E	£292-900	
Byron School, Cambridge	A: 1-12		B, E	£120-£360	
Cambridge Academy of English	A: 1-12 J: 7-8	9-14, 14-16 yrs	B	£240-£490	GBC, Arels
Cambridge Centre for English Studies	A: 1-12 J: 6-8	14-16 yrs	B	£105-£115	
Cambridge Centre for Languages	A: 1-12 J: 7-8	10-17 yrs	B, F, E	£200-£1290	
Cambridge International Study Centre	A: 1-12 J: 1-12	13 yrs +	B, E	£250-£400	
Cambridge Language & Activity Courses	J: 7-8	8-13, 13-17 yrs		£1040**/2wks	GBC
Cambridge Language Services	A: 9-6			£70-£85	
Cambridge School of Languages	A: 1-12 J: 6-8	10-16 yrs	B, E	£157.50-£201.50	GBC, Arels
Central Language School, Cambridge	A: 1-12			£99-£110	
Centre for English Language & British Studies	A: 1-12		E	£135-£239	Baleap
Churchill House English Home Tuition Courses	A: 1-12 J: 1-12 (1-1 only)	7 yrs +	B, T, F, H, C, E	£450-£780**	

Institution Name	Availability	Junior Ages	Specials	Price /week	Status
Colchester English Study Centre	A: 1-12 J: 7-8	8-18 yrs	B, T, F, C, E	£236-£264**	GBC, Arels
Colchester Institute	A: 9-6		B, T, C	£77.75	GBC, Baselt
EF International School of English	A: 1-12		B, E	£450** (summer)	GBC, Arels
Embassy CES Newnham	A: 1-12 J: 7-8	14-18 yrs	B, T, F, E	£120-£1440	GBC, Arels
English Business (The)	A: 1-12		B, T, F, H, C, E	£150-£830	
English Language Holidays	A: 1-12 (1-1 only)		B, E	£300-£400**	
Eurocentre, Cambridge	A: 1-12			£130-£205	
Euroyouth	J: 1-12			On application	
Friday Bridge School of English	A: 7-9			£150-£215**	
Harlow College	A: 1-12			On application	
Homestay Hertfordshire	A: 1-12 J: 1-12 (1-1 only)	9-13 yrs	B	£425-£725**	
I H Rickmansworth -ELCO	J: 7-8	11-17 yrs		£255-£380**	GBC, Arels
ICS	A: 1-12			£99-£220	ABLS
International Language Academy	A: 1-12		B, E	£145+	
Infuion Languages	A: 1-12 J: 1-12 (1-1 only)	14-18 yrs	B, T, F, C, E	£555-£1040**	GBC, Arels
Kids Klub	J: 1-12	6-17 yrs	T	£259-£329**	BAHA
Language Studies International	A: 1-12 J: 7-8			On application	
Language Tree (UK) Ltd (The)	J: 7-8	10-18 yrs		£275-£310**	
Live & Learn English	A: 7-8 J: 7-8			On application	
Living English	A: 1-12 (1-1 only)		B	£1240-£1682	
New School of English	A: 1-12		B	£370/2wks, £1830/12wks	GBC, Arels
North Hertfordshire College	A: 1-12			£12-£60	

Institution Name	Availability	Junior Ages	Specials	Price /week	Status
Norwich Institute for Language Education (NILE)	A: 1-12 (closed groups)		B, E	On application	GBC, Arels
Oaklands College	A: 1-12		B, T, C, E	£557 per term (EU) £1080 (world)	GBC, Bcselt
Peterborough College of Adult Education	A: 9-6			On application	Local Authority
Peterborough Regional College	A: 9-6		B	£70 approx.	GBC, Arels
Rectory School of Business English (The)	A: 1-12		B, T, F, H, E	£250-£400	
Select English	A: 1-12 J: 7-8	8-16 yrs		£265-£390**	GBC
South East Essex College	A: 9-12, 1-6, 7		B	£100/semester	
St. Andrew's	A: 1-12 J: 7-8			On application	
St. Edmund's College	J: 7-8	9-15 yrs	E	£420**	
Studio Cambridge	A: 1-12 J: 7-8	10-17 yrs	B, C, E	£165-£180+	GBC, Arels
Suffolk Country Courses	J: 3-9	8-18 yrs		£320-£400**	
T.L.S. - The Language School	A: 1-12 (1-1 only)		B, E	£750-£2750**	GBC, Bcselt
Thurrock College	A: 9-6		T, H, C	£124	Baleap
University of Essex	A: 1, 4, 7, 8, 9, 10		E	£150-£250	
University of Hertfordshire	A: 9-5, 6-9		B, E	Variable	
University of Luton	A: 1-12		B, E	£150-£200	GBC, Bcselt
West Herts College	A: 9-7		B, T, H	£14-£135	
Whitehill Estate School of English	A: 3-9 J: 6-8	12-15 yrs		£165-£225**	

9 NORTH WEST

Includes Cheshire, Greater Manchester, Lancashire, Merseyside.

Manchester and Liverpool, home of the Beatles, are the two main cities of this region. Both have good shopping facilities, bars, restaurants and a lively nightlife.

Southeast of Manchester lies the Peak District, offering great countryside for those who enjoy moderately strenuous walks.

Further south, the town of Chester is encircled by a two-mile ring of medieval and Roman walls. The town itself is a delightful combination of Tudor and Victorian buildings.

Pour ceux qui aiment faire de bonnes randonnées, le Peak District est une destination parfaite. Pour ceux qui préfèrent les villes, Manchester et Liverpool offrent une grande variété de distractions, tandis que l'ancienne ville de Chester est connue pour ses bâtiments Tudor et Victoriens.

Für diejenigen, die ausgedehnte Spaziergänge und das Land lieben, ist der Peak District ein besonders geeignetes Ziel. Für diejenigen, die lieber in Städte reisen, bieten Liverpool und Manchester ein großes Vergnügungsangebot, während Chester für seine Tudor und viktorianischen Gebäude bekannt ist.

Para los que disfrutan del campo y del camina, ésta región es ideal. Para los que prefieren las ciudades, están Manchester y Liverpool que ofrecen todo tipo de diversiones. La antigua ciudad de Chester es famosa por sus casas que datan de las épocas Tudor y Victoriana.

Il Peak District è la destinazione ideale per gli amanti delle camminate in campagna. Per coloro che invece preferiscono la città, Manchester e Liverpool offrono una grande varietà di intrattenimenti, mentre Chester è rinomata per i suoi palazzi in stile Tudor e Vittoriano.

 SIGHTS

Blackpool Sea Life Centre
Underwater walk-through tunnel, containing tropical sharks.
Blackpool, Lancs. Tel: 01253 22445

Jodrell Bank Science Centre
Planetarium and the Lovell telescope, used to look deep into space. Lower Withington, Cheshire.
Tel: 01477 71339

Boat Museum
Largest collection of floating boats in the world! Ellesmere Port, Cheshire.
Tel: 0151 355 5017

Albert Dock
Britain's largest grade I listed building, with shops and a maritime museum. Liverpool.
Tel: 0151 708 7334

For further information on these or other sights, contact the North West Tourist Board, Swan House, Swan Meadow Road, Wigan Pier, Wigan. WN3 5BB.
Tel: 01942 821222

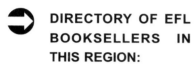

DIRECTORY OF EFL BOOKSELLERS IN THIS REGION:

(NB: Many bookshops hold a good selection of EFL material, even if they are not listed below. Moreover, if the particular book you are looking for is not in stock, they can order it for you.)

Askews Library Services
218-222 North Road, Preston PR1 1SY
Tel: 01772 555947 Fax: 01772 254860
Web: http://www.askews.co.uk

Blackwell's University Bookshop
Alsop Building, Brownlow Hill
Liverpool L3 5TX
Tel: 0151 709 8146 Fax: 0151 709 6653
Web: http://bookshop.blackwell.co.uk

Bookland & Company
University College Chester
Cheyney Road, Chester CH1 4WA
Tel: 01244 372715 Fax: 01244 372715
Web: http://www.bookland.co.uk

Broadhurst of Southport Ltd
5-7 Market Street, Southport PR8 1HD
Tel: 01704 532064 Fax: 01704 542009
Web: http://www.ckbroadhurst.com

Blackwell's University Bookshop
University Library Building
52 St. Peter's Square, Preston PR1 2HZ
Tel: 01772 254462 Fax: 01772 202313
Web: http://bookshop.blackwell.co.uk

Blackwell's University Bookshop
The Precinct Centre, Oxford Road
Manchester M13 9RN
Tel: 0161 274 3331 Fax: 0161 274 3228
Web: http://bookshop.blackwell.co.uk

College Bookshop
University College of St Martins
Bowerham Road, Lancaster LA1 3JD
Tel: 01524 60125 Fax: 01524 845004

Guardian Gifts
P O Box 36, Altrincham WA15 8PX
Tel: 0161 904 9000 Fax: 0161 903 8224
Web: http://www.guardiangifts.com

Hammicks Bookshops
4 Cornmarket, Marketgate Shopping Centre
Lancaster LA1 1AL
Tel: 01524 842561 Fax: 01524 844131
Web: http://www.hammicks-bookshops.co.uk

The Holt Jackson Book Company Ltd
Preston Road, Lytham St Annes FY8 5AX
Tel: 01253 737464 Fax: 01253 733361
Web: http://www.holtjackson.co.uk

Jarrold & Sons Ltd
5 London Street, Norwich NR2 1JF
Tel: 01603 660661 Fax: 01603 611295
http://www.jarrold-department-stores.co.uk

Ottakar's Bookstore
19 Victoria Street, Crewe CW1 2HF
Tel: 01270 580022 Fax: 01270 580034
Web: http://www.ottakars.co.uk

SPCK Bookshop
Liverpool Hope University College
Green Lane North, Liverpool L16 8ND
Tel: 0151 722 2784 Fax: 0151 738 0762
Web: http://www.spck.org.uk

Tattersall's Bookshop
5 Duke's Court Mill Street
Macclesfield SK11 6NN
Tel: 01625 614741 Fax: 01625 614741

W H Smith Ltd
8-12 George Street, Altrincham WA14 1SF
Tel: 0161 928 3745
Web: http://www.whsmith.co.uk

Waterstone's
2-4 St Ann's Square, Manchester M2 7HH
Tel: 0161 832 0424 Fax: 0161 831 7786
Web: http://www.waterstones.co.uk

DIRECTORY OF COURSES IN THIS REGION

PRIVATE SCHOOLS / ORGANISATIONS

Action Holidays
Robinwood, Jumps Road
Todmorden OL14 8HJ
Tel: 01706 814554   Fax: 01706 816680

Berlitz
28th Floor, Sunley Tower
Piccadilly Plaza, Manchester M1 4BW
Tel: 0161 228 3607

**Churchill House English Home Tuition
Courses** - *See South East display for details*

Communicaid English
The Business Exchange, 121 Deansgate
Manchester M3 2BX
Tel: 0800 1691310   Fax:
Email: info@communicaid.com
http://www.communicaid.com

Eaton Language Centre
York Hse, 32 York Road, Sale
Manchester M33 6UU
Tel: 0161 962 3105   Fax: 0161 905 2476
Email: english@eaton-languages.co.uk
http://www.eaton-languages.co.uk

Educare College
Santaidd, Burnage Lane
Manchester M19 1DR
Tel: 0161 442 0858   Fax: 0161 443 2357
Email: info@educare.demon.co.uk
http://www.educare.demon.co.uk

English in Chester
9-11 Stanley Place,
Chester CH1 2LU
Tel: 01244 318913   Fax: 01244 320091
Email: study@english-in-chester.co.uk
http://www.english-in-chester.co.uk

European Languages Centre
Northern House, 43-45 Pembroke Place
Liverpool L3 5PH
Tel: 0151 708 7071   Fax: 0151 707 1919
Email: sderham@eurolang.com
http://www.eurolang.com

Inlingua College Courses
12 Meadowgate, Urmston
Manchester M31 1LB
Tel: 0161 748 2621   Fax: 0161 746 8385

InTuition Languages - *See London display
for details*

Lancashire College
Southport Road,
Chorley PR7 1NB
Tel: 01257 260909   Fax: 01257 241370
Email: insight@lancscollege.u-net.com
http://www.learningbreaks.org.uk/

Lancaster Learning and Leisure
10 Maple Road,
Garstang PR3 1WN
Tel: 01995 600980   Fax: 01995 600980
Email: info@english-language.co.uk
http://www.english-language.co.uk

Manchester Academy of English
St. Margaret's Chambers, 5 Newton St.
Manchester M1 1HL
Tel: 0161 237 5619   Fax: 0161 237 9016
Email: english@manacad.co.uk
http://www.manacad.co.uk
See display for further details

Manchester Language School
Moor Cottage, Grange Lane Didsbury
Manchester M20 6RW
Tel: 0161 448 8372   Fax: 0161 448 9343
Email: mls@isite.co.uk
http://www.manchesterlanguageschool.co.uk
See display for further details

Nord Anglia ILA
10 Eden Place,
Cheadle SK8 1AT
Tel: 0161 491 4191   Fax: 0161 491 4410
Email: marketing@nord-anglia.co.uk
http://www.language-academies.com

Rossall International Study Centre
Rossall School, Broadway
Fleetwood FY7 8JW
Tel: 01253 774204   Fax: 01253 779415
Email: director@rossall-isc.org.uk
http://www.rossall-isc.org.uk

Sandgrown School of English Ltd.
59 Cartmell Road,
Lytham St. Annes FY8 1DF
Tel: 01253 711212   Fax: 01253 712561
Email: Sandgrown@mcintyre50.freeserve.co.uk
http://www.sandgrown.co.uk

TW Languages for Business Ltd
PO Box 281,
Altrincham WA14 4GS
Tel: 0161 928 7283   Fax: 0161 928 7201
Email: info@twlanguages.com
http://www.twlanguages.com

Universal Language Centre
36 Canal St.,
Manchester M1 3WD
Tel: 0161 236 5331   Fax: 0161 263 7734
Email: info@languagecentre.co.uk
http://www.languagecentre.co.uk
See display for further details

STATE COLLEGES / UNIVERSITIES

Accrington & Rossendale College
Sandy Lane,
Accrington BB5 2AW
Tel: 01254 389933

Blackburn College
Feilden Street,
Blackburn BB2 1LH
Tel: 01254 292251   Fax:
Email: m.kershaw@blackburn.ac.uk

Blackpool & the Fylde College
Ashfield Road,
Bispham FY8 5EB
Tel: 01253 352352   Fax: 01253 356127
Email: visitors@blackpool.ac.uk
http://www.blackpool.ac.uk

Bolton College
Manchester Road,
Bolton BL2 1ER
Tel: 01204 453458

Bury College
Millennium Centre, Market St.
Bury BL9 0BG
Tel: 0161 280 8451   Fax: 0161 280 8228
Email: vivien.finney@burycollege.ac.uk
http://www.burycollege.ac.uk

Chester College
The Language Centre, Cheyney Road
Chester CH1 4BJ
Tel: 01244 375444

City College Manchester
International Office, 141 Barlow Moor Road,
West Didsbury
Manchester M20 2PQ
Tel: 0161 957 1609   Fax: 0161957 1609
Email: rspriggs@ccm.ac.uk
http://www.ccm.ac.uk

Halton College of Further Education
Kingsway,
Widnes WA8 7QQ
Tel: 0151 423 1391   Fax: 0151 420 7855
Email: peter.adams@haltoncollege.ac.uk
http://www.haltoncollege.ac.uk

Hopwood Hall College
Rochdale Road,
Middleton M24 6XH
Tel: 0161 643 7560   Fax: 0161 643 2114
Email: enquiries@hopwood.ac.uk
http://www.hopwood.ac.uk

Lancaster University
LAMEL, Bowland College
Lancaster LA1 4YT
Tel: 01524 593045   Fax: 01524 843085
Email: linguistics@lancaster.ac.uk
http://www.iling.lancs.ac.uk

Language College
Bishop Heber County High School, Malpas
Nr. Chester SY14 8JD
Tel: 01948 860571   Fax: 01948 860962

Liverpool Community College
Riversdale Centre, Riversdale Road
Liverpool L19 3QR
Tel: 0151 252 4711   Fax: 0151252 4708
Email: karen.finley@liv-coll.ac.uk
http://www.liv-coll.ac.uk/efl/default.htm

Macclesfield College
Park Lane,
Macclesfield SK11 8LF
Tel: 01625 427744

Manchester College of Arts & Technology
EFL Unit, The John Unsworth Building,
Lower Hardman St.
Manchester M3 3ER
Tel: 0161 455 2434   Fax: 0161 953 2259
Email: international@mancat.ac.uk
http://www.mancat.ac.uk

Nelson & Colne College
Scotland Road,
Nelson BB9 7YT
Tel: 01282 603151

Oldham College
Rochdale Road,
Oldham OL9 6AA
Tel: 0161 624 5214

Preston College
International Office, St. Vincents Rd
Fulwood, Preston PR2 8UR
Tel: 01772 225286   Fax: 01772 225283
Email: international@preston.ac.uk
http://www.4internationalstudents.com

Shena Simon College
34 Whitworth Street,
Manchester M1 3HB
Tel: 0161 236 3418   Fax: 0161 237 5621
Email: enquiries@shenasimon.ac.uk
http://www.shenasimon.ac.uk/acis/acis.htm

South Trafford College
Manchester Road, West Timperley
Altrincham WA14 5PQ
Tel: 0161 952 4720   Fax: 0161952 4672
Email: languages@stcoll.ac.uk
http://www.stcoll.ac.uk

Southport College
Mornington Road,
Southport PR9 0TT
Tel: 01704 500606

St. Helens College
Brook Street,
St. Helens WA10 1PZ
Tel: 01744 733766

Tameside College
Beaufort Road,
Ashton-under-Lyne OL6 6NX
Tel: 0161 708 6782   Fax: 0161 904 6611
Email: sultan.ahmed@tamesidecollege.ac.uk
http://www.tamesidecollege.co.uk

UMIST, ELTC

Sessional and Summer Courses.
General, Academic, Business and
Technical English. Foundation Year.
Cambridge and IELTS examination
Centre. Access to the internet and
email, multimedia laboratory and self-
access centre. University library and
recreational facilities.

PO Box 88, Manchester M60 1QD

Tel: +44 (0) 161 200 3397
Fax: +44 (0) 161 200 3396
Email: eltc@umist.ac.uk
Web: http://www.eltc.umist.ac.uk

UMIST, ELTC
PO Box 88,
Manchester M60 1QD
Tel: 0161 200 3397   Fax: 0161 200 3396
Email: eltc@umist.ac.uk
http://www.eltc.umist.ac.uk
See display for further details

University of Central Lancashire
Dept. of Languages, Fylde Buildings
Preston PR1 2HE
Tel: 01772 893130   Fax: 01772 892909
Email: c.barwood@uclan.ac.uk

University of Liverpool
AELSU, Dept. English Lang., Modern
Languages Building Chatham St.
Liverpool L69 3BX
Tel: 0151 794 2734   Fax: 0151 794 2739
Email: glester@liv.ac.uk

University of Manchester
English Language Programmes, Art
Building, Oxford Road
Manchester M13 9PL
Tel: 0161 275 3482   Fax: 0161 275 3435
Email: englang@man.ac.uk
http://langcent.man.ac.uk

University of Manchester, Owens Park
293 Wilmslow Road, Fallowfield
Manchester M14 6HD
Tel: 0161 248 3000   Fax: 0161 248 3032

Warrington Collegiate Institute
Language Ctre, Winwick Road,
Warrington WA2 8QA
Tel: 01925 494494   Fax: 01925 418328
Email: c.jones@warr.ac.uk

West Cheshire College
International Study Centre, Eaton Rd,
Handbridge
Chester CH4 7ER
Tel: 01244 670566   Fax: 01244 670611
Email: international@west-cheshire.ac.uk
http://www.west-cheshire.ac.uk

Wigan & Leigh College
PO Box 53, Parsons Walk
Wigan WN1 1RS
Tel: 01942 761563   Fax: 01942 761572
Email: f.brogan@wigan-leigh.ac.uk
http://www.wigan-leigh.ac.uk

Wirral Metropolitan College
ELU, Conway Park Campus, Europa Blvd
Birkenhead
Wirral CH41 4NT
Tel: 0151 551 7088   Fax: 0151 551 7001
Email: elu@wmc.ac.uk
http://www.wmc.ac.uk/esol

Youth & Community Education
Chaucer Street,
Oldham OL1 1BA
Tel: 0161 624 3957

Institution Name	Availability	Junior Ages	Specials	Price /week	Status
Action Holidays	J: 7-8			On application	
Blackburn College	A: 9-6		E	Free-£102	
Blackpool & the Fylde College	A: 1-12		E	On application	
Bolton College	A: 9-6			On application	
Bury College	A: 1-12		E	On application	
Churchill House English Home Tuition Courses	A: 1-12 J: 1-12 (1-1 only)	7 yrs +	B, T, F, H, C, E	£450-£780**	GBC, Baselt
City College Manchester	A: 1-12		E	£75-£100	
Communicaid English	A: 1-12		B, T, F, H, C, E	£845-£1845	
Eaton Language Centre	A: 1-12 J: 7-8	14 yrs +	B, T, F, E	£145-£195 (£250 summer)	GBC, Arels
Educare College	A: 1-12		F, H, C, E	£100-£350+	
English in Chester	A: 1-12 J: 7-8	14-16 yrs	B, T, F	£120-£175	
European Languages Centre	A: 1-12 J: 6-9	8-15 yrs	B, T, F, H, C, E	£129-£199	GBC, Arels
Halton College of Further Education	A: 9-6		C, E	£85	
Hopwood Hall College	A: 1-12		B, C, E	On application	
Inlingua College Courses	A: 7-8			On application	
InTuition Languages	A: 1-12 J: 1-12 (1-1 only)	14-18 yrs	B, T, F, C, E	£555-£1040**	GBC, Arels
Lancashire College	A: 1-12			On application	
Lancaster Learning and Leisure	A: 4-7, 9-10		T	£660-£810**	
Liverpool Community College	A: 9-6			£100-£120	GBC, Baselt
Manchester Academy of English	A: 1-12		B, E	£112-£235	GBC, Arels
Manchester College of Arts & Technology	A: 1-12		B, H, E	£1300/term	GBC, Baselt
Manchester Language School	A: 1-12 J: 7-8	17 yrs +	B, T	£135 (£875**)	ABLS

Institution Name	Availability	Junior Ages	Specials	Price /week	Status
Nord Anglia ILA	A: 1-12 J: 6-9	8-18 yrs	B, F, C, E	£120-£184	
Preston College	A: 9-6, 7-8 J: 9-6, 7-8	16-18 yrs (14-16 with accompanying staff)		Free-£130	
Rossall International Study Centre	J: 9-12, 1-6	11-16 yrs		£6550**/term	
Sandgrown School of English Ltd.	A: 1-12 J: 3-4, 6-8	11-18 yrs	B, T, H, C	£250-£500**	
Sheena Simon College	A: 1-12		B, E	£75-£125	GBC, Baselt
South Trafford College	A: 9-6		B, T, F, H, C	£90 approx. (less for EU students)	GBC, Baselt
Tameside College	A: 1-12			Free	
TW Languages for Business Ltd	A: 1-12		B, T, F, H, C, E	£125-£900	
UMIST, ELTC	A: 1-12		B, C, E	£160-£200	Baleap
Universal Language Centre	A: 1-12 J: 1-12	14-15 yrs	B, T, F, E	£99-£185	
University of Central Lancashire	A: 1-12			On application	
University of Liverpool	A: 7-9			On application	
University of Manchester	A: 1-12		E	£165	GBC, Baselt, Baleap
Warrington Collegiate Institute	A: 9-6			£5	
West Cheshire College	A: 1-12		B, T, E	£90-£130	GBC, Baselt
Wigan & Leigh College	A: 1-12		B, E	£50-£100	GBC, Baselt
Wirral Metropolitan College	A: 1-12		B	£110	GBC, Baselt
Youth & Community Education	A: 1-12				

10 YORKSHIRE & HUMBERSIDE

Includes North, South and West Yorkshire, Humberside.

Yorkshire is England's largest county and has much to offer: the Yorkshire Dales, home of the Brönte sisters, are a beautiful area of hills and valleys; the North York Moors are the largest expanse of heather-clad moorland in the country. Finally, the Yorkshire coastline is famous for its rugged cliffs and old smugglers' villages.

The city of York, with its spectacular Minster Cathedral (the largest Gothic cathedral in England), its medieval streets and buildings, is a must for any visitor.

With over 100 museums, ranging from small folk museums to large prize winning centres, this region has fascinating attractions for all.

Région célèbre pour les Yorkshire Dales avec ses superbes collines et vallées ainsi que de larges espaces de landes sauvages. Aussi renommée pour sa ville médiévale de York qui a une magnifique cathédrale gothique.

Diese Gegend ist berühmt für ihre Yorkshire Dales mit ihrer wunderschönen Berg- und Tallandschaft und das unberührte Moor. Nicht minder bekannt ist die mittelalterliche Stadt York mit ihrer überwältigenden, gothischen Kathedrale.

Célebre por los Yorkshire Dales, con valles y colinas magníficas y además con muchos páramos vírgenes, la ciudad de York es muy conocida por su suntuosa catedral gótica.

Regione famosa per le Yorkshire Dales, con monti, valli e molte zone di brughiera incontaminata. Rinomata anche per la città medievale di York, con la sua stupenda cattedrale gotica.

 SIGHTS

Jorvik Viking Centre
Recreation of Viking York, with excavations of houses and objects found. Coppergate, York.
Tel: 01904 643211

Fountains Abbey & Studley Royal Park
The largest monastic ruin in Britain, founded in 1132.
Ripon, North Yorks. Tel: 01765 608888

Pleasure Island Fun Park
Amusement Park, with many rides including wave swinger, boomerang and dream boat! King's Road, Cleethorpes. Tel: 01472 211511

Thrybergh County Park

63 acre park with 35 acre lake. Activities include sailing, windsurfing, canoeing & fishing. Doncaster Road, Thrybergh, Rotherham. Tel: 01709 850353

For further information on these or other sights, contact the Yorkshire & Humberside Tourist Board, 312 Tadcaster Road, York. YO2 2HF Tel: 01904 707961

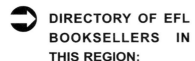

DIRECTORY OF EFL BOOKSELLERS IN THIS REGION:

(NB: Many bookshops hold a good selection of EFL material, even if they are not listed below. Moreover, if the particular book you are looking for is not in stock, they can order it for you.)

1853 Gallery
Salts Mill, Victoria Road, Saltaire
Shipley BD18 3LB
Tel: 01274 531163 Fax: 01274 531184
Web: http://www.saltsmill.org.uk

Blackwell's
21 Blenheim Terrace, Woodhouse Lane
Leeds LS2 9HJ
Tel: 0113 243 2446 Fax: 0113 243 0661
Web: http://bookshop.blackwell.co.uk

Blackwell's University Bookshop
University of Sheffield
Mappin Street, Sheffield S1 4DT
Tel: 0114 278 7211 Fax: 0114 278 7629
Web: http://bookshop.blackwell.co.uk

Blackwell's University Bookshop
City Campus, Pond Street
Sheffield S1 1WB
Tel: 0114 275 2152 Fax: 0114 279 8950
Web: http://bookshop.blackwell.co.uk

College Bookshop
High Melton, Doncaster DN5 7SZ
Tel: 01302 553788 Fax: 01302 553788

James Thin Ltd
5 New Street, Huddersfield HD1 2AX
Tel: 01484 544836 Fax: 01484 451758
Web: http://www.jamesthin.com

Leeds University Union Bookshop
Students' Union Buildings
P O Box 157, Leeds LS1 1UH
Tel: 0113 244 4974 Fax: 0113 244 8786

Ottakar's Bookstore
41-43 New Street, Huddersfield HD1 2BQ
Tel: 01484 431051 Fax: 01484 432795
Web: http://www.ottakars.co.uk

Page One Books
9 Princes Avenue, Hull HU5 3RX
Tel: 01482 341925 Fax: 01482 494770
Web: http://www.page1.co.uk/

Waterstone's
36-38 Albion Street, Leeds LS1 6HX
Tel: 0113 242 0839 Fax: 0113 242 2825
Web: http://www.waterstones.co.uk

Waterstone's
93-97 Albion Street, Leeds LS1 5AP
Tel: 0113 244 4588 Fax: 0113 247 0282
Web: http://www.waterstones.co.uk

Waterstone's
Grand Buildings, Jameson Street
Hull HU1 3JX
Tel: 01482 580234 Fax: 01482 227824
Web: http://www.waterstones.co.uk

Waterstone's
24-26 Orchard Square, Sheffield S1 2FB
Tel: 0114 272 8971 Fax: 0114 275 3905
Web: http://www.waterstones.co.uk

Waterstone's
9-10 High Ousegate, York YO1 8RZ
Tel: 01904 610044 Fax: 01904 654065
Web: http://www.waterstones.co.uk

Waterstone's
University of Hull, University House
Hull HU6 7RX
Tel: 01482 444190 Fax: 01482 492000
Web: http://www.waterstones.co.uk

DIRECTORY OF COURSES IN THIS REGION

PRIVATE SCHOOLS / ORGANISATIONS

Anglolang Academy of English
20 Avenue Road,
Scarborough YO12 5JX
Tel: 01723 367141   Fax: 01723 378698
Email: communicate@anglolang.co.uk
http://www.anglolang.co.uk

Beverley English Centre
The Old Hall, Vicar Lane
Beverley HU17 8DF
Tel: 01482 679928
Email: mary@beverleyenglishcentre.co.uk
http://www.beverleyenglishcentre.co.uk

Carl Duisberg Language Centre Sheffield
19-33 Bells Court,
Sheffield S1 2FY
Tel: 0114 272 7937   Fax: 0114 275 9688
Email: info@cdcsheffield.co.uk
http://www.cdcsheffield.co.uk

**Churchill House English Home Tuition
Courses** - *See South East display for details*

Dales English Language Holidays
Ebor House, Burtersett Road
Hawes DL8 3NT
Tel: 01969 667337   Fax: 01969 667337
Email: info@dalesenglish.co.uk
http://www.dalesenglish.co.uk

**English Adventure - UK - Based
Language Summer Courses**
19 Roman Gardens,
Leeds LS8 2AJ
Tel: 0113 266 0701
Email: info@english-adventure.co.uk
http://www.english-adventure.co.uk

English in York
38-40 Coney St.,
York YO1 1ND
Tel: 01904 636771   Fax: 01904 641214
Email: lorraine@english-in-york.co.uk
http://www.english-in-york.co.uk

English Language Centre (The)
5 New Street,
York YO1 8RA
Tel: 01904 672243   Fax: 01904 672200
Email: english@elcyork.com
http://www.elcyork.com

Functional English
5 Chubb Hill, Whitby YO21 1JU
Tel: 01947 603933   Fax: 01947 820703
Email: office@funenglish.co.uk
http://www.funenglish.co.uk

Harrogate International Language Centre
Woodcroft, High Bond End
Knaresborough HG5 9BS
Tel: 01423 864447   Fax: 01423 860297

**Harrogate International Language Centre
at Ashville College**
Green Lane, Harrogate HG2 9JP
Tel: 01423 566358   Fax: 01423 505142
Email: ashville@kma.co.uk

Harrogate Language Academy
8A Royal Parade, Harrogate HG1 2SZ
Tel: 01423 531969   Fax: 01423 531064
Email: enquiry@hla.co.uk
http://www.hla.co.uk

Harrogate Tutorial College
2 The Oval, Harrogate HG2 9BA
Tel: 01423 501041   Fax: 01423 531110
Email: study@htcuk.org
http://www.htcuk.org

International Language Institute
County House, Vicar Lane
Leeds LS1 7JH
Tel: 0113 242 8893   Fax: 0113 2347543
Email: 101322.1376@compuserve.com
http://www.vitalo.com/ili

InTuition Languages - *See London display
for details*

Leeds Languages
19 Roman Gardens,
Leeds LS8 2AJ
Tel: 0113 266 0701   Fax: 0113 266 0701
Email: info@leedslanguages.cjb.net
http://www.leedslanguages.cjb.net

Live English
21 Bagdale, Whitby YO22 4PP
Tel: 01947 880955   Fax: 01947 880955
Email: magda@live-english.demon.co.uk
http://www.live-english.demon.co.uk

Melton College
137 Holgate Rd,
York YO24 4DH
Tel: 01904 622250   Fax: 01904 629233
Email: efl@melton-college.co.uk
http://www.melton-college.co.uk

Scarborough International School
37 Stepney Road,
Scarborough YO12 5BN
Tel: 01723 362879   Fax: 01723 366458
Email: info@english-language.uk.com
http://www.english-language.uk.com

York Associates
Peasholme House, St.Saviours Place
York YO1 7PJ
Tel: 01904 624246   Fax: 01904 646971
Email: training@yorkassoc.go-ed.com
http://www.york-associates.co.uk

STATE COLLEGES / UNIVERSITIES

Airedale & Wharfedale College
Calverley Lane, Horsforth
Leeds LS18 4RQ
Tel: 0113 258 1723

Avenues Adult Education Centre
Park Avenue, Hull HU5 4DA
Tel: 01482 331680   Fax: 01482 331688
Email: avenues.adulted@hullcc.gov.uk
http://www.hullcc.gov.uk/adulteducation/

Barnsley College
PO Box 266, Church St.
Barnsley S70 2YW
Tel: 01226 216182   Fax: 01226 216724
Email: ecu@barnsley.ac.uk
http://www.barnsley.ac.uk

Bradford College
ELC, Old Building Gt. Horton Rd
Bradford BD7 1AY
Tel: 01274 753207   Fax: 01274 741553
Email: elc@bilk.ac.uk
http://www.bilk.ac.uk

Calderdale College
Francis Street, Halifax HX1 3UZ
Tel: 01422 399329   Fax: 01422 399320

Grimsby College
Nuns Corner, Grimsby DN34 5BQ
Tel: 01472 279222   Fax: 01472 897724

Huddersfield Technical College
New North Road,
Huddersfield HD1 5NN
Tel: 01484 536521   Fax: 01484 511885
Email: international@huddcoll.ac.uk
http://www.huddcoll.ac.uk

Hull College
Park Street Centre, Park Street
Hull HU2 8RR
Tel: 01482 598955   Fax: 01482 598989
Email: cmiddleton@hull-college.co.uk
http://www.hull-college.co.uuk

John Leggott Sixth Form College
West Common Lane,
Scunthorpe DN17 1DS
Tel: 01724 282998

Joseph Priestley College
Alec Beevers Centre, Burton Ave
Leeds LS11 5ER
Tel: 0113 307 6111   Fax: 0113 271 3456
Email: helpline@joseph-priestley.ac.uk
http://www.joseph-priestley.ac.uk

Keighley College
Cavendish Street,
Keighley BD21 3DF
Tel: 01535 618600
Email: guidance@keighley.ac.uk
http://www.keighley.ac.uk

Kitson College
Cookridge St., Leeds LS2 8BL
Tel: 0113 2430381

Leeds Metropolitan University
Centre for Language Study, Beckett Park
Leeds LS13 2JQ
Tel: 0113 283 7440   Fax: 0113 274 5966
Email: cls@lmu.ac.uk
http://www.lmu.ac.uk/cls
See display for further details

Mid Cheshire College
Hartford Campus, Northwich CW8 1LJ
Tel: 01606 74444   Fax: 01606 75101
Email: Admin@midchesh.u.net.com

Notre Dame Sixth Form College
St.Mark's Avenue, Leeds LS2 9BL
Tel: 0113 294 6644   Fax: 0113 294 6006
Email: m.corbett@notredamecoll.ac.uk
http://www.notredamecoll.ac.uk

Park Lane College
Park Lane, Leeds LS3 1AA
Tel: 0113 216 2032   Fax: 0113 216 2020
Email: international@mail.parklanecoll.ac.uk
http://www.parklanecoll.ac.uk

Sheffield College
Overseas Business Unit, Castle Centre
Granville Rd, Sheffield S2 2RL
Tel: 0114 260 2676   Fax: 0114 260 2169
Email: international.office@sheffcol.ac.uk
http://www.sheffcol.ac.uk

Sheffield Hallam University
TESOL Centre, 36 Collegiate Crescent
Campus, Sheffield S10 2BP
Tel: 0114 225 2365   Fax: 0114 225 2280
Email: tesol@shu.ac.uk
http://www.shu.ac.uk/tesol/

LEEDS   METROPOLITAN   UNIVERSITY

TEFL Courses

Preparation courses leading to Cambridge CELTA (4 week intensive) or Trinity College TESOL (one year part-time) qualifications.
Overseas career prospects are excellent.

Postgraduate TESOL Courses

- MA Materials Development for Language Teaching
- PhD Research
- MA Professional Development for Language Education (Joint with NILE)
- MA Language Teaching

English Language Courses

- General English
- Undergraduate Foundation
- Pre-Masters
- Cambridge & IELTS Exam

For further details of these courses, please contact:

THE BRITISH ASSOCIATION OF STATE
ENGLISH LANGUAGE TEACHING

The Centre for Language Study (EP), Leeds Metropolitan University, Beckett Park Campus, Leeds LS6 3QS
Tel: +44 (0)113 283 7440
Fax: +44 (0)113 274 5966
e.mail: cls@lmu.ac.uk   web: http://www.lmu.ac.uk/cls

University of Huddersfield
International & European Office,
Queensgate, Huddersfield HD1 3DH
Tel: 01484 473153   Fax: 01484 450408
Email: m.j.hemsley@hud.ac.uk
http://www.hud.ac.uk

University of Hull
The Language Institute, Cottingham Road
Hull HU6 7RX
Tel: 01482 465900   Fax: 01482 466180
Email: langinst@hull.ac.uk
http://www.hull.ac.uk

University of Leeds
Language Centre, Leeds LS2 9JT
Tel: 0113 343 3251   Fax: 0113 343 3252
Email: langc@leeds.ac.uk
http://www.leeds.ac.uk/languages/lc_home.html

University of Salford
EFL, School of Languages
Maxwell Building, Salford M5 4WT
Tel: 0161 295 5751   Fax: 0161 295 5135
Email: efl-languages@salford.ac.uk
http://www.salford.ac.uk/intinst/

University of Sheffield
ELT Centre, 9 Northumberland Road
Sheffield S10 2TT
Tel: 0114 222 1781   Fax: 0114 2739907
Email: elt@sheffield.ac.uk

University of York
EFL Unit, Language Teaching Centre
Heslington, York YO10 5DD
Tel: 01904 432480   Fax: 01904 432481
Email: efl@york.ac.uk
http://www.york.ac.uk/efl/

Wakefield College
Margaret Street, Wakefield WF1 2DH
Tel: 01924 370501

Wyke College
Grammar School Road, Hull HU5 4NX
Tel: 01482 346347   Fax: 01482 473336
Email: office@wyke.ac.uk
http://www.wyke.ac.uk

York College of F&HE
Tadcaster Road, York YO2 1UA
Tel: 01904 770366   Fax: 01904 770363
Email: efl@yorkcollege.com
http://www.yorkcollege.com

York St. John College
Lord Mayor's Walk, York YO31 7EX
Tel: 01904 716684   Fax: 01904 716929
Email: iscc@yorksj.ac.uk
http://www.yorksj.ac.uk

Institution Name	Availability	Junior Ages	Specials	Price /week	Status
Anglolang Academy of English	A: 1-12 J: 6-8	14 yrs +	B, T, F, H, C, E	£160-£965	GBC, Arels
Avenues Adult Education Centre	A: 1-12		C	On application	
Barnsley College	A: 1-12		B, E	£97-£125	
Beverley English Centre	A: 1-12 J: 1-12	10-15 yrs	B, T, F, H, C, E	£100-£350	
Bradford College	A: 1-12		B, T, H, C, E	£100-£105.50	GBC, Baselt
Calderdale College	A: 1-7, 9-12			On application	
Carl Duisberg Language Centre Sheffield	A: 1-12 J: 4-8	12-16 yrs	B, T, F, H, E	£135-£1429	GBC
Churchill House English Home Tuition Courses	A: 1-12 J: 1-12 (1-1 only)	7 yrs +	B, T, F, H, C, E	£450-£780**	
Dales English Language Holidays	A: 7-9			£325-£385**	
English in York	A: 1-12		B, T, F, H, E	£120-£1050	GBC, Arels
English Language Centre (The)	A: 1-12 J: 6-8	12-15 yrs		£90-£195	GBC, Arels
Functional English	A: 1-12 J: 7-8	12-16 yrs	B	£158-£178	GBC, Arels
Harrogate Language Academy	A: 1-12 J: 5-6	13-16 yrs	B, T, F, H, E	£145-£190	GBC, Arels
Harrogate Tutorial College	A: 1-12 J: 6-8	12-16 yrs	B, C, E	£95-£190	GBC, Arels, BAC, CIFE
Huddersfield Technical College	A: 1-12		B, T, H, C, E	£45-£110	GBC, Baselt
Hull College	A: 9-6			£120	GBC, Baselt
International Language Institute	A: 1-12		E	£98-£375+	
InTuition Languages	A: 1-12 J: 1-12 (1-1 only)	14-18 yrs	B, T, F, C, E	£555-£1040**	GBC, Arels
Joseph Priestley College	A: 9-6			On application	
Leeds Languages	A: 1-12 J: 7-8	12-18 yrs	B, E	£100-£300	
Leeds Metropolitan University	A: 1-12		B, T, H, C, E	£125-£220	GBC, Baselt
Live English	A: 4-9 J: 6-8	8-17 yrs	B, C	£100-£400	

Institution Name	Availability	Junior Ages	Specials	Price /week	Status
Melton College	A: 1-12 J: 4	12-18 yrs	E	£140-£195	GBC, Arels
Mid Cheshire College	A: 1-6, 9-12			On application	
Park Lane College	A: 9-6		B, T, E	£100-£125	GBC, Baselt
Scarborough International School	A: 1-12 J: 6-8	5-12 yrs	B, E	£147-£630	GBC, Arels
Sheffield College	A: 1-12		B, C	£125-£175	GBC, Baselt
Sheffield Hallam University	A: 1,4, 6,7, 8, 9		E	£130-£250	GBC, Baselt
University of Huddersfield	A: 1-12		B, H, C, E	£120-£200	
University of Hull	A: 1-12		B, E	£141-£166	
University of Leeds	A: 1-12		E	£190-£199	GBC
University of Salford	A: 1-12		B, C, E	£150-£170	GBC, Baselt
University of York	A: 7,8,9		E	£171-£185	Baleap
Wyke College	A: 10-6		B, E	£25-£75	
York Associates	A: 1-12		B	On application	
York College of F&HE	A: 9-8			On application	
York St. John College	A: 1-12		B, T, F, H, C, E	£140-£250	GBC, Baselt

11 NORTHUMBRIA & CUMBRIA

Newcastle

Durham

Carlisle

Windermere

Isle of Man

Includes Cleveland, County Durham, Northumberland, Tyne & Wear, Cumbria, the English Lakeland and the Isle of Man.

Unspoilt and wild, this beautiful region delights visitors with its views of magnificent countryside and coastline.

The Lake District in Cumbria is a heaven for walkers, and has inspired many writers, particularly the poet William Wordsworth and Beatrice Potter.

The Northumberland National Park, one of the last extents of wilderness left in England, is another popular destination for nature lovers. Visitors can relax and enjoy a drink at one of the many 'old-world inns', or explore some of the picturesque villages that lie nestled in the hills.

Alternatively, you could visit Hadrian's Wall which runs across northern England. Constructed by the Romans, it was designed to prevent an invasion from Scotland, but now provides an interesting back drop to the beautiful scenery.

For city life, head to Newcastle-upon-Tyne, a bustling city and the region's capital, or Durham, a university town, with its magnificent 12th century Cathedral.

Northumbria: Belle région avec des contrées intérieures et une côte superbes. Le mur Hadrian, construit par les Romains, et la grande ville universitaire de Durham sont parmi les attraits de ce territoire.

Cumbria: Bien connue pour son Lake District, le plus grand parc national en Angleterre, cette charmante région est idéale pour ceux qui aiment la nature et les randonnées.

Northumbria: Schöne Umgebung und Küstenlandschaft in einer wunderbaren Region. Hadrian's Mauer, von den Römern erbaut, und die große Universitätsstadt Durham sind nur zwei der Attraktionen dieser Gegend.

Cumbria: Diese Region ist für den Lake District, Englands größten Nationalpark, bekannt und ist daher für den Naturliebenden oder den Entspannungssuchenden besonders geeignet.

Northumbria: Bonita región con un campo y costas preciosas. El Muro de Hadrian, construido por los romanos y la importante ciudad universitaria de Durham son tan sólo algunas de las atracciones que ofrece esta parte de Inglaterra.

Cumbria: Región muy conocida por el Distrito de los Lagos, el parque nacional más grande de Inglaterra. Es una región encantadora, sobre todo para los que aprecian descansar en un ambiente de naturaleza espléndida.

Northumbria: Bella regione dalla magnifica campagna e litorale. Il muro d'Adriano, costruito dai romani, e la grande città universitaria di Durham costituiscono solo un esempio delle attarazioni da essa offerte.

Cumbria: Rinomata per il Lake District, - il distretto dei laghi - questa incantevole regione è il luogo ideale per gli amanti della natura in cerca di relax, in quanto vanta il più grande parco nazionale dell' Inghilterra.

 DIRECTORY OF EFL BOOKSELLERS IN THIS REGION:

(NB: Many bookshops hold a good selection of EFL material, even if they are not listed below. Moreover, if the particular book you are looking for is not in stock, they can order it for you.)

Blackwell's
141 Percy Street
Newcastle-upon-Tyne NE1 7RS
Tel: 0191 232 642Fax: 0191 260 2536
Web: http://bookshop.blackwell.co.uk

Ottakar's Bookstore
25 Portland Walk
Barrow-in-Furness LA14 1D
Tel: 01229 871693 Fax: 01229 871694
Web: http://www.ottakars.co.uk

Ottakar's Bookstore
Unit 2 21-25 Strand Street
Douglas, Isle of Man IM1 2EF
Tel: 01624 679051 Fax: 01624 679075
Web: http://www.ottakars.co.uk

Ottakar's Bookstore
7 Westmorland Centre
Kendal LA9 4LR
Tel: 01539 741771 Fax: 01539 741772
Web: http://www.ottakars.co.uk

Ottakar's Bookstore
Unit 9, The Bridges Shopping Centre
Sunderland SR1 3RB
Tel: 0191 567 4331

Ottakar's Bookstore
1 Cornmill Centre
Darlington DL1 1LS
Tel: 01325 465666 Fax: 01325 465888
Web: http://www.ottakars.co.uk

Waterstone's
17 The Parade The Metro Centre
Gateshead, Tyne & Wear NE11 9YJ
Tel: 0191 493 2715 Fax: 0191 460 3101
Web: http://www.waterstones.co.uk

Waterstone's
Emerson Chambers
Blackett Street
Newcastle-upon-Tyne NE1 7JF
Tel: 0191 261 7757 Fax: 0191 232 0069
Web: http://www.waterstones.co.uk

Well Read Bookshop
University of Northumbria Students Union
2 Sandyford Road
Newcastle-upon-Tyne NE1 8SB
Tel: 0191 227 3400 Fax: 0191 232 7279

A ➡️ Z   DIRECTORY OF COURSES IN THIS REGION

PRIVATE SCHOOLS / ORGANISATIONS

Anglo Language Academy
'Woodlea' Winster, Windermere LA23 3NY
Tel: 015395 68809   Fax: 015395 68809
Email: learning@anglolang.demon.co.uk

Churchill House English Home Tuition Courses - *See South East display for details*

Communicaid English
Churchill House, 12 Mosley Street
Newcastle Upon Tyne NE1 1DE
Tel: 0800 1691310   Fax:
Email: info@communicaid.com
http://www.communicaid.com

Durham Language Services
Blakelow, Bar Road, Baslow DE45 1SF
Tel: 01246 583366   Fax: 01246 583091
Email: enquiries@d-l-s.co.uk
http://www.d-l-s.co.uk

English International
4 South Cliff, Whitley Bay
Newcastle upon Tyne NE26 2PB
Tel: 0191 253 7367   Fax: 0191 251 3121
Email: englishinternational@eudoramail.com
http://www.englishinternational.com

English Language in the Lakes
Nab Cottage, Rydal, Ambleside LA22 9SD
Tel: 015394 35311   Fax: 015394 35493
Email: ell@nab.dial.lakesnet.co.uk
http://www.nabcottage.com
See display for further details

International House, Newcastle
14-18 Stowell St.,
Newcastle-upon-Tyne NE1 4XQ
Tel: 0191 232 9551   Fax: 0191 232 1126
Email: info@ihnewcastle.com
http://www.ihnewcastle.com

InTuition Languages - *See London display for details*

Newcastle Language Institute
Hawthorn House, Forth Banks
Newcastle-upon-Tyne NE1 3SG
Tel: 0191 232 4978   Fax: 1912610760

North-East.org.uk
7 Mersey Place,
Gateshead NE8 3ST
Tel: 0191 477 8718   Fax: 0191 477 8718
Email: drjcobi@aol.com
http://www.North-East.org.uk
See display for further details

ENGLISH FOR BUSINESS AND MEDICINE

North-East.org.uk

Intensive one-on-one residential homestays are now available for distinguished Entrepreneurs and Senior Medical Doctors. Similar options abound for Pharmaceutical Industry workers and other Health-related sector staff.

Tuition: £2500 per week (fully inclusive of meals, entertainment and accommodation). You will live with your tutor and speak English 24 hours a day.

"Travelling - Teacher" facilities are also on offer to corporations and individuals who would rather have the tutor come to them instead.

For more details please kindly contact:

Dr Joseph C. Obi MBBS MPH DSC FRIPH
Principal TEFL Tutor and Dean of Studies

+ 44 7957 638611   e-mail: drjcobi@aol.com
website: http://www.North-East.org.uk

ENGLISH LANGUAGE IN THE LAKES

Innovative, intensive, dynamic courses for adults, in one of the most beautifully situated schools in England.

Live with your teachers.

Very small classes.

British Council accredited.

Members of ARELS and TANDEM.

Contact: Tim Melling
E.L.L., Nab Cottage, Rydal,
Ambleside, Cumbria. LA22 9SD

Tel: +44 (0) 15394 35311
Fax: +44 (0) 15394 35493
Email: ell@nab.dial.lakesnet.co.uk
http://www.nabcottage.com

STATE COLLEGES / UNIVERSITIES

Darlington College of Technology
Cleveland Avenue,
Darlington DL3 7BB
Tel: 01325 503050   Fax: 01325 503000
Email: enquire@darlington.ac.uk
http://www.darlington.ac.uk

Gateshead Training Consultancy
Gateshead College, Durham Road
Gateshead NE9 5BN
Tel: 0191 490 2260   Fax: 0191 490 2315
Email: international@gateshead.ac.uk
http://www.gateshead.ac.uk

Hartlepool College of Further Education
Stockton Street,
Hartlepool TS25 7NT
Tel: 01429 275453

Isle of Man College
Homefield Road, Douglas
Isle of Man IM2 6RB
Tel: 01624 623113

Longlands College of Further Education
Douglas Street,
Middlesbrough TS4 2JW
Tel: 01642 248351

Middlesbrough College
Roman Road,
Middlesbrough TS5 5PJ
Tel: 01642 333333   Fax: 01642 333310
Email: r.smith@mbro.ac.uk
http://www.mbro.ac.uk

New College Durham
Framwellgate Moor Centre,
Durham DH1 5ES
Tel: 0191 375 4383   Fax: 0191 375 4333
Email: jo.fayram@newdur.ac.uk
http://intra.newdur.ac.uk

Newcastle College
International Office, Rye Hill Campus,
Scotswood Road
Newcastle Upon Tyne NE4 7SA
Tel: 0191 200 4068   Fax: 0191220 4474
Email: international@ncl-coll.ac.uk
http://www.ncl-coll.ac.uk

North Tyneside College
Embleton Avenue,
Wallsend NE28 9NJ
Tel: 0191 262 5000

South Tyneside College
St. George's Avenue,
South Shields NE33 6ET
Tel: 0191 455 8075   Fax: 0191 455 8075
Email: annstc@hotmail.com
http://www.stc.ac.uk

University of Durham
Language Ctre, Elvet Riverside New Elvet
Durham DH1 3JT
Tel: 0191 374 3716   Fax: 0191 374 7790
Email: language.centre@durham.ac.uk
http://www.durham.ac.uk

University of Newcastle-upon-Tyne
Language Centre,
Newcastle-upon-Tyne NE1 7RU
Tel: 0191 222 7535   Fax: 0191 222 5239
Email: language.centre@ncl.ac.uk
http://www.ncl.ac.uk/langcen/

University of Northumbria at Newcastle
EFL Division, Lipman Building
Newcastle upon Tyne NE1 8ST
Tel: 0191 227 4919   Fax: 0191227 4439
Email: andrea.percival@unn.ac.uk

University of Sunderland
English Language Unit, Forster Building
Chester Road
Sunderland SR1 3SD
Tel: 0191 515 2166   Fax: 0191 515 2105
Email: joan.cutting@sunderland.ac.uk

West Cumbria College
Park Lane,
Workington CA14 2RW
Tel: 01900 64331

Institution Name	Availability	Junior Ages	Specials	Price /week	Status
Anglo Language Academy	A: 1-12		B, T	£450-£1250	
Churchill House English Home Tuition Courses	A: 1-12 J: 1-12 (1-1 only)	7 yrs +	B, T, F, H, C, E	£450-£780**	
Communicaid English	A: 1-12		B, T, F, H, C, E	£845-£1845	
Darlington College of Technology	A: 1-12		E	£100-£125	GBC, Baselt
Durham Language Services	A: 7-8 J: 7-8	10-16 yrs		£290-£300**	
English International	A: 1-12		B	£220 or £320+**	
English Language in the Lakes	A: 4-10			£325-£395**	GBC, Arels
Gateshead Training Consultancy	A: 9-6		B, T, C, E	On application	
International House, Newcastle	A: 1-12		B, T, H, C, E	£125-£200	GBC, Arels, Eaquals
Intuition Languages	A: 1-12 J: 1-12 (1-1 only)	14-18 yrs	B, T, F, C, E	£555-£1040**	GBC, Arels
Middlesbrough College	A: 9-7			£30 (EU) £100 (others)	GBC
New College Durham	A: 1-12		B, T, E	£3.30-£116	
Newcastle College	A: 1-12		B, E	££125-£200	GBC, Baselt
North-East.org.uk	A: 1-12 (1-1 only)		B Also medicine	£2500-£3000**	
South Tyneside College	A: 9-7		C, E	On application	
University of Durham	A: 1-12		B, E	£410/3wks (summer)	Baleap
University of Newcastle-upon-Tyne	A: 1-12		B, F, C, E	£190	Baleap
University of Northumbria at Newcastle	A: 1-12				

12 SCOTLAND

Includes Borders, Central, Dumfries & Galloway, Fife, Grampian, Highland, Lothian, Orkney, Shetland, Strathclyde, Tayside, Western Isles.

Though part of the United Kingdom, Scotland is a country within a country, with its own laws, culture and traditions. Breathtaking scenery, imposing castles wrapped up in mysterious mist, valleys, mountains and lochs conjure up a very romantic picture. Edinburgh, Scotland's capital city, offers a wealth of interesting sites, entertainment and many all year round high quality learning programmes.

Glasgow, a cosmopolitan city, is the arts centre of Scotland, with the headquarters of the Scottish Opera, Scottish Ballet and the Royal Scottish National Orchestra.

Dundee, St. Andrews and Aberdeen are all famous cities which have much to offer the foreign student.

The whole of this beautiful country is well worth visiting and of course, one can sample some of the finest whiskies in the world or enjoy a pleasant round of golf on one of Scotland's many courses.

L'Ecosse - Un pays superbe avec des lacs, des montagnes et de mystérieux châteaux. Les grandes villes d'Edimbourg et de Glasgow offrent des évenements culturels toute l'année, attirant des visiteurs du monde entier.

Schottland - Ein tolles Land der Seen, Berge und mysteriösen Schlösser. Die Großstädte Edinburgh und Glasgow bieten das ganze Jahr über kulturelle Veranstaltungen, die Besucher aus aller Welt anlocken.

Escocia - Un país magnífico con lagos, montañas y castillos misteriosos. Las ciudades importantes de Edimburgo y Glasgow ofrecen todo el año diversiones culturales que atraen a visitantes de todas partes del mundo.

Scozia - Stupendo paese ricco di laghi, montagne e castelli misteriosi. Le città principali, Edinburgo e Glasgow, offrono eventi culturali che richiamano visitatori da ogni parte del mondo durante tutto l'arco dell' anno.

 SIGHTS

Edinburgh Castle
Impressive fortress housing the crown jewels of Scotland. Castlehill, Edinburgh. Tel: 0131 668 8800

Royal Museum of Scotland
Truly splendid Victorian building, containing rich international collections. Chambers St., Edinburgh. Tel: 0131 225 7534

Museum and Art Gallery, Kelvingrove

One of the finest municipal collections of paintings in Britain. Glasgow.

For further information contact the Edinburgh and Scotland Information Centre, 3 Princes Street, Edinburgh. EH2 2QP
Tel: 0131 557 1700

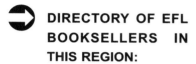 DIRECTORY OF EFL BOOKSELLERS IN THIS REGION:

(NB: Many bookshops hold a good selection of EFL material, even if they are not listed below. Moreover, if the particular book you are looking for is not in stock, they can order it for you.)

Bauermeister Booksellers
19 George IV Bridge, Edinburgh, EH1 1EH
Tel: 0131 226 5561 Fax: 0131 220 0679
Web: http://www.bauermeister.co.uk

James Thin Ltd
27 Buccleuch Street, Edinburgh EH8 9JR
Tel: 0131 556 6743 Fax: 0131 556 6743
Web: http://www.jamesthin.com

James Thin Ltd
53-59 South Bridge, Edinburgh EHl 1YS
Tel: 0131 662 8222 Fax: 0131 557 8149
Web: http://www.jamesthin.com

John Smith & Son Ltd
John McIntyre Building
University of Glasgow, Glasgow G12 8PP
Tel: 0141 339 1463 Fax: 0141 339 3690
Web: http://www.johnsmith.co.uk

John Smith & Son Ltd
127 Market Street, St Andrews KY16 9PE
Tel: 01334 475122 Fax: 01334 478035
Web: http://www.johnsmith.co.uk

John Smith & Son Ltd
Strathclyde University Bookshop
100 Cathedral Street, Glasgow G4 0RD
Tel: 0141 552 3377 Fax: 0141 552 7454
Web: http://www.johnsmith.co.uk

Ottakar's Bookstore
3-7 Union Bridge, Aberdeen AB11 6BG
Tel: 01224 592440 Fax: 01224 592442
Web: http://www.ottakars.co.uk

Ottakar's Bookstore
16 Cameron Toll Shopping Centre
6 Lady Road, Edinburgh EH16 5PB
Tel: 0131 666 1866 Fax: 0131 666 1873
Web: http://www.ottakars.co.uk

Ottakar's Bookstore
Unit 1, Upper Mall, Princes Square
East Kilbride G74 1LJ
Tel: 01355 271835 Fax: 01335 271840
Web: http://www.ottakars.co.uk

Ottakar's Bookstore
38 The Avenue at Mearns
Newton Mearns G77 6EY
Tel: 0141 616 3933
Fax: 0141 616 3255
Web: http://www.ottakars.co.uk

Ottakar's Bookstore
175 High Street, Kirkcaldy KY1 1JA
Tel: 01592 263755 Fax: 01592 263811
Web: http://www.ottakars.co.uk

Ottakar's Bookstore
Unit 6 Buchanan Galleries
Buchanan Street, Glasgow G1 2FF
Tel: 0141 353 1500 Fax: 0141 353 0649
Web: http://www.ottakars.co.uk

DIRECTORY OF COURSES IN THIS REGION

PRIVATE SCHOOLS / ORGANISATIONS

Aberdeen Centre for English
68 Polmuir Road,
Aberdeen AB11 7TH
Tel: 01224 580968   Fax: 01224 575655
Email: english@acescotland.co.uk
http://www.acescotland.co.uk

Aspect ILA Edinburgh
11 Great Stuart St.,
Edinburgh EH3 7TP
Tel: 01202 638100   Fax: 01202 438900
Email: enquires@aspectworld.com
http://www.aspectworld.com

Balliliesk
Muckhart,
New Dollar FK14 7JW
Tel: 01259 781293   Fax: 01259 781293

Basil Paterson Edinburgh
22 Abercromby Place,
Edinburgh EH3 6QE
Tel: 0131 556 7695   Fax: 0131 557 8503
Email: courses@bp-coll.demon.co.uk
http://www.basilpaterson.co.uk

Berlitz Language Centre
26 Frederick St.,
Edinburgh EH2 2JR
Tel: 0131 226 7198   Fax: 0131 225 2918
Email: edinburgh@languagecentres.com

Carrick Language Courses
P.O. Box 16191,
Glasgow G14 9YT
Tel: 0141 950 1171   Fax: 0141 579 1303
Email: english@carrick-
courses.demon.co.uk
http://www.carrick-courses.demon.co.uk

**Churchill House English Home Tuition
Courses** - *See South East display for details*

Communicaid English
10 Sandyford Place,
Glasgow G3 7NB
Tel: 0800 1691310
Email: info@communicaid.com
http://www.communicaid.com

ECS Scotland
43-45 Circus Lane,
Edinburgh EH3 6SU
Tel: 0131 226 5262   Fax: 0131 343 6507
Email: info@ecsscotlang.sol.co.uk
http://www.sol.co.uk/e/ecsscotlang/

Edinburgh School of English
271 Canongate, The Royal Mile
Edinburgh EH8 8BQ
Tel: 0131 557 9200   Fax: 0131 557 9192
Email: europa@edinburghschool.ac.uk
http://www.edinburghschool.ac.uk

English Language Institute
69 Nile Grove, Morningside
Edinburgh EH10 4SN
Tel: 0131 447 2398   Fax: 0131 447 7131
Email: info@eli.co.uk
http://www.eli.co.uk

English Tutorials in Edinburgh
25 St. Ronans Terrace,
Edinburgh EH10 5PG
Tel: 0131 466 0242   Fax: 0131 466 0737
Email: c.smith@cont.demon.co.uk
http://www.englishtutorials.co.uk

English-in-Scotland
Viewvale, 9 New Road, Bannockburn
Stirling FK7 8LP
Tel: 01786 818456
Email: scotgene@lycos.co.uk

Glasgow International English & Business School
2nd Floor, 180 Hope St.,
Glasgow G2 2UE
Tel: 0141 332 8889   Fax: 0141 332 8881
Email: giebs@globalconnects.com
http://www.globalconnects.com

Hamilton School of English
c/o Capielaw nr. Rosewell,
Midlothian EH24 9EE
Tel: 0131 440 3301   Fax: 0131 440 3301
Email: hamiltonschool@edent.c.uk
http://www.ednet.co.uk/~hamiltonschool

Highland Language Centre
12 Marine Terrace, Rosemarkie
Ross-shire IV10 8UL
Tel: 01381 620598   Fax: 01381 621247
Email: info@hlc.co.uk
http://www.hlc.co.uk

InTuition Languages - *See London display for details*

K.I.L.T.
8 Roseburn Avenue,
Edinburgh EH12 5PA
Tel: 0131 337 3554   Fax: 0131 337 3554
Email: kiltedin@hotmail.com
http://www.kiltedin.co.uk

LinguaScot
Orwell House, Carberry Road Leven
Fife KY8 4JH
Tel: 01333 426070   Fax: 01333 426070
Email: linguascot@blueyonder.co.uk

Loch Ness English
Inchnacardoch,
Fort Augustus PH32 4BN
Tel: 01320 366376   Fax: 01320 366376
Email: info@lochnessenglish.com
http://www.lochnessenglish.com

Lochcarron School of English
Pathend, Main Street Lochcarron
Srathcarron IV54 8YB
Tel: 01520 722733   Fax: 01520 722733
Email: LochcarronSchool@aol.com
http://www.speakingenglish.co.uk

Mackintosh School of English Language
2 / 71 St Vincent Crescent,
Glasgow G3 8NQ
Tel: 0141 248 3026   Fax: 0141 248 3026
Email: enquiries@the-mackintosh-school.co.uk
http://www.the-mackintosh-school.co.uk

Randolph School of English
63 Frederick St.,
Edinburgh EH2 1LH
Tel: 0131 226 5004   Fax: 0131 226 5003
Email: randolphSE@aol.com
http://members.aol.com/randolphse

Regent Edinburgh
29 Chester St.,
Edinburgh EH3 7EN
Tel: 0131 225 9888   Fax: 0131 225 2133
Email: edinburgh@regent.org.uk
http://www.regent.org.uk

Scot-Ed Courses
6 Blinkbonny Gardens,
Edinburgh EH4 3HG
Tel: 0131 332 1060   Fax: 0131 623 2154
Email: scot-ed@blueyonder.co.uk
http://www.go-ed.com/scot-ed

St. Andrew's International School of English
30 Buchanan Gardens, St Andrews
Fife KY16 9LU
Tel: 01334 473625

Wallace College
12 George IV Bridge,
Edinburgh EH1 1EE
Tel: 0131 220 3634   Fax: 0131 220 3633
Email: wallacecollege@btinternet.com
http://www.wallacecollege.co.uk
See display for further details

THE WALLACE COLLEGE
Edinburgh's City Centre
Language School.
Friendly welcoming staff.
Small classes.
An English course to suit your needs.
Courses start weekly.
Accommodation arranged with a
selected host family or in a guest house.

12 George IV Bridge
Edinburgh EH1 1EE

Tel: +44 (0) 131 220 3634
Fax: +44 (0) 131 220 3633
Email: wallacecollege@btinternet.com
http://www.wallacecollege.btinternet.co.uk

STATE COLLEGES / UNIVERSITIES

Aberdeen College
Gallowgate Centre, Gallowgate
Aberdeen AB25 1BN
Tel: 01224 612000   Fax: 01224 612001
Email: enquiry@abcol.ac.uk
http://www.abcol.ac.uk

Anniesland College
19 Hatfield Drive,
Glasgow G12 0YE
Tel: 0141 357 6082   Fax: 0141 357 6063
Email: internationaloffice@anniesland.ac.uk
http://www.anniesland.ac.uk

Ayr College
Dam Park,
Ayr KA8 0EU
Tel: 01292 265184   Fax: 01292 263889
Email: webmaster@ayrcoll.ac.uk
http://www.ayrcoll.ac.uk

Cardonald College
690 Mosspark Drive,
Glasgow G52 3AY
Tel: 0141 272 3333   Fax: 0141 272 3444
Email: iross@cardonald.ac.uk
http://www.cardonald.ac.uk

Dundee College
Melrose Terrace,
Dundee DD3 7QX
Tel: 01382 834898   Fax: 01382 458153
Email: dci@dundeecoll.ac.uk
http://www.dundeecoll.ac.uk

Edinburgh's Telford College
ESOL - Languages dept., Crewe Toll
Edinburgh EH4 2NZ
Tel: 0131 332 2491   Fax: 0131 343 1218
http://www.ed-coll.ac.uk

Heriot-Watt University
Riccarton,
Edinburgh EH14 4AS
Tel: 0131 451 4201   Fax: 0131 451 3079
Email: O.Alexander@hw.ac.uk
http://www.hw.ac.uk/langWWW/english
See display for further details

Heriot-Watt University
Edinburgh
School of Languages

▶ English for: Study - Business - Science and Engineering - Interpreting and Technical Translation. Introduction to TEFL.

▶ The School of Languages at Heriot-Watt University, Edinburgh offers English courses year round in support of the university's core disciplines of languages, business studies, science and technology.

▶ Consultancy services available to individuals and companies requiring tailor-made courses, either in-house or on our parkland campus.

▶ 13 kilometres from the centre of Edinburgh.

Riccarton, Edinburgh EH14 4AS UK
Tel: 0131 451 8189
Fax: 0131 451 3079
Email: O.Alexander@hw.ac.uk
Web: http://www.hw.ac.uk/langWWW/english

Inverness College
School of Social Sciences & Languages,
Longman Road South
Inverness IV1 1SA
Tel: 01463 256046   Fax: 01463 220079
Email: PdeLima/IC@fc.uhi.ac.uk
http://www.uhi.ac.uk/inverness

Kilmarnock College
Holehouse Road,
Kilmarnock KA3 7AT
Tel: 01563 23501

Langside College
50 Prospecthill Road,
Glasgow G42 9LB
Tel: 0141 649 4991   Fax: 0141 632 5252
Email: jboyle@perseus.langside.ac.uk
http://www.langside.ac.uk

Lauder College, Dunfermline
Halbeath, Dunfermline
Fife KY11 5DY
Tel: 01383 726201   Fax: 01383 621449

Moray House English Language Centre
University of Edinburgh, 37 Holyrood Road
Edinburgh EH8 8AQ
Tel: 0131 558 6332   Fax: 0131 557 5138
Email: elc@mhie.ac.uk
http://www.education.ed.ac.uk/

Motherwell College
Dalzell Drive,
Motherwell ML1 2DD
Tel: 01698 232323   Fax: 01698 275430

Perth College
Crieff Road,
Perth PH1 2NX
Tel: 01738 877000   Fax: 01738 877016
Email: english@perth.ac.uk
http://www.perth.ac.uk

Queen Margaret University College
Clerwood Terrace,
Edinburgh EH12 8TS
Tel: 0131 317 3292   Fax: 0131 317 3292
Email: sbannerman@qmuc.ac.uk
http://elu.qmuc.ac.uk

Stevenson College
Bankhead Avenue, Sighthill
Edinburgh EN11 4DE
Tel: 0131 535 4700   Fax: 0131 535 4708
Email: info@stevenson.ac.uk
http://www.stevenson.ac.uk/sections/elt/
index.htm

University of Aberdeen
Regent Walk,
Aberdeen AB24 3FY
Tel: 01224 272536   Fax: 01224 276730
Email: langcen@abdn.ac.uk
http://www.abdn.ac.uk/langcentre

University of Dundee
Caird House,
Dundee DD1 4HN
Tel: 01382 344532   Fax: 01382 227858
Email: info@cals.dundee.ac.uk
http://www.dundee.ac.uk/languagestudies/
esp2.htm

University of Edinburgh
Institute of Applied Language Studies,
21 Hill Place
Edinburgh EH8 9DP
Tel: 0131 650 6200   Fax: 0131 667 5927
Email: ials.enquiries@ed.ac.uk
http://www.ials.ed.ac.uk

University of Glasgow
EFL Unit, Hetherington Buildings Bute
Gardens
Glasgow G12 8RS
Tel: 0141 330 4220   Fax: 0141 330 3381
Email: enquiries@efl.arts.gla.ac.uk
http://www.efl.arts.gla.ac.uk

University of St. Andrews
ELT Ctre, Butts Wynd
St. Andrews KY16 9AL
Tel: 01334 462258   Fax: 01334 462270
Email: afa@st-and.ac.uk
http://www.st-and.ac.uk/services/elt/
home.html

University of Stirling
Centre for English Language Teaching,
Stirling FK9 4LA
Tel: 01786 467934   Fax: 01786 466131
Email: celt@stir.ac.uk
http://www.celt.stir.ac.uk

University of Strathclyde
English Language Teaching Division,
Jordanhill Campus, Southbrae Drive
Glasgow G13 1PP
Tel: 0141 950 3620   Fax: 0141 950 3268

University of Strathclyde
English Language Teaching Division, 26
Richmond St.
Glasgow G1 1XH
Tel: 0141 548 3065   Fax: 0141 553 4122
Email: eltd.les@strath.ac.uk
http://www.strath.ac.uk/Departments/ELTD/
inex.html

Institution Name	Availability	Junior Ages	Specials	Price /week	Status
Aberdeen Centre for English	A: 1-12		B, E	£95-£180	
Aberdeen College	A: 9-7		E	£50-£100	GBC, Baselt
Anniesland College	A: 8-6			£20-£105	GBC
Aspect ILA Edinburgh	A: 1-12		B	£123-£161+	
Ayr College	A: 8-6			£9	
Basil Paterson Edinburgh	A: 1-12		B, T, F, E	£74-£1000	GBC, Arels
Berlitz Language Centre	A: 1-12			On application	
Cardonald College	A: 1-12			On application	GBC, Baselt
Carrick Language Courses	A: 7-8 J: 7-8	10-17 yrs	B, H, T, F, C	£148-£419	
Churchill House English Home Tuition Courses	A: 1-12 J: 1-12 (1-1 only)	7 yrs +	B, T, F, H, C, E	£450-£780**	
Communicaid English	A: 1-12		B, T, F, H, C, E	£845-£1845	
Dundee College	A: 1-11 J: 7	10-15 yrs		£25-£150	GBC, Baselt
ECS Scotland	A: 1-12		B, F, H, E	£110-£700	GBC
Edinburgh School of English	A: 1-12 J: 4, 6-8	9-17 yrs	B, T, E	£160-£552	GBC, Arels
English Language Institute	A: 1-12		B, T, F, H, C, E	£145	
English Tutorials in Edinburgh	A: 1-12 (1-1 to 3-1 only)		B, T, F, H, C, E	£140-£700	
English-in-Scotland				On application	
Glasgow International English & Business School	A: 1-12		B, E	£45-£55	
Hamilton School of English	J: 7-8	12-18 yrs		£220-£275**	GBC, Arels
Heriot-Watt University	A: 1-12		E	£170-£380	
Highland Language Centre	A: 1-12 (1-1 only)		B, T, F	£1390-£1795**	
InTuition Languages	A: 1-12 J: 1-12 (1-1 only)	14-18 yrs	B, T, F, C, E	£555-£1040**	GBC, Arels
Inverness College	A: 9-6			£6-£25	

Institution Name	Availability	Junior Ages	Specials	Price /week	Status
K.I.L.T.	A: 3-4, 7-10		T	£250-£500	
Langside College	A: 1-12		B	On application	
LinguaScot	A: 3-9 (mostly 1-1)			£425-£475**	
Loch Ness English	A: 1-12		B, T, F, H, C, E	£236-£480	JAOLS
Lochcarron School of English	A: 1-12		B, T, F, H, C, E	£150-£600	
Moray House English Language Centre	A: 1-12 J: 1-12			On application	
Motherwell College	A: 1-12 J: 6-8			On application	
Perth College	A: 1-12			£107-£175**	GBC, Baselt
Queen Margaret University College	A: 2-12		B, T, F, H, C, E	£145-£175	
Randolph School of English	A: 7-9		B	£145-£240	
Regent Edinburgh	A: 1-12		B, T, F, C, E	£105-£265	GBC, Arels
Scot-Ed Courses	J: 7-8	12-19 yrs		£260-£280**	GBC, Arels
Stevenson College	A: 1-12		B, E	£260/7wks (EU) £840/7wks (non EU)	GBC, Baselt
The Mackintosh School of English Language	A: 1-12		B, T, F, E	£160-£630	
University of Aberdeen	A: 8-9		E	£130	
University of Dundee	A: 1-12		B, E	£165-£196	GBC, Baselt
University of Edinburgh	A: 1-12 J: 7-8	16-18 yrs	B, E	£135-£340	GBC, Baselt
University of Glasgow	A: 1-12			On application	Balcapp
University of St. Andrews	A: 1-12 J: 7			On application	Balcapp
University of Stirling	A: 1-12		B, E	£160	
University of Strathclyde	A: 1-12		B, E	£150-£250	Balcapp
Wallace College	A: 1-12 J 4, 6-9	9-16 yrs	B	£125-£146	

EFL CORRESPONDENCE COURSES

Learning English at home is a good way of building your confidence before coming to Britain, or of maintaining your skills after your visit.

The following pages contain comprehensive details of some of the correspondence courses on offer, all of which are accredited by the Open & Distance Learning Quality Council. Write directly to the institution of your choice for a brochure and further details.

Etudes à la maison et cours par correspondance: Apprendre l'anglais chez soi est un bon moyen de consolider sa confiance avant de partir ou bien de maintenir son niveau après le retour. Pour plus amples détails de ces cours, s'addresser directement à l'organisation choisie.

Heim- und Fernkurse: Englisch zu Hause zu lernen ist eine gute Sache, um zuerst Vertrauen zur Sprache zu bekommen, bevor Sie nach England reisen, oder um erlernte Kenntnisse zuhause zu vertiefen. Um weitere Informationen zu den einzelnen Kursen zu bekommen, schreiben Sie direkt an das Institut Ihrer Wahl.

Cursos por correspondencia: Aprender inglés en su casa es un buen medio para adquirir mas confianza en sí mismo antes de visitar Inglaterra; también es muy cómodo para mantener su conocimiento después de terminada la visita. Para más detalles se puede escribir directamente a la organización escogida por Vd.

Corsi per corrispondenza: Studiare l'inglese a casa propria è un buon modo per acquistare confidenza con la lingua prima di intraprendere un viaggio di studio in Gran Bretagna ed è inoltre utile per mantenere il livello raggiunto. Per ulteriori informazioni sui corsi elencati, vi preghiamo di scrivere direttamente all' organizzazione di vostra scelta.

BUSINESS TRAINING LTD
Sevendale House, 7 Dale Street. Manchester M1 1JB
Tel: 0161 228 6735/6   Fax: 0161 236 9440
E-Mail: studentservices@buinesstraining.co.uk
Web: http://www.buinesstraining.co.uk

○   **Business English Course - With Spoken English**

Course designed for non-native speakers. Consists of 7 sections:

Grammar Made Easy - Grammar Completed - Writing Business Letters - Business Writing & Punctuation - Correct Expression, Word Formation & Specialist Letters - Comprehension & Report Writing - Summaries, Business Meetings.

Students are supplied with books and 3 x C60 cassettes, plus tutorial support. Course should take approximately 9 to 12 months to complete. Leads to Business Training's Diploma in Business English. PRICE: £154 (can be paid in instalments).

○   **English For Secretaries Diploma Course -**
     Including Spoken English

Course designed for non-native speakers. Consists of 6 sections (based on the Business English Course):

Grammar Made Easy - Grammar Completed, Business Letters & Letter Layout - Letters Continued, Punctuation - Vocabulary, Spelling, Other Written Communications & Specimen Letters for Secretaries - Comprehension & Summary - Reports for Secretaries, Meetings, Agenda & Minute Writing.

Students are supplied with books and 3 x C60 cassettes, plus tutorial support. Course should take approximately 7 to 10 months to complete. Leads to Business Training's English for Secretaries Diploma.   PRICE: £154 (can be paid in instalments).

○   **The Art of Spoken English - With Personal Tuition**

Course designed for students who need to improve their pronunciation and conversational abilities.

Tape cassettes provide 212 pronunciation/ conversation exercises and 39 conversations.
Topics covered include: stress and rhythm exercises, role-playing, common idioms and expressions, business discussions, English for travel, shopping etc.

Students are supplied with four cassettes and study booklets, with 255 minutes of playback time. Two progress assignments are completed on blank tapes which are assessed by your tutor. Course takes approximately 4 months to complete. Certificate is awarded on successful completion of course. PRICE: £110 (can be paid in instalments).

○ **Advanced Business English Diploma Course**

Course designed for students who already have a reasonable command of English. Consists of 10 sections:

Introduction to the course - Writing Style & Techniques I - Writing Style & Techniques II - How to Write Effective Letters - Writing Sales Letters & Direct Mail - Writing Notes & Memos - Report Writing - Presenting Visual Information - Curriculum Vitae (CV), Testimonials & References - Writing Newsletters, Articles & Press Releases.

Students are supplied with books and tutorial support. Course should take approximately 6 months to complete. Leads to Business Training's Diploma in Advanced Business English. PRICE: £154 (can be paid in instalments).

○ **Professional Business Writing**

Course designed for students who already have a reasonable command of English. Consists of 12 sections:

Introduction - Writing Style & Techniques I - Writing Style & Techniques II - How to Write Effective Letters - Writing Sales & Direct Mail - Writing Notices & Memos - How to Make Notes & Summarise Information - Report Writing Techniques - Presenting Visual Information - Preparing Agendas & the Minutes of Meetings - Filling a Job Vacancy - Writing Newsletters.

Students are supplied with books and tutorial support. Course should take 12 months to complete. PRICE: £154 (can be paid in instalments).

CAMBRIDGE INTERNATIONAL COLLEGE
College House, Leoville, St. Ouen, PO Box 530, Jersey JE3 2DB
Tel: 01534 485052   Fax: 01534 485071
E-Mail: learn@cambridgetraining.com
Web: http://www.cambridgetraining.com

A Diploma from the college is issued on satisfactory completion of courses. Prices shown include tutorial support.

PRICES: £130 / $210 / €210 per course.

○ **Primary English**

Aimed at students with only a very basic level of English, this course is better if the student has some help from an English speaking friend or relative. The course material is available in a range of languages.

Contents include:
The English alphabet, how to form simple sentences, questions and commands. Introduction to nouns, verbs, adjectives and adverbs. English Pronunciation (includes cassette).

○ **Secondary English**

Aimed at students who are already proficient in basic English.

Contents include:
English letters and words, how to use an English-English dictionnary (supplied as part of course), writing and comprehension, letter writing.

○ **Professional English - for everyday and business use**

Contents include:
English words; punctuation, sentences and their essential parts; nouns, pronouns and adjectives; verbs and adverbs; idiomatic expressions and proverbs; introduction to letter writing; business letters.

○ **Business English and Letter Writing**

Aimed at managers and business people who want to master the art of writing effective business letters.

Contents include:
General features of a business letter; enquiries, estimates, orders and trade references; letters seeking employment; correspondence between employees; sales letters; letters concerning accounting matters.

CHELTENHAM TUTORIAL COLLEGE
292 High Street, Cheltenham GL50 3HQ
Tel: 01242 241279   Fax: 01242 234256
E-mail: info@cheltenhamlearning.co.uk
Web: http://www.cheltenhamlearning.co.uk

O   Business English 1

Topics include:
- Making and answering enquiries
- confirming information
- business letters and memos
- reports
- telecommunications and electronic mail.

Qualifications: Prepares students for LCCI English for Business (first level); LCCI English for Commerce (first level); Pitman English for Business Communications (elementary); Pitman English for Office Skills (elementary); RSA Communications in Business (stage 1).

PRICE: In the UK: £145 (with tuition) £85 (without tuition)
        Overseas: £170 (with tuition) £100 (without tuition)

O   Business English 2

For the more experienced user of English in a business environment. It offers full guidance and practice on correspondence, report writing, summaries and comprehension and examines in detail the processes of communication in business organisations.

Qualifications: Prepares students for LCCI English for Business (second level); LCCI English for Commerce (second level); LCCI Secretarial Studies Certificate - Use of English paper; Pitman English for Business Communications (Intermediate); Pitman English for Office Skills (Intermediate); RSA Communications in Business (stage 2).

PRICE: In the UK: £145 (with tuition) £85 (without tuition)
         Overseas: £170 (with tuition) £100 (without tuition)

O   Business English 3

Suitable for able and experienced communicators wishing to extend and polish their skills. It deals with reports, minutes of meetings, summary writing and expansion, essays and business letters. Comprehensive advice on grammar, punctuation, spelling and choice of words is also provided.

Qualifications: Prepares students for LCCI English for Business (third level); LCCI English for Commerce (third level); LCCI Private Secretary's Certificate - Communication paper; Pitman English for Business Communications (advanced); RSA Communications in Business (stage 3).

PRICE: In the UK: £145 (with tuition) £85 (without tuition)
         Overseas: £170 (with tuition) £100 (without tuition)

○ Effective Business Communication

Course for supervisors and managers, its aim is to improve workplace communication skills. The course covers the underlying theory and the practicalities of written, spoken and visual communication and pays particular attention to important business situations, such as interviews and meetings. The courses includes examples and case studies, plus guidance on common problems of grammar, spelling, punctuation and vocabulary. The role of information technology in business communication is also covered at length.

PRICE: In the UK: £145. Overseas: £170

The Cheltenham Tutorial College also offers a wide range of other courses, including marketing, computing, accounting, 'A' level English Language & Literature and an MBA in conjunction with Leicester University.

THE LONDON SCHOOL OF JOURNALISM
22, Upbrook Mews, London W2 3HG
Tel: 020 7706 3790 Fax: 020 7706 3870
E-Mail: Enquiry@lsjournalism.com
Web: http://www.lsjournalism.com

All prices include tutorial support. Upon successful completion of courses a certificate is issued.

○ Improve Your English

Topics covered include:

General points of style - Sentence structure - Nouns & pronouns - Using adjectives - Verbs & adverbs - Prepositions & conjunctions - Punctuation - Final briefing

The course consists of eight modules, each with its own grammatical exercises and essay questions on related topics. The duration of the course is 4 to 9 months, during which time students will be set 23 assignments.

PRICE: £215 (UK) £230 (outside UK) £210 for Online Tuition

○ English For Business

Topics covered include:

Writing for business - Developing a good style - Communicating - Layouts & letters - Factual presentation - Writing summaries - Using statistics -

Writing reports - Advertising & promotions - Sources of information - Interviews & CVs

The course consists of 11 modules, with over 40 assignments during a 9 to 12 month period.

PRICE: £295 (UK) £325 (outside UK)   £285 for Online Tuition

Other courses offered by the London School of Journalism include: Enjoying English Literature, An Appreciation of English Poetry, Understanding English History, Journalism and News-writing.

MERCERS COLLEGE
Ware, Hertfordshire. SG12 9DZ
Tel: 01920 465926 Fax: 01920 484909

Mercers College helps students to prepare for the following University of Cambridge Examinations:

- **Preliminary English Test (PET)**
- **First Certificate in English (FCE)**
- **Certificate in Advanced English (CAE)**
- **Certificate of Proficiency in English (CPE)**

Candidates should contact a local registered examination centre before enrolling with the college. These are normally institutions such as an International School, British Council premises or private educational establishments.

PRICES: PET: £185, FCE: £200, CAE: £245, CPE: £275

The above prices include tuition, textbooks and postage and packing costs. The FCE course includes two cassettes to prepare candidates for the listening comprehension.

Candidates taking the CPE can also have tuition for the optional additional paper in English Literature, which involves studying 3 texts. This option costs an extra £55.

NATIONAL EXTENSION COLLEGE
The Michael Young Centre, Purbeck Road, Cambridge. CB2 2HN
Tel: 01223 400200   Fax: 01223 400325
E-Mail: info@nec.ac.uk   Web: http://www.nec.ac.uk

Note: All National Extension College home study courses include tutorial support, and students have up to two years from the date of enrolment to complete their course assignments.

Price of all courses: £115 in the UK (Add £30 for EU residents, or £45 for all other countries.) Enrol on two back to basics courses for £195, three for £275 or all four for £350.

○ Back to Basics

Course designed for those who lack confidence in reading or writing.

Back to Basics - Grammar
A full introduction to the rules of grammar and how to use them. The topics include being exact, choosing the right word and being consistent.
Consists of personal tuition, with 5 marked assignments.

Back to Basics - Spelling
Designed to improve your spelling skills, the course covers a wide range of topics, including silent letters, root words and confusing letters.
Consists of personal tuition, with 5 marked assignments.

Back to Basics - Punctuation
A practical guide to punctuation, this course covers topics such as sentences, commas, paragraphs and dialogue.
Consists of personal tuition, with 5 marked assignments.

Back to Basics - Reading
Develops a range of reading skills, including comprehension, critical reading and using reference books.

Consists of personal tuition, with 5 marked assignments.

The National Extension College also provides tuition for the following exams from the Institute of Linguists:

- Diploma in Translation (post-graduate level qualification entitling holder to use the designation 'Dip.TransIoL')

- Diploma in English (degree equivalent)

- ELIC Programme: Intermediate Diploma, Diploma in Languages for International Communication (degree equivalent).

The Diplomas in Translation, English and Languages for International Communication enable successful candidates to apply for Membership of the Institute (MIL). For further details contact the Institute of Linguists (address supplied in chapter on exams).

EFL EXAMINATIONS

English language exams not only enable you to provide evidence of your abilities, but also present a useful goal for you to achieve during your stay, providing an incitement to learn.

Below, you will find most of the major exams open to foreign students. They are divided into the examination boards, and the level of English required is in ascending order (i.e. the easier exams are listed at the beginning and the harder ones at the end of each section.)

Further details can be obtained directly from the exam boards, the addresses of which are given at the end of this chapter. Once you have decided on the type of exam that is best suited to your requirements (i.e. on your level of English, amount of time you will study for the exam, any preferences made by your employers/ educational establishment) you should check to see a) if your language school offers preparation for the exams b) when you will be able to sit the exam.

Most schools would also be able to offer you help and guidance if you are unsure.

Etudier pour un examen non seulement donne des qualifications mais aussi un but pour un séjour linguistique. Ci-dessous, liste d'examens avec détails de niveaux de compétence contrôlés.

Eine Prüfung am Ende des Kurses bescheinigt die erreichte Qualifikation und sorgt für Motivation während des Kurses. Untenstehend sind die wichtigsten Prüfungen und ihre Inhalte aufgeführt.

Estudiar para un examen otorga una calificación de provecho y también un objetivo al final del curso. Más abajo hay una lista de exámenes y diferentes niveles.

La preparazione ad un esame non solo offre l'opportunità di ottenere un utile certificato, ma rappresenta anche una motivazione in più allo studio della lingua. Qui sotto troverete un elenco dei principali esami offerti, con dettagli sui programmi di ciascuno di essi.

QUICK REFERENCE CHART

For examination dates, see the following page.

Key to Symbols Used:

= Reading = Writing = Listening = Speaking

Type of Exam			
LONDON CHAMBER OF COMMERCE (LCCIEB) *(all the exams are work related)*				
Practical Business English: Preliminary	✓	✓		
English For Business:				
First Level	✓	✓		
Second Level	✓	✓		(✓)
Third Level	✓	✓		(✓)
Forth Level	✓	✓		(✓)
English For Commerce:				
First Level	✓	✓		
Second Level	✓	✓		(✓)
Third Level	✓	✓		(✓)
Spoken English For Industry and Commerce:				
Preliminary			✓	✓
First Level	✓		✓	✓
Third Level	✓		✓	✓
Forth Level	✓		✓	✓
Written English for Tourism Industry:				
First Level	✓	✓		
Second Level	✓	✓		
PITMAN QUALIFICATIONS English for Speakers of Other Languages:				
Basic	✓	✓	✓	
Elementary	✓	✓	✓	
Intermediate	✓	✓	✓	
Higher Intermediate	✓	✓	✓	
Advanced	✓	✓	✓	

Type of Exam	📖	✏️	👂	💬
Pitman cont.				
Spoken English for Speakers of Other Languages:				
Basic				✓
Elementary				✓
Intermediate				✓
Higher Intermediate				✓
Advanced		✓		
English for Business Communications:				
Level One	✓	✓		
Level Two	✓	✓		
Level Three	✓	✓		
English for Office Skills:				
Level One	✓	✓	✓	
Level Two	✓	✓	✓	
Communication in Technical English: Advanced	✓	✓		
UNIVERSITY OF CAMBRIDGE (UCLES)				
Key English Test	✓	✓	✓	✓
Preliminary English Test	✓	✓	✓	✓
Business English Certificates Preliminary	✓	✓	✓	✓
Certificates in Communicative Skills I	✓	✓	✓	✓
First Certificate in English	✓	✓	✓	✓
Business English Certificates Vantage	✓	✓	✓	✓
Certificates in Communicative Skills II	✓	✓	✓	✓
Certificate in Advanced English	✓	✓	✓	✓
Business English Certificates Higher	✓	✓	✓	✓
Certificates in Communicative Skills III	✓	✓	✓	✓
Certificate of Proficiency in English	✓	✓	✓	✓
Certificates in Communicative Skills IV	✓	✓	✓	✓
UNIVERSITY OF OXFORD (UODLE)				
Arels Spoken English				
Preliminary Level			✓	✓
Higher Level			✓	✓
Diploma			✓	✓
Oxford Written Exams				
Preliminary Level	✓	✓		
Higher Level	✓	✓		

EXAMINATION DATES

London Chamber of Commerce and Industry (LCCIEB)

Practical Business English: Preliminary. *Available on demand throughout the year.*
English for Business: Levels 1 to 3. *Available in March, May, June/ July and November/December.*
English for Commerce: Levels 1 to 3. *Available in March (except level 3), April/May, June/July and November/December. Also available on demand throughout the year.*
Spoken English for Industry and Commerce: Levels 1 to 4. *Available on demand, if one month's notice is given.*
Spoken English For the Tourism Industry: Intermediate. *Available on demand, if one month's notice is given.*
Written English for the Tourism Industry: Levels 1 & 2. *Available in March, April/May, June and November. Also available on demand throughout the year.*

Pitman Qualifications

Dates for all Pitman exams are set by the individual examination centres, of which there are 5000+ around the world.

University of Cambridge (UCLES)

Key Stage and Preliminary English Tests 6 dates in the year, normally March, May, twice in June, November and December.
First Certificate in English, Certificate in Advanced English and Certificate in Proficiency in English Available in June and December.
Certificates in Communicative Skills: Levels 1 to 4. Available in May/June and November/December.
Business English Certificates: March, May, June, July, November/ December

University of Oxford (UODLE)

Spoken English: Levels 1 to 3, Written Exams: Preliminary & Higher Level. Available in May and November.

OTHER EXAMINATIONS

ASSESSMENT AND QUALIFICATIONS ALLIANCE (AQA)

The AQA offers the following qualifications: Junior English Tests "JET" - Levels 1-4 (level 1 for 7/8 yrs, 2 for 9/10 yrs, 3 for 11/12 yrs for 12/13yrs). Senior English Tests "SET" - Levels 1-2 (level 1 for 14/15 yrs and 2 for 15/ 16 yrs). Exams can be taken at registered AQA centres in the UK.

CENTRA

Test in English Language Skills, at basic and intermediate levels. The exam assesses the candidate's ability to use the type of factual English needed for work, as opposed to social English. All four language skills are tested. Exams take place mid-May to mid-June at registered centres.

ENGLISH SPEAKING BOARD

Oral assessments in English as an Acquired Language (EAL) for all ages and professions.
Levels covered in the main EAL syllabus range from Pre-Foundation, through Intermediate to Advanced, with three stages in each range.
A Higher Certificate in EAL and a Certificate in Professional Skills for Language School Teachers (International) are also available, together with the Diploma in EAL which entitles holders to use the initials Dip.ESB (EAL).

ESB's EAL examinations can be taken in a range of centres in the UK and overseas. Contact the ESB for more details.

GENERAL MEDICAL COUNCIL (GMC)

Overseas doctors wishing to work in the UK have to sit the Professional and Linguistic Assessments Board (PLAB) test, which assesses candidates' communication skills in clinical situations. Before taking the PLAB, candidates must first achieve a minimum overall band score of 7.0 in the IELTS test, with a minimum score of 6.0 in each on the four individual sections. (See below for further details of IELTS.)   The PLAB test is divided into two separate parts :

1) Multiple choice questions, Clinical problem solving & Photographic material examinations.

2) Objective Structured Clinical and Oral Examinations (OSCOE), designed to test the candidate's ability to communicate with patients, medical colleagues, etc. For further information contact the GMC (address given at end of this chapter).

INSTITUTE OF LINGUISTS

Diploma in Public Service Interpreting *(held every June)*
Diploma in Translation *(held every November - post-grad. level qualification)*

Diploma in English for International Communication *(held every May - degree level qualification)*

Successful diploma candidates can apply for Membership of the Institute - MIL

LONDON CHAMBER OF COMMERCE AND INDUSTRY EXAMINATIONS BOARD (LCCIEB)

As shown in the chart plus:

Communication - Use of English (Private Secretary's Certificate, Second Certificate for Legal Secretaries, Second Certificate in Office Technology). *Post 'A'-level qualification, which demonstrates the candidate's ability to operate in a middle to senior management environment.*

Communication - Use of English (Private and Executive Secretary's Diploma). *Postgraduate level qualification for those working at senior secretarial / administrative level.*

English Language Skills Assessment - ELSA
Multiple-choice proficiency test developed to evaluate the overall English language skills of a candidate. Covers reading, writing, listening and speaking (each may be separately tested and scored). Scores are accompanied by an explanation which predicts performance in a business context.

LONDON EXAMINATIONS – EDEXCEL INTERNATIONAL

Communicative language tests Six progressive levels.
Part of the European Certificate project.

TOEIC - Test of English for International Communication

Used by multi-national corporations, often in the Far East, to assess English communication skills. The exam consists of a multiple choice, covering listening comprehension and reading. TOEIC uses North American English.

TRINITY COLLEGE LONDON

Trinity administers the only full range of entirely oral examinations for learners of English. This 12 level, 1-to-1 assessment scheme is available in over 50 countries, for all age groups.

UNIVERSITY OF CAMBRIDGE LOCAL EXAMINATIONS SYNDICATE

As shown in the chart plus:

Cambridge Young Learners Tests
This series comprises three levels of assessment (Starters, Mover and

Flyers) from Beginner to Waystage level, and is designed for learners aged 7 to 11 years.

Cambridge Examination in English for Language Teachers (CEELT) Levels I and II.

Exam for teachers whose first language is not English, available at two levels. All four language skills are tested (reading, writing, listening & speaking). Candidates sit three papers (oral, listening & reading/writing). Includes a video based oral test.

Also from UCLES:

Business Language Testing Service (BULATS)

Assessment service specifically for the use of companies and organisations which need a reliable way of assessing the language ability of employees or trainees. Includes tests in a number of European languages. Institutions wishing to use the service must contact their local BULATS agent. Contact UCLES for more details.

CommuniCAT

Computer based language testing system, aimed at schools and universities. Assesses a student's language ability to help in placements, progress reports etc.. Suitable for all levels, from beginners to advanced.

LEVEL OF ENGLISH REQUIRED TO STUDY AT A BRITISH UNIVERSITY/ INSTITUTE OF HIGHER EDUCATION

Students wishing to undertake graduate or postgraduate studies at a British university, will need to prove that their English is of a high enough level to be able to complete the course. The level of English required varies from one university to another, and also depends on the subject to be studied (for example, a maths course will not entail the same linguistic requirements as a literary course.) The following exams are the most widely accepted as proof of a student's language skills. However, it is vital to check with your chosen university/ institute of higher education to ensure you meet the correct entry criteria.

Niveau d'anglais requis pour étudier dans une université britannique: *Les examens ci-dessous sont acceptés par la plupart des universités. Cependant vous devriez vérifier les criters exacts de l'université de votre choix.*

Die erforderlichen Englischkenntnisse, um an einer englischen Universität zu studieren: Die folgenden Prüfungen sind an den meisten Universitäten anerkannt. Dennoch sollten Sie mit jeder einzelnen Universität abklären, was ihre Zulassungskriterien sind.

Nivel de inglés necesario para estudiar en una universidad británica. Los exámenes nombrados más adelante son aceptados en la mayoría de las universidades, pero es importante verificar con cada una de ellas acerca de los criterios de matrícula.

Livello di conoscenza dell' inglese richiesto per accedere ad una università britannica: I seguenti esami vengono riconosciuti dalla maggior parte delle università, tuttavia vi consigliamo di verificare con ognuna di esse quali siano i loro criteri d'ammissione.

■ **Certificate of Attainment in English (Levels 4 to 6)** - (EDEXCEL)

Skills tested: Reading, Writing, Listening and Speaking (optional).

■ **First Certificate in English** - (UCLES)

Skills tested: Reading, Writing, Listening and Speaking. Candidates must sit five papers. Required results: Grade A

■ **Certificate in Advanced English** - (UCLES)

Skills tested: Reading, Writing, Listening and Speaking. Candidates must sit five papers. Required results: Pass

■ **Certificate of Proficiency in English -** (UCLES)

Skills tested: Reading, Writing, Listening and Speaking. Candidates must sit five papers. Required results: Pass

■ **English for Speakers of Other Languages** (Pitman Qualifications)

Higher Intermediate or Advanced Certificates. Skills tested: Reading, Writing & Listening. Required results: Pass

■ **English for Business** - (LCCIEB)

Level 3 Candidates must take the optional oral component, in addition to the standard written papers.

■ **Higher Level Certificate -** (ARELS and UODLE)

Both certificates are needed (one from ARELS and one from UODLE) in order to test all four language skills. Required results: Pass in the ARELS higher certificate and pass/ credit in the Oxford higher certificate.

■   **International English Language Testing System (IELTS)** -
(British Council/ UCLES/ International Development Program of Australian Universities and Colleges.)

Exam specifically aimed at those wanting to study or train in the medium of English. All four language skills (reading, writing, speaking, listening) are tested. Results are given in the form of a nine-band scale, with 9 indicating the highest level of achievement.

The test can be taken both in the UK and world-wide, available according to demand. Required results: Most common requirement is 6.0 or 6.5. However, level depends on the institution in which you wish to study and the type of course you will be taking.

■   **University Entrance Test for Speakers of Other Languages (UETESOL)** - (Assessment and Qualifications Alliance - AQA)

The exam tests skills in a context as close as possible to that likely to be encountered in an undergraduate course. It is particularly suitable for candidates who wish to undertake studies in the areas of science, engineering, business studies or social sciences. It is not appropriate for those who wish to pursue literary studies.

Five skills areas are assessed: writing, editing, reading, listening and speaking. Exam consists of a written paper of 2 ¾ hours (covering writing, editing & reading skills), a listening comprehension of approx. 45 mins and an oral test of approx. 10 mins. Required Overall Result: Pass (equivalent to a minimum score of B,B,B,C,C in all sections)
NB: The test will not be available after June 2002.

■   **Test in English for Educational Purposes (TEEP)** -
(University of Reading, Testing and Evaluation Unit)

For undergraduate or postgraduate students wishing to study at a UK university. It tests English language proficiency in reading academic texts, listening to lectures and writing on academic topics. Skills tested: Reading, Writing, Listening and spoken English if requested.   The test lasts 2 hours (excluding the speaking section). It is available on the first Wednesday of every term at Reading University or at other times on payment of a surcharge.

Plus:

For students wishing to study at an American College or University, a **TOEFL** (Test of English as a Foreign Language) score of 550 is widely accepted. This test uses North American English and is computer-based.   Many UK universities will accept a TOEFL score of 580-600, plus proof of spoken and written skills.   The test costs US $110 and can be taken at centres around the world. For more details, see the TOEFL website:
http://www.toefl.org

CONTACT ADDRESSES OF EXAM BOARDS:

THE ASSESSMENT AND QUALIFICATIONS ALLIANCE
Stag Hill House, Guildford Surrey, GU2 7XJ
Tel: 01483 506506 Fax: 01483 300152
E-Mail jetset@aqa.org.uk *(for JET and SET)*

also

Devas Street, Manchester M15 6EX
Tel: 0161 953 1180 Fax: 0161 273 7572
Web site http://www.aqa.org.uk/ *(for UETESOL)*

CENTRA
Examinations and Assessments Services
Duxbury Park, Duxbury Hall Road, Chorley, Lancashire PR7 4AT
Tel: 01257 241428 Fax: 01257 260357

ENGLISH SPEAKING BOARD (International) Ltd.
26a Princes Street, Southport, Merseyside. PR8 1EQ
Tel: 01704 501730 Fax: 01704 539637
E-Mail: admin@esbuk.demon.co.uk
Web: http://www.esbuk.demon.co.uk

GENERAL MEDICAL COUNCIL (GMC)
178 Great Portland St, London. W1N 6JE.
Tel: 020 7580 7642 Fax: 020 7915 3565

INSTITUTE OF LINGUISTS (IoL)
Saxon House, 48 Southwark Street, London SE1 1UN
Tel: 020 7940 3100 Fax: 020 7940 3101
E-Mail: info@iol.org.uk
Web: http://www.iol.org.uk

LONDON CHAMBER OF COMMERCE & INDUSTRY EXAMINATIONS
BOARD (LCCIEB)
112 Station Road, Sidcup, Kent. DA15 7BJ
Tel: 020 8302 0261 Fax: 020 8302 4169 E-Mail: custserv@lccieb.org.uk
Web: http://www.lccieb.org.uk

LONDON EXAMINATIONS – EDEXCEL INTERNATIONAL
Stewart House, 32 Russell Square, London. WC1B 5DN.
Tel: 020 7331 4021 Fax: 020 7331 4022
Web: http://www.edexcel.org.uk/

PITMAN QUALIFICATIONS
1 Giltspur Street, London EC1A 9DD
Tel: 020 7294 2471 Fax: 020 7294 2400
Web: http://www.city-and-guilds.co.uk/pitman

TOEIC - International Communications (UK) Ltd.
TOEIC House, 129 Wendell Road, London W12 9SD
Tel: O20 8740 6282 Fax: 020 8740 5207
E-Mail: toeicinuk@aol.com
Web: http://www.toeic.com

TRINITY COLLEGE LONDON
89 Albert Embankment, London. SE1 7TP
Tel: 020 7720 6100 Fax: 020 7720 6161
E-Mail: info@trinitycollege.co.uk
Web: http://www.trinitycollege.co.uk

UNIVERSITY OF CAMBRIDGE LOCAL EXAMINATIONS SYNDICATE
(UCLES)
1 Hills Road, Cambridge. CB1 2EU
Tel: 01223 553311 Fax: 01223 460278
E-Mail: efl@ucles.org.uk
Web: http://www.cambridge-efl.org.uk

UNIVERSITY OF OXFORD DELEGACY OF LOCAL EXAMINATIONS
(UODLE)/ ARELS
1 Hills Road, Cambridge. CB1 2EU
Tel: 01223 553311 Fax: 01223 460278
E-Mail: efl@ucles.org.uk or uodle.vdq@ucles.org.uk
Web: http://www.uodle.org.uk

UNIVERSITY OF READING
Testing and Evaluation Unit,
Centre for Applied Language Studies, Whiteknights
PO Box 218, Reading RG6 2AA
Tel: 0118 931 6719   Fax: 0118 975 6506
E-Mail: b.e.osullivan@reading.ac.uk
Web: http://www.rdg.ac.uk/slals/teep

PART II

TEACHING ENGLISH IN BRITAIN

Teaching English as a Foreign Language Courses
(TEFL)

TEACHING ENGLISH AS A FOREIGN LANGUAGE (TEFL)

TEFL QUALIFICATIONS

Language schools, both in the UK and abroad, increasingly expect their teachers to have TEFL qualifications. There are numerous exams on offer, the two most widely accepted being the <u>Certificate in English Language Teaching to Adults (CELTA formerly CTEFLA)</u> and the <u>Certificate in Teaching English to Speakers of Other Languages (Cert. TESOL)</u>. The details of these exams are given below, as are those of the other main qualifications available.

<u>Please note:</u> TEFL Certificates and Diplomas do not confer Qualified Teacher Status (QTS). This means that holders of these qualifications will be unable to work in British state schools, unless they have a relevant B.Ed. or P.G.C.E.

Certificate in English Language Teaching to Adults (CELTA)
Exam Board: UCLES

The certificate forms part of the new CILTS (Cambridge Integrated Language Teaching Syllabus) and replaces the old Certificate in Teaching English as a Foreign Language (Cert. TEFLA). It is aimed at those without ELT experience, but with a standard of education which would allow entry to Higher Education. Candidates must be at least 20 years old at the start of the course. Courses have a minimum length of 100 contact hours, 6 hours supervised practice teaching and 8 hours directed observation of live lessons. Full-time courses last four to five weeks. Part-time up to one year.

Certificate in Teaching English to Speakers of Other Languages (Cert. TESOL)   Exam Board: Trinity College London

A first qualification for those with little or no previous experience. It qualifies the trainee to teach both adults and children and is available to both native and non-native speakers. Courses usually last for 1 month (intensive) or part-time from 3 months to 1 year. (Trinity College stipulates a min. of 130 hours of tuition, with at least 6 practical teaching experience.) Each institution sets its own entry requirements, but a good standard of general education is expected by all of them. In general, preference is given to students aged 20+.

 OTHER TEFL QUALIFICATIONS

Certificate in English Language Teaching to Young Learners (CELTYL) Exam Board: UCLES

The CELTYL is an introductory course for candidates who have little or no previous experience of teaching languages. Entry requirements follow those of the CELTA. The Certificate course programme focuses on teaching young learners either from 5-10, 11-16, or 8-13 years old. It involves a minimum of 100 contact hours, 6 hours supervised teaching practice and 8 hours directed observation of lessons taught by experienced ELT professionals. Full-time courses last 4 weeks, part-time courses last 4 to 5 months to a year.

Certificate of Endorsement in English Language Teaching to Young Learners Exam Board: UCLES

This pilot extension course allows recently qualified holders of a CELTA to extend this to work with young learners. Full-time courses last 2 weeks. Part-time up to 6 months.

Certificate for Overseas Teachers of English (COTE) Exam Board: UCLES

COTE is an in-service training course for practising teachers who have relevant classroom experience with children or adults. It is aimed at non-native speakers of English outside the UK. Candidates should have a level of English approximately equivalent to Cambridge First Certificate in English or Certificate in Communicative Skills in English, Level 2. Courses are usually a minimum of 150 hours and run part-time over six months or a year.

Diploma in English Language Teaching to Adults (DELTA) Exam Board: UCLES

The Diploma in English Language Teaching to Adults (DELTA) forms part of the CILTS review and replaces the Diploma in Teaching

English as a Foreign Language to Adults (DTEFLA) and the Diploma in Overseas Teaching of English (DOTE).

It is an in-service qualification for those with at least two years full-time (1200 hours) experience of teaching English as a foreign language. Candidates should have a standard of education which would allow entry to higher education and will normally have formal ELT training.

Courses have a minimum length of 120 contact hours, 10 hours teaching of ELT to adults (4 of which are supervised) and 10 hours directed observation of lessons. Candidates are expected to give substantial time to reading, research and assignments. Part-time courses tend to last about 8 months, but some centres also offer an intensive 10-12 week course.

Diploma in English Language Teaching to Young Learners (DELTYL) Exam Board: UCLES

The Diploma course is intended for candidates who have substantial experience of teaching English to young learners and has the same general entry requirements as the DELTA. The courses includes 120 contact hours, 10 hours teaching practice, 4 of which are assessed by a course tutor, 10 hours directed observation of young learner lessons and 150 hours of reading, research and assignments. Courses will be available on a full-time or part-time basis.

Diploma in Business and Professional English Language Teaching (DipBPE) Exam Board: UCLES

Currently in pilot, the DipBPE has the same entry requirements as DELTA but additionally candidates should have substantial business English teaching experience, and be over 21 years of age by the course start date. The course is a minimum of 140 hours. Courses will be available on a full-time or part-time basis.

Advanced Diploma in English Language Teaching Management (ADLTM) Exam Board: UCLES

The Advanced Diploma is an award at a higher level than DELTA, DELTYL and DipBPE. The focus is shifted away from the practicalities of the classroom to more specialised areas of management and planning. The course involves 100 hours course contact time, 220 hours guided study and 130 hours to complete assessed course work. Full-time courses last 3 months, part-time courses up to a maximum of 2 years.

International Diploma in English Language Teaching Management (IDLTM) Exam Board: UCLES

325 hour course which enables English Language teaching professionals to apply skills derived from management theory and practice to their work as Language Teaching managers. Candidates must have a degree or equivalent, a minimum of three years' language teaching experience or 5 years' working experience in a language teaching context.

Certificate in Teaching English to Young Learners (TEYL)
Exam Board: Trinity College

Intended for practising teachers of primary level children who wish to add a TESOL specialism to their existing skills. Trainees must follow an approved course. Minimum tuition time: 140 hours (20 of which are teaching practice), usually over a six week course (full-time). Open to native and non-native speakers.

Specialist Certificate in Teaching English for Industry and Commerce (CertTEfIC) Exam Board: Trinity College

This certificate was launched in the summer of 1998. The course is open to candidates with at least 6 months full time teaching experience who hold an initial TEFL qualification. It consists of 50 hours tuition plus a post-course project.

Licentiate Diploma in TESOL (LTCL TESOL)
Exam Board: Trinity College London

For teachers with at least two years teaching experience, wishing to pursue a career in TESOL. The examination is open to anyone with the relevant experience, but it is recommended that candidates follow an approved course. These normally last eight to ten weeks (intensive) or 1 year part-time.

Exam consists of two written papers (on the nature and use of the English language + the practical aspects of teaching), an oral interview (on the characteristics of spoken English + aspects of language teaching) and classroom teaching observation (1 full lesson). Open to native & non-native speakers.

NB: This qualification has just been revised. Key changes include the replacement of the written examination Paper 2 with a coursework portfolio and the inclusion of internal assessment by the course providers. City College Manchester is the first centre to receive provisional validation for course provision of the revised LTCL Diploma TESOL. Email the college for details (aspencer@ccm.ac.uk).

Diploma in the Teaching of English to Speakers of Asian Languages (DipTESAL) Exam Board: Trinity College

Developed with Curtin University, Australia, for experienced teachers working or intending to work in Asia. The 150 hour programme includes observed and assessed teaching, a classroom research project and practical assignments. It is of an equivalent standard to the LTCL (TESOL).

Foundation Certificate for Teachers of Business English (FTBE) Exam Board: London Chamber of Commerce and Industry

For qualified general EFL teachers intending to specialise in teaching English for Business Purposes. Open to both native and non-native speakers.

Certificate in Teaching English for Business (CertTEB) Exam Board: London Chamber of Commerce and Industry/Arels

For teachers with little or no experience of teaching English for Business (50 hours tuition)

Certificate in Professional Skills for Language School Teachers (International) Exam Board: English Speaking Board (International) Ltd.

Exam for non-native speakers wishing to update their spoken English.

The ARELS Certificate in Teaching One-to-One Exam Board: ARELS / Trinity College

For candidates with an initial TEFL qualification, and preferably some experience of teaching one-to-one. The course lasts 25 hours (1 week full-time) plus a follow-up project. Contact ARELS for more details (see address section at end of the book).

ARELS Diploma in ELT Management Designed for the UK ELT sector of the market, looking at UK legislation for employment, health & safety etc. The course runs from September to June and consists of 10 intensive one day training sessions in London combined with self study. All assignments are practical and of direct relevance to the organisation in which the course participant is working. There is no final exam and no purely academic essays.

There is also a vast array of university certificates, diplomas and Masters degree courses. Many tend to be of a more theoretical nature and do not always provide students with actual teaching practice. This is fine if the student already has some 'hands-on' experience, but for those who have not taught before, it is important to check that the course offers a teaching component.

A ➡ Z DIRECTORY OF TEFL COURSES IN BRITAIN

TEFL qualifications can be prepared for in a wide range of schools and colleges throughout the country. The following pages contain a directory of some of these institutions, and the qualifications for which you are prepared.

F/T = Full-time, P/T = Part-time

Aberdeen College
Gallowgate Centre, Gallowgate
Aberdeen AB25 1BN
Tel: 01224 612000   Fax: 01224 612001
Email: enquiry@abcol.ac.uk
http://www.abcol.ac.uk
P/T Cert. TESOL. Also F/T & P/T Intro. Course
Price: On application

Aberystwyth, The University of Wales
Language & Learning Ctre, Llandinam
Building Penglais Campus
Aberystwyth SY23 3DB
Tel: 01970 622545   Fax: 01970 622546
Email: language+learning@aber.ac.uk
http://www.aber.ac.uk/language+learning
F/T Cert. TESOL. Also F/T Teacher Development Course.
Price: £950 for 4½ wk Cert. TESOL Course
See display in region 5

Abingdon & Witney College
Wootton Road, Abingdon OX14 1GG
Tel: 01235 555585   Fax: 01235 553168
Email: inquiry@abingdon-witney.ac.uk
http://www.abingdon-witney.ac.uk
P/T Intro. Course
Price: £60 per course

Acton & West London College
Mill Hill Road, Acton London W3 8UX
Tel: 020 8231 6220   Fax: 020 8993 2725
Email: susie.kusnierz@wlc.ac.uk
http://www.westlondoncollege.ac.uk
P/T CELTA & P/T Intro. Course
Price: £595 for CELTA. £100 for 30hr intro. to teaching ESOL.

Albion International Study Centre
Bocardo House, 24b St Michael's St.
Oxford OX1 2EB
Tel: 01865 244470   Fax: 01865 244112
Email: info@albionschools.co.uk
http://www.albionschools.co.uk
Intro. Course
Price: £190/wk

Anglia Polytechnic University
Centre for English Language Studies
East Road, Cambridge CB1 1PT
Tel: 01223 417716   Fax: 01223 417717
Email: efl@apu.ac.uk
http://www.apu.ac.uk/efl
F/T & P/T CELTA
Price: £970 per course

Anglo-Continental
29-35 Wimborne Road,
Bournemouth BH2 6NA
Tel: 01202 557414   Fax: 01202 556156
Email: english@anglo-continental.com
http://www.anglo-continental.com
F/T CELTA, P/T Cert. TESOL
Price: £958 for CELTA.

Anglolang Academy of English
20 Avenue Road,
Scarborough YO12 5JX
Tel: 01723 367141   Fax: 01723 378698
Email: communicate@anglolang.co.uk
http://www.anglolang.co.uk
F/T Cert. TESOL
Price: £950 per course

Angloschool
146 Church Road,
London SE19 2NT
Tel: 020 8653 7285   Fax: 020 8653 9667
Email: Linda@angloschool.co.uk
http://www.angloschool.co.uk
P/T DELTA
Price: £800 (approx.) + exam fee
See display in region 3

Anniesland College
19 Hatfield Drive,
Glasgow G12 0YE
Tel: 0141 357 6082   Fax: 014 357 6063
Email: internationaloffice@anniesland.ac.uk
http://www.anniesland.ac.uk
P/T Intro Course
Price: £70 per course

Aston University
Language Studies Unit, Aston Triangle
Birmingham B4 7ET
Tel: 0121 359 3611 ex4242 Fax: 0121 359 2725
Email: lsu@aston.ac.uk
Cert, Dip. & MSc - master's by distance
learning
Price: On application

Barnet College
Montagu Road,
London N2 0JY
Tel: 020 8266 4365   Fax: 020 8202 6727
Email: int_enq@barnet.ac.uk
http://www.barnet.ac.uk
P/T CELTA & DELTA
Price: On application

Barnet College
Wood St.,
Barnet EN5 4AZ
Tel: 020 8440 6321   Fax: 020 8441 5236
Email: stsald@barnet.ac.uk
http://www.barnet.ac.uk
F/T & P/T CELTA
Price: £750/ per course

Basil Paterson Edinburgh
22 Abercromby Place,
Edinburgh EH3 6QE
Tel: 0131 556 7695   Fax: 0131 557 8503
Email: courses@bp-coll.demon.co.uk
http://www.basilpaterson.co.uk
F/T CELTA
Price: £900 per course

Basingstoke College of Technology
Worthing Road,
Basingstoke RG21 8TN
Tel: 01256 306350   Fax: 01256 306444
Email: Annabel.Stowe@bcot.ac.uk
http://www.bcot.ac.uk

F/T & P/T Cert. TESOL. Also 4 day Intro.
Course (Easter only).
Price: £719 for Cert. TESOL courses.

Bath Spa University College
Newton St. Loe,
Bath BA2 9BN
Tel: 01225 875845   Fax: 01225 875501
Email: international-office@bathspa.ac.uk
http://www.bathspa.ac.uk
F/T CELTA
Price: £995 per course

Bedford College
Cauldwell Street,
Bedford MK42 9AH
Tel: 01234 291000   Fax: 01234 342674
Email: hweaver@bedford.ac.uk
http://www.bedford.ac.uk
P/T CELTA. Also P/T Intro Course
Price: £800 for CELTA course

BEET Language Centre
Nortoft Road, Charminster
Bournemouth BH8 8PY
Tel: 01202 397721   Fax: 01202 309662
Email: admin@beet.co.uk
http://www.beet.co.uk
Refresher course for non-native teachers
Price: On application
See display in region 2

Bell Language School
Red Cross Lane,
Cambridge CB2 2QX
Tel: 01223 247242   Fax: 01223 412410
Email: info@bell-schools.ac.uk
http://www.bell-schools.ac.uk
F/T CELTA
Price: £890 for 4wk course.
BATQI accredited.

Bell Language School
South Road,
Saffron Walden CB11 3DP
Tel: 01799 522918   Fax: 01799 526949
Email: info@bell-centres.com
http://www.bell-centres.com
F/T DELTA
Price: £1395 for 10wk course

Bell Norwich
Bowthorpe Hall, Bowthorpe
Norwich NR5 9AA
Tel: 01603 745615   Fax: 01603 747669
Email: info@bell-schools.ac.uk
http://www.bell-schools.ac.uk
F/T CELTA / DELTA. F/T Intro. Course. Also
Primary & Computer teacher training courses.
Price: £890 for 4wk CELTA course, £1250
for 9wk DELTA.

Blackburn College
Feilden Street,
Blackburn BB2 1LH
Tel: 01254 292251   Fax:
Email: m.kershaw@blackburn.ac.uk
P/T CELTA
Price: £439 per course

Blackpool & the Fylde College
Ashfield Road,
Bispham FY8 5EB
Tel: 01253 352352   Fax: 01253 356127
Email: visitors@blackpool.ac.uk
http://www.blackpool.ac.uk
P/T Cert. TESOL
Price: £650 per course

Bolton College
Manchester Road, Bolton BL2 1ER
Tel: 01204 453458
P/T Cert. TESOL
Price: £600 approx.

Bournemouth & Poole College of Further Education
International Operations, Lansdown Centre
Bournemouth BH1 3JJ
Tel: 01202 205656   Fax: 01202 205991
Email: intops.bpcfe@dial.pipex.com
http://www.thecollege.co.uk
P/T CELTA. Also P/T Intro. Course
Price: £750 for CELTA, £75 for Intro.

Bournemouth International Language College
4 Trinity, 161 Old Christchurch Road
Bournemouth BH1 1JU
Tel: 01202 318269   Fax: 01202 318269
Email: tefl@bilc.co.uk
http://www.bilk.co.uk/tefl.htm
F/T Cert. TEB. Also F/T Intro. Course
Price: £300 for 2 wks

Bracknell & Wokingham College
Montague House, Broad St.
Wokingham RG40 1AU
Tel: 0118 902 9150   Fax: 0118 902 9160
Email: international@bracknell.ac.uk
http://www.bracknell.ac.uk
F/T & P/T Cert.TESOL, P/T Dip. TESOL & P/T Intro. Course
Price: £675 per course

Bradford College
ELC, Old Building Gt. Horton Rd
Bradford BD7 1AY
Tel: 01274 753207   Fax: 01274 741553
Email: elc@bilk.ac.uk
http://www.bilk.ac.uk
P/T Cert.TESOL
Price: £700 per course

Brasshouse Centre
50 Sheepcote St.,
Birmingham B16 8AJ
Tel: 0121 303 0114   Fax: 0121 464 5375
Email: brasshouse@birmingham.gov.uk
http://www.birmingham.gov.uk/brasshouse
F/T & P/T CELTA. P/T DELTA.
Also F/T Intro. Course
Price: £750 for 10wk CELTA, £900 for 4wk CELTA.
See display in region 6

Brighton College of Technology
Pelham Street,
Brighton BN1 4FA
Tel: 01273 667788   Fax: 01273 667703
Email: info@bricoltech.ac.uk
http://www.bricoltech.ac.uk
P/T Cert.TESOL
Price: £6.90-£10 per week

Britannia Academy of English
1517a London Road,
Norbury SW16 4AE
Tel: 020 8239 1515   Fax: 020 8239 1551
Email: study@britanniaacademy.co.uk
http://www.britanniaacademy.co.uk
F/T TESOL Cert (ACTDEC)
Price: £125-£350

Bromley College
Rookery Lane,
Bromley BR2 8HE
Tel: 020 8295 7031   Fax: 020 8295 7051
Email: international@bromley.ac.uk
http://www.bromley.ac.uk/
P/T CELTA
Price: £25-£100
See display in region 3

Bromley Language Centre
240 High St.,
Bromley BR1 1PQ
Tel: 020 8464 5149   Fax: 020 8325 2276
Email: bromlang@yahoo.co.uk
http://www.bromleylanguage.freeserve.co.uk
In-house TEFL diploma
Price: £96 per week
See display in region 3

Bromley School of English
2 Park Road,
Bromley BR1 3HP
Tel: 020 8313 0308   Fax: 020 8313 3957
Email: info@bromleyschool.com
http://www.bromleyschool.com
F/T CELTA
Price: £795

Brooklands College
Heath Rd,
Weybridge KT13 8TT
Tel: 01932 797739   Fax: 01932 797800
Email: uover@brooklands.ac.uk
http://www.brooklands.ac.uk
P/T Cert. TESOL (Wed. 9.15am-3.15pm)
Price: £680 for 22 wks course

Burlington School of English
1-3 Chesilton Road,
London SW6 5AA
Tel: 020 7736 9621   Fax: 020 7371 8131
Email: marketing@burlingtonschool.co.uk
http://www.burlington-school.co.uk
English for overseas teachers.
Price: £780 for 4wks with 20hrs per week.

Bury College
Millennium Centre, Market St.
Bury BL9 0BG
Tel: 0161 280 8451   Fax: 0161 280 8228
Email: vivien.finney@burycollege.ac.uk
http://www.burycollege.ac.uk
F/T & P/T Cert. TESOL
Price: £625 per course

Calderdale College
Francis Street,
Halifax HX1 3UZ
Tel: 01422 399329   Fax: 01422 399320
P/T Cert. TESOL
Price: £650 / per course

Cambridge International Study Centre
St Mary's College, 2 Brookside
Cambridge CB2 1JE
Tel: 01223 305698   Fax: 01223 307352
Email: director@stmaryscambridge.com
http://www.stmaryscambridge.com
F/T St.Mary's College TEFL course.
Price: £800 for 4wk course.

Canterbury Christ Church University College
International Office, North Holmes Road
Canterbury CT1 1QU
Tel: Tel: 01227 767700 Fax: 01227 781558
Email: ipol@cant.ac.uk
http://www.cant.ac.uk/io
P/T CELTA. Cert., Dip. & MA in TESOL
Price: On application. BATQI accredited.

Cardiff University
English Language Centre, 53 Park Place
Cardiff CF10 3AT
Tel: 029 2087 6587   Fax: 029 2023 1968
Email: elt@cardiff.ac.uk
http://www.cardiff.ac.uk/elsis
F/T Cert. TESOL
Price: £975 per course

Cardonald College
690 Mosspark Drive,
Glasgow G52 3AY
Tel: 0141 272 3333   Fax: 0141 272 3444
Email: iross@cardonald.ac.uk
http://www.cardonald.ac.uk
P/T Intro. Course
Price: On application

Centre for English Language & British Studies
University of East Anglia,
Norwich NR4 7TJ
Tel: 01603 592977   Fax: 01603 250200
Email: s.burge@uea.ac.uk
http://www.uea.ac.uk/llt/ceb
P/T CELTA (Jan.to April)
Price: £1192 per course
See display in region 8

Charles Keene College
Painter St.,
Leicester LE10 3WA
Tel: 0116 251 6037   Fax: 0116 262 0592
Email: advice@ckeene.ac.uk
http://www.ckeen.ac.uk
P/T Cert. TESOL
Price: On application

Cheltenham International Language Centre
Dunholme Villa, The Park
Cheltenham GL50 2QF
Tel: 01242 532925   Fax: 01242 532926
Email: cilc@glos.ac.uk
http://www.glos.ac.uk/cilc
F/T & P/T CELTA
Price: £995 per course

Chichester College of Arts, Science & Technology
Westgate Fields,
Chichester PO19 1SB
Tel: 01243 536294   Fax: 01243 775783
Email: intunit@chichester.ac.uk
http://www.chichester.ac.uk
P/T CELTA
Price: On application

Churchill House English Home Tuition Courses
Spencer Square (137),
Ramsgate CT11 9EQ
Tel: 01843 586833   Fax: 01843 584827
Email: ehtc@churchillhouse.co.uk
http://www.churchillhouse.co.uk
Arels Cert. in 1-1 teaching
Price: £295

Churchill House School of English Language
Spencer Square (137),
Ramsgate CT11 9EQ
Tel: 01843 586833   Fax: 01843 584827
Email: welcome@churchillhouse.co.uk
http://www.churchillhouse.co.uk
F/T Refresher Course - Arels 1 to 1 Teaching Certificate
Price: £980 /4wks
See display in region 4

City College Manchester
International Office, 141 Barlow Moor Road, West Didsbury
Manchester M20 2PQ
Tel: 0161 957 1609   Fax: 0161957 1609
Email: rspriggs@ccm.ac.uk
http://www.ccm.ac.uk
F/T & P/T Cert. TESOL. Also preliminary cert. in TESOL.
Price: £605-£800 per course. £75 (£15 if on benefits) for the preliminary course (1 term).

City of Bath College
Avon Street,
Bath BA1 1UP
Tel: 01225 312191   Fax: 01225 328864
Email: intstudent@citybathcoll.ac.uk
http://www.citybathcoll.ac.uk
F/T & P/T CELTA Also F/T DELTA
Price: On application

City of Bristol College
Brunel Centre, Ashley Down Road
Bristol BS7 9BU
Tel: 0117 904 5163   Fax: 0117 904 5180
Email: emmanuel.raud@cityofbristol.ac.uk
http://www.cityofbristol.ac.uk
P/T CELTA
Price: £999 for 12wk course (2 days/wk)

City of Islington College
Finsbury Park Ctre, Prah Rd
London N4 2RA
Tel: 020 7288 4922   Fax: 020 7359 8769
Email: celta@candi.ac.uk
http://www.candi.ac.uk
P/T CELTA
Price: £19.41

Class Languages
Cotswold House, 28 Cambray Place,
Cheltenham GL50 1JN
Tel: 01242 520046   Fax: 01242 256707
Email: enquiries@classlanguages.com
http://www.classlanguages.com
F/T & P/T Intro. Course + tailor-made in house course
Price: £100-£500

Colchester English Study Centre
19 Lexden Road,
Colchester CO3 3PW
Tel: 01206 544422   Fax: 01206 761849
Email: info@cesc.co.uk
http://www.cesc.co.uk
F/T Intro. Course
Price: £200 for 1wk course

Colchester Institute
Sheepen Road,
Colchester CO3 3LL
Tel: 01206 518765   Fax: 01206 518186
Email: efl@colch-inst.ac.uk
http://www.colch-inst.ac.uk
F/T Cert. TESOL
Price: £820 for 7wk course

Coleg Menai
Friddoedd Road,
Bangor LL56 4UQ
Tel: 01248 383324   Fax: 01248 370052
Email: carl.mather@menai.ac.uk
http://www.menai.ac.uk
F/T & P/T CELTA. Also F/T & P/T Intro.
Price: On application

College of North West London
Kilburn Centre, Priory Park Road
London NW6 7UJ
Tel: 020 8208 5131   Fax: 020 8208 5151
Email: international.admin@cnwl.ac.uk
http://www.cnwl.ac.uk
P/T CELTA
Price: £550

Computing and Business College
Metropolitan Business Centre, Suite B010
Enfield Road
London N1 5AZ
Tel: 020 7923 7466   Fax: 020 7249 0500
Email: cbcedu@aol.com
CELTA, Cert & Dip. TEB
Price: On application

Cornwall College
Pool TR15 3RD
Tel: 01209 616213   Fax: 01209 616214
Email: languages@cornwall.ac.uk
http://www.cornwall.ac..uk
F/T Cert. TESOL
Price: £187.50

Coventry Technical College English Centre
Butts, Coventry CV1 3GD
Tel: 024 7652 6742   Fax: 024 7652 6743
Email: language@covcollege.ac.uk
http://www.covcollege.ac.uk
F/T & P/T Cert.TESOL
Price: £695 per course

Crawley College
College Road,
Crawley RH10 1HR
Tel: 01293 442295   Fax: 01293 442399
Email: crawcol@rmplc.co.uk
P/T CELTA
Price: On application

**Croydon Continuing Education &
Training Service**
South Norwood Centre, Sandown Rd
London SE25 4XE
Tel: 020 8656 6620   Fax: 020 8662 1828
P/T CELTA
Price: £700 approx.

Culture-Link UK
2 Keast Ct, Heron Clse
Weymouth DT3 6SX
Tel: 01305 834166   Fax:
Email: RachelTouray@aol.com
1 week familiarisation course.
Price: £150

Darlington College of Technology
Cleveland Avenue,
Darlington DL3 7BB
Tel: 01325 503050   Fax: 01325 503000
Email: enquire@darlington.ac.uk
http://www.darlington.ac.uk
P/T Cert. TESOL
Price: £300 approx.

Dorset International College
Cambridge House, 7 Knyveton Road
Bournemouth BH1 3QF
Tel: 01202 316611   Fax: 01202 318811
Email: info@dorsetinternationalcollege.co.uk
http://www.dorsetinternationalcollege.co.uk
Language Development for Qualified
Teachers
Price: £696 per course

Dundee College
Melrose Terrace,
Dundee DD3 7QX
Tel: 01382 834898   Fax: 01382 458153
Email: dci@dundeecoll.ac.uk
http://www.dundeecoll.ac.uk
F/T & P/T CELTA
Price: £795

East Berkshire College
Claremont Road,
Windsor SL4 3AZ
Tel: 01753 793000   Fax: 01753 793119
Email: audreyrenton@eastberks.ac.uk
http://www.eastberks.ac.uk
F/T & P/T Cert. TESOL
Price: On application

East Berkshire College
Station Road,
Langley SL3 8BY
Tel: 01753 793000
P/T Cert. TESOL
Price: On application

**Eastbourne College of Arts and
Technology**
Cross Levels Way,
Eastbourne BN21 2UF
Tel: 01323 637637   Fax: 01323 637472
Email: info@ecat.ac.uk
http://www.ecat.ac.uk/overseas
F/T & P/T CELTA
Price: On application

Eastbourne School of English
8 Trinity Trees,
Eastbourne BN21 3LD
Tel: 01323 721759   Fax: 01323 639271
Email: english@esoe.co.uk
http://www.esoe.co.uk
P/T DELTA (Oct-June).
Price: £1000 per course
BATQI accredited.

Eastleigh College
Chestnut Avenue,
Eastleigh SO50 5HT
Tel: 023 8032 6326   Fax: 023 80399912
Email: sdowner@eastleigh.ac.uk
http://www.eastleigh.ac.uk
F/T & P/T CELTA
Price: £625 approx. / per course

Edgware Academy of Languages
205 Edgware Road,
London W2 1ES
Tel: 020 7262 0944   Fax: 020 7262 0948
Email: info@english-courses.co.uk
http://www.english-courses.co.uk
P/T Intro. Course + CELTA
Price: £15-£30

EF English First
1-3 Farman Street,
Hove BN3 1AL
Tel: 01273 201412   Fax: 01273 748566
Email: languages.gb@ef.com
http://www. ef.com
F/T Cert.TESOL
Price: £850 per course

ELT Banbury
49 Oxford Road,
Banbury OX16 9AH
Tel: 01295 263480   Fax: 01295 271658
Email: info@elt-banbury.com
http://www.elt-banbury.com
F/T CELTA & Cert. TESOL
Price: £250

Embassy CES Hastings
White Rock,
Hastings TN34 1JY
Tel: 01424 720100   Fax: 01424 720323
Email: hastings@embassyces.com
http://www.embassyces.com
F/T CELTA & DELTA. Also Teaching English to
young learners + range of other short courses.
Price: £820 for CELTA, £1455 for 8wk
DELTA or £1590 for 9wk course. £530 for
2wk young learner course.

Embassy CES Newnham
8 Grange Road,
Cambridge CB3 9DU
Tel: 01223 311344   Fax: 01223 461411
Email: cambridge@embassyces.com
http://www.embassyces.com
F/T CELTA. Also practical methodology
course.
Price: £940 for CELTA

English in Chester
9-11 Stanley Place,
Chester CH1 2LU
Tel: 01244 318913   Fax: 01244 320091
Email: study@english-in-chester.co.uk
http://www.english-in-chester.co.uk
DELTA
Price: On application

English International
4 South Cliff, Whitley Bay
Newcastle upon Tyne NE26 2PB
Tel: 0191 253 7367   Fax: 0191 251 3121
Email: englishinternational@eudoramail.com
http://www.englishinternational.com
Intro & Refresher courses.
Price: On application

English Language Centre
6B Church St.,
Reading RG1 2SB
Tel: 0118 939 1833   Fax: 0118 939 1833
Email: katepepper@ntlworld.com
F/T & P/T CELTA.
Price: £725 for 6wk course

English Language Centre (The)
5 New Street,
York YO1 8RA
Tel: 01904 672243   Fax: 01904 672200
Email: english@elcyork.com
http://www.elcyork.com
F/T & P/T CELTA & DELTA
Price: £895 per course

English Language Support Centre
Millbrook Centre, Mill End Road
High Wycombe HP12 4BA
Tel: 01494 522021   Fax: 01494 522021

C&G 9281 (02) Initial Cert. in Teaching
Basic Communication Skills to Adults
Price: Free in exchange for volunteering to
teach ESOL for 1yr on a 1-1 basis.

English Plus @ Canterbury
35 Henry Court, Gordon Road,
Canterbury CT1 3PL
Tel: 01227 831041   Fax: 01227 831041
Email: english-plus@hotmail.com
http:// www.englishplus.freeuk.com
F/T & P/T CELTA, Cert. TESOL
Price: £250-£700

English Training Centre (The)
The Guildhall, Box 104, University of
Birmingham
Edgbaston Park Road
Birmingham B15 2TU
Fax: 0121 449 2221
Email: psimmonds@englishtc.co.uk
http://www.englishtc.co.uk
P/T Intro. Course by distance learning
Price: £220-£250 per course.
*See section on Distance Learning for more
details.*

Eurocentres Business Institute
56 Eccleston Square,
London SW1V 1PH
Tel: 020 7834 4155 Fax: 020 7834 1866
Email: ebi-info@eurocentres.com
http://www.eurocentres.com
F/T Cert. TEB
Price: £272-£300

Eurocentres, Lee Green
21 Meadowcourt Road,
London SE3 9EU
Tel: 020 8318 5633 Fax: 020 8318 9057
Email: sgibbons@eurocentres.com
http://www.eurocentres.com
F/T Refresher course for overseas teachers
Price: £257

European Languages Centre
Northern House, 43-45 Pembroke Place
Liverpool L3 5PH
Tel: 0151 708 7071 Fax: 0151 707 1919
Email: sderham@eurolang.com
http://www.eurolang.com
F/T & P/T TESOL Course (leads to centre's
own cert.)
Price: £990 for F/T course

European Link
Kent Adult Education, Avebury Avenue
Tonbridge TN9 1TG
Tel: 01732 361181 Fax: 01732 361185
Email: kaeselink@aol.com
F/T for foreign teachers only
Price: On application

Evendine College
22 Grosvenor Gardens,
London SW1W 0DH
Tel: 020 7730 4070 Fax: 020 7881 0852
Email: evendine@evendine.com
http://www.evendine.com
F/T & P/T Cert. & Dip. TESOL. Also
teaching business Eng. & Intro. Course.
Price: £649 for Cert. TESOL course

Farnborough College
Boundary Road,
Farnborough GU14 6SB
Tel: 01252 407307 Fax: 01252 407041
Email: info@farn-ct.ac.uk
http://www.farn-ct.ac.uk
P/T CELTA
Price: £750 for 30wk course

Filton College Bristol
International Students Ctre, Filton Avenue
Bristol BS34 7AT
Tel: 0117 909 2279 Fax: 0117 931 2637
Email: international@filton-college.ac.uk
http://www.filton-college.ac.uk

P/T CELTA. Also P/T Intro. Course
Price: £975 for P/T CELTA

Gateshead Training Consultancy
Gateshead College, Durham Road
Gateshead NE9 5BN
Tel: 0191 490 0300 Fax: 0191 490 2315
Email: ucan@gateshead.ac.uk
http://www.gateshead.ac.uk
P/T Cert. TESOL (Sept. to May)
Price: On application.

GEOS English Academy
55-61 Portland Road,
Brighton & Hove BN3 5DQ
Tel: 01273 735975 Fax: 01273 732884
Email: info@geos-brighton.com
http://www.geos-brighton.com
F/T CELTA
Price: £870 for 4wk course
See display in region 4

Globe English Centre
31 St. David's Hill,
Exeter EX4 4DA
Tel: 01392 271036 Fax: 01392 427559
Email: study@globeenglish.co.uk
http://www.GlobeEnglish.co.uk
Teacher Refresher Course
Price: £295 a week

Gloscat
Princess Elizabeth Way,
Cheltenham GL51 7SJ
Tel: 01242 532144 Fax: 01242 532196
Email: woodmj@gloscat.ac.uk
http://www.gloscat.ac.uk
F/T & P/T CELTA
Price: £998 per course

Golders Green College
11 Golders Green Road,
London NW11 8DY
Tel: 020 8731 0963 Fax: 020 8455 6528
Email: teachertraining@ggcol.fsnet.co.uk
http://www.clct.co.uk/ttc
F/T & P/T Cert. TESOL, P/T Dip. TESOL
Price: £699 for Cert. TESOL, £800 for Dip.

Grimsby College
Nuns Corner, Grimsby DN34 5BQ
Tel: 01472 279222 Fax: 01472 897724
P/T Cert. TESOL
Price: On application

Grove House Language Centre
Carlton Avenue,
Greenhithe DA9 9DR
Tel: 01322 386826 Fax: 01322 386347
Email: EFL@grovehouse.com
http://www.grovehouse.com

F/T Cert.TESOL. Also F/T Intro. Course
Price: £875 for 4 wk course

Guildford College
Stoke Park,
Guildford GU1 1EZ
Tel: 01483 448688   Fax: 01483 448689
Email: international@guildford.ac.uk
http://www.guildford.ac.uk/int/welcom.htm
P/T Cert.TESOL
Price: £600 per course

Hammersmith & West London College
Gliddon Road, Barons Court
London W14 9BL
Tel: 020 8563 0063   Fax: 020 8563 8247
Email: cic@hwlc.ac.uk
http://www.hwlc.ac.uk
F/T & P/T CELTA + P/T DELTA
Price: £695 for CELTA. £895 for DELTA.
BATQI accredited.

Handsworth College
Soho Road, Handsworth
Birmingham B21 9DP
Tel: 0121 551 6031   Fax: 0121 523 4447
Email: l.webster@handsworth.ac.uk
http://www.handsworth.ac.uk
P/T CELTA
Price: £400 approx.

Harrogate Tutorial College
2 The Oval,
Harrogate HG2 9BA
Tel: 01423 501041   Fax: 01423 531110
Email: study@htcuk.org
http://www.htcuk.org
F/T Teacher refresher course
Price: £215 per week

Harrow College
Temple House, 221-225 Station Road
Harrow HA1 2XL
Tel: 020 8909 6594   Fax: 020 8909 6061
Email: lkoten@harrow.ac.uk
http://www.harrow.ac.uk
P/T CELTA
Price: £590 approx.

**Harrow House International College
London**
103 Palace Road, Hampton Court
London KT8 9DU
Tel: 01929 424421   Fax: 01929 427175
Email: karin.abarrow@lds.co.uk
http://www.harrowhouse.com
F/T CELTA
Price: £1276 per course
See display in region 2

Harrow House International Colleges
Harrow Drive,
Swanage BH19 1PE
Tel: 01929 424421   Fax: 01929 427175
Email: karin.abarrow@lds.co.uk
http://www.harrowhouse.com
F/T CELTA
Price: £1276 per course
See display in region 2

Hart Villages Centre
Robert May's School, West St. Odiham
Basingstoke RG24 1NA
Tel: 01256 703808   Fax: 01256 703012
P/T Cert. TESOL
Price: On application

Hastings College of Arts & Technology
Archery Road,
St. Leonards-on-Sea TN38 0HX
Tel: 01424 445400   Fax: 01424 424804
Email: studentadvisers@hastings.ac.uk
http://www.hastings.ac.uk
P/T Cert.TESOL
Price: £300 per course.

Heriot-Watt University
Riccarton,
Edinburgh EH14 4AS
Tel: 0131 451 4201   Fax: 0131 451 3079
Email: O.Alexander@hw.ac.uk
http://www.hw.ac.uk/langWWW/english
F/T & P/T Intro. Course
Price: £175 per course
See display in region 12

Hopwood Hall College
Rochdale Road,
Middleton M24 6XH
Tel: 01706 345346
Email: enquiries@hopwood.ac.uk
http://www.hopwood.ac.uk
P/T Cert. TESOL
Price: £560 per course

Hounslow Community Education
The Civic Centre, Lampton Road
Hounslow TW3 4DN
Tel: 020 8862 5388   Fax: 020 8862 5064
Email: info@education.hounslow.gov.uk
http://www.hounslowlea.org.uk
P/T Teaching Eng. To Adults Course
Price: £3.80

Hove School of English
9 The Drive, Hove
Brighton BN3 3JE
Tel: 01273 723781   Fax: 01273 771222
Email: hse@ukstudies.co.uk
http://www.ukstudies.co.uk

Teacher training for overseas teachers
Price: £300 per week

Hull College
Park Street Centre, Park Street
Hull HU2 8RR
Tel: 01482 598955   Fax: 01482 598989
Email: cmiddleton@hull-college.co.uk
http://www.hull-college.co.uuk
P/T Cert. TESOL
Price: £270 for 11 wk course (UK student price)

i-to-i UK
9 Blenheim Terrace,
Leeds LS2 9HZ
Tel: 0870 333 2332   Fax: 0113 242 2171
Email: frances.moriarty@i-to-i.com
http://www.i-to-i.com
W/end & Online Courses
Price: £195 per course

Inlingua Cheltenham
Rodney Lodge, Rodney Road
Cheltenham GL50 1HX
Tel: 01242 250493   Fax: 01242 250495
Email: training@inlingua-cheltenham.co.uk
http://www.inlingua-cheltenham.co.uk
F/T & P/T Cert. TESOL, P/T Dip. TESOL.
Also LCCI Foundation Cert. & Intro. Course
Price: £995 for F/T Cert. TESOL course.

Institute of Education
University of London, CCS 20 Bedford Way
London WC1H 0AL
Tel: 020 7612 6504   Fax: 020 7612 6177
Email: m.scott@ioe.ac.uk
http://www.ioe.ac.uk
F/T & P/T MA TESOL.
Price: On application
BATQI accredited.
See section on distance learning.

Intensive School of English & Business Communication
34 Duke St,
Brighton BN1 1BS
Tel: 01273 384800   Fax: 01273 236872
Email: info@ise.uk.com
http://www.ise.uk.com
F/T & P/T CELTA. Also F/T & P/T Cert.
TESOL & Foundation Certificate for
Teachers of Business English.
Price: £850 for CELTA

International College of English
27, Chalton Lane, Clanfield
Portsmouth PO8 0PP
Tel: 023 9259 6989   Fax: 023 9259 6989
Email: mel596989@aol.com
F/T & P/T Intro. Course
Price: £90-£110

International House
106 Piccadilly,
London W1V 9FL
Tel: 020 7491 2598   Fax: 020 7409 0959
Email: info@ihondon.co.uk
http://www.ihlondon.com
F/T & P/T CELTA / DELTA, Cert.TEB & IH
Foundation in Business English teaching.
Also range of other F/T short courses
Price: On application
BATQI accredited.

International House, Newcastle
14-18 Stowell St.,
Newcastle-upon-Tyne NE1 4XQ
Tel: 0191 232 9551   Fax: 0191 232 1126
Email: info@ihnewcastle.co.uk
http://www.ihnewcastle.com
F/T CELTA/DELTA. Also F/T Intro. Course &
Overseas teachers course.
Price: £945/4wk CELTA, £1400/8wk DELTA,
£450/2wk overseas teachers course.

International Language Institute
County House, Vicar Lane
Leeds LS1 7JH
Tel: 0113 242 8893   Fax: 0113 2347543
Email: 101322.1376@compuserve.com
http://www.vitalo.com/ili
F/T CELTA & Dip. TESOL
Price: £970 approx. / per course

International School (The)
1-3 Mount Radford Crescent,
Exeter EX2 4EW
Tel: 01392 254102   Fax: 01392 434432
Email: study@internationalschool.co.uk
http://www.internationalschool.co.uk
F/T Cert. TESOL
Price: £900 per course

International Study Programmes
The Manor, Hazleton
Cheltenham GL54 4EB
Tel: 01451 860379   Fax: 01451 860482
Email: Discover@International-Study-Programmes.org.uk
http://International-Study-Programmes.org.uk
F/T 2wk course for overseas (non native)
teachers of English
Price: £630 per course including accomm.

International Training Network
28 Howard Rd,
Bournemouth BH8 9EA
Tel: 01202 516872   Fax: 01202 516872
F/T Cert. TESOL
Price: On application

ITS English School
43-45 Cambridge Gardens,
Hastings TN34 1EN
Tel: 01424 438025   Fax: 01424 438050
Email: itsbest@its-hastings.co.uk
http://www.its-hastings.co.uk
F/T Cert. TESOL & P/T Dip. TESOL. Also
Intro. course & courses for overseas teachers.
Price: On application.
BATQI accredited.

ITTC

Training for English language teaching
- Cambridge CELTA every month
- Cambridge DELTA 3 per year

LCCI & ARELS Business Teaching
Certificate

Refresher Courses for Overseas Teachers
of English - Comenius approved.

Nortoft Road, Charminster
Bournemouth BH8 8PY

Tel: +44 1202 397721
Fax: +44 1202 309662
E-Mail: tefl@ittc.co.uk
Website: http://www.ittc.co.uk

ITTC
Nortoft Road, Charminster
Bournemouth BH8 8PY
Tel: 01202 397721   Fax: 01202 309662
Email: tefl@ittc.co.uk
http://www.ittc.co.uk
F/T CELTA, F/T & P/T DELTA. Also LCCI
Foundation Cert. TBE & LCCI/Arels Cert. in
Teaching Business English
Price: £1100 for F/T 4wk CELTA course.
See display for further details

Joseph Priestley College
Alec Beevers Centre, Burton Ave
Leeds LS11 5ER
Tel: 0113 307 6111   Fax: 0113 271 3456
Email: helpline@joseph-priestley.ac.uk
http://www.joseph-priestley.ac.uk
P/T Cert. TESOL
Price: £600 approx.

Keele University
English Language Unit, c/o Dept. of
Academic Affairs,
Keele ST5 5BG   Tel: 01782 584293
Email: eltu@keele.ac.uk
http://www.keele.ac.uk/depts/aa/elu
F/T & P/T Intro. Course
Price: £135 for 25hr course

Kent School of English
3/5, 10/12 Granville Avenue,
Broadstairs CT10 1QD
Tel: 01843 874870   Fax: 01843 860418
Email: enquiries@kentschool.co.uk
http://www. kentschool.co.uk
F/T Cert. TESOL
Price: £750 per course

King's College London
English Language Ctre, Strand
London WC2R 2LS
Tel: 020 7848 1600   Fax: 020 7848 1601
Email: elc@kcl.ac.uk
http://www.kcl.ac.uk/elc
P/T DELTA
Price: £895

**Kingston Community Adult Education &
Training**
King Charles Centre, King Charles Road
Surbiton KT5 9AL
Tel: 020 8547 6875   Fax: 020 8547 6874
Email: gill.ellis@rbk.kingston.gov.uk
http://www.kingston.gov.uk/adulteducation
P/T CELTA
Price: £700 per course

Lancaster University
LAMEL, Bowland College
Lancaster LA1 4YT
Tel: 01524 593045   Fax: 01524 843085
Email: linguistics@lancaster.ac.uk
http://www.iling.lancs.ac.uk
BA with TEFL element. Also MA in TESOL.
Price: On application

Language Link
181 Earls Court Rd,
London SW5 9RB
Tel: 020 7225 1065   Fax: 020 7584 3518
Email: languagelink@compuserve.com
http://www.languagelink.co.uk
F/T & P/T CELTA, DELTA (4wks intensive +
8mths guided revision), Cert. TESOL, F/T
Intro. Course, Overseas teachers refresher
Price: £850 approx. for CELTA. £430 for
2wk refresher.

Language Link
21 Harrington Road,
London SW7 3EU
Tel: 020 7225 1065   Fax: 020 7584 3518
Email: languagelink@compuserve.com
http://www.languagelink.co.uk
F/T & P/T CELTA, DELTA (4wks intensive
+ 8mths guided revision), Cert. TESOL,
F/T Intro. Course, Overseas teachers
refresher
Price: £850 approx. for CELTA. £430 for
2wk refresher.

Language Project (The)
27 Oakfield Road, Clifton
Bristol BS8 2AT
Tel: 0117 909 0911   Fax: 0117 907 7181
Email: info@languageproject.co.uk
http://www.languageproject.co.uk
F/T Cert. TESOL. F/T & P/T Dip. TESOL.
Also F/T Intro. Course & English for foreign
teachers course.
Price: £180 for 1wk Intro. course. £235 for
1wk foreign teachers course.

Languages Training & Development
116 Corn Street, Witney
Oxford OX28 6BU
Tel: 01993 894710   Fax: 01993 706066
Email: info@ltdoxford.com
http//www. ltdoxford.com
F/T Cert.TESOL. Also LCCI FTBE (distance
learning)
Price: £900 for Cert. TESOL, £300 for LCCI
FTBE. Centre can help students with
funding/grants.

Leeds Metropolitan University
Centre for Language Study, Beckett Park
Leeds LS13 2JQ
Tel: 0113 283 7440   Fax: 0113 274 5966
Email: cls@lmu.ac.uk
http://www.lmu.ac.uk/cls
F/T CELTA, P/T Cert. TESOL. Also Cert. &
MA courses.
Price: £450-£950 for Cert. courses
See display in region 10 for full details

Lewisham College
EFL Dept., Lewisham Way
London SE4 1UT
Tel: 020 8694 3295   Fax: 020 8694 3349
http://www.lewisham.ac.uk
F/T & P/T CELTA
Price: £700 per course

Lochcarron School of English
Pathend, Main Street Lochcarron
Srathcarron IV54 8YB
Tel: 01520 722733   Fax: 01520 722733
Email: LochcarronSchool@aol.com
http://www.speakingenglish.co.uk
Intro. Course
Price: £500 per course

London Guildhall University
English Language Centre, Old Castle St.
London E1 7NT
Tel: 020 7320 1251   Fax: 020 7320 1253
Email: elc@lgu.ac.uk
http://www.lgu.ac.uk/elc
F/T Cert.TEB.
Price: £210-£260

London Study Centre
Munster House, 676 Fulham Road
London SW6 5SA
Tel: 020 7731 3549   Fax: 020 7731 6060
Email: lsc.uk@compuserve.com
http://www.londonstudycentre.com
F/T & P/T Cert.TESOL
Price: £800 per course

London Teacher Training Centre
140 Ashley Crescent,
London SW11 5QZ
Tel: 01323 488357   Fax: 01323 488357
Email: lttc@teachenglish.co.uk
http://www.teachenglish.co.uk
Distance learning courses by post or
Internet. LTTC Cert./Dip. in teaching young
learners, Cert.in teaching business English.
Also M.A. in TESOL.
Price: £185 for Cert. in teaching young
learners, £260 for the Dip.

Lydbury English Centre
Lydbury North SY7 8AU
Tel: 01588 681000   Fax: 01588 681018
Email: enquiry@lydbury.co.uk
http://www.lydbury.co.uk
LCCI Cert. TEB
Price: £550 per course

Management International
63-69 Eltham Road,
London SE12 8UF
Tel: 020 8852 1261   Fax: 020 8297 0514
Email: info@managementinternational.co.uk
http://managementinternational.co.uk
F/T Intro. Course
Price: £135-£225

Manchester Academy of English
St. Margaret's Chambers, 5 Newton St.
Manchester M1 1HL
Tel: 0161 237 5619   Fax: 0161 237 9016
Email: english@manacad.co.uk
http://www. manacad.co.uk
F/T Cert. TESOL.
Price: On application
See display in region 9

**Manchester College of Arts &
Technology**
EFL Unit, The John Unsworth Building,
Lower Hardman St.
Manchester M3 3ER
Tel: 0161 455 2434   Fax: 0161 953 2259
Email: international@mancat.ac.uk
http://www.mancat.ac.uk
F/T & P/T Cert. TESOL (F/T June/July, P/T
Sept.-Apr.)
Price: £620 P/T or £550 F/T

Marble Arch Intensive English - M.A.I.E.
21 Star St.,
London W2 1QB
Tel: 020 7402 9273   Fax: 020 7724 2219
Email: skola@easynet.co.uk
http://www.skola.co.uk
P/T CELTA
Price: £799 per course

Marjon International
Derriford Road,
Plymouth PL6 8BH
Tel: 01752 636821   Fax: 01752 636802
Email: inted@marjon.ac.uk
http://www.marjon.ac.uk/about/international_ed/
Range of short (2-4wk) courses in Teacher
Development, Trainer Development, TEYL,
TESP, EMI (Using English as a Medium of
Instruction)
Price: £710 for 3 wk course.
BATQI accredited.

Mid Kent College
Oakwood Park Centre, Language Services
Tonbridge Road
Maidstone ME16 8AQ
Tel: 01622 691555   Fax: 01622 695049
Email: clare.harrison@midkent.ac.uk
http://www.midkent.ac.uk
F/T & P/T CELTA
Price: £710 per course

Middlesbrough College
Roman Road,
Middlesbrough TS5 5PJ
Tel: 01642 333333   Fax: 01642 333310
Email: r.smith@mbro.ac.uk
http://www.mbro.ac.uk
P/T Cert. TESOL
Price: £400 per course (lasts academic yr)

Middlesex University
White Hart Lane, Tottenham
London N17 8HR
Tel: 020 8411 6722   Fax: 020 84116655
Email: p.fanning@mdx.ac.uk
http://www.ilrs.mdx.ac.uk/lang/eng_non
F/T & P/T Intro. courses. Also 3yr BA
TEFL, & 9mth P/T TEFL course for
graduates (equiv. to a P/T CELTA course)
Price: £800 for 9mth course
BATQI accredited.

MLS International College
MLS House, 8 Verulam Place,
Bournemouth BH1 1DW
Tel: 01202 291556   Fax: 01202 293846
Email: admin@mls-college.co.uk
http://www.mls-college.co.uk
Specialised Teacher Training programmes
for groups / on site visits
Price: £165 per week

Moray House English Language Centre
The University of Edinburgh,
37 Holyrood Road, Edinburgh EH8 8AQ
Tel: 0131 558 6332   Fax: 0131 557 5138
Email: scie@mhie.ac.uk
http://www.education.ed.ac.uk/
F/T CELTA. BEd (hons) & MEd TESOL (F/T
or distance learning - *see section on
distance learning for more info.*)
Price: On application
BATQI accredited.

Multi Lingua
Abbot Hse, Sydenham Rd
Guilford GU1 3RL
Tel: 01483 535118   Fax: 01483 534777
Email: mail@multi-lingua.co.uk
http://www.multi-lingua.co.uk
F/T CELTA. Also F/T & P/T Mult-Lingua
Cert. & Prep. TEFL.
Price: £750 for CELTA.

NetLearn Languages
28 Appledore Avenue,
Ruislip HA4 0UU
Tel: 020 8845 5555   Fax: 07092 106305
Email: enquiries@netlearnlanguages.com
http://www.colte.com
Certificate in the Online Teaching of English
(COLTE)
Price: £295 per course

New College Durham
Framwellgate Moor Centre,
Durham DH1 5ES
Tel: 0191 375 4383   Fax: 0191 375 4333
Email: jo.fayram@newdur.ac.uk
http://intra.newdur.ac.uk
P/T Cert. TESOL . P/T Intro. Course (lasting
123 hrs)
Price: £375 for 1yr course

New College Nottingham
Clarendon City College, The Adams
Building, Stoney St.
Nottingham NG1 2LJ
Tel: 0115 910 4610   Fax: 0115 910 4611
Email: enquiry@ncn.ac.uk
http://www.ncn.ac.uk
F/T & P/T CELTA
Price: £790

New Horizons
40 Dalmeny Road, Southbourne
Bournemouth BH6 4BW
Tel: 01202 425298   Fax: 01202 425298
F/T & P/T CELTA
Price: On application

Newbold College
St. Mark's Road, Binfield
Bracknell RG42 4AN
Tel: 01344 407421   Fax: 01344 407405
Email: admissions@newbold.ac.uk
http://www.newbold.ac.uk
F/T Cert. TESOL
Price: £1000 per course

Newcastle College
International Office, Rye Hill Campus,
Scotswood Road
Newcastle Upon Tyne NE4 7SA
Tel: 0191 200 4068   Fax: 0191220 4474
Email: sjohnson@ncl-coll.ac.uk
http://www. ncl-coll.ac.uk
P/T CELTA
Price: £795

Newham College of Further Education
High Street South, East Ham
London E6 3AB
Tel: 020 8257 4293   Fax: 020 8257 4306
Email: pam.fleisch@newham.ac.uk
P/T CELTA
Price: On application

North Lindsey College
Kingsway,
Scunthorpe DN17 1AJ
Tel: 01724 281111   Fax: 01724 294020
P/T Cert. TESOL
Price: sjohnson@ncl-coll.ac.uk

North Trafford College
Talbort Rd, Stretford
Manchester M32 0XH
Tel: 0161 886 7070   Fax: 0161 872 7921
Email: admissions@northtrafford.ac.uk
http://www.northtrafford.ac.uk
P/T CELTA
Price: £695

Northampton College
Language Centre, Booth Lane
Northampton NN3 3RF
Tel: 01604 734270   Fax: 01604 734207
Email: heleny@northamptoncollege.ac.uk
P/T Cert. TESOL. P/T Intro. course
Price: On application

Northbrook College
International Office, Union Place
Worthing BN11 1LG
Tel: 01903 606107   Fax: 01903 606113
Email: international@nbcol.ac.uk
http://www.northbrook.ac.uk
F/T & P/T Cert. TESOL, P/T Dip. TESOL.

Also Intro. course, young learners course &
Arels Cert. in 1-1 teaching.
Price: £549 for Cert. TESOL (concessions
£352) £550 for Dip.TESOL. £285 for Arels
course.

**Norwich Institute for Language
Education (NILE)**
PO Box 2000,
Norwich NR2 1LE
Tel: 01603 664473   Fax: 01603 664493
Email: marketing@nile-elt.com
http://www.nile-elt.com
Wide range of courses for teachers,
including Master's level, all of which qualify
for Lingua/Comenius funding.
Price: On application

Norwood English
20 Hadley Gardens, Norwood Green
Southall UB2 5SQ
Tel: 020 8893 6253   Fax: 020 8893 6253
Email: norwoodeng@aol.com
http://members.aol.com/norwoodeng/
Intro. Course & Distance Learning Course
Price: £160-£220

Nottingham Trent University
Nottingham Language Centre, Burton St.
Nottingham NG1 4BU
Tel: 0115 848 6156   Fax: 0115 848 6513
Email: nlc@ntu.ac.uk
http://nlc.ntu.ac.uk
F/T & P/T CELTA / DELTA. Also Intro. Course
Price: £900 for F/T CELTA

Oaklands College
International Office, St. Peter's Road,
St. Albans AL1 3RX
Tel: 01727 737175   Fax: 01727 737273
Email: international@oaklans.ac.uk
http://www.oaklands.ac.uk
F/T & P/T Cert / Dip TESOL
Price: On application

**OISE London Intensive School of
English**
19-23 Oxford St.,
London W1R 1RF
Tel: 020 7494 3456   Fax: 020 7494 3366
Email: admissions.london@oise.net
P/T Intro. Course
Price: On application

Oxford Brookes University
International Centre for English Language
Studies
Gipsy Lane Campus, Headington
Oxford OX3 0BP
Tel: 01865 483874   Fax: 01865 484377

Email: icels@sol.brookes.ac.uk
http://www.brookes.ac.uk/sol/home/icels.html
P/T CELTA, MA + Diploma in ELT
Price: £1200 approx.

Oxford College of Further Education
City Centre Campus, Oxpens Road
Oxford OX1 1SA
Tel: 01865 269268   Fax: 01865 269412
Email: enquiries_oxford@oxfe.ac.uk
http://www.oxfe.ac.uk
F/T & P/T CELTA + P/T DELTA.
Price: £775 for P/T CELTA

Oxford House College
28 Market Place, Oxford Circus
London W1W 8AW
Tel: 020 7580 9785   Fax: 020 7323 4582
Email: english@oxfordhouse.co.uk
http://wwww.oxfordhousecollege.co.uk
F/T & P/T Cert. TESOL. P/T Dip.TESOL.
Also ELT Academic Management,
Overseas Teachers Methodology &
Professional Development courses.
Price: £650 for F/T Cert.TESOL course.
BATQI accredited.

Park Lane College
Park Lane,
Leeds LS3 1AA
Tel: 0113 216 2032   Fax: 0113 216 2020
Email: enquiry@mail.parklanecoll.ac.uk
http://www.parklanecoll.ac.uk
P/T Cert. TESOL
Price: £450 approx.

Plymouth College of Further Education
Academic & Continuing Studies, Goschen
Centre, Saltash Road
Plymouth PL2 2DP
Tel: 01752 305290   Fax: 01752 305065
Email: ggodfrey@pcfe.ac.uk
http://www.pcfe.ac.uk/
F/T & P/T Cert. TESOL
Price: £1050 per course.

Polyglot Language Centre
214 Trinity Road,
London SW17 7HP
Tel: 020 8767 9113   Fax: 020 8767 9104
Email: english@polyglot.co.uk
http://www.polyglot.co.uk
F/T CELTA
Price: £835 for 4wk course
See display in region 3

Queen Margaret University College
Clerwood Terrace,
Edinburgh EH12 8TS
Tel: 0131 317 3292   Fax: 0131 317 3292

Email: sbannerman@qmuc.ac.uk
http://elu.qmuc.ac.uk
P/T Intro. Course
Price: £20-£25

Radcliffe College
185 Oxford St.,
London W1R 1TA
Tel: 020 7734 4214   Fax: 020 7734 4218
Email: cambridge@radcliffe-college.com
http://www.radcliffecollege.co.uk
F/T CELTA, F/T Cert/Dip. TESOL & F/T
Intro. Course
Price: On application
See display in region 3

Radcliffe College
53 Oxford St.,
London W1R 1RD
Tel: 020 7494 1083   Fax: 020 7494 1084
Email: cambridge@radcliffe-college.com
http://www.radcliffecollege.co.uk
F/T CELTA, F/T Cert/Dip. TESOL & F/T
Intro. Course
Price: On application
See display in region 3

Randolph School of English
63 Frederick St.,
Edinburgh EH2 1LH
Tel: 0131 226 5004   Fax: 0131 226 5003
Email: randolphSE@aol.com
http://members.aol.com/randolphse
F/T & P/T CELTA
Price: £850 for 4 wk course

**Reading College & School of Arts &
Design**
Crescent Road,
Reading RG1 5RQ
Tel: 0118 967 5442   Fax: 0118 967 5441
Email: spargoc@reading-college.ac.uk
http://www.reading-college.ac.uk
F/T & P/T CELTA, P/T DELTA
Price: £640 for CELTA (either P/T or 4 wk
F/T), £210 for DELTA

Red Dragon Languages Consultancy
109 Victoria Road,
Bournemouth BH1 4RS
Tel: 01202 398879   Fax: 01202 566764
Email: redragonlanguages@hotmail.com
http://www.rdlc.co.uk
F/T & P/T Intro. Course
Price: £150 for 1wk course

Regency School of English
Royal Crescent,
Ramsgate CT11 9PE
Tel: 01843 591212   Fax: 01843 850035

Email: andrew@regencyschool.co.uk
http://www.regencyschool.co.uk
P/T Dip. TESOL
Price: On application.

Regent Edinburgh
29 Chester St.,
Edinburgh EH3 7EN
Tel: 0131 225 9888   Fax: 0131 225 2133
Email: edinburgh@regent.org.uk
http://www.regent.org.uk
F/T Cert. TESOL
Price: £850 per course

Regent London
12 Buckingham St,
London WC2N 6DF
Tel: 020 7872 6620   Fax: 020 7872 6630
Email: london@regent.org.uk
http://www.regent.org.uk
F/T & P/T CELTA. Also Overseas Teachers'
Refresher Course
Price: £800 for CELTA.

Regent Oxford
90 Banbury Road,
Oxford OX2 6JT
Tel: 01865 515566   Fax: 01865 512538
Email: oxford@regent.org.uk
http://www.regent.org.uk
F/T CELTA.
Price: £750 per course

RLI Language Services
122 Coldershaw Road,
London W13 9DT
Tel: 020 8567 3988   Fax: 020 8840 9287
Email: info@language-tuition.co.uk
http://www.language-tuition.co.uk
F/T & P/T Intro. Course
Price: £400 for 45hrs
See display in region 3

Sandgrown School of English Ltd.
59 Cartmell Road,
Lytham St. Annes FY8 1DF
Tel: 01253 711212   Fax: 01253 712561
Email: Sandgrown@mcintyre50.freeserve.co.uk
http://www.sandgrown.co.uk
F/T & P/T Intro. Course
Price: £250-£500

Sandwell College
Crocketts Lane,
Smethwick B66 3BU
Tel: 0121 253 6306   Fax: 0121253 6322
Email: ulla.stede@sandwell.ac.uk
http://www.sandwell.ac.uk
P/T Cert. TESOL
Price: £700 per course

Scarborough International School
37 Stepney Road,
Scarborough YO12 5BN
Tel: 01723 362879   Fax: 01723 366458
Email: info@ english-language.uk.com
http://www.english-language.uk.com
Overseas teachers refresher course
Price: £252 / wk

SCOLA Community College
St Nicholas Way,
Sutton SM1 1EA
Tel: 020 8770 6901   Fax: 020 8770 6933
Email: scola@suttonlea.org
P/T Cert. TESOL
Price: On application (but free if UB40 &
L.B.Sutton resident)

Shane English School London
59 South Molton St.,
London W1K 5SN
Tel: 020 7499 8533   Fax: 020 7499 9374
Email: marketing@shane-english.co.uk
http://www.shane-english.co.uk
F/T CELTA
Price: £759 per course

Sheffield Hallam University
TESOL Centre, 36 Collegiate Crescent
Campus
Sheffield S10 2BP
Tel: 0114 225 2365   Fax: 0114 225 2280
Email: tesol@shu.ac.uk
http://www.shu.ac.uk/tesol/
F/T & P/T Cert/Dip. TESOL (can also be
taken as part distance learning, part face-to-
face).   F/T & P/T Intro. Course
Price: £925 for F/T Cert. TESOL course

Sidmouth International School
May Cottage,
Sidmouth EX10 8EN
Tel: 01395 516754   Fax: 01395 579270
Email: efl@sidmouth-int.co.uk
http://www.sidmouth-int.co.uk
F/T Cert. TESOL. Also P/T Dip. TESOL
Price: £895 for 4wk course

SOAS
University of London, 4 Gower St.
London WC1E 6HA
Tel: 020 7580 8272   Fax: 020 7631 3043
Email: english@soas.ac.uk
http://www.soas.ac.uk/elu
F/T CELTA
Price: £880 per course

Solihull College
Centre for International Development,
Blossomfield Road
Solihull B91 1SB
Tel: 0121 678 7172   Fax: 0121 711 2316
Email: intenqu@solihull.ac.uk
F/T & P/T CELTA. Also F/T DELTA
Price: £750 for CELTA. £950 for 10wk
DELTA.

Somerset College of Arts & Technology
Wellington Road,
Tauton TA1 5AX
Tel: 01823 366366   Fax: 01823 366418
Email: jem@somerset.ac.uk
http://www.somerset.ac.uk
F/T & P/T NOCN TEFL
Price: £28.88

South Devon College
Language Centre, Newton Road
Torquay TQ2 5BY
Tel: 01803 386338   Fax: 01803 386333
Email: ddavies@s-devon.ac.uk
http://www.s-devon.ac.uk
P/T CELTA
Price: On application

South Downs College
College Road, Purbrook Way
Havant PO7 8AA
Tel: 023 9279 7979   Fax: 023 92356124
Email: college@southdowns.ac.uk
http://www.southdowns.ac.uk
P/T Intro. Course
Price: £4.20

South East Essex College
Carnarvon Road,
Southend on Sea SS2 6LS
Tel: 01702 220448   Fax: 01702 432320
Email: marketing@se-essex-college.ac.uk
http://www.se-essex-college.ac.uk
P/T Cert. TESOL (32wks)
Price: £750

South Kent College
European Business & Language Centre,
Maison Dieu Road
Dover CT16 1DH
Tel: 01304 204573   Fax: 01304 204573
F/T & P/T Cert. TESOL
Price: On application

South Thames College
50-52 Putney Hill,
London SW15 6QX
Tel: 020 8918 7380   Fax: 020 8918 7347
Email: eis@south-thames.ac.uk
http://www.south-thames.ac.uk

F/T & P/T CELTA
Price: £650-£760 for either F/T or P/T
course

South Trafford College
Manchester Road, West Timperley
Altrincham WA14 5PQ
Tel: 0161 952 4720   Fax: 0161952 4672
Email: languages@stcoll.ac.uk
http://www.stcoll.ac.uk
P/T CELTA. Also P/T Foundation course
Price: £625 for CELTA.

Southwark College
The Cut,
London SE1 8LE
Tel: 020 7815 1682   Fax: 020 7261 1301
Email: info@southwark.ac.uk
http://www.southwark.ac.uk
P/T Cert. TESOL. Also 1wk Intro. Course
Price: £720 for Cert. TESOL.

St Giles International Brighton
3 Marlborough Place,
Brighton BN1 1UB
Tel: 01273 682747   Fax: 01273 689808
Email: stgiles@pavilion.co.uk
http://www.stgiles-international.com
F/T CELTA
Price: On application

St Giles International London Central
154 Southampton Row,
London WC1B 5AX
Tel: 020 7837 0404   Fax: 020 7837 4099
Email: londoncentral@stgiles.co.uk
http://www.stgiles-international.com
F/T Cert. TESOL
Price: On application

St Giles International London Highgate
51 Shepherds Hill,
London N6 5QP
Tel: 020 8340 0828   Fax: 020 8348 9389
Email: edtrust@stgiles.co.uk
http://www.tefl-stgiles.com
F/T & P/T CELTA
Price: £750 per course

St. Brelade's College
Mont Les Vaux, St. Aubin
JERSEY JE2 8AF
Tel: 01534 741305   Fax: 01534 741159
Email: sbc@itl.net
http://www.st-brelades-college.co.uk
F/T Cert. & Dip. TESOL
Price: £830 approx. for Cert. course.

St. George International
76 Mortimer St.,
London W1N 7DE
Tel: 020 7299 1707   Fax: 020 7299 1711
Email: teflenq@stgeorges.co.uk
http://www.stgeorges.co.uk
F/T & P/T Cert. TESOL. F/T Dip. TESOL
Price: £495 for F/T Cert., £545 for P/T
Cert. £895 for Dip. Exam fees not included
in any course.

St. Martin's College, Lancaster
Languages Development Centre,
Lancaster LA1 3JD
Tel: 01524 384488   Fax: 01524 384492
Email: c.lucas@ucsm.ac.uk
http://www.ucsm.ac.uk
P/T Intro. Course. Also St. Martin's own 4
wk certificate course
Price: £59-£185

St. Mary's College
Waldegrave Rd, Strawberry Hill
Twickenham TW1 4SX
Tel: 020 8240 4346   Fax: 020 8240 4365
Email: grantk@smuc.ac.uk
http://www.smuc.ac.uk
F/T Cert.TESOL. Also MA in Applied
Linguistics & ELT
Price: £780 +£75 moderation fee for
Cert.TESOL course. MA costs £2400 (UK/
EU) or £6000 for overseas students

Stanton School of English
167 Queensway,
London W2 4SB
Tel: 020 7221 7259   Fax: 020 7792 9047
Email: study@stanton-school.co.uk
http://www.stanton-school.co.uk
F/T CELTA, P/T DELTA, F/T Intro. Course &
2wk teacher training course for non-native
teachers
Price: £698 for 4wk CELTA course

Stevenson College
Bankhead Avenue, Sighthill
Edinburgh EN11 4DE
Tel: 0131 535 4700 Fax: 0131 535 4708
Email: info@stevenson.ac.uk
http://www.stevenson.ac.uk
P/T CELTA. Also P/T Intro Course.
Price: £750 for CELTA. £48 for Intro

Stockport College
Wellington Road South,
Stockport SK1 3UQ
Tel: 0161 958 3100   Fax: 0161 480 6636
Email: Liz.O'Reilly@stockport.ac.uk
http://www.stockport.ac.uk
P/T Cert. TESOL
Price: £800 approx. for 8mth course

Stoke-on-Trent College
Stoke Rd, Shelton
Stoke-on-Trent ST4 2DG
Tel: 01782 208208   Fax: 01782 603504
Email: dston@stokecoll.ac.uk
http://www.stokecoll.ac.uk
P/T CELTA
Price: £850

Students International Ltd
158 Dalby Rd,
Melton Mowbray LE13 0BJ
Tel: 01664 481997   Fax: 01664 563332
Email: studentsint@aol.com
http://www.studentsint.com
F/T & P/T Cert. TESOL
Price: £795 for F/T 4 wk course

Studio Cambridge
6 Salisbury Villas, Station Road
Cambridge CB1 2JF
Tel: 01223 369701   Fax: 01223 314944
Email: information@studiocambridge.co.uk
http://www.studiocambridge.co.uk
F/T CELTA
Price: £880 for 4wk course

Surrey Adult Education Centre
19 Esher Green,
Esher KT10 8AA
Tel: 01372 465374   Fax: 01372 463696
P/T Cert & Dip TESOL
Price: On application

Surrey Language Training
Sandford House, 39 West Street
Farnham GU9 7DR
Tel: 01252 723494   Fax: 01252 733519
Email: slc@surreylanguage.co.uk
http://www.surreylanguage.co.uk/slc/slc.html
F/T Cert./Dip. TESOL
Price: £720 for 4wk Cert. course.
£850+£120 moderation fee for Dip. course.

Sussex Downs College
Mountfield Road,
Lewes BN7 2XH
Tel: 01273 483188   Fax: 01273 488974
Email: international@sussexdowns.ac.uk
http://www.sussexdowns.ac.uk
P/T CELTA
Price: £850 for 1yr course

Sussex Language Institute, University of Sussex
Arts A, Falmer
Brighton BN1 9QN
Tel: 01273 678006   Fax: 01273 678476
Email: A.Loske@sussex.ac.uk
http://www.sussex.ac.uk/langc/tefl.html

F/T Cert. TESOL. Also Intro. Course
Price: £840 for Cert. TESOL course. £140
for Intro.

Swansea College
Tycoch Rd,
Swansea SA2 9EB
Tel: 01792 284000   Fax: 01792 284074
Email: p.p.@swancoll.ac.uk
http://www.swancoll.ac.uk
P/T Open College Network
Price: On application

SYAES Waverley Area
25 West St.,
Farnham GU9 8DH
Tel: 01252 723888   Fax: 01252 712927
P/T Cert. TESOL
Price: On application

Torbay Language Centre
Conway Road,
Paignton TQ4 5LH
Tel: 01803 558555   Fax: 01803 666998
Email: TLC@lalschool.org
http://www.lalgroup.com
F/T CELTA. P/T Intro. Course
Price: £960 for 4wk CELTA course. £60 for
1wk intro.

Totnes European School
4 Birdwood Court,
Totnes TQ9 5SG
Tel: 01803 868123   Fax: 01803 868223
Email: selsacs@eclipse.co.uk
http://www.selsacs.co.uk/tes
F/T & P/T DELTA, Cert.TESOL & Intro.
Price: £130-£160

Truro College
Haven House, Quay St
Truro TR1 2UY
Tel: 01872 240986   Fax: 01872 261145
Email: pamelas@trurocollege.ac.uk
http://www.trurocollege.ac.uk
National Open College Network (South
West) TEFL Course
Price: £250 for P/T Course

TTI School of English
148-150 Camden High Street,
London NW1 0NE
Tel: 0800 174031   Fax: 020 7419 2299
Email: Info@ttischool.com
http://www.ttischool.com
P/T Teacher Training International Cert.
Price: £91.66

Universal Language Training
Woking College, Rydens Way
Woking GU22 9DL
Tel: 01483 770911   Fax: 01483 770848
Email: enquiry@universal-language.co.uk
http://www.universal-language.co.uk
F/T & P/T Cert. TESOL. Also free intro.
seminars.
Price: £695 for both course + exam fee
BATQI accredited.

University College Chichester
The Dome, Upper Bognor Road
Bognor Regis PO21 1HR
Tel: 01243 816271   Fax: 01243 816272
Email: g.lloyd@ucc.ac.uk
http://www.ucc.ac.uk
Teaching English to young learners.
Teaching Eng. in secondary schools.
CEELT + range of other courses.
Price: On application
BATQI accredited.

University of Bath
English Language Centre, Claverton Down
Bath BA2 7AY
Tel: 01225 323024   Fax: 01225 323135
Email: english@bath.ac.uk
http://www.bath.ac.uk/elc
P/T DELTA. Also MA in TEFL.
Price: On application

University of Brighton
School of Languages, Falmer
Brighton BN1 9PH
Tel: 01273 643339   Fax: 01273 690710
Email: slweb@bton.ac.uk
http://www.bton.ac.uk/
F/T & P/T Dip. TESOL (uni. own). Also, MA
TESOL, MA in media assisted language
teaching and refresher course.
Price: On application
BATQI accredited.

University of Bristol
Graduate School of Education
35 Berkeley Square
Bristol BS8 1JA
Tel: 0117 928 7093   Fax: 0117925 1537
Email: G.M.Clibbon@bristol.ac.uk
http://www.bristol.ac.uk/Depts/LangCent/
efl/efl.htm
F/T& P/T M.Ed TEFL. Also Intro. Course
Price: On application

University of Central Lancashire
Dept. of Languages, Fylde Buildings
Preston PR1 2HE
Tel: 01772 893130 Fax: 01772 892909
Email: c.barwood@uclan.ac.uk
MA - Teaching English for International
Business
Price: On application

University of Durham
Language Ctre, Elvet Riverside New Elvet
Durham DH1 3JT
Tel: 0191 374 3716 Fax: 0191 374 7790
Email: language.centre@durham.ac.uk
http://www.durham.ac.uk
F/T CELTA & DELTA. Also MA Applied
Linguistics
Price: £975 for CELTA, £1400 for DELTA

University of Edinburgh
Institute of Applied Language Studies
21 Hill Place
Edinburgh EH8 9DP
Tel: 0131 650 6200   Fax: 0131 667 5927
Email: ials.enquiries@ed.ac.uk
http://www.ials.ed.ac.uk
F/T DELTA. Also Intro. Course
Price: £1700 for DELTA
BATQI accredited.

University of Essex
ELT Centre, Wivenhoe Park
Colchester CO4 3SQ
Tel: 01206 872217 Fax: 01206 873107
Email: dilly@essex.ac.uk
http://www.essex.ac.uk/eltc
PG Uni. Cert./Dip.
Price: On application

University of Glamorgan
Centre for Language Studies,
Pontypridd CF37 1DL
Tel: 01443 480480 Fax: 01443 480558
Email: jrwalter@glam.ac.uk
F/T & P/T CELTA & Cert. TESOL
Price: On application

University of Glasgow
EFL Unit, Hetherington Buildings Bute
Gardens
Glasgow G12 8RS
Tel: 0141 330 4220 Fax: 0141 330 3381
Email: enquiries@efl.arts.gla.ac.uk
http://www.efl.arts.gla.ac.uk/CELTA.html
P/T CELTA
Price: On application

University of Hertfordshire
Admissions Office, Hatfield Campus
College Lane , Hatfield AL10 9AB
Tel: 01707 284421 Fax: 01707 285274
Email: admissions@herts.ac.uk
http://www.herts.ac.uk
F/T & P/T DELTA. Also MA in ELT &
Applied Lings.
Price: Variable

University of Hull
The Language Institute, Cottingham Road
Hull HU6 7RX
Tel: 01482 465900 Fax: 01482 466180
Email: langinst@hull.ac.uk
http://www.hull.ac.uk
P/T MEd in ICT (Information and
Communication Technology) for TESOL
(distance learning over the Internet)
Price: Approx. £4200

University of Leeds
Language Centre,
Leeds LS2 9JT
Tel: 0113 343 3251 Fax: 0113 343 3252
Email: TESOL@education.leeds.ac.uk
http://www.education.leeds.ac.uk/TESOL
Intro. Course (5 days, runs April & June
only) MEd TESOL (also available as
distance learning), MEd TESOL Young
Learners, Certificate in Teaching English to
Young Learner,
Price: £110 for 5 day Intro. Course. Other
prices on request.

University of Liverpool
AELSU, Dept. English Lang., Modern
Languages Building
Chatham St., Liverpool L69 3BX
Tel: 0151 794 2734   Fax: 0151 794 2739
Email: glester@liv.ac.uk
F/T & P/T Cert. TEFL (Uni. of Liverpool)
Price: On application
BATQI accredited.

University of Luton
EFL Suite, 3rd floor, Vicarage Street Campus
Vicarage Street, Luton LU1 3AJ
Tel: 01582 743205 Fax: 01582 743221
Email: efl@luton.ac.uk
http://www.luton.ac.uk
Teaching EFL BA (Hons). P/T Cert.
TESOL & F/T Cert in TEFL (uni's own
course, runs in July)
Price: On application

University of Manchester
Faculty of Education, Oxford Road
Manchester M13 9PL
Tel: 0161 275 3467 Fax: 0161 275 3480
Email: langlit@man.ac.uk
http://www.man.ac.uk/langlit/ELT.htm
Range of distance learning M.Eds. *See end of chapter for more details.*
BATQI accredited.

University of Northumbria at Newcastle
EFL Division, Lipman Building
Newcastle upon Tyne NE1 8ST
Tel: 0191 227 4919 Fax: 0191 227 4439
Email: andrea.percival@unn.ac.uk
P/T & F/T CELTA & Dip. TEFLA
Price: On application

University of Portsmouth
Language Centre, Park Building
King Henry I Street
Portsmouth PO1 2DZ
Tel: 023 9284 6112 Fax: 023 9284 6156
Email: language.centre@port.ac.uk
http://www.port.ac.uk/english@portsmouth
F/T TEFL refresher. Also F/T Primary
English Language Teaching Course.
Price: £520 for 2 week refresher course
See display in region 2

University of Reading
School of Linguistics & Applied Lang.
Studies, Whiteknights
PO Box 241, Reading RG6 6WB
Tel: 0118 931 8511 Fax: 1189756506
Email: SLALS@reading.ac.uk
http://www.rdg.ac.uk/AcaDepts/cl/SLALS/index.htm
F/T MA TEFL . (Also available P/T through distance learning)
Price: On application
BATQI Accredited

University of Salford
EFL, School of Languages,
Maxwell Building, Salford M5 4WT
Tel: 0161 295 5751 Fax: 0161 295 5135
Email: efl-languages@salford.ac.uk
http://www.salford.ac.uk/intinst/
F/T MA TEFL
Price: On application

University of St. Andrews
ELT Ctre, Butts Wynd
St. Andrews KY16 9AL
Tel: 01334 462258 Fax: 01334 462270
Email: amm3@st-and.ac.uk
http://www.st-and.ac.uk/services/elt/home.html
F/T Cert. TESOL. Also Uni.'s own 1 wk
TEFL course (runs June/July only).
Price: £900 for Cert. TESOL. £175 for 1 wk course

University of Stirling
Centre for English Language Teaching,
Stirling FK9 4LA
Tel: 01786 467934 Fax: 01786 466131
Email: celt@stir.ac.uk
http://www.celt.stir.ac.uk
MSc/PgDip. in TESOL, BA in English
Language Teaching
Price: On application

University of Strathclyde
English Language Teaching Division,
26 Richmond St.
Glasgow G1 1XH
Tel: 0141 950 3620 Fax: 0141 950 3219
Email: eltd.les@strath.ac.uk
http://www.strath.ac.uk/Departments/ELTD/index.html
F/T & P/T Intro. Course
Price: £195 per course

University of Surrey
English Language Institute,
Guildford GU2 5XH
Tel: 01483 259911 Fax: 01483 259507
Email: eli@surrey.ac.uk
P/ T distance learning MA / MSc
Price: On application

University of the West of England
Fac. of Languages, Coldharbour Lane
Frenchay, Bristol BS16 1QY
Tel: 0117 334 2392 Fax: 0117 334 2820
Email: george.mann@uwe.ac.uk
http://www.uwe.ac.uk
F/T Cert. TESOL, MA in Tesol & linguistics,
Intro. Course
Price: £975 for Cert. TESOL

University of Wales, Swansea
Centre for Applied Language Studies,
North Arts, Swansea SA2 8PP
Tel: 01792 295391 Fax: 01792 295641
Email: K.A.Frith@swansea.ac.uk
http://www.swansea.ac.uk/cals/clasx.html
F/T Intro. Course
Price: £244

University of Westminster
309 Regent Street,
London W1B 2UW
Tel: 020 7915 5401 Fax: 020 7911 5001
Email: efl@wmin.ac.uk
http://www.wmin.ac.uk/efl
F/T & P/T CELTA
Price: £890 for F/T course

University of Wolverhampton
School of Humanities, Languages & Social
Sciences, Wulfruna Street
Wolverhampton WV1 1SB
Tel: 01902 322770   Fax: 01902 322 739
Email: efl@wlv.ac.uk
http://www.wlv.ac.uk/efl
P/T Cert. TESOL
Price: On application

University of York
EFL Unit, Language Teaching Centre
Heslington
York YO10 5DD
Tel: 01904 432483   Fax: 01904 432481
Email: efl2@york.ac.uk
http://www.york.ac.uk/efl/
MA in Teaching English to Young Learners
(2 yr P/T distance learning course, with 2
wk on site tuition in July)
Price: £6480 for 2yrs.

Uxbridge College
Park Road,
Uxbridge UB8 1NQ
Tel: 01895 853300   Fax: 01895 853377
Email: pmcann@uxbridge.ac.uk
http://www.uxbridge.ac.uk
F/T & P/T CELTA
Price: On application

Waltham Forest College
Forest Road,
London E17 4JB
Tel: 020 8501 8091   Fax: 020 8501 8001
Email: international@waltham.ac.uk
http://www.waltham.ac.uk
F/T & P/T CELTA, P/T DELTA.
Price: £650 for CELTA

West Cheshire College
International Study Centre, Eaton Rd
Handbridge
Chester CH4 7ER
Tel: 01244 670566   Fax: 01244 670611
Email: international@west-cheshire.ac.uk
http://www.west-cheshire.ac.uk
F/T & P/T CELTA. Also methodology update
for non-native teachers
Price: £750 for CELTA course

West Herts College
Cassio Campus, Langley Road
Watford WD1 3RH
Tel: 01923 812049   Fax: 01923 812284
Email: admissions@westherts.ac.uk
http://westherts.ac.uk
P/T CELTA
Price: £735 per 23wk course

West Kent College
Brook St.,
Tonbridge TN9 2PW
Tel: 01732 358101   Fax: 01732 771415
Email: judyhebert@wkc.ac.uk
P/T CELTA
Price: £800 per course

Westbourne English Language School
24 Westover Road,
Bournemouth BH1 2BZ
Tel: 01202 294054   Fax: 01202 294054
Email: welschool@bournemouth-net.co.uk
http://www.artisan-inter.net/wels/
P/T ACTDEC Distance Learning
Price: £345-£415 per course

Westminster Kingsway College
School of Languages, Peter St.
London W1V 4HS
Tel: 020 7437 8536   Fax: 020 7287 0711
Email: linda.roberts@westking.ac.uk
http://www.westking.ac.uk
F/T CELTA & P/T DELTA
Price: On application

Weston College
Knightstone Road,
Weston-super-Mare BS23 2AL
Tel: 01934 411411   Fax: 01934 411410
Email: MKTG@weston.ac.uk
http://www.weston.ac.uk
Intro. Course
Price: £190 per course

Wigan & Leigh College
PO Box 53, Parsons Walk
Wigan WN1 1RS
Tel: 01942 761563   Fax: 01942 761572
Email: f.brogan@wigan-leigh.ac.uk
http://www.wigan-leigh.ac.uk
P/T CELTA & DELTA. Also Intro. Course
Price: £600 + exam fee

Windsor Schools
21 Osborne Road,
Windsor SL4 3EG
Tel: 01753 858995   Fax: 01753 831726
Email: info@windsorschools.co.uk
http://www.windsorenglish.com
F/T & P/T Cert.TESOL
Price: £884 per course

Wirral Metropolitan College
ELU, Conway Park Campus, Europa Blvd,
Birkenhead
Wirral CH41 4NT
Tel: 0151 551 7088   Fax: 0151 551 7001
Email: elu@wmc.ac.uk
http://www.wmc.ac.uk/esol
P/T Cert. TESOL
Price: £620 for 2 term course

Wold School of English
Ivy House, Main St, Osgodby
Market Rasen LN8 3PA
Tel: 01673 828539   Fax: 01673 828539
Email: hrosser@fsbdial.co.uk
http://www.woldschool.com
Teacher refresher courses
Price: £500 for 2wk course

Woolwich College
Villas Rd, Plumstead
London SE18 7PN
Tel: 020 8488 4800   Fax: 020 8488 4899
F/T & P/T CELTA
Price: £580 per course

York Associates
Peasholme House, St.Saviours Place
York YO1 7PJ
Tel: 01904 624246   Fax: 01904 646971
Email: training@yorkassoc.go-ed.com
http://www.york-associates.co.uk
Business English Cert. courses, lasting
50hrs & accredited by London Guildhall Uni.
Price: On application

York College of F&HE
Tadcaster Road,
York YO2 1UA
Tel: 01904 770366   Fax: 01904 770363
Email: efl@yorkcollege.com
http://www.yorkcollege.com
P/T CELTA
Price: £800 approx.

 TEFL DISTANCE LEARNING COURSES

Recognised Validating Bodies

There are numerous organisations offering TEFL qualifications by correspondence. Students should be careful, however, to avoid courses which do not lead to a recognised examination, or which are not accredited by a recognised external body. Finding employment with only an in-house certificate or diploma which no-one has heard of can be very difficult, so beware.

Apart from the main TEFL qualifications listed at the beginning of this chapter, the other recognised validating bodies are: The College of Teachers and ACTDEC.

The College of Teachers
(Formerly known as the College of Preceptors)

The Chartered Body of the Teaching Profession
Coppice Row, Theydon Bois, Epping, Essex. CM16 7DN
Tel: 01992 812727   Fax: 01992 814690
E-Mail: collegeofteachers@mailbox.ulcc.ac.uk
Web: http://www.collegeofteachers.ac.uk/TESOL.htm

Under the terms of its Royal Charter of 1849, the College is empowered to provide professional qualifications for teachers in the UK and overseas. The status of the qualifications awarded under the terms of this charter is the same as that of qualifications awarded by British universities.

The College offers the following qualifications in TESOL:

Distance Learning Only

Certificate of Educational Studies in TESOL, COES (TESOL)

For candidates seeking an introduction to the world of teaching English to speakers of other languages.

Associate of the College of Teachers ACoT (TESOL)

For practising teachers of ESOL or new entrants to the profession seeking the award as part I of the Advanced Certificate in TESOL.

College of Teachers Diploma Dip.CoT (TESOL)

In-service award for experienced teachers of ESOL.

Fellow of the College of Teachers FCoT (TESOL)

M.Phil level award for candidates successfully completing an in-service distance study programme. Courses usually in two parts: a 450-hour distance programme leading to the Dip.CoT (TESOL) or award of the Advanced Diploma in TESOL followed by a distance case studies unit and a 36-week research phase ending with a 18,000 -20,000 word project.

Distance Learning plus Face-to-Face Component

Advanced Certificate in TESOL A.Cert. (TESOL)

Pre-service award for new entrants to the profession. Accredited courses leading to this qualification consist of 325 hours distance-training in the theory and methodology of TESOL, followed by 75 hours face-to-face work including teaching practice.

Advanced Diploma in TESOL A.Dip. (TESOL)

For experienced practising teachers of ESOL. Accredited courses leading to this qualification consist of 450 hours distance learning in the theory and methodology of TESOL, 75 hours of classroom-centred research and 115 hours practical work including advanced teaching practice. Also fulfils the requirements for Part I of the programme leading to the FCoT (TESOL).

ACTDEC -
The Accreditation Council for TESOL Distance Education Courses

Non-profit making organisation which accredits the following distance learning TESOL qualifications:

1) Preliminary Certificate of Educational Studies in TESOL
- Pre-Cert.(ES) TESOL *(Study time: 70 hours)*

2) Certificate of Educational Studies in TESOL - Cert.(ES) TESOL
(Study time: 120-150 hours)

3) Certificate in the Theory and Methodology of TESOL -
Cert.(TM) TESOL *(Study time: 250 hours)*

4) Diploma in the Theory and Methodology of TESOL or TESP
- Dip.(TM) TESOL or Dip.(TM) TESP
(Study time: 400-450 hours. Open to candidates who have at least 2 years teaching experience)

Distance-trained candidates who are qualified Associate Teachers, i.e. holders of the Certificate of Educational Studies in TESOL (an ACTDEC level 2 qualification), but without teaching practice experience, are provided with a TP-portfolio. Schools willing to offer supervised teaching practice, under the scheme, work with associate teachers to complete the portfolio record of achievement. Where a school is recognised as proficient, and accredited by ACTDEC, the teacher, having satisfactorily completed the schedule of teaching practice laid down by ACTDEC, receives an additional practical teaching certificate issued by the Council.

A copy of the ACTDEC Code of Practice, Information and list of members can be obtained from:

The Secretary, ACTDEC, 21 Wessex Gardens, Dore,
Sheffield S17 3PQ   Fax: 0114 236 0774
E-Mail: info@ACTDEC.org.uk
Web: http://www.ACTDEC.org.uk

There are also ACTDEC members in America and Spain. Contact ACTDEC for further details.

 TEFL Distance Learning Course Providers

Eurolink Teacher Training / Training Link International
3, Abbeydale Road South, Millhouses, Sheffield. S7 2QL
Tel: 0114 262 1522   Fax: 0114 236 0774
E-Mail: info@eurolinkcourses.co.uk
Web: http://www.eurolinkcourses.co.uk

Training Link offers courses leading to the following ACTDEC qualifications:

Pre-Cert.(ES) TESOL
Price: UK £216 Europe £234 Rest of World £252

Cert.(ES) TESOL
Price: UK £363 Europe £408 Rest of World £453

Certificate in Practical Phonetics:
Price: UK £175 Europe £187 Rest of World £199

Eurolink Teacher Training offers courses leading to the following College of Teachers and ACTDEC qualifications:

Cert.(TM) TESOL and ACoT (TESOL)
Price: UK: £519   Europe: £567 Rest of World: £667

Advanced Certificate in TESOL (A.Cert.TESOL)
Price: UK: £898   Europe: £946 Rest of World: £1037

Dip. (TM) TESOL and Dip.CoT (TESOL)
Price: UK: £658 Europe: £697 Rest of World: £780

Advanced Diploma in TESOL (A.Dip TESOL)
Price: UK: £1115   Europe: £1154   Rest of World: £1237

Combined Dip. (TM) TESOL/Dip.CoT (TESOL) & FCoT (TESOL)
Price: UK: £1594   Europe: £1632   Rest of World: £1715

Masters' level FCoT (Part 2 only).
Fast track for holders of other acceptable Part 1 qualifications.
Price: UK: £1020   Europe: £1020   Rest of World: £1020

Payment can also be made by instalments - contact Eurolink Teacher Training for further details.

For the College of Teachers' Advanced Certificate in TESOL, the Teaching Practice and face-to-face component is provided by the Carl Duisberg Language Centre Sheffield, 19-33 Bells Court, Bells Square, Sheffield S1 2FY

Teaching Practice is also available in Germany and Spain.
See www.eurolinkcourses.co.uk for details.

INTESOL
4 Higher Downs, Knutsford, Cheshire WA16 8AW
Tel: 01565 631743 Fax: 01565 631366
E-Mail: Lynda@intesol.freeserve.co.uk
Web: http://www.intesoltesoltraining.com

INTESOL runs the following ACTDEC accredited course:

Cert.(ES) TESOL
Price: UK: £365 *(or £395 if paid in 3 instalments)*
Europe: £385 *(or £415 if paid in 3 instalments)*
Rest of World: £395 *(or £425 if paid in 3 instalments)*

Courses start at any time of year.

INTESOL also offers a four week Cert.(ES) TESOL intensive course, with two weeks distance learning and two weeks face-to-face tuition. Course takes place at Regents College in Nantwich, Cheshire.

Price: £695 (non-residential)   £895 (residential)

Also available is a Certificate in English for Specific Purposes (ESP) This consists of 9 units and take approx. 90hrs to complete.

Price: £195 (UK) £220 (EU) £240 (rest of world)

Teaching Practice Certificate
After completing the Cert. of Educational Studies in TESOL, students can do a week's teaching practice at the English Language Centre in Regents College, in Nantwich. This costs £125 or £195 with accommodation.

 ## Other Distance Learning TEFL Courses

The **National Extension College (NEC)** offers an 'Introduction to TEFL' distance learning course.

Designed to help students prepare for a TEFL Certificate course, it covers the two central exam topics of language and learning awareness. Prospective students will need a good level of general education, including an English 'A' level.

Course consists of individual tuition with 6 marked assignments. PRICE: £215 (payment by instalments also possible.)

For the NEC address and contact details, see the chapter on 'EFL Correspondence Courses'.

The **Montessori Centre International Ltd** runs a 'Teaching English as an Additional Language (TEAL)' Certificate, designed to give educators a Montessori perspective on TESL.

There are two types of certificate: Stage I and Stage II. The Stage I assessment is entirely marked by coursework, whereas the Stage II certificate includes a two week TEAL workshop and examination.

PRICE: £400 for a Stage I certificate. For Stage II add the cost of the workshop, £490 (inclusive of £90 non-refundable registration fee) and £65 for the written paper examination.

For more details contact: Montessori Centre International Ltd,
18 Balderton Street, London W1K 6TG
Tel: 020 7493 0165   Fax: 020 7629 7808.
Email: mci@montessori.ac.uk   Web: http://www.montessori.ac.uk

The English Training Centre (ETC)

The ETC was established in 1997 by two tutors who are founder members of BIELT (The British Institute of English Language Teachers). The Centre offers a Certificate Course in Teaching English as a Foreign Language, which is suitable for people considering teaching, or for teachers with less than two years experience in TEFL.

The course consists of 3 modules ("The Fundamentals", "Teaching the Four Language Skills" and "Practical Skills for the EFL teacher") sub-divided into 12 units. The course duration is usually 10 to 24 weeks (recommended length is 12 weeks).

PRICE: Registration and Module 1: £120 by post or email. Modules 2 and 3: £130 by post / £100 by email (i.e. a total of £250 by post or £220 by email).

For more details contact: The English Training Centre
The Guildhall, Box 104, University of Birmingham,
Edgbaston Park Road, Birmingham B15 2TU
Fax: 0121 449 2221   Email: psimmonds@englishtc.co.uk
Web: http://www.englishtc.co.uk

Plus: *(see main TEFL course listing for addresses)*

Aston University: *distance learning Dip./ MSc in TESOL/TESP*
Duration: 2 to 5 years. Course start dates: Jan, Apr, July, Oct.
Price: on application.   Email: lsu@aston.ac.uk
Web: http://www.aston.ac.uk/pg/pros/lestptesol.htm

International House: *Distance Learning DELTA*
Produced in conjunction with The British Council.
£1610 plus Cambridge exam registration fee of approx. £200
Duration: 8 months (studying for about 10 hrs a week)
Web: http://www.thedistancedelta.com/

Institute of Education (London): *Online distance learning MA TESOL*
Duration: 2 years min. to 4 years max. (studying 10 hours /wk)
Price: £5250   Email: c.croft@ioe.ac.uk
Web: http://k1.ioe.ac.uk/lie/tesoldl.html

<u>Moray House:</u> *distance learning MEd TESOL*
Duration: 3 years (average) to 6 years max. Price: on application.
Web: http://www.education.ed.ac.uk/crd/tesol/MEd-distance.html

<u>University of Birmingham:</u> *distance learning MA TEFL/TESL*
Duration: 30 months. Price: on application.

<u>University of Manchester:</u> *MEd in ELT* and *MEd in Educational Technology and ELT*   Duration of both: 3 to 4 years part-time
Can either be studied by distance learning or on-site.
Email: education.enquiries@man.ac.uk
Tel: 0161 275 3467 Fax: 0161 275 3480
Web: http://www.education.man.ac.uk/langlit/EdTech/ETechCourses.htm

<u>University of Sheffield:</u> *MEd in English Language Teaching*
Duration: 2-4 years Price: £1980 per year (payable first two years only)
Web: http://www.shef.ac.uk/education/courses/MEdELT.shtml

<u>University of Surrey:</u> *distance learning Dip./MA in Linguistics (TESOL) & MSc in English Language Teaching Management*
Price: £5600
Web: http://www.surrey.ac.uk/ELI/ma.html
also Dip./MSc in English Language Teaching Management
Duration: 17-27 months. Price: £6960
Web: http://www.surrey.ac.uk/ELI/msc.html

<u>University of York:</u> *distance learning MA in Teaching English to Young Learners*   Duration: 2 yrs part-time. Price: £3150 per year (i.e. £6300 in total)
Web: http://www.york.ac.uk/inst/ltc/efl/courses/ma/mateyl.htm#Restructuring

 USEFUL TEFL ADDRESSES:
(in alphabetical order)

<u>GENERAL:</u>

BATQI - *the British Association of TESOL Qualifying Institutions*
Gerard Gilpin, 35 Barclay Square, Bristol BS8 1JA
Tel 0117 928 7093   Fax: 0117 925 1537
Email: G.M.Clibbon@ bristol.ac.uk   Web: http://www.batqi.org

BIELT - The British Institute of English Language Teachers
Web: http://www.bielt.org.uk

The British Council
English Language Information Section Medlock Street, Manchester, M15 4AA
Tel: 0161 957 7137 Fax: 0161 957 7168 Web: http://www.britcoun.org

Department for Education and Employment (DfEE)
Mowden Hall, Darlington DL3 9BG   Tel: 01325 460155   Fax: 01325 392695

EL Gazette: *Trade journal*
Dilke House, 1 Malet Street, London W1 7JA
Tel: 020 7255 1969 Fax: 020 7255 1972   Web: http://www.elgazette.com

IATELF -
International Association of Teachers of English as a Foreign Language
3, Kingsdown Chambers, Kingsdown Park, Whitstable, Kent. CT5 2DJ
Tel: 01227 276528 Fax: 01227 274415   Web: http://www.iatefl.org/

NATECLA - *National Association for Teaching English and other Community Languages to Adults*
National Centre, South Birmingham College, 524 Stratford Road, Birmingham B11 4AJ
Tel: 0121 694 5000 Fax: 0121 694 5007

RECRUITMENT AGENCIES / VOLUNTARY ORGANISATIONS:

Central Bureau for Educational Visits & Exchanges
Organises the 'English Language Assistants Programme' which places British assistants in schools and colleges overseas for one academic year to help with the teaching of English. (Usually language students.)
Seymour Mews, London W1H 9PE.   Tel: 020 7389 4764 (England & Wales)
or 0131 447 8024 (Scotland)   or 01232 664418 (Northern Ireland)

CfBT (Centre for British Teachers) Education Services
Recruiters of qualified EFL teachers
1, The Chambers, East Street, Reading RG1 4JD
Tel: 0118 952 3900 Fax: 0118 952 3939   Web: http://www.cfbt.com

Christians Abroad
Offers advice about opportunities to work overseas for people of any faith.
1 Stockwell Green, London SW9 9HP
Tel: 020 7737 7811   Fax: 020 77373237
E-mail: projects@cabroad.org.uk   Web: http://www.cabroad.org.uk

Council on International Educational Exchange
Graduates (with or without a TEFL qualification) for teaching posts in China.
52 Poland Street, London W1V 4JQ
Tel: 020 7478 2000   Fax: 020 7734 7322 E-mail: InfoUK@ciee.org

The East European Partnership
Places selected graduate volunteers in Central & Eastern Europe and the former Soviet Union.   Carlton House, 27A Carlton Drive, London SW15 2BS
Tel: 020 8780 2841   Fax: 020 8780 9592

ELT Banbury
TEFL recruitment for Europe, Far and Middle East.
49, Oxford Road, Banbury, Oxfordshire. OX16 9AH
Tel: 01295 263480 Fax: 01295 271658   E-mail: 100760.2247@compuserve.com

English World-wide - *EFL recruitment agency*
The Italian Building, Dockhead, London SE1 2BS
Tel: 020 7252 1402 Fax: 020 72318002 Email: nfo.eww@pop3.hiway.co.uk

ILC Recruitment - *Recruitment agency for the UK & overseas*
White Rock, Hastings, East Sussex. TN43 1JY
Tel: 01424 720109   Fax: 01424 720323 Web: http://www.ilcgroup.com

International House
Language school chain, with branches around the world.
106 Piccadilly, London W1V 9FL
Tel: 020 7491 2598 Fax: 020 7409 095 http://www.ihlondon.com

The Japan Exchange & Teaching (JET) Programme
Recruits English speakers to work as assistant teachers in Japanese schools.
The Council for International Exchange, 33, Seymour Place
London W1H 6AT Tel: 020 7224 8896

Linguarama
*Large chain of language schools looking for teachers for Germany
and Austria.*   89, High Street, Alton, Hants. GU34 1LG   Tel: 01420 80899
E-mail: personnel@linguarama.com   Web: http://www.linguarama.com

Nova Group
Runs over 270 language schools in Japan. Send CV and covering letter to:
Carrington House, 126-130 Regent Street, London W1R 5FE.
Tel: 020 7734 2727   Fax: 020 7734 3001   Web: http://www.nova-group.com

The Project Trust
Educational charity placing 17-19 year olds in schools around the world.
St. John Street, London EC1M 4AA
Tel: 020 7490 8764   Fax: 020 7490 8759 E-mail: projecttrust@compuserve.com

Saxoncourt Recruitment
*Recruits EFL teachers for positions in Asia, Western/Eastern Europe, Latin American
and the Middle East.*   59 South Molton Street, London. W1Y 1HH
Tel: 020 7499 8533 Fax: 020 7499 9374 E-mail: recruit@saxoncourt.com

VSO (Voluntary Service Overseas)
*Places nearly 2000 volunteers in developing countries around the world. Volunteers
only receive a local salary, but are provided with flights and accommodation.*
317, Putney Bridge Road, London, SW15 2PN
Tel: 020 8780 2266 Fax: 020 8780 1326   Web: http://www.vso.org.uk

For more TEFL job opportunities, see the chapter on Internet Sites.

PART III

GENERAL INFORMATION

for both EFL and TEFL

EFL PUBLISHERS

The following pages contain a directory of the main EFL publishers in the United Kingdom. Information about their current titles and prices can be obtained by contacting them directly. Publishers of CALL (Computer Assisted Language Learning) material are also listed.

Liste de maisons d'édition spécialistes de l'anglais pour étrangers. Contacter ces maisons directement pour recevoir des renseignements sur leurs livres.

Verlage, die Bücher zum Thema 'Englisch als Fremdsprache' publizieren. Setzen Sie sich mit den entsprechenden Firmen direkt in Kontakt, um Informationen zu ihren Büchern zu bekommen.

Lista de editores de publicaciones sobre la lengua inglesa como idioma para extranjeros. Póngase en contacto directamente con las compañías para recibir informaciones sobre sus libros.

Elenco delle case editrici di pubblicazioni didattriche per l'apprendimento della lingua inglese per stranieri. Contattare direttamente le case editrici per ottenere informazioni sulle loro pubblicazioni.

AMCD Publications Ltd
PO Box 182, Altrincham, Cheshire WA15 9UA
Tel/Fax: 0161 434 5105

The Anglo - American Book Co.
Crown Buildings, Bancyfelin, Carmarthenshire SA33 5ND
Tel: 01267 211880 Fax: 01267 211882
Web: http://www.anglo-american.co.uk

Ann Arbor Publishers Ltd.
PO Box 1, Bedford, Northumberland NE70 7JX
Tel: 01668 214460   Fax: 01668 214484
Web: http://www.annarbor.co.uk

Avanti Books
8 Parsons Green, Boulton Road, Stevenage, Herts. SG1 4QG
Tel: 01438 350155   Fax: 01438 741131

Barefoot Books
18 Highbury Terrace, London N5 1NP
Tel: 020 7704 6492 Fax: 020 7359 5798
Web: http://www.barefoot-books.com

Robert Beard
Lowden Manor Cottage, Lowden Hill, Chippenham, Wilts. SN15 2BX
Tel/Fax: 01249 659792

Berlitz Publishing Ltd.
9-13 Grosvenor Street, London W1X 9FB
Tel: 020 7518 8300 Fax: 020 7518 8310 Web: http://www.berlitz.com

Bogle L'Ouverture Publications Ltd
PO Box 2186, London W13 9Q2 Tel/Fax: 020 8579 4920

Broadcast Books
4 Cotham Vale, Bristol BS6 6HR
Web: http://www.broadcastbooks.demon.co.uk

Cambridge University Press
The Edinburgh Building, Shaftesbury Road, Cambridge CB2 2RU
Tel: 01223 312393 Fax: 01223 315052
Web: http://www.cup.cam.ac.uk/elt and www.cambridge.org/elt

Carel Press
4 Hewson Street, Carlisle CA2 5AU
Tel: 01228 538928   Fax: 01228 591816
Web: http://ourworld.compuserve.com/homepages/Carel_Press

Centre for Information on Language Teaching & Research
20 Bedfordbury , London WC2N 4JB
Tel: 020 7379 5101 Fax: 020 7379 5082 Web: http://www.cilt.org.uk

Centre for Language Teaching in Primary Education
Webber Street, London SE1 8QW
Tel: 020 7401 3382   Fax: 020 7928 4624 Web: http://www.cple.co.uk

Chancerel International Publishers Ltd
120 Long Acre, London WC2E 9PA
Tel: 020 7240 2811   Fax: 020 7836 4186

Child's Play (International) Ltd
Ashworth Road, Bridgemead, Swindon, Wilts SN5 7YD
Tel: 01793 616286   Fax: 01793 512795 Web: http://www.childs-play.com

Clifton Press
PO Box 100, Manchester M20 6GZ
Tel: 0161 432 5811 Fax: 0161 443 2766   Web: http://www.mantrex.co.uk

Peter Collin Publishing Ltd.
1 Cambridge Road, Teddington, Middlesex TW11 8DT
Tel: 020 8943 3386 Fax: 020 8943 1673   Web: http://www.pcp.co.uk

Crown House Publishing Ltd
Crown Buildings, Bancyfelin, Carmarthenshire SA33 5ND
Tel: 01267 211345   Fax: 01267 211882
Web: http://www.crownhouse.co.uk

CYP Ltd
The Fairway, Bush Fair, Harlow, Essex CM18 6LY
Tel: 01279 444707 Fax: 01279 445570

DELTA Publishing
39 Alexandra Road, Addlestone, Surrey KT15 2PQ, UK
Tel: 01932 854776 Fax: 01932 849528
Web: http://www.deltabooks.co.uk

Dorling Kindersley Holdings PLC
9 Henrietta Street, London WC2E 8PS
Tel: 020 7836 5411 Fax: 020 7836 7570   http://www.dk.com

Drake Educational Associates Ltd.
St. Fagans Road, Fairwater, Cardiff CF5 3AE
Tel: 029 2056 0333 Fax: 029 2055 4909
Web: http://www.drakegroup.co.uk

Drake International Services
Market House, Market Place, Deddington, Oxon OX15 0SE
Tel: 01869 338240   Fax: 01869 338310

Educational Software Products
PO Box 1152, Oxford OX2 9YU
Tel/Fax: 01865 864224   Web: http://www.educationalsoftware.co.uk

EuroTalk Ltd   (CALL)
315-317 New Kings Road, Fulham, London SW6 4RF
Tel: 020 7371 7711 Fax: 020 7371 7781

Express Publishing
Liberty House, New Greenham Park, Newbury G19 6HW
Tel: 01635 817363 Fax: 01635 817463
Web: http://www.expresspublishing.co.uk

Gerald Duckworth & Co. Ltd
61 Frith Street, London W1V 5TA
Tel: 020 7434 4242   Fax: 020 7434 4420
Web: http://www.duckworth-publishers.co.uk

Educational Explorers
11 Crown Street, Reading, Berks. RG1 2TQ
Tel: 0118 987 3101   Fax: 0118 987 3103

ELM Publications
Seaton House, Kings Ripton, Huntingdon PE17 2NJ
Tel: 01487 773254   Fax: 01487 773359

Englang Books
17 Bond Road, Bitterne Park, Southampton S018 1LR
Tel/Fax: 023 8058 5411

European Schoolbooks Ltd
Ashville Trading Estate, The Runnings, Cheltenham GL51 9PQ
Tel: 01242 245252   Fax: 01242 224137
Web: http://www.eurobooks.co.uk

Express Publishing
3 Roman Bridge Close, Blackpool, Swansea SA3 5BE
Tel: 01792 404855   Fax: 01792 404886
Web: http://www.expresspublishing.co.uk

David Fulton Publisher Ltd
26-27 Boswell Street, London WC1N 3JD
Tel: 020 7405 5606   Fax: 020 7831 4840 Web: http://www.fultonbooks.co.uk

Garnet Publishing Ltd
8 Southern Court, South Street, Reading RG1 4QS
Tel: 0118 959 7847   Fax: 020 959 7356
Web: http://www.garnet-ithaca.demon.co.uk

Georgian Press
56 Sandy Lane, Leyland, Preston PR5 1ED
Tel: 01772 431790   Fax: 01772 431378
Web: http://www.georgianpress.co.uk

Haan Associates
PO Box 607, London SW16 1EB
Tel: 020 8793 4262 Fax: 020 8497 0309 Web: http://www.haan.co.uk

Harcourt College Publishers
Harcourt Place, 32 Jamestown Road, London NW1 7BY
Tel: 020 7424 4200   Fax: 020 7482 2293

Harper-Collins Publishers Ltd.
77-85 Fulham Palace Road, London W6 8JB
Tel: 020 8741 7070 Fax: 020 8307 4440
Web: http://www.fireandwater.com

Hodder & Stoughton
338 Euston Road, London NW1 3BH
Tel: 020 7873 6400 Fax: 020 7873 6299
Web: http://www.madaboutbooks.com

Hope Education
Orb Mill, Huddersfield Road, Oldham OL4 2ST
Tel: 0161 633 6611   Fax: 0161 633 3431
Web: http://www.hope-education.co.uk

Hilda King Educational
Ashwells, Manor Drive, Penn, High Wycombe HP10 8EU
Tel/Fax: 01494 813947 Web: http://www.hildaking.clara.net

IBI Multimedia
PO Box 2449, Chelmsford CM2 7PA
Tel: 01245 437434 Fax: 01245 472722 Web: http://www.englishlive.co.uk

Impart Books
Gwelfryn, Llanidloes Road, Newtown, Powys SY16 4HX
Tel: 01686 623484   Fax: 01686 623784

Information Transfer
Burleigh House, 15 Newmarket Road, Cambridge CB5 8EG
Tel: 01223 312227 Fax: 01223 327017   http://www.intran.co.k

International Business Images
PO Box 2449, Chelmsford CM2 7PA
Tel: 01245 473434 Fax: 01245 472722
Web: http://www.business-english.co.uk

Kingfisher Publications Ltd.
New Penderel House, 283-288 High Holborn, London WC1B 7HZ
Tel: 020 7903 9999 Fax: 020 7242 4979

Kingscourt Publishing Ltd
20 British Grove, Chiswick, London W4 2NL
Tel: 020 8741 2533   Fax: 020 8741 2533
Web: http://www.kingscourt.co.uk

Koch Distribution
Thomas House, Hampshire International Business Park, Crockford
Lane, Chineham, Berks RG24 8WH
Tel: 01256 707767   Fax: 01256 707277
Web: http://www.kochdistribution.co.uk

Kogan Page Ltd
120 Pentonville Road, London N1 9JN
Tel: 020 7278 0433 Fax: 020 7837 6348
Web: http://www.kogan-page.co.uk

Language Teaching Publications
114A Church Road, Hove BN3 2EB
Tel: 01273 736344 Fax: 01273 775361 Web: http://www.ltpwebsite.com

Letterland International Ltd
33 New Road, Barton, Cambridge, CB3 7AY
Tel: 01223 262675 Fax: 01223 264126 Web: http://www.letterland.com

Letts Educational
Aldine House, Aldine Place, London W12 8AW
Tel: 0208 740 2266 Fax: 0208 743 8451 Web: http://www.lettsed.co.uk

Linguaphone Institute Ltd.
111 Upper Richmond Road, Putney, London SW15 2TJ
Tel: 020 8333 4900 Fax: 020 8333 4833
Web: http://www.linguaphone.co.co.uk

London Chamber of Commerce and Industry Examination Board
6 Graphite Square, London SE11 5EE
Tel: 020 7793 3850 Fax: 020 7582 1806 Web: http://www.lccieb.org.uk

McGraw Hill Publishing Company
McGraw Hill House, Shoppenhangers Road, Maidenhead SL6 2QL
Tel: 01628 502500 Fax: 01628 502167   Web: http://www.mcgraw-hill.co.uk

Mac Millan Education Ltd
Between Towns Road, Oxford OX4 3PP
Tel: 01865 405700 Fax: 01865 405701 Web: http://www.mhelt.com

MFP Publications
PO Box 501, Watford, WD1 3LQ Tel/Fax: 01923 222740

Mini Flash Card Language Games
PO Box 1526, London W7 3LQ Tel: 020 8567 1076 Fax: 020 8566 3930

Multi Lingua
Park House, 13 Charlotte Street, Bristol, BS1 5PP
Tel: 0117 925 7575 Fax: 0117 925 5825 Web: http://www.lingua.co.uk

National Association for the Teaching of English
50 Broadfield Road, Broadfield Business Centre, Sheffield. S8 OJX
Tel: 0114 255 5419 Fax: 0114 255 5296 Web: http://www.nate.org.uk

New Era Publications (UK) Ltd
Saint Hill Manor, Saint Hill, East Grinstead RH19 4JY
Tel: 01342 314846   Fax: 01342 314857

Nottingham University Press
Manor Farm, Main Street, Thrumpton, Nottingham NG11 0AX
Tel: 0115 983 1001   Fax: 0115 983 1003 Web: http://www.nup.com

Oriflamme Publishing
60 Charteris Road, London N4 3AB Tel/Fax: 020 7281 8501

Oxford University Press
Oxford University Press, ELT Division, Great Clarendon Street,
Oxford OX2 6DP
Tel: 01865 556767 Fax: 01865 556646   Web: http://www.oup.com

Packard Publishing Ltd
Forum House, Stirling Road, Chichester PO19 2EN
Tel/Fax: 01243 537977

Pastest
Egerton Court, Parkgate Estate, Knutsford WA16 8DX
Tel: 01565 755226 Fax: 01565 650264 Web: http://www.pastest.co.uk

Pearson Education Ltd
PO Box 88, Edinburgh Gate, Harlow CM20 2JE
Tel: 01279 623923   Fax: 01279 623627
Web: http://www.pearsoned-ema.com and http://www.longman-elt.com

Penguin Longman Publishing
5 Bentinck Street, London W1M 5RN
Tel: 0207 487 6000 Fax: 0207 486 4204
Web: http://www.penguinreaders.com

Philograph Publications Ltd
North Way, Walworth Industrial Estate, Andover SP10 5BA
Tel: 01264 332226 Fax: 01264 332171

Pomegranate Press
Church Cottage, Westmeston, Hassocks BN6 8RH
Tel/Fax: 01273 846743

Richmond Publishing
19 Berghem Mews, Blythe Road, London W14 0HN
Tel: 0207 371 3976 Fax: 0207 371 3824 Web: http://www.richmondelt.com

The Robinswood Presss
South Avenue, Stourbridge DY8 3XY
Tel: 01384 397475 Fax: 01384 440443
Web: http://www.robinswood.co.uk

Schofield and Sims Ltd
Dogley Mill, Fency Bridge, Huddersfield HD8 0NQ
Tel: 01484 607080 Fax: 01484 606815

Sherwood Forest
PO Box 10, Nottingham NG1 1LZ   Tel: 0115 953 2010

Studymates
Unit 5, Dolphin Building, Queen Anne's Battery, Plymouth PL4 0LP
Tel: 01752 262626 Fax: 01752 262641 Web: http://www.studymates.co.uk

Summertown Publishing
26 Grove Street, Oxford OX2 7JT
Tel: 01865 514770 Fax: 01865 513924 Web: http://www.summertown.co.uk

Vektor Ltd
6-10 Hanover Street, Manchester M4 4AH
Tel: 0161 828 3000 Fax: 0161 828 3001 Web: http://www.vektor.com

Verulam Publishing Ltd.
152a Park Street Lane, Park Street, St. Albans, Herts. AL2 2AU
Tel: 01727 872770   Fax: 01727 873866
Web: http://www.verulampub.demon.co.uk

Winslow Press Ltd.
Telford Road, Bicester, Oxon OX6 0TS
Tel: 01869 244644 Fax: 01869 320040
Web: http://www.winslow-press.co.uk

DIRECTORY OF EFL INTERNET SITES

The internet provides a vast array of language learning resources. It is possible to use on-line dictionaries, complete grammar exercises or get into contact with other language learners, so that you can exchange ideas and information.

One of the first sites you should look at is, of course, the Europa Pages home page! The address is:

http://www.europa-pages.com

You will find some of the information contained in this book, as well as details of other European language courses. Many of the links below are also provided on our site.
(Please note: In the fast moving world of the internet, it is likely that some of the site addresses given will have changed by the time you try to access them. Most should contain, however, a link to the new site.)

L'Internet offre un énorme choix de resourses pour apprendre des langues étrangères. On peut utiliser des dictionnaires, faire des exercices de grammaire ou bien entrer en contact avec d'autres étudiants pour échanger idées et renseignements. Le premier site que vous devriez choisir est le nôtre!:
http://www.europa-pages.com

Das Internet liefert eine große Anzahl an Informationen über Hilfsmittel zur Spracherlernung oder Lehrmittel. Es ist möglich, Wörterbücher oder komplette Grammatiklektionen abzurufen oder mit anderen Sprachschülern in Kontakt zu treten, um Ideen und Informationen auszutauschen. Eine der Seiten, die Sie zuerst einsehen sollten, ist die homepage von Europa Pages!:
http://www.europa-pages.com

La Internet proporciona una amplia gama de facilidades para aprender idiomas. Es posible usar diccionarios, ejercicios de gramática o ponerse en contacto con otros estudiantes para intercombiar ideas e informaciones.

El primer 'home page' tiene que ser lo de Europa Pages. La señas son:
http://www.europa-pages.com

L'Internet offre un'ampia gamma di risorse per l'apprendimento delle lingue straniere. È possibile accedere a dizionari, esercizi di grammatica o addirittura mettersi in contatto con altri studenti di lingue, in modo da scambiarsi idee e informazioni. Controllare innanzitutto 'Europa Pages home page'! L'indirizzo è:
http://www.europa-pages.com

 Sites with lots of links to other EFL web pages:

AAA EFL Links
Links to resources for English students and teachers of English.
http://www.aaaefl.co.uk

About.com Guide to English as 2nd Language
Comprehensive guide to using the Net as an English learning/teaching resource. *http://esl.about.com*

Dave's ESL Café
Probably the most extensive ESL site on the web. *http://www.eslcafe.com*

ESL Flow
Loads of links from around the world, presented in the style of a learning level flow chart. Divided into elementary, pre-intermediate and intermediate levels.
http://www.homestead.com/ESLflow/Index.html

ESL Home Page
A collection of ESL links and resources on the Web.
http://www.lang.uiuc.edu/r-li5/esl/

Europa Pages
English Language & UK Travel Links
http://www.europa-pages.com/links/english_links.html

The Human Languages Page   http://www.june29.com/HLP

Language Learning Resource Centre   http://ml.hss.cmu.edu/llrc

Lingua Center
English and ESL resources for students and teachers.
http://deil.lang.uiuc.edu/ LinguaCenter

Multilingual Circus: http://www.multilinguals.com.au

Dictionaries / Thesauri / Reference

Acronym Dictionary
Constantly updated - you can even add new acronyms yourself!
http://www.ucc.ie/info/net/acronyms/acro.html

Acronym Finder
Over 55,000 acronyms and their meanings.   *http://www.mtnds.com/af*

ARTFL Project
A searchable forms-based Roget's Thesaurus.
http://humanities.uchicago.edu/forms_unrest/ROGET.html

Babelfish
Translate single words, phrases or entire web pages to or from French,
German, Italian or Spanish to English.   *http://babelfish.altavista.com*

Bartlett's Book of Familiar Quotations
A searchable list of familiar quotations. Also finds the quote's author.
http://www.columbia.edu/acis/bartleby/bartlett

British/American English dictionary
http://www.peak.org/~jeremy/dictionary/dict.html

The Internet Dictionary Project
Multi-lingual dictionary - English to a wide range of other languages
http://www.june29.com/IDP/IDPsearch.html

The LOGOS Dictionary
Can Translate into 24 languages. Includes audio files to help with
pronunciation.   *http://www.logos.it/owa-s/dictionary_dba.sp?lg=EN*

OneLook Dictionaries
Searchable index of over 100 Internet-accessible online dictionaries/
glossaries. Dictionaries are arranged by topic, but you can search them
all at once.   *http://www.onelook.com/*

The Oxford English Dictionary Online: *http://www.oed.com/*

Rhyming Dictionary
Enter an English word, it returns a list of words which rhyme.
http://bobo.link.cs.cmu.edu/cgi-bin/dougb/rhyme.cgi

Roget'S Thesaurus
Searchable version Roget's Thesaurus. *http://www.thesaurus.com*

Webster's Revised Unabridged Dictionary
1913 edition. Searchable English dictionary. From the ARTFL Project.
http://humanities.uchicago.edu/forms_unrest/webster.form.html

Grammar

CNN Newsroom and Worldview for ESL
Grammar and vocabulary exercises, as well as speaking or writing
discussion questions for ESL students.
http://lc.byuh.edu/cnn_n/cnn-n_page.html

An Elementary English Grammar
Descriptions and examples of aspects of English grammar.
http://www.hiway.co.uk/~ei/intro.html

Englishclub.net
Grammar, reference and other resources.   *http://www.englishclub.net*

The English Zone
Idioms, grammar, written comprehension etc.
http://home.earthlink.net/~emallory/index.html

Grammar and Style Notes
For university level students.
http://andromeda.rutgers.edu/~jlynch/Writing

Grammar Help Page   *http://www.hut.fi/~rvilmi/help/grammar_help/*

Grammar NOW!
Your grammar questions answered!   *http://www.grammarnow.com*

GWYNI (Grammar When You Need It)
For beginners to advanced.
http://www.geocities.com/Athens/Olympus/7583/

Guide to Grammar and Writing
Advanced level aimed at potential university students.
http://webster.commnet.edu/HP/pages/darling/grammar.htm

HyperGrammar   - English grammar course.
http://www.uottawa.ca/academic/arts/writcent/hypergrammar/grammar.html

On-Line English Grammar
On-line English grammar site, with information about English grammar,
question-and-answer pages etc. *http://www.edunet.com/english/grammar*

Online Grammar Tutor
Free lessons covering range of grammatical topics.
http://nz.com/webnz/checkers/grammar2.html

Reading & Writing

The Able Writer: A Rhetoric & Handbook
For university level students.   *http://www.odu.edu/~jpb/ablewriter.html*

Bangkok Post
Exercises and vocabulary explanations to help users read an English newspaper.
http://www.bangkokpost.com/education

BookLink Home Page
Extensive online bookshop for ESL teaching materials including over 3000 titles from more than 50 publishers.
http://www.intac.com/~booklink/esl.htm

The Children's Literature WWW Page
http://www.ucalgary.ca/~dkbrown/index.html

The Curmudgeon's Stylebook - English usage and style guide.
http://www.theslot.com/contents.html

Glossary of Poetic Terms
Glossary of poetic literary terms with English definitions.
http://shoga.wwa.com/~rgs/glossary.html

The On-Line Books Page.
Library with over 5,000 texts. *http://www.cs.cmu.edu/books.html*

Project Gutenberg
Over 10,000 public domain texts are held on this site. *http://sailor.gutenberg.org*

Writing Den
Rules and advice for intermediate level students.
http://www2.actden.com/writ_den/tips/contents.htm

Listening & speaking

Tip:
In order to listen to most sites, you will need to install 'Real Player'.
This can be downloaded from: *http://www.real.com*

All Things Considered - National Public Radio
Listen to individual stories or an entire broadcast.
http://www.npr.org/programs/atc/

American Accent Training   http://www.americanaccent.com

Audio Books
All types of books read in English.   *http://www.audioNet.com/books/*

Audio Net
Books, items from the news, interviews etc. *http://www.audionet.com*

BBC World Service
http://www.bbc.co.uk/worldservice/audio/index.htm
Also: *http://www.bbc.co.uk/worldservice/BBC_English/words/index.htm*
Which has vocabulary explanations.

Book Radi
Interviews with authors discussing their latest titles.
http://www.BookRadio.com

British English Pronunciation
http://www.engl.polyu.edu.hk/MATERIALS/Pronunciation/1a-index.htm

Broadcast.com
Sports, books, travel, news and a wide range of other topics covered.
Very extensive site.   *http://www.broadcast.com*

The CMU Pronouncing Dictionary -
Look up the pronunciation of American English words. (Dictionary is also
available to download.) *http://www.speech.cs.cmu.edu/cgi-bin/cmudict*

Cyber Listening Lab
Interactive listening exercises and quizzes.   *http://www.esl-lab.com*

The English Listening Lounge
Listening comprehension using recordings made for ESL learners.
http://www.EnglishListening.com

English Pronunciation   http://www.faceweb.okanagan.bc.ca/pron/

History Channel - Famous speeches that have changed the world.
http://www.historychannel.com/speeches/index.html

Interactive Listening Comprehension
Listen to a text and then answer questions on it.
http://deil.lang.uiuc.edu/LCRA/

International Phonetic Association
http://www.arts.gla.ac.uk/IPA/ipa.html

Learning Oral English Online
An online conversation book for intermediate ESL learners.
http://www.lang.uiuc.edu/r-li5/book/

New York Times - Listen to a range of Interviews.
http://www.nytimes.com/books/specials/audio.html

Pseudo.com - TV you can't get on TV!
Audio and video programmes, on a range of topics.
http://www.pseudo.com

Royale Software   *http://www.royalesoft.com*

Sounds of English
Focuses on American pronunciation.
http://mason.gmu.edu/~swidmaye/sounds.htm

 Vocabulary

A.Word.A.Day Home Page
New word introduced everyday, with explanation and sound clip.
http://www.wordsmith.org/words/today.html

American Slanguages
US slang explained.   *http://www.slanguage.com/index.html*

Britspeak
cultural and linguistic differences between British English and American
English. Includes problem words for English speakers.
http://pages.prodigy.com/NY/NYC/britspk/main.html

The Dialectizer
Translate English to cockney, jive, redneck etc. Crazy but fun!
http://rinkworks.com/dialect/

Focusing on Words
A series to improve your vocabulary by learning the Greek/Latin roots of
English words.   *http://www.wordfocus.com/*

Foreign Languages for Travellers
Basic phrases, vocabulary etc.   *http://www.travlang.com/languages*

Idioms: Introduction   *http://www.eslcafe.com/idioms*

University of Tampere
Focuses on idioms.   *http://www.uta.fi/FAST/US8/us8sked.html*

Vocabulary University
This site is actually aimed at children, but is good for non-native speakers. *http://www.vocabulary.com/index.html*

Word Play
Index of sites that feature fun with words. Includes anagrams, cool words, poetry, and more. *http://homepage.interaccess.com/~wolinsky/word.htm*

The Word Wizard
English education and entertainment site. Periodic contests, questions & answers about English, word-a-day, and more. Requires free registration. *http://wordwizard.com/*

 English for Specific Purposes (ESP)

Business English Resources
Extensive list of useful links.
http://babel.uoregon.edu/aei/esp/tcis_biblio.html

Compendium of Environmental Acronyms
http://www.umr.edu/~aeg/arco/arco.html

Computing Dictionary
Comprehensive online computing dictionary.
http://wombat.doc.ic.ac.uk/foldoc/index.html

Cutting Edge
UK and US English business and finance terms.
http://homepages.enterprise.net/edge/GlossUK.html

EMP - English for Medical Purposes
http://www.unav.es/emp/emp.html

English for Academic Purposes
http://sun1.bham.ac.uk/johnstf/timeap3.htm

Internet and Unix Dictionary
Dictionary of Internet and Unix terms.
http://www.msg.net/kadow/answers.html

Online Guide to Scientific Presentations
For EFL students.
http://www.jaist.ac.jp/~mark/ScientificPresentation.html

Online Technical Writing
http://www.io.com/~hcexres/tcm1603/acchtml/acctoc.html

What is?
Technological reference site.   *http://whatis.com*

 Test your English

Better English Business Exercises - Range of grammar and vocabulary
tests.   *http://www.better-english.com/exerciselist.html*

English Learner
Games and quizzes.   *http://www.englishlearner.com*

Quick Placement Test
Produced by the Cambridge Exam board and the Oxford University
Press, this test helps students to judge their current level of English.
http://www.oup.com/elt/global/catalogue/exams/quickplacementtest/

ESL Cafe's Quiz Page
Quizzes on a range of ESL topics.
http://www.pacificnet.net/~sperling/quiz

Self-Study Quizzes for ESL Students
http://www.aitech.ac.jp/~iteslj/quizzes/index.html

Schumann's foreign language tests
Range of vocabulary tests for English and other languages.
http://ourworld.compuserve.com/homepages/JOSCHU

Test your English level
An informal test offered by Liverpool's John Moores University
http://www.livjm.ac.uk/language/engtest.htm

TOEFL Practice Questions
http://web1.toefl.org/abttoefl.html#testsect

also: *http://web1.toefl.org/abttoefl.html*
for general information on the TOEFL exam.

Chat / Pen Friends

CRIBE (Chat Room In Broken English)
Real time text chat room for non-native English users.
http://www.cup.com/bm7/cribe.htm

EF Chat Pool
Two chat rooms - one on set topics other open discussions.
http://www.englishtown.com/master/community/penpals/

ESL Café's Chat   http://www.eslcafe.com/chat/chatpro.cgi

ESL Hub Chat   http://www.soltec.net/esltutor/chat.htm

ESL Hub's Keypal Email Exchange
Find a pen-pal or leave a message.
http://www.soltec.net/esltutor/wwwboard/wwwboard.html

International ESL/EFL email student discussion lists
http://www.latrobe.edu.au/www/education/sl/sl.html

International Pen-pals
Browse the list of people looking for pen-pals, or add your own entry.
http://www.europa-pages.com/penpal_form.html

Schools' International Pen-pals
For teachers looking for pen-pals for their classes / students.
http://www.europa-pages.com/school_form.html

 TEFL / TESOL Resources

Adult Education ESL Teacher's Guide - Includes lesson plans.
http://humanities.byu.edu/elc/Teacher/TeacherGuideMain

Collin's Cobuild   http://titania.cobuild.collins.co.uk

Chorus - Software review, including CALL materials.
http://www-writing.berkeley.edu/chorus

EF Teachers' Inn - Jobs, lesson plans, news etc.
http://www.englishtown.com/master/community/teachers/

English Direct
Service for teachers and students of English as a foreign language, with country/culture information and downloadable teaching   materials as shareware. *http://ourworld.compuserve.com/homepages/English_Direct/*

English to Go
Free lesson plans based on current news articles, including handouts, notes and activities. *http://www.english-to-go.com*

English Teaching Materials
Links for teachers and students. *http://eleaston.com*

ESL Forums Network
Links, book links, games, activities etc.
http://members.xoom.com/esl_forum

ESL Partyland
Forums, lesson plans, quizzes and more.
http://www.eslpartyland.com/home.htm

ESL Playhouse
Activities and games for young learners.
http://members.tripod.com/~ESL4Kids

ESL SuperStore
ESL product information from over 35 publishers. *http://eslss.com*

Homepage for TESL-EJ - Teaching English as a Second Language Electronic Journal.
http://www.kyoto-su.ac.jp/information/tesl-ej/index.html

IATEFL
The International Association of Teachers of English as a Foreign Language *http://www.iatefl.org*

Language & Learning Awareness
Online course from the National Extension College. An introduction to TEFL from a teacher's perspective. *http://www.edunet.com/nec/*

One World - One People
Lessons and games. *http://members.aol.com/Jakajk/ESLLessons.html*

Pizzaz
Creative writing handouts.
http://darkwing.uoregon.edu/~leslieob/pizzaz.html

Sarah and John's TEFL Pitstop
Yet more help with those lesson plans!
http://www.lingolex.com/jstefl.htm

TEFL Farm
Reviews and lots of other information for TEFL teachers.
http://www.teflfarm.com

TESOL Online
Trade association site, with information on joining etc.
http://www.tesol.edu/

The Virtual English Language Centre
Resources for English as a second language (ESL) students and teachers.
http://www.comenius.com/index.html

 TEFL Employment

Agora Employment   http://www.agoralang.com/agora/employment.html

Better Resource
Jobs in Korea.   *http://www.eslkorea.com/*

Canadian Institute for Teaching Overseas (CITO)
http://www.nsis.com/~cito/CITO.html

Chat-4-Job
Real-time chat page for potential employees / employers.
http://chat4job.com/

Chronicle of Higher Education
College and university ESL jobs.   *http://chronicle.com/jobs/*

ELT News - Jobs
Jobs in Japan.   *http://www.eltnews.com/eltjobs.shtml*

ESL Café's Job Links   - Large list of links and job offers from around the world. *http://www.eslcafe.com/search/Jobs*

International Job Centre
Post a free job wanted announcement and/or view the list of ELT job offers from around the world. Employers can also post their vacancies for free.   *http://www.europa-pages.com/jobs*

J & S Resource
For teachers wishing to work in Korea.
http://www.interlog.com/~resource/

O-Hayo Sensei
For vacancies and news on teaching in Japan.
http://www.ohayosensei.com/

Taiwan Teacher   *http://www.geocities.com/Athens/Delphi/1979/*

Teach English in Mexico   *http://www.teach-english-mexico.com*

Teach English (ESL) in South Korea   *http://www.net-link.net/~us2korea/*

The Teacher's Employment Network
For working in the States.   *http://www.teachingjobs.com/*

TEFL Nation
Job offers / wanted.   *http://www.teflnetnation.com/jobs/jobindex.htm*

TEFL.net
Job offers and other TEFL news.   *http://www.tefl.net*

TEFL Professional Network   *http://tefl.com/*

TESL Job Opportunities
Job offers.   *http://www.linguistic-funland.com/tesljob.html*

Thai-American International
For Americans wishing to teach in Thailand.   *http://www.taiteach.com*

Tower of English
Jobs wanted / offered.
http://members.tripod.com/~towerofenglish/job.htm

 On-line Newspapers, Magazines and Journals

EFL Web Home Page
English as a Foreign Language online magazine.
http://www.u-net.com/eflweb/

The Interrnet TESL Journal
Articles, news, papers, ideas, and links about teaching ESL
http://www.aitech.ac.jp/~iteslj/

SOON - News in World-wide English
Site written using easy-English as an aid to those learning English. Current events, stories, English help and teachers' pages for students/teachers of English. *http://www.soon.org.uk/*

World Wide Words
Articles on Aspects of English. Essays on English usage, phrases, words, etc. *http://clever.net/quinion/words/index.htm*

UK National Press

The Times   http://www.the-times.co.uk

The Guardian http://www.guardian.co.uk

The Telegraph http://www.telegraph.co.uk

The Financial Times http://www.ft.com

The Economist http://www.economist.com

 Miscellaneous Resources

The British Council   http://www.britcoun.org

Grants to Study in the UK
A guide for overseas students   *http://www.d-s-c.demon.co.uk/suk1.html*

The Open University - http://www.open.ac.uk

Wolverhampton University - Hypertext map of British universities
http://www.scit.wlv.ac.uk/ukinfo/uk.map.html

 UK Travel and Tourism

British Tourist Authority - http://www.bta.org.uk

Wales/ Cymru - http://www.tourism.wales.gov.uk

Scottish Tourist Board - http://www.holiday.scotland.net/

Welcome to Britain - http://www.britain.co.uk

Virtual London - http://www.a-london-guide.co.uk

Visit Britain
Special service from the British Tourist Authority, with the latest information on tourist attractions and events around the country.
http://www.open.visitbritain.com

Official London Theatre Guide
Find out what's on in London's West End.
http://www.officiallondontheatre.co.uk

Information Britain
A site for tourists dedicated to promoting the history and culture of the UK.
http://www.information-britain.co.uk

ISTC - International Student Travel Confederation
http://www.istc.org/

Eurotrip
For budget independent travel in Europe
http://www.eurotrip.com

Excite City Net
Tourist information for cities world-wide
http://www.city.net

Car Hire 4 Less
Discounted car rental in the UK, with online booking.
http://www.carhire4less.co.uk

The Automobile Association UK - Where to stay, where to eat.
Find a hotel, B&B or restaurant in this searchable guide covering the whole of the UK.   *http://www.theaa.co.uk/hotels/*

About.com - United Kingdom for Visitiors
Covers hotels, nightlife, guides to all main UK cities etc.
http://gouk.about.com/travel/gouk/mbody.htm

AU PAIR WORK

Working as an au pair for an English family is an ideal way of learning the language.

The job usually involves some baby-sitting in the evenings, looking after the children in the day, and light housework.

In return, the au pair receives "pocket-money", and is provided with meals and a room.

Most families expect their au pairs to have a basic command of English, and want them to stay for at least six months, so it is work best suited for longer term visitors. However, during the summer holidays, it is possible to find shorter term posts, lasting between one to three months.

In general, there are three types of au pair positions:

1. **Demi-au pairs:** They work for about 3 hours a day, and receive approximately £20-£25 a week pocket money, plus accommodation and meals.

2. **Au pairs**: They work for about 5 hours a day, and earn around £30 - £35 a week, plus accommodation and meals.

3. **Au pair plus:** They work slightly longer hours of 6-7 a day, but earn approximately £50 a week, in addition to accommodation and meals.

Au Pairing: It's a man's world too!

Whilst this is traditionally a job for girls, young men are now allowed to become au pairs as well. Most families do, however, still prefer to have female au pairs, but some are prepared to take on young men, particularly if all their children are boys. So it is worth while checking in advance for available positions before arriving in the UK.

Regulations

There are certain regulations which apply to those seeking au pair work in Britain.

The would-be au pair must:

a) Be single and without dependants
b) Aged 17 to 27 years old
c) Hold a passport from one of the countries listed in the box.

> *Andorra, Austria, Belgium, Bosnia-Herzegovina, Croatia, Cyprus, Czech Republic, Denmark, Finland, France, Germany, Greece, Greenland, Hungary, Iceland, Ireland, Italy, Liechtenstein, Luxembourg, Macedonia, Malta, Monaco, Norway, Portugal, San Marino, Slovak Republic, Slovenia, Spain, Sweden, Switzerland, The Faroes, The Netherlands, Turkey.*

Au pair work can be found through specialised agencies, either based in your own country or in the UK. Another source of au pairing posts is 'The Lady' magazine, printed weekly (39-40 Bedford Street, London WC2E 9ER Tel: 020 7379 4717).

Would-be au pairs, and families looking for au pairs, can also visit our on-line Au pair Centre: http://www.europa-pages.com/au_pair

Enrolment procedures vary from one agency to another, but usually the would-be au pair completes a questionnaire, writes a letter presenting themselves to the family, and supplies references supporting their ability to look after children.

It is important that the au pair receives written confirmation of the work she is supposed to undertake, as misunderstandings can lead to difficulties once the stay has begun. The au pair should also ensure that she has enough free time to attend a language lessons - remembering that her time off might not correspond with the courses available.

In order to enter Britain, the au pair agency or family should write a letter confirming your position, and then you will be allowed to stay in the UK for up to two years.

Below you will find a list of some au pair agencies in Britain. It is worth while to contact several of them, in order to compare their terms.

Habiter avec une famille anglaise en aidant avec les enfants est un bon moyen d'apprendre la langue. Cependant, il faut être célibataire, âgé(e) de 17 à 27 et appartenant à l'un des pays dans la case. Pour plus de renseignements, écrivez à l'une des agences ci-dessous.

Wenn man bei einer englischen Familie wohnt und Kinder betreut, ist dies ein guter Weg, um die Sprache zu erlernen. Die Voraussetzungen hierzu: Sie müssen ledig, zwischen 17 und 27 Jahre alt und einer der in dem Kasten aufgelisteten Länder zugehörig sein. Wünschen Sie weitere Informationen, schreiben Sie an eine der unten aufgelisteten Au-Pair Agenturen.

Vivir con una familia inglesa y ayudar con los niños es un buen ambiente para aprender el idioma. Para ser "au pair" se necesita tener entre 17 y 27 años, soltero(a) y perteneciendo a uno de los países enumerados en la casilla. Para más informaciones escriba a cualquiera de las agencias de la lista más adelante.

Soggiornare presso una famiglia inglese referenziata e prendersi cura dei bambini è un ottimo modo per imparare la lingua. Questa alternativa è riservata alle ragazze nubili dai 17 ai 27 anni d'età e appartenenti ad uno dei paesi citati nel riquadro che segue. Per ulteriori informazioni, scrivere alle agenzie au-pair sottocitate.

 AU PAIR AGENCIES

A1 KIDSCARE UK

Arranges placements in: United Kingdom, Western Europe and U.S.A.

Accepts applicants from: Andorra, Austria, Belgium, Bosnia-Herzegovina, Croatia, Cyprus, Czech Republic, Denmark, Finland, France, Germany, Greece, Greenland, Hungary, Iceland, Ireland, Italy, Liechtenstein, Luxembourg, Macedonia, Malta, Monaco, Norway, Portugal, San Marino, Slovak Republic, Slovenia, Spain, Sweden, Switzerland, The Faroes, The Netherlands, Turkey

General Conditions: All families must provide the Au-Pair with a room, food, pocket money according to guidelines and opportunity to attend language classes. All Au-Pairs must have experience with children. Minimum pocket money £45/wk. Nanny, Mother's Helps & Baby-sitting positions are also available.

Other Comments: Free service for Au-Pairs, Nannies & Baby-sitters. No registration fee for families. No.1 for efficient instant application processing. For further information and application forms please visit our website or contact us via freephone, fax or e-mail.

Email: info@a1kidscare.co.uk Web: http://www.a1kidscare.co.uk
Contact: Alena Udovic-Korutaro Tel: UK freephone: 0800 096 4916 / 00 44 (0)121 622 5671 Fax: 00 44 (0)121 622 5671
Address: 3rd Floor, Suite D, Smithfield House, Digbeth, Birmingham, UK B5 6BS

ABC LEANA AU PAIRS

Arranges placements in: U.K., mainly London and Surrey.

Accepts applicants from: EU member states, Hungary, Slovakia, Czech Republic. Representatives in Sweden, Italy and Spain.

General Conditions: Ideal age 19-24. Experience with children preferable, willingness to do light housework, and ironing. Should have at least simple conversational English language ability. Flexibility to fit into family life. Minimum length of stay 6 months.

Other Comments: We have over 10 years' experience of matching au pairs and families. We offer reception meetings in London, introductions and provide information and advice to families and au pairs in order to make the arrangement a success.

Contact: Vivienne Colchester
Email: vivienne@abc-aupairs.co.uk
Web: http://www.abc-aupairs.co.uk
Tel: +44 (0)20 8299 3052   Fax: +44 (0)20 8299 6086
Address: 42 Underhill Road, London SE22 0QT. UK.

ALMONDBURY AUPAIR AGENCY

Arranges placements in: Everywhere

Accepts applicants from: Everywhere

General Conditions: No fees to aupairs. Free replacements to families

Other Comments: Job vacancies at can seen at -
http://aupair-agency.com/job-vacancies.htm

Contact: Damian Kirkwood
Email: Office@aupair-agency.com   Web: http://www.aupair-agency.com
Tel: +44 (0)1288 359159   Fax:+44 (0)1288 359159
Address: 4 Napier Road, Holland Park, London W14 8LQ. UK.

THE LONDON AU PAIR & NANNY AGENCY

Arranges placements in: Most of host-families live in London.

Accepts applicants from: E.U., Switzerland, Czech Republic & Slovakia,
Macedonia, Hungary, Bosnia-Herzegovina, Slovenia, Croatia.

General Conditions: Preferably aged 19-25. Minimum stay 6 months.
Love of children, tolerance & willingness to help with housework
essential. Our excellent after-care service includes a contact list of
other local Au Pairs on arrival & advice about language courses.
Friendly host-families very welcome.

Other Comments: For 23 years we have been placing Au Pairs
with friendly host-families in and around London. We have an
excellent reputation and our after-care service continues for Au Pairs
and Families throughout the Au Pair stay. We are happy to give
you references from previous Au Pairs and Host Families.

Contact: Maggie Dyer
Email: info@londonaupair.co.uk
Web: http://www.londonaupair.co.uk
Tel: +44 (0)20 7435 3891   Fax: +44 (0)20 7794 2700
Address: 4 Sunnyside, Childs Hill, London. NW2 2QN. U.K.

MIDSHIRES AU PAIR BUREAU

Arranges placements in: All over the UK , including England, Scotland, Wales, Northern Ireland.

Accepts applicants from: EU Member States, Bosnia, Croatia, Czech Republic, Greenland, Hungary, Macedonia, Slovak, Republic, Slovenia, Switzerland.

General Conditions: Must have at least a basic knowledge of English, childcare experience, aged between 18-27 years, willing to assist in both childcare and domestic duties, minimum stay of 6 months, willing to help in the family home for 25 hours per week plus babysitting if needed for pocket money of £45 per week .

Other Comments: Midshires place au pairs all over the UK, no fees are charged to the au pair. We offer a friendly caring service to all parties to ensure that placements run smoothly. Au pair circles, Special offers, advice on English courses, Helpline, Travel, Quarterly Newsletter etc. Established since 1995.

Contact: Lindsay Doughty
Email: enquiries@midshires-aupairs.co.uk
Web: http://www.midshires-aupairs.co.uk
Tel: +44 (01455 285503 Fax: + 44 (0) 1455 286676
Address: Willowbrook House, Cosby Road, Broughton Astley, Leicester. LE9 6PA. UK.

Other agencies:

Tip: If you want to live in a specific part of the UK, contact an agency nearest to that area - they are more likely to have a family.

ABC Nannies
62 Halkett Place, St. Helier, Jersey, Channel Isles. JE2 4WG
Tel: 01534 519990 Fax: 01534 768899
Email: help@abcnannies.net Web: http://www.abcnannies.net

ACE Au-Pairs
27 Chickerell Road, Park North, Swindon, Wiltshire SN3 2RQ
Tel/Fax: 01793 430091
Email: info@aceaupairs.co.uk Web: http://www.aceaupairs.co.uk

ACE Recruitment (au-pair and nanny service)
Jordon House, Hemp Lane, Wigginton, Nr Tring, Herts HP23 6HQ
Tel/Fax: 01442 828277
Email: info@ace-jobs.co.uk Web: http://www.ace-jobs.co.uk

A-One Au-Pairs & Nannies
Suite 216, The Commercial Centre, Picket Piece, Andover, Hampshire SP11 6RU
Tel: 01264 332500 Fax: 01264 362050
Email: info@aupairsetc.co.uk Web: http://www.aupairsetc.co.uk

Abacus Au Pair Agency
1a Ruskin Road, Hove, East Sussex BN35HA Tel / Fax: 01273 203803
Email: info@abacusaupairagency.co.uk Web: http://www.abacusaupairagency.co.uk

The Au-Pair Agency
231 Hale Lane, Edgware HA8 9QF Tel: 020 8958 1750 Fax: 020 8958 5261
Email: elaine@aupairagency.com Web: http://www.aupairagency.com

Au Pairs & Nannies Online
56 Mansfield Road, London NW3 2HT Tel/Fax: 020 7419 9972
Email: mail@aupairsonline.com Web: http://www.aupairsonline.com

Aupairmatch.co.uk
Combermere Road, Morden, Surrey SM4 6RD Tel: 0208 646 8853
Email: dora@aupairmatch.co.uk Web: http://www.aupairmatch.co.uk

Busy Bee Au Pairs
The Laurels, Meadow Close, Blackwater, Camberley, Surrey. GU17 9DB
Tel / Fax: 01276 38580
Email: jill@busybee-aupairs.co.uk Web: http://www.busybee-aupairs.co.uk

Choice Au Pairs
17 Khasiaberry, Walnut Tree, Milton Keynes MK7 7DR Tel/Fax: 01908 671067
Email: rachel@choiceaupairs.co.uk Web: http://www.choiceaupairs.co.uk

Cross Country Au Pairs
1 Bridgegate Business Park, Gatehouse Way, Aylesbury, Bucks. HP19 8XN
Tel/Fax: 01296 331552
Email: info@eur-aupair.com Web: http://www.eur-aupair.com

Ecoline Ltd
18 The Paddocks, Great Totham, Maldon, Essex Tel/Fax: 01621 893888
Email: seanbenn@ecoline.org.uk Web: http://www.ecoline.org.uk

Edgware Au Pair Agency
1565 Stratford Road, Hall Green, Birmingham B28 9JA
Tel: 0121 733 6444 Fax: 0121 733 6555
Email: solihull@100s-aupairs.co.uk Web: http://www.100s-aupairs.co.uk

Muswell Hill Au-Pairs
42 Woodland Rise, Muswell Hill, London N10 3UG
Tel: 020 8883 7594 Fax: 020 8372 6043
Email: au-pairs@muswell-hill.com Web: http://www.muswell-hill.com

Premier Global Au-Pairs
14 Burleigh Close, Addlestone, Surrey KT15 1PW
Tel: 01932 855327 Fax: 0870 063 3096
Email: Contact@globalaupairs.com Web: http://www.globalaupairs.com

A TO Z OF COMMON ELT ACRONYMS

A

ABEEB - Association of British ESOL Examining Boards

ABLS - Association of British Language Schools

ADLTM - Advanced Diploma in English Language Teaching Management (UCLES)

ACoT - Associate of the College of Teachers

ACE - Adult and Community Education

ACP (TESOL) - Associate of the College of Preceptors (now ACoT Tesol)

A.Cert.TESOL - Advanced Certificate in TESOL (College of Teachers / Preceptors)

ACTDEC - Accreditation Council for TESOL Distance Education Courses

AE - Adult Education

AEB - Associated Examining Board

AEI - Adult Education Institute

ALTE - Association of Language Testers in Europe

ALTO - Association of Language Travel Organisations

ARELS - Association of Recognised English Language Services

B

BAAL - British Association for Applied Linguistics

BACC - British Accreditation Council for Further & Higher Education

BALEAP - British Association of Lecturers in English for Academic Purposes

BALT - British Association for Language Teaching

BASELT - British Association of State English Language Teaching

BATQI - British Association of TESOL Qualifying Institutions

BC - British Council

BEC - Business English Certificate (UCLES)

BIELT: British Institute of English Language Teaching

BTEC - Business and Technology Education Council

BULATS - Business Language Testing Service (UCLES)

C

CAE - Certificate in Advanced English (UCLES)

CALL - Computer Assisted Language Learning

CBEVE - Central Bureau for Educational Visits and Exchanges

CCSE - Certificates in Communicative Skills in English (UCLES)

CEELT - Cambridge Examination in English for Language Teachers (UCLES)

CEIBT - Certificate in English for International Business and Trade (UCLES)

CELTA - Certificate in English Language Teaching to Adults (UCLES)

CELTYL - Certificate in English Language Teaching to Young Learners (UCLES)

Cert(ES) TESOL - Certificate of Educational Studies in TESOL (ACTDEC)

CertTEfIC - Specialist Certificate in Teaching English for Industry and Commerce (Trinity College)

CertTIB - Certificate in Teaching English for Business (LCCIEB)

Cert (TM) TESOL - Certificate in the Theory and Methodology of TESOL (ACTDEC)

CfBT - Centre for British Teachers

CGLI - City and Guilds of London Institute

CILT - Centre for Information on Language Teaching and Research

CILTS - Cambridge Integrated Language Teaching Schemes (UCLES)

CNAA - Council for National Academic Awards

COTE - Certificate for Overseas Teachers of English (UCLES)

CPE - Certificate of Proficiency in English (UCLES)

CRELS - Combined Registered English Language Schools (New Zealand)

CTEFLA - Certificate in Teaching English as a Foreign Language to Adults (UCLES - *replaced by CELTA*)

D

DELTA - Diploma in English Language Teaching to Adults (UCLES)

DELTYL - Diploma in English Language Teaching to Young Learners (UCLES)

DES - Diploma in English Studies (UCLES)

DFEE - Department for Education and Employment

Dip.BPE - Diploma in Business and Professional English Language Teaching (UCLES)

Dip.CoT - Diploma of the College of Teachers

Dip.CP (TESOL) - Diploma of the College of Preceptors (*now Dip.CoT Tesol*)

Dip.TESAL - Diploma in the Teaching of English to Speakers of Asian Languages (Trinity College)

Dip.TIB - Diploma in Teaching English for Business (LCCIEB)

Dip (TM) TESOL - Diploma in the Theory and Methodology of TESOL (ACTDEC)
Dip (TM) TESP - Diploma in the Theory and Methodology of TESP (ACTDEC)
DOTE - Diploma for Overseas Teachers of English (UCLES - *replaced by DELTA*)
DTEFLA - Diploma in Teaching English as a Foreign Language to Adults (UCLES – *replaced by DELTA*)

E

EAP - English for Academic Purposes
EAQUALS - European Association for Quality Language Services
EAT - European Association of Teachers
EFB - English for Business (LCCIEB)
EFC - English for Commerce (LCCIEB)
EFL - English as a Foreign Language
EFTI - English for the Tourism Industry (LCCIEB)
ELICOS - English Language Intensive Courses to Overseas Students *(Australia)*
ELSA - English Language Skills Assessment (LCCIEB)
ELT - English Language Teaching
ESB - English Speaking Board
ESL - English as a Second Language
ESOL - English to Speakers of Other Languages
ESP - English for Specific Purposes
ESU - English Speaking Union

F

FCoT - Fellow of the College of Teachers
FCE - First Certificate in English (UCLES)
FE - Further Education
FIELS - Federation of Independent English Language Schools *(New Zealand)*
FIRST - Association of British language schools.
FIYTO - Federation of International Youth Travel Organisations
FLIC - Foreign Languages for Industry and Commerce (LCCIEB)
FTBE - Foundation Certificate for Teachers of Business English (LCCIEB)

G

GNVQ - General National Vocational Qualification

H

HE - Higher Education
HNC - Higher National Certificate (BTEC)
HND - Higher National Diploma (BTEC)
HPA - Home Providers Association

I

IATEFL - International Association of Teachers of English as a Foreign Language
IB - International Baccalaureate
IDLTM - International Diploma in English Language Teaching Management (UCLES)
IELTDHE - Institute for English Language Teacher Development in Higher Education
IELTS - International English Language Testing System (UCLES-BC-IDP)
IoL - Institute of Linguists

J

JCLA - Joint Council of Language Associations
JET - Japan Exchange and Teaching Programme

K

KET - Key English Test (UCLES)

L

LAGB - Linguistics Association of Great Britain
LCCIEB - London Chamber of Commerce and Industry Examinations Board

M

MLA - Modern Language Association

N

NAAE - National Association of Advisors in English
NALA - National Association of Language Advisors
NATE - National Association for the Teaching of English
NATECLA - National Association for the Teaching of English and Community Languages to Adults
NATEFLI - National Association of TEFL in Ireland
NATESOL - National Association of Teachers of English for Speakers of Other Languages (United States)
NATFHE - National Association of Teachers in Further and Higher Education
NCILT - National Centre for Industrial Language Training
NCLE - National Congress on Languages in Education
NCML - National Council for Modern Languages in Higher and Further Education
NCVQ - National Council for Vocational

Qualifications
ND - National Diploma (BTEC)
NEAB - Northern Examinations and Assessment Board
NELLE - Networking English Language Learning in Europe
NESB - Non-English Speaking Background
NIACE - National Institute of Adult Continuing Education
NVQ - National Vocational Qualification

O

ODL - Open and Distant Learning
OFSTED - Office for Standards in Education
OIBEC - Oxford International Business English Certificate (UODLE)
OL - Open Learning
OU - Open University

P

PBE - Practical Business English (LCCIEB)
PEI - Pitman Examinations Institute
PET - Preliminary English Test (UCLES)
PGCE - Post Graduate Certificate in Education
Pre-Cert (ES) TESOL - Preliminary Certificate of Educational Studies in TESOL (ACTDEC)

Q

QTS - Qualified Teacher Status

R

RELSA - Recognised English Language Schools Association (Ireland)
RSA - Royal Society of Arts

S

SALT - Scottish Association for Language Teaching
SATEFL - Scottish Association for the Teaching of English as a Foreign Language
SATESL - Scottish Association for the Teaching of English as a Second Language
SCOTTESOL - Scottish TESOL Association
SEFIC - Spoken English for Industry and Commerce (LCCIEB)
SESOL - Spoken English for Speakers of Other Languages (Trinity College)
SIETAR - Society of International English Cultural Training and Research
SNVQ - Scottish National Vocational Qualification

T

TEC - Training and Enterprise Council
TEEP - Test of English for Educational Purposes
TEFL - Teaching English as a Foreign Language
TEP - Tourism English Proficiency (UODLE)
TESL - Teaching English as a Second Language
TESOL - Teaching English to Speakers of Other Languages
TEVAC - Teaching English for Vacation and Activity Courses
TOEFL - Test of English as a Foreign Language
TP - Teaching Practice

U

UCLES - University of Cambridge Local Examinations Syndicate
UETESOL - University Entrance Test for Speakers of Other Languages (NEAB)
UKCOSA - United Kingdom Council for Overseas Student Affairs
ULEAC - University of London Examinations and Assessment Council
UODLE - University of Oxford Delegacy of Examinations

V

VSO - Voluntary Services Overseas

W

WEFT - Written English for the Tourism Industry (LCCIEB)
WYSTC - The World Youth and Student Travel Conference

WORK PLACEMENTS

Eagle UK
Eagle House, 177 Stourbridge Road,
Halesowen, West Midlands B63 3UD
Tel: 0121 585 6177
Fax: 0121 585 7441
Email : info@eagle-uk.demon.co.uk
http://www.eagle-uk.demon.co.uk
*Work placements in the UK for 1 month to
1 year for students and graduates only.
Marketing, sales, import/export and
tourism.*

EWEP (European Work Experience Programme)
Unit 9 , Red Lion Court, Alexandra Road,
Hounslow - Middx TW3 1JS
Tel: 020 8572 29 93
Fax: 020 8572 1114
Email: sales@ewep.com
http://www.ewep.com
*Arranges placements for 18 to 25 year olds
for 2 months to 1 year in hotels, restaurants
and shops. Covers London and the
surrounding areas, but also other parts of
UK. EWEP has an accommodation
service, providing rooms with British
families or houses shared with other
students. Prices range from £55.00 to
£65.00 a week including bills.*

International Work UK
42 Studley Avenue, London E4 9PS
Tel: 020 8523 4426
Fax: 020 8503 3177
*Arranges jobs in a range of sectors for 4-24
wks.*

LAF (UK)
91 Western Road, Brighton BN1 2NW
Tel: 01273 746932
Fax: 01273 204580
E-mail: Cameron.laf@btinternet.com
*Placements from 1 to 6 months. Minimum
age 18 years. Range of sectors including
finance, tourism and marketing.*

MI - Management International
63-69 Eltham Road, London SE12 8UF
Tel: 020 8852 1261
Fax: 020 8297 0514
Email: info@managementinternational.co.uk
http://www.managementinternational.co.uk
*Placements from 4 weeks to 1 year in
marketing, finance, PR, banking, law,
hotels etc. Mostly arranged in London but
also offered around UK and Ireland.*

Trident Transnational
Saffron Court, 14b St Cross Street,
London EC1N 8XA
Tel: 020 7242 1515
Fax: 020 7430 2975
Email : transnational@trid.demon.co.uk
http://www.TheTridentTrust.org.uk
*Finds jobs in the UK for 4 weeks to 1 year.
Covers range of jobs including marketing,
sales, PR, tourism, banking, finance,
administration and computing.*

LOW COST ACCOMMODATION

Youth Hostels Association of England and Wales

*230 hostels around England and Wales,
from basic shared rooms in the
countryside, to en-suite private rooms in
city centres. Not just for the young!*
Contact: YHA (England and Wales) Ltd
Trevelyan House, Dimple Road, Matlock,
Derbyshire DE4 3YH
Tel: 0870 870 8808
Fax: 0629 592702
Email: customerservices@yha.org.uk
Web: http://www.yha.org.uk/

YMCA England
*Hostel accommodation around the country
for all sexes, ages and religious faiths.*
Contact: 640 Forest Road, London E17 3DZ
Tel: 020 8520 5599
Fax: 020 8509 3190
E-mail: info@england.ymca.org.uk
Web: http://www.ymca.org.uk

University Accommodation
*Universities around the country often rent
out their student rooms during the holidays.
(B & B = Bed and Breakfast)*

Cardiff University
*B & B and self-catering apartments
available during the Summer.*
Tel: 029 2087 5117
Email: conference@cardiff.ac.uk

King's Conference & Vacation Bureau
*B & B and self-catering apartments
available during Easter and Summer.*
Tel: 020 7848 1700 Email:
vac.bureau@kcl.ac.uk

London School of Economics
*B & B and self-catering apartments
available during Easter and Summer.*
Tel: 020 7955 7575
Email: vacation@lse.ac.uk
http://www.http://www.lse.ac.uk/vacations

Middlesex University
*B & B and self-catering apartments
available during the Summer.*
Tel: 020 8362 6513
Email: l.kalcher@mdx.ac.uk

Queen Mary, University of London
*B & B and self-catering apartments
available during the Summer.*
Tel: 020 7882 3642
Email: holiday@qmw.ac.uk
http://www.qmw.ac.uk/conferences

University College, London
*B & B and self-catering apartments
available during the Summer.*
Tel: 020 7833 8175
Email: residences@ucl.ac.uk

University of Bath
*B & B and self-catering apartments
available all year.*
Tel: 01225 826622
Email: c.d.marshall@bath.ac.uk
http://www.bath.ac.uk/conferences

University of Bristol
*B & B and self-catering apartments
available during the Summer.*
Tel: 0117 954 5501
Email: conference-office@bris.ac.uk
http://www.bris.ac.uk/Depts/Conferences

University of Durham
*B & B and self-catering apartments
available during Easter and Summer.*
Tel: 0191 3743 454
Email: conference.tourisrm@durham.ac.uk
http://www.dur.ac.uk/conference_tourism

University of Edinburgh
*B & B and self-catering apartments
available during Easter and Summer.*
Tel: 0131 651 2055
Email: edinburgh.first@ed.ac.uk
http://www.http://www.edinburghfirst.com

University of Exeter
*B & B and self-catering apartments
available during Easter and Summer.*
Tel: 01392215566
Email: conferences@exeter.ac.uk
http://www.ex.ac.uk/hospitality

University of Kent at Canterbury
*B & B and self-catering apartments
available during Easter and Summer.*
Tel: 01227 828000
Email: hospitality-enquiry@ukc.ac.uk
http://www.ukc.ac.uk/hospitality

University of Liverpool
*B & B and self-catering apartments
available during Easter and Summer.*
Tel: 0151 7946440
Email: confoff@liv.ac.uk
http://www.livuniconferences.co.uk

University of Luton
*B & B and self-catering apartments
available during the Summer.*
Tel: 01582743917
Email: gill.Lawrence@luton.ac.uk

University of North London
*B & B and self-catering apartments
available during the Summer.*
Tel: 020 7607 5417
Email: summerlets@unl.ac.uk
http://www.unl.ac.uk/accommodation/summer

University of Portsmouth
*B & B and self-catering apartments
available during the Summer.*
Tel: 023 9284 4321
Email: reservations@port.ac.uk

University of St. Andrews
*B & B and self-catering apartments
available during the Summer.*
Tel: 01334 462000
Email: holidays@st-andrews.ac.uk

University of Strathclyde
*B & B and self-catering apartments
available during the Summer.*
Tel: 0141 5534148
Email: rescat@mis.strath.ac.uk
http://www.rescat.strath.ac.uk

University of Stirling
*B & B and self-catering apartments
available Jan.to Feb. and Summer.*
Tel: 01786 467140 Email:
hohdays@stir.ac.uk
http://www.Holidays.stir.ac.uk

University of Wales Aberystwyth
*B & B and self-catering apartments
available during Easter and Summer.*
Tel: 01970 6 21960
Email: holidays@aber.ac.uk
http://www.aber.ac.uk/visitors

University of York
*B & B and self-catering apartments
available all year.*
Tel: 0190 443 2040
Email: conferences@york.ac.uk
http://www.york.ac.uk/univ/conf

*For details of these and other venues,
contact VenueMasters (formed from the
merger of BUAC - the British Universities
Accommodation Consortium and Connect
Venues):*

VenueMasters
The Workstation, Paternoster Row,
Sheffield S1 2BX
Tel: 0114 249 3090
Fax: 0114 249 3091
Email: inf@venuemasters.co.uk
Web: http://www.venuemasters.co.uk

The Experiment in International Living
EIL, 287 Worcester Road, Malvern,
Worcs. WR14 1AB.
Tel: 0800 018 4015 or 01684 562577
Fax: 01684 562212
Email: info@eiluk.org
http://www.eiluk.org (UK site)
http://www.experiment.org/ (International
Site - has branches around the world)

*An international non-profit organisation
promoting intercultural learning through
homestays, educational group travel, study
abroad, language training, work exchange,
and other cultural immersion programmes.
EIL can arrange accommodation with UK
families. Price: £213.00 for 1 week,
£555.00 for 4 weeks (£235 to £643 if
staying with a family in London). Price
includes meals.*

Other useful addresses:

BABSSCO - British Association of
Boarding School Summer Courses
c/o Harrow School, 5 High Street,
Harrow HA1 3HP
Tel: 020 8426 4638
Fax: 020 8867 7180
Email: info@babssco.org.uk
http://www.babssco.co.uk
*Arranges 2 to 4 week courses for juniors
at a range of boarding schools in the UK.
(Dulwich College for 14-18 yrs, Heathfield
School for 8 to 17 years, Harrow School
for 14 to 17 years, Rugby School for 14 to
17 years, Christ College Brecon for 9 to 15
years. Prices are approx. £970 for 2 weeks,
all inclusive.*

Eurolingua Institute SA
265 alleé du Nouveau Monde
34000 Montpellier, France
Tel: +33 467 15 04 73
Fax: +33 467 15 04 73
Email: enquiry@eurolingua.com
http://www.eurolingua.com
*Arranges homestay courses in numerous
countries around the world, including the
UK.*

Home Language International
20 avenue de Fontvieille
MC98000 Monaco
 Tel: + 377 97 70 74 72
Fax: + 377 97 70 74 71
Email: hli@monaco.mc
http://www.hli.co.uk
*Arranges homestay courses for adults and
juniors around the UK and a wide range of
other countries. Prices range from £470
to £770 per week, including 1-1 tuition and
accommodation. It is also possible to book
host family accommodation only, without
tuition.*

The Homestay Providers' Association.
*Independent association of homestay and
home tuition providers in the UK*
Email: enquiry@h-p-a.org.uk
http://www.h-p-a.org.uk/

English as a Foreign Language Organisations:

ARELS -

The Association of Recognised English Language Services
2 Pontypool Place, Valentines Place
London SE1 8QF
Tel: 020 7242 3136
Fax: 020 7928 9378
E-Mail: info@arels.org.uk
Web: http://www.arels.org.uk

BASELT -

British Association of
State English Language Teaching
Cheltenham & Gloucester College
of Higher Education
Francis Close Hall, Swindon Road
Cheltenham GL50 4AZ
Tel: 01242 227099
Fax: 01242 227055
E-Mail: baselt@chelt.ac.uk
Web: http://www.baselt.org.uk

British Council (Headquarters)

10 Spring Gardens
London SW1A 2BN
Tel: 020 7930 8466
Fax: 020 7839 6347
Web: http://www.britcoun.org
For information on language courses recognised by the GBC, and general advice about living and studying in Britain.

BALEAP -

British Association of Lecturers in English for Academic Purposes
Language Institute, Arts A,
University of Sussex,
Falmer, Brighton BN1 9QN
Tel: 01273 678006
Fax: 01273 678476
E-mail: M.Khidhayir@sussex.ac.uk
http://www.baleap.org.uk

EAQUALS -

The European Association for Quality Language Services
5 Chemin des Maggenberg
1700 Fribourg
Switzerland
Tel / Fax: + 41 26 4814665
http://www.eaquals.org

General contact for students:

UKCOSA -

United Kingdom Council for Overseas Students
9-17 St. Albans Place
London N1 ONX
Tel: 020 7226 3762
Fax: 020 7226 3373
Student Helpline: 020 7354 5210
(Mon-Fri, 1-4pm)
E-Mail: enquiries@ukcosa.org.uk
Web: http://www.ukcosa.org.uk
Advice for international students on: UK immigration control, regulations on fees, awards & loans, financial aid & sources of funding, rights of EEA students studying in the UK.